REVENUE STAMPS.

The Abolition of Stamp Taxes—What Articles Require Yet to be Stamped—Information of Importance.

There seems to be a prevalent opinion that revenue stamps have been abolished by a late act of Congress and are no longer required, and hence some persons have ceased to use them. In the first place the act of Congress referred to does not take effect until the first day of October next; and secondly, revenue stamps have not been entirely abolished. Every man is supposed to know the law, and he who violates it cannot plead ignorance on extenuation of his offense. He is still liable to punishment, even though he may have erred ignorantly. For the purpose of informing our readers on the subject we give the new law, which is as follows:

"SECTION 36. *That on and after the first day of October*, 1872, all the taxes imposed by stamps under and by virtue of schedule B. of section 170 of the act approved June 30, 1864, and the several acts amendatory thereof, be and the same are hereby repealed, excepting only the tax of two cents on bank checks, drafts, or orders. Provided that where any mortgage has been executed and recorded, before the first day of October, 1872, to secure the payment of bonds or obligations that may be made and issued from time to time, and such mortgage not being stamped, all such bonds or obligations so made and issued on and after the first day of October, 1872, shall not be subject to any stamp duty, but only such of their bonds or obligations as may have been made before the last day aforesaid: And provided further that in the meantime the holder of any instrument of writing of whatsoever kind of description which has been made without being duly stamped or with a defunct stamp, may make application to any collector of internal revenue, and that upon such application such collector shall thereupon affix the stamp provided by such holder upon such instrument of writing as is required by law to be put upon the same, and subject to the provisions of section 158 of the internal revenue laws."

We are indebted to Mr. Jacob Cooke, Deputy Assessor of Internal Revenue, for the following careful epitome of instruments which now require stamps, and upon which

STAMPS ARE TO BE ABOLISHED.

Contracts for insurance against accidental injuries.

Affidavits.

All agreements or contracts, or renewals of the same.

Appraisements of value or damage, or for any other purpose.

Assignments of a lease, mortgage, policy of insurance, or anything else.

Bills of exchange, foreign, inland, letters of credit, or anything of that kind now taxed by stamps.

Bills of lading, and receipts, in the United States for anywhere else.

Bills of sale of any kind.

Bonds of indemnification of any kind.

Bonds of administrator or guardian, or anything that has the name of bond in it, and now taxed by stamp.

Brokers' notes.

Certificates of stock, profits, damage, deposit, or any other kind of certificate now taxed by stamp.

Charter, or its renewal, or a charter-party of any kind.

All contracts or agreements.

Conveyance, any part of the work of conveying.

Indorsement of any negotiable or not negotiable instrument.

Entry, for consumption, warehousing or withdrawal.

Gaugers' returns.

Insurance policies, contracts, tickets, renewals, etc., (life, marine, inland and fire).

Lease. All through the lease list is abolished.

Legal documents. Writ or other process, confession of judgment, cognovit, appeals, warrants, etc., letters of administration, testamentary, etc.

Manifests at custom-house, or anywhere else, or for any purpose.

Mortgage, of any kind.

Passage ticket, to any place in the world.

Pawners' checks.

Power of attorney for any purpose.

Probate of will, of any kind.

Promissory note for anything.

Protest of any kind.

Quit claim deed.

Receipt. Now generally exempted, and if included in present law in any case, will be hereafter exempted.

Sheriff's return.

Trust deed.

Warehouse receipt.

Warrant of attorney.

Weigher's return of any character.

STAMPS RETAINED.

The tax of two cents on checks, drafts and orders is all of Schedule B that is retained.

SCHEDULE C.

The duties on the articles named in this schedule have not been changed by the late act. The following named articles should be stamped as before:

All proprietary medicines.

All perfumery and cosmetics.

All friction matches.

Wax tapers.

Cigar lights.

Playing cards.

EMERSON'S

Internal Revenue Guide

1867,

Containing the Law of June 30, 1864,

AS AMENDED

MARCH 3, 1865, JULY 13, 1866, AND MARCH 2, 1867,

WITH SECTIONS CODIFIED AND ARRANGED IN THEIR APPROPRIATE PLACES, WITH

AMENDMENTS SUBSTITUTED FOR SECTIONS OR PARTS OF SECTIONS REPEALED WITH DECISIONS, RULINGS, CIRCULARS, SCHEDULES OF RATES OF TAX, EXEMPTIONS, STAMP DUTIES, WITH ANALYSIS AND FULL DIRECTIONS FOR THE PENDING ASSESSMENT OF

THE INCOME TAX,

WITH

Complete Digest and Alphabetical Index.

BY CHARLES N. EMERSON,
Counsellor at Law, and Assessor 10th Mass. Dist.

SPRINGFIELD, MASS.:
SAMUEL BOWLES & COMPANY.
1867.

Samuel Bowles & Company, Printers and Electrotypers.

Preface

TO THIS EDITION OF "THE GUIDE" FOR 1867.

THE Law of June 30, 1864, as amended July 13, 1866, was again amended on the 2d of March, 1867; and the Editor and Compiler of this work, still desirous of fulfilling his original purpose of giving to subordinate revenue officers and the public such assistance as his experience might dictate, in the administration and proper understanding of a complex system, adds to his humble labors in this direction, the late amendatory enactments of 1867, with notes and comments, and such rulings and decisions made by the Department since July 13, 1866, as are deemed of importance in the understanding of the Statute of that date, and illustrative of the principles of construction which will be applicable to the amendments of the present winter.

These amendments are not very numerous, but most of them are highly important.

They may be briefly analyzed as follows, viz:

SECTION 1 changes the time for the assessment of the Income Tax, the Special Tax, (formerly styled "Licenses,") and the other annual taxes, from May to March, and the date of collection of the same, from June to April, and changes the tax upon Cotton produced within the United States.

SECTION 2, applies the same principle of a "Special Tax in proportion to the amount of sales," of apothecaries, butchers, confectioners, plumbers and gas fitters, as now applies to the case of "Wholesale Dealers."

SECTION 3, prescribes certain duties to be performed by District Attorneys of the United States, in reporting pending suits and proceedings in connection with the Internal Revenue, and authorizing the Commissioner of Internal Revenue to establish certain rules and regulations respecting each suit.

SECTION 4, gives to the Commissioner of Internal Revenue certain charge and control of real estate set off, &c., to the United States, in payment of debts on account of the Internal Revenue, to give releases of the same, &c.

SECTION 5, prescribes, in addition to other penalties imposed on manufactures of articles requiring stamps, that it shall be the duty of the proper Assessor or Assistant Assessor to estimate the amount of the tax so due, in certain cases, and assess it.

SECTION 6, empowers the Commissioner to designate Assistant Assessors, to make and report assessments in any part of the collection district, when so directed.

SECTION 7, appropriates $100,000 to be expended in detecting and bringing to trial, persons guilty of violating the revenue laws.

SECTION 8, reduces the penalty of ten per cent. now levied for failure to pay certain revenue taxes, to five per cent., and interest till paid, at the rate of one per cent. per month.

SECTION 9, makes certain amendments to the Law of 1864 as amended; substantially as follows, viz:

(a) Gives Assistant Assessors five instead of four dollars daily compensation, and repeals the provision of Statute of 1866 for "Office Rent."

(b) Gives commission on "other articles," in addition to spirits and cotton shipped in bond, and sold in other districts.

(c) Makes amended provision for vacancy in the Collector's office.

(d) Provides additional penalty for failure to pay the proper "Special Tax;" and additional provisions in relation to particular occupations subject to Special Taxes.

(e) Includes tobacco, snuff and cigars, under the provisions in relation to distilled spirits, and forfeiture and sale of same.

(f) Strikes out the former limitation of "April 1867," from the Gas tax; giving these companies the right to add the tax to the price charged consumers, or due upon contracts.

(g) Changes the tax upon leather, glass, woolen goods, sugars, and sugar refineries, wood screws and gunpowder, boots and shoes, and other articles set forth in the Schedules, as amended, (q. v.)

(h) Abolishes the ad valorem tax on cigars, and levies a uniform tax of five dollars per thousand.

(i) Modifies the stamp taxes of Schedule "B."

SECTION 10, makes certain modifications of the Law of July 13, 1866, and fully detailed.

SECTION 11, makes extensive additions to the Schedule of articles exempt from taxation.

SECTION 12, imposes a tax on brandy from grapes of one dollar per gallon, with severe penalties for fraudulent description of the article.

SECTION 13, essentially amends the Income Tax, the principal modifications being:

1. The increase of the amount deducted from $600 to $1000.

2. Making five per cent. the uniform rate of tax on all income in excess of $1000.

3. A more specific detail of the items to be included in estimating this tax, and the proper deductions.

SECTIONS 14 to 27 inclusive, provide new and more stringent regulations in relation to the importation and bonding of distilled spirits, and severe penalties for fraud or attempted fraud in connection therewith.

SECTION 28, makes it a felony on the part of any person, with severe punishment, for falsely representing himself to be a revenue officer, and receiving money, &c., under pretence of a violation of the Revenue Laws.

SECTION 29, makes it a misdemeanor to mix Naphtha and illuminating oils, or sell, or offer for sale, oil made from petroleum, inflammable at certain temperatures or fire tests.

SECTION 30, provides severe penalties for conspiring to defraud the United States in revenue matters.

SECTION 31, requires all inspectors to give bonds.

SECTION 32, provides penalties for fraudulent use of empty

cigar boxes, or for selling the same, or offering them for sale, without defacing or destroying the stamps.

SECTION 33, enacts that tonnage duties shall be levied but once within one year.

SECTION 34, which concludes the amendatory Law of 1867, repeals the tax upon advertisements, and gross receipts of toll roads, with the usual saving clause for accrued rights and penalties under all former acts relating to the Internal Revenue.

This rapid analysis of the Law of 1867, will give some idea of the topics which have engaged the attention of Congress in its enactment.

The Compiler has retained in this edition of the work the entire Law of 1864 as amended in 1866, with the full body of notes and references of other editions, superadding as a Supplement the Statute of the present winter, and a carefully prepared collection of the leading decisions and rulings of the Commissioner, Hon. E. A. Rollins, and his efficient Deputies, who, from their extended experience in the administration of the system, and their unremitting labors, have afforded the subordinate officers of the revenue invaluable assistance, and the country the fullest guaranty of a faithful and wise performance of important and arduous duties.

In the Appendix will be found extracts from carefully prepared circular instructions issued by the Department, portions of which are to some extent inapplicable to the present Law, but all useful for reference and guide, and quite essential to be thoroughly understood by all revenue officers.

The immediate assessment of the Annual Tax, with its engrossing duties devolved upon an Assessor, and the limited time allowed the Editor to prepare a treatise upon topics far more deserving of greater research, and better analysis, must be his apology for the errors, omissions and incompleteness, which may here be discovered. He submits this third compilation of the Revenue Law, to the public, trusting it will be found convenient and useful. CHARLES N. EMERSON.

PITTSFIELD, March 10, 1867.

Contents.

Explanatory.

The numbers of the sections of the act of June 30, 1864, as amended by the act of March 3, 1865, are herein retained. Also the numbers of the unrepealed sections of these acts, and of such acts of Congress deemed applicable to the Internal Revenue Law, which were incorporated by the Treasury Department in the official copy of the act of 1864.

The provisions of the law of July 13, 1866, whether as new and complete sections, or as amendment of previous statutes, are printed in brackets, thus, [ ] and inserted in their appropriate places.

The law of March 2, 1867, is published in order of sections, at beginning of Supplement.

ERRATA.

The law of 1864 as amended was printed, in part, from manuscript, and a few errors escaped notice, viz:

On page 27, three lines from foot, for "two years" read fifteen months.

On page 132, two lines from foot, read "proposed but not finally adopted in the Senate," in place of "effected." (The change *was* effected by act of March 2, 1867, q. v.)

On page 180, line 25, erase "pumps."

Internal Revenue Guide.

LAW OF 1866.

AN ACT*

TO REDUCE INTERNAL TAXATION, AND TO AMEND AN ACT ENTITLED "AN ACT TO PROVIDE INTERNAL REVENUE TO SUPPORT THE GOVERNMENT, TO PAY INTEREST ON THE PUBLIC DEBT, AND FOR OTHER PURPOSES," APPROVED JUNE THIRTIETH, EIGHTEEN HUNDRED AND SIXTY-FOUR, AND ACTS AMENDATORY THEREOF.

Commissioner of Internal Revenue.† *His Salary, Duties and Powers.*

Be it enacted by the Senate and House of Representatives of the United States of America in Congress assembled, That, for the pur-

* The "Excise," or "Internal Revenue Law," was enacted by Congress July 1, 1862, and contained 119 Sections. On the 14th of July, 1862, it was provided that the portion of it relating to Stamps should not take effect till September 1, 1862; and that portion relating to the appointment of Assessors and Collectors, should take effect on the 21st of July. By joint resolution of July 17, Section 77 of the Act was amended, substituting August 1 for May 1, 1862, as the date from and after which certain duties should be levied and paid upon carriages, yachts and billiard tables; and further providing that certain matters required by the act to be done, either on or before the 1st days of July or August, should be postponed to such time as might be fixed and determined on by the Secretary of the Treasury; he to give public notice of the time when the law should take effect. This provision, somewhat anomalous in the enactment of General Laws, became necessary, in order properly to arrange the machinery for the efficient operation of a novel and important system of taxation. Under this joint resolution, the Secretary of the Treasury gave notice that the Law would take effect on September 1, 1862.

On the 3d of March, 1863, important amendments were adopted by Congress,

† The first Commissioner was Hon. George S. Boutwell, of Massachusetts. To him and to the Deputy, C. F. Estee, of New York, is due, in great measure, the admirable system of forms and details, which have required but little change since they originated them, and have only been essentially modified to meet the changes in the law itself. He was succeeded by Hon. Joseph J. Lewis, of Pennsylvania, who brought to the position much experience and discriminating legal acumen. He held the office till 1865, when he was succeeded by William Orton, Esq., of New York city, a gentleman of much business capacity, and great familiarity with the practical operation of the system. He, however, resigned in a few months, and was succeeded by Hon. E. A. Rollins, of New Hampshire, the present incumbent, who was the Deputy Commissioner under Judge Lewis, and is an efficient and accomplished officer.

pose of superintending the collection of internal duties, stamp duties, licenses, or taxes, imposed by this act, or which may hereafter be imposed, and of assessing the same, the Commissioner of Internal Revenue, whose annual salary shall be [six] thousand dollars, shall be charged, under the direction of the Secretary of the Treasury, with preparing all the instructions, regulations, directions, forms, blanks, stamps, and licenses, and distributing the same, or any part thereof, and all other matters pertaining to the assessment and collection of the duties, stamp duties, licenses, and taxes which may be necessary to carry this act into effect, and with the general superintendence of his office, as aforesaid, and shall have authority, and hereby is authorized and required, to provide cotton marks, hydrometers, and proper and sufficient adhesive stamps, and stamps or dies for expressing and denoting the several stamp duties, or the amount thereof in the case of percentage duties, imposed by this act, and to alter and renew or replace such stamps, from time to time, as occasion shall require. He may also contract for or procure the printing of requisite forms, decisions, regulations, and advertisements; but the printing of such forms, decisions, and regulations shall be done at the public printing office, unless the public printer shall be unable to perform the work. (And the Secretary of the Treasury may, at any time prior to the first day of July, eighteen hundred and sixty-six, assign to the office of the Commissioner of Internal Revenue such number of clerks as he may deem necessary, or the exigencies of the

---

both in the machinery of the law and the rates of duty. On the 30th of June, 1864, after a most thorough review and examination of its details, in the Committee of Ways and Means in the House, and the Finance Committee of the Senate, the law was substantially remodeled; regard being had in its modified provisions, as well to the defects in the practical workings of the system as to the necessity for increased taxation. On the 3d of March, 1865, the law was again essentially amended, and the rates of tax in most respects greatly increased, and additional subjects of taxation provided for.

In July, 1866, the present law was established, and a substantial reduction made in the rates of duty upon some articles; others which had been subject to taxes, either burdensome or impolitic, omitted, and an estimated reduction made in the aggregate revenues from internal duties, of some seventy millions of dollars. Congress was greatly aided in establishing this amended system, by the labors and reports of a Board of Commissioners raised by Congress, to inquire "into the manner and efficiency of the present and past methods of collecting the Internal Revenue and to take testimony." The country owes a vast debt of gratitude to that Board for their exhausting and efficient services, and their reports are models of careful analysis and philosophical conclusions. (Vide reports of Hon. D. A. Wells, Chairman.)

In the first ten months of the operation of the original Law of 1862, as amended in 1863, it realized for the Treasury something less than $40,000,000. In the second year, ending June 30, 1864, about $125,000,000. For the year ending June 30, 1865, about $211,000,000; while it is estimated that the receipts for the fiscal year ending June 30, 1866, will fall but little short of $300,000,000. (It appears by the returns of the Treasury at the end of this fiscal year—on 30th of June—to be actually in excess of $311,000,000.) This vast revenue has been realized with but little embarrassment to the industrial pursuits of the country; the people have cheerfully responded to this unprecedented burden upon their resources; and its success as a financial measure has excited the astonishment and admiration of foreign nations.

public service may require;* and the privilege of franking all letters and documents pertaining to the duties of his office, and of receiving free of postage all such letters and documents, is hereby extended to said Commissioner.)—March 3, 1865, Section 20.

General Provisions. Mode of Keeping and Auditing of Accounts. Inspection of Money by Secretary of Treasury and Comptrollers. Commissioner's Bond.

SEC. 2. *And be it further enacted*, That it shall be the duty of the Commissioner of Internal Revenue to pay over daily to the Treasurer of the United States all public moneys which may come into his possession, for which the Treasurer shall give proper receipts and keep a faithful account; and at the end of each month the said Commissioner shall render true and faithful accounts of all public moneys received or paid out, or paid to the Treasurer of the United States, exhibiting proper vouchers therefor, and the same shall be received and examined by the Fifth Auditor of the Treasury, who shall thereafter certify the balance, if any, and transmit the accounts, with the vouchers and certificate, to the First Comptroller for his decision thereon; and the said Commissioner, when such accounts are settled as herein provided for, shall transmit a copy thereof to the Secretary of the Treasury. He shall at all times submit to the Secretary of the Treasury and the Comptroller, or either of them, the inspection of moneys in his hands, and shall, prior to the entering upon the duties of his office, execute a bond, with sufficient sureties, to be approved by the Secretary of the Treasury and by the First Comptroller, in a sum of not less than one hundred thousand dollars, payable to the United States, conditioned that said Commissioner shall faithfully perform the duties of his office according to law, and shall justly and faithfully account for and pay over to the United States, in obedience to law and in compliance with the order or regulations of the Secretary of the Treasury, all public moneys which may come into his hands or possession, and for the safe-keeping and faithful account of all stamps, adhesive stamps, or vellum, parchment or paper bearing a stamp denoting any duty thereon, which bond shall be filed in the office of the First Comptroller of the Treasury. And such Commissioner shall, from time to time, renew, strengthen, and increase his official bond as the Secretary of the Treasury may direct.

Taxes to be paid daily into the Treasury. Certificate of Deposit returned to Commissioner.

(SEC. 3. Act of March 3, 1865.) *And be it further enacted*, That from and after the thirtieth day of June, eighteen hundred and sixty-five, the gross amount of all duties, taxes, and revenues received or collected by virtue of the several acts to provide internal revenue to sup-

*See Section 65, Act of July, 1866, reorganizing the office of the Commissioner of Internal Revenue, *infra*.

port the government and to pay the interest on the public debt, and of any other act or acts that may now or hereafter be in force connected with the internal revenues, shall be paid by the officers, collectors or agents receiving or collecting the same daily into the Treasury of the United States, under the instructions of the Secretary of the Treasury, without any abatement or deduction on account of salary, compensation, fees, costs, charges, expenses, or claims of any description whatever, anything in any law to the contrary notwithstanding. And all moneys now directed by law to be paid to the Commissioner of Internal Revenue, including those derived from the sale of stamps, shall be paid into the treasury of the United States by the party making such payment; and a certificate of such payment, stating the name of the depositor, and the specific account on which the deposit was made, signed by the treasurer, assistant treasurer, designated depositary or proper officer of a deposit bank, and transmitted to and received by the Commissioner of Internal Revenue, shall be deemed a compliance with the law requiring payment to be made to the Commissioner, any law to the contrary notwithstanding: *Provided*, That in districts where from the distance of the officer, collector or agent receiving or collecting such duties, taxes, and revenues from a proper government depository, the Secretary of the Treasury may deem it proper, he may extend the time for making such payment, not exceeding, however, in any case, a period of one month.

*Deputy Commissioner and Duties and Powers.**

SEC. 3. *And be it further enacted*, That the Deputy Commissioner of Internal Revenue, whose annual salary shall be twenty-five hundred dollars, shall be charged with such duties in the Bureau of Internal Revenue as may be prescribed by the Secretary of the Treasury, or as may be required by law, and shall act as Commissioner of Internal Revenue in the absence of that officer, and exercise the privilege of franking all letters and documents pertaining to the office of Internal Revenue.

Revenue Agents.† Duties and Compensation.

SEC. 4. *And be it further enacted*, That the Secretary of the Treasury may appoint not exceeding ten revenue agents, whose duties shall

---

*The Deputy Commissioner is vested, in the absence of the Commissioner, with all the powers, and performs all the duties of the latter. The present Deputy is Hon. D. C. Whitman, who has had long experience in the details of the Department.

†Revenue Agents and Inspectors send their accounts monthly to the Commissioner of Internal Revenue to be audited and paid.

CIRCULAR 22—REVISED.

SEE APPENDIX.

By Section 37 of the Act of June 30, 1864, the Revenue Agent is empowered to examine the books and papers of any person whom he may have reason to suspect of attempting to defraud the revenue. This, however, he is

be, under the direction of the Secretary of the Treasury, to aid in the prevention, detection, and punishment of frauds upon the internal revenue, and in the enforcement of the collection thereof, who shall be paid, in addition to the expenses necessarily incurred by them, such compensation as the Secretary of the Treasury may deem just and reasonable, not exceeding two thousand dollars per annum. The above salaries to be paid in the same manner as are other expenses for collecting the revenue.

Inspectors. Duties and Compensation. Penalty for extortion, &c.

SEC. 5. *And be it further enacted*, That the Secretary of the Treas-

---

expected to exercise with discretion. No officer is warranted in making inquisition into the operation and proceeds of a man's private business without probable cause to believe that some wrong has been done to the Government. An investigation without probable cause, for the purpose of gratifying a personal curiosity or a private pique, would be criminal in the officers.

He may render important assistance to the assessor by suggesting the course of the inquiry, examining and cross-examining witnesses, collecting and following accounts, &c. When evidence is obtained he submits the facts to the assessor, and *he* must act; but his duties are ended when he has discovered the fraud, and the collector attends to the prosecution.—*Dept. Circular, June* 21, 1865. *Int. Rev. Record, Vol. III., p.* 146.

"In answer to an inquiry we would state that no Revenue Agent or Inspector, Assessor or Assistant Assessor, possesses any authority of law to receive money or checks in payment of taxes or of liabilities due to the United States. Nor have Revenue Agents, Inspectors, Collectors, or Deputy Collectors any authority of law to estimate or fix the amount of tax due from any individual. Assessors and Assistant Assessors can alone make assessment by law. No Revenue Agent or Inspector can, consistent with law, be at the same time a Deputy Collector, or have delegated to them the power to receive money on behalf of Collectors in payment of taxes or liabilities to the United States."—*Letter of Commissioner* ——, 1865.

It will be seen that the following constitute the class of officers charged with the superintendence of the assessment and the collection of the Internal Revenue: The Commissioner and Deputy Commissioner, the Cashier, the Assessor and his Assistants, the Collector and such Deputies as he may see fit to appoint, responsible immediately to him, with their remuneration fixed and paid by him; ten Revenue Agents appointed by the Secretary of the Treasury, and acting as the police of the law, and charged with its enforcement in the several districts, and also such numbers of Inspectors in each Collection District as the Secretary of the Treasury may deem necessary, who are charged with the general enforcement of the law and the detection of frauds. For the inspection of Distilled Spirits and Tobacco and Cigars there are appointed in the districts, when necessary, a corps of Inspectors, whose duties will be fully detailed in the proper place.

THE ASSESSOR.

The work of initiating and assessing the taxes of course devolves upon the assessor and his assistants. By the provisions of the law as originally enacted and substantially continued in the various re-enactments and amendments, the President was authorized to divide the States and Territories into convenient Collection Districts, in each of which an Assessor and Collector was nominated and commissioned, subject to confirmation by the Senate.

ury may appoint inspectors in any assessment district where in his judgment it may be necessary for the purposes of a proper enforcement of the internal revenue laws or the detection of frauds, and such inspectors and revenue agents aforesaid shall be subject to the rules and regulations of the said Secretary, and have all the powers conferred upon any other officers of internal revenue in making any examination of persons, books and premises which may be necessary in the discharge of the duties of their office. And the compensation of such inspectors shall be fixed and paid for such time as they may be actually employed, not exceeding four dollars per day, and their just and proper traveling expenses.

[And any inspector, or revenue agent, or any special agent, appointed

---

These districts generally correspond to the Congressional Districts. The exceptions were that in California two additional Districts were authorized corresponding to the number of Senators as well as Representatives, and extra districts, when needed, from the great size or importance of the Congressional Districts, as in the lower wards of the city of New York.—*Law of* 1862, *Section* 2.

The duties of the assessor and his assistants are extensive and comprehensive; and as they correspond to the various provisions of the law in relation to the assessment, they are with great particularity and fullness detailed in the text of the law itself. We will allude, however, generally to his official duties and the routine of his office.

1. He divides his district into convenient assessment divisions, in each of which he nominates, subject to the approval of the Commissioner and the Secretary of the Treasury, an assistant assessor.

2. Before entering upon the actual performance of the duties of his office he takes the oath of allegiance provided by the law of 1862, chapter 128, together with the appropriate oath of office for the diligent and faithful performance of his official trust.

3. After establishing his several sub-districts, with definite boundaries, he gives public notice of such divisions, with the name of the assistant assigned to each.

4. His assistants act under his general superintendence; he supplies them with stationery, forms, blanks and instructions, and makes himself as familiar as possible with the progress of their work, the manner which it is performed, &c.

5. He receives and hears appeals made to him from the assessment of his assistants upon their annual or other lists.

6. He issues summons to all persons who refuse or neglect upon notice to make required lists or returns, or who are suspected of making false, fraudulent, or understated returns or valuations, requiring the production of accounts, books, or entries upon such books, and to give testimony in the premises, and answer interrogatories; and in case of disobedience he makes application to the proper authority for a warrant of attachment. Vide Section 14, passim, Section 19.

7. He returns to the collector certified copies of annual, monthly and special lists.

8. He keeps his office or principal place of business always open during business hours, for the hearing of appeals by parties who voluntarily appear before him. Sections 14–26.

9. He is bound by the instructions and regulations of the Department, in the performance of all duties enjoined upon him under the law, and to instruct his assistants accordingly. Sections 14–19.

10. If he enters upon his official duties without having taken the required

by the Secretary of the Treasury, who shall demand or receive any compensation, fee, or reward, other than such as are provided by law for, or in regard to, the performance of his official duties, or shall be guilty of any extortion or willful oppression in the discharge of such duties, shall, upon conviction thereof in any circuit or district court of the United States having jurisdiction thereof, be subject to a fine of not exceeding one thousand dollars, or to imprisonment for not exceeding one year, or both, at the discretion of the court, and shall be dismissed from office, and shall be forever disqualified from holding any office under the government of the United States. And one-half of the fine so imposed shall be for the use of the United States, and the other half for the use of the person, to be ascertained by the judgment of the court,

---

oaths, or shall willfully fail to perform any prescribed duty, or shall make fraudulent valuation or assessment, or shall demand any fee, compensation or reward for the performance of any official duty, or shall be guilty of extortion or willful oppression in office, he is made subject to heavy penalties and fine, and is made liable in damages, at the suit of any party injured by his malfeasance in office, upon conviction thereof.

11. He is authorized to enter in the day time, any brewery, distillery, factory or other place or building where articles of property or objects of taxation are made, produced or kept, within his district, to examine the same or inspect the accounts of the same.

12. His compensation is a salary of $1,500 per year, payable quarterly; and in addition thereto, a commission graded by the amount of actual collections in his district, in no case, however, to exceed the sum of $2,500, requiring an aggregate of collections of $1,200,000 annually, (or a maximum compensation of $4,000.) He is also allowed his necessary disbursements, for rent of office, not exceeding $500 per year; also his reasonable charges for clerk hire—(those allowances, last named, vary greatly in different districts; from $300 or $350 in some of the smallest rural districts, to $5,000 or more in the large city districts.) He is allowed for his stationery, blank books and postage in official business. Extra compensation is authorized by the law when a district embraces more than a single congressional district, and in some of the Southern and Western States, where the cost of living and traveling is greater than ordinary. The Assessor is made liable to the severe penalty of summary dismissal from office and a fine of not less than $500 for fraud in the appointment of an assistant, or for demanding or receiving from him any part of his pay as a condition of his appointment to, or continuance in office.

13. He approves the accounts of his assistants, which he duly certifies to the Collector, who is authorized upon this certificate to pay them; or he may disapprove the account, leaving the assistant to his appeal to the commissioner. Should the assessor negligently approve an improper or exorbitant account, the amount of the same is deducted from his own compensation.

The above comprise the general duties of an assessor. Very much depends upon his faithfulness, industry and integrity. His position, although comparatively humble, is to the last degree important and responsible. The reward he has to gain, is not in the applause of the multitude, for his duties rather tend in the direction of reproach and popular enmity; not in the pages of a showy record of honor, for his only record is in the ledger sheets of heavy burdens and impositions; not in extravagant salary or commissions, for in view of the weary and exhausting labors of his office, they are but meager; but his fame and reward must be found in the consciousness that he has been faithful, impartial, firm and unswerving—that without fear or favor, he has, so far as in him lay, done equal justice to the humblest artisan and the richest capitalist of his district. [Instructions, Series 2: No. 1. See Appendix.]

who shall first give the information whereby any such fine may be imposed.]

*Cashier.** *Salary, Duties and Powers, Bond of, &c.*

SEC. 6. *And be it further enacted,* That the cashier of internal duties, who shall hereafter be called cashier of internal revenue, and whose annual salary shall be twenty-five hundred dollars, shall perform such duties as may be assigned to his office by the Commissioner of Internal Revenue, under the regulations of the Secretary of the Treasury, and shall give a bond, with sufficient sureties, to be approved by the Secretary of the Treasury, and by the Solicitor, that he will faithfully account for all the moneys or other articles of value belonging to the United States which may come into his hands, and perform all the duties enjoined upon his office, according to law and regulations, as aforesaid; which bond shall be deposited with the First Comptroller of the Treasury.

Collection Districts, and Appointment of Assessors and Collectors.

SEC. 7. *And be it further enacted,* That the second section of an act entitled "An act to provide internal revenue to support the government and to pay interest on the public debt," approved July one, eighteen hundred and sixty-two, shall remain and continue in full force; and the President is hereby authorized to alter the respective collection districts provided for in said section as the public interests may require.

Same Subject. Limitation of Districts.

(SEC. 2. Act of July 1, 1862.) *And be it further enacted,* That for the purpose of assessing, levying, and collecting the duties or taxes hereinafter prescribed by this act, the President of the United States be, and he is hereby, authorized to divide, respectively the States and Territories of the United States and the District of Columbia into convenient collection districts, and to nominate, and, by and with the advice and consent of the Senate, to appoint an assessor and a collector for each such district, who shall be residents within the same: *Provided,* That any of said States and Territories and the District of Columbia may, if the President shall deem it proper, be erected into and included in one district: *Provided,* That the number of Districts in any State shall not exceed the number of Representatives to which such State shall be entitled in the present Congress, except in such States as are entitled to an increased representation in the thirty-eighth Congress, in which States the number of districts shall not exceed the number of Representatives to which any such State may be so entitled: *And provided further,* That in the State of California the President may establish a number of districts, not exceeding the number of Senators and Representatives to which said State is entitled in the present Congress.

* See Section 65 of the Act of 1866, in which, it seems, the *Cashier* is not retained in the reorganization of the Internal Revenue Department.

*Division of Assessment Districts. Appointment of Assistants, Vacancies, &c.**

SEC. 8. *And be it further enacted*, That each assessor shall divide his district into a convenient number of assessment districts, which may be changed as often as may be deemed necessary, subject to such regulations and limitations as may be imposed by the Commissioner of In-

---

*ASSISTANT ASSESSORS.

As stated in a previous note in relation to the duties of the assessor, the duties of his assistant are co-extensive with the various provisions of the law in relation to the assessment, and will be to a great extent detailed in the text; but it may be useful to analyze generally the routine of his office, and the duties devolving upon him:

1. Before entering upon the performance of any official duty, his appointment and the limits of his assessment division are published in some newspaper printed in the district, and if one is printed in his division, it should properly appear in *that*.

2. He takes the prescribed oaths and causes them to be filed with the assessor and collector, to be duly transmitted to the department.

3. He makes a carefully prepared list of the names of every person in his division subject to license tax, or engaged in the manufacture of any taxed production or article; also of every state corporation liable to assessment, and of any and all persons liable to any duty, tax or assessment; and monthly, at least, to *revise* such list, that he may have continually before him an intimate knowledge of his division, with its shops, factories, storehouses and stores, railroads, banks, insurance offices, bridges, ferries, &c.

4. He should keep careful record of all persons who decease in his division, that he may at the proper time assess "legacies and successions," and in this behalf he should, as often as once a quarter, examine the records of the Surrogate's Courts and Courts of Probate of Wills, &c.; also the Registry of Deeds for the transfer of any estates which may be liable to the tax upon successions, upon "voluntary and other conveyances."

5. Provision should be made for keeping a room or office in his division, and a notification to the public of its location. In the present law it is provided that an allowance may be made for the rent of such office in such divisions as the commissioner may authorize. (Vide Section 22.)

6. He should devote his whole time to the duties of his office, to the exclusion of other employment, rendering his bills for his services promptly to the assessor on the first day of every month.

7. The proper performance of his important duties demands of him a familiar and thorough knowledge of the provisions of the statute, and the rulings and instructions of the department as communicated to him by the Assessor or otherwise.

8. On the first day of May annually he should be prepared to commence his annual assessment, and furnish every person in his division who may be liable to license duty or income assessment with the appropriate blanks, keeping careful lists of each blank or notice which he may issue, personally serving all notices which may be the ground of assessment on failure of due return of the person liable, that he may, if need be, verify such service.

9. On the first of every month he should supply manufacturers and others with the proper blanks, and insist upon a literal compliance with the provisions of the law in every respect, that he may be prepared on the fifteenth of the month, or at such other times as required to forward his monthly or other list to his principal.

In the preparation of the annual (May) list, the greatest care and diligence are required of the assistant. Many persons, of course, pay no taxes of any kind during the year, and are not liable to any; but the assistant cannot know

ternal Revenue, within each of which the assessor, whenever there shall be a vacancy, shall appoint, with the approval of said Commissioner, one or more assistant assessors, who shall be a resident of such assessment district; and in case of a vacancy occurring in the office of assessor by reason of death or any other cause, the assistant assessor of the assessment district in which the assessor resided at the time of the vacancy

---

this fact intuitively; and it becomes necessary, and is made obligatory by the terms of the law, that his annual visitation should extend to every part of his subdivision, which would seem to extend to every household, shop, store, factory, mill, warehouse, or other place of business in such subdivision. If he finds the occupants absent, he leaves a notice addressed to him requiring a sworn list or return, within ten days. Upon such notice, or refusal, or neglect to make the return within the time required, he is subject to be summoned before the assessor of the district, and to severe penalties for failure to obey the summons, or for a false or fraudulent return.

The assistant assessor is also vested with authority to enter upon premises where property is situate, not owned or possessed by, or under the care of any person within his division, and take such view thereof as may be necessary to make lists of the same, and assess the tax due, which list being subscribed by him, is deemed a sufficient list for all legal purposes.

It is also further provided, that a person having taxable property in another district than that where he resides, may make a return to the assistant assessor in the district where he actually has his home or place of business. This list is transmitted to the assistant of the district where the property is situate for examination and approval, or alteration, modification or additions; and then returned to the assistant from whom it was received, who proceeds to make the assessment, upon the return, in all respects as if the list had been taken by himself. This provision is for the convenience of the tax-payer, enabling him to pay his tax at his place of residence.

It is apparent, that practically the assistant has personally to perform much labor premised by the law, to be performed by the person liable to the tax. Very many persons, unfamiliar with business, and totally unfamiliar or ignorant of the law, are wholly unable to make out a proper return or list, however willing and desirous they may be to conform to every requirement; and are unable to procure the services of others, more competent for this purpose; many are uncertain or doubtful as to their liability to assessment, and seek a personal interview with the assistant, that he may "explain matters," and if a return is necessary, get the latter to make out the list or return. Some (they are, we are happy to say, but few,) seek to evade taxation, and it becomes necessary to "ferret them out," and procure from them such list or return, as will enable the assistant to determine the tax to be imposed. A faithful and diligent assistant will find all his time fully occupied in the performance of the duties imposed upon him by the law, and those thrown upon him by the forgetfulness, the negligence or the dishonesty of tax-payers. The experience of all principal assessors is uniform, that the aggregate of the assessments of his district, is materially increased or lessened, in the proportion that his assistants are faithful and industrious, or on the other hand lacking in energy, firmness and zeal. (Special assistants are appointed to have charge of distilleries, who receive the same pay as other assistants.)

The accounts of assessors for expenses and commissions are rendered quarterly, on the first days of January, April, July and October, embodied in Form 82, to be sent by the assessor to the Commissioner, immediately after the close of each quarter. When the account is audited, the amount found due is paid to the assessor, either by a draft on the Treasury or by an order on the collector or disbursing agent. (Circular 22, revised. October, 1865. Appendix, Series 2, No. 2.)

The monthly pay of the assessor and his expenses for clerical service, is

occurring shall act as assessor until an appointment filling the vacancy shall be made.

Collectors' Bonds. Renewal of Same.

SEC. 9. *And be it further enacted,* That before any collector shall enter upon the duties of his office, he shall execute a bond for such

---

included in the collector's monthly estimate or Form 54. There is allowed for his clerk hire each month, one twelfth of the annual allowance, theretofore fixed by the 1st Comptroller, and the Secretary of the Treasury. (Circular 22, Revised. Appendix, Series 2, No.)

As to the duty of the assessor in relation to false or fraudulent returns, see Special Circular No. 12 of January 9, 1865. (Int. Rev. Rec., Vol. I., p. 19.)

All assessors in the several districts, at the close of each month, should transmit severally to the Secretary of the Treasury and to the Commissioner, statements showing the true amounts of the assessments, certified by them to the collectors of the several districts for collection. (Treasury Regulations of June 20, 1865. II. Int. Rev. Rec. 4. Series 2, No. 2.

For full detail of respective and distinctive duties of assessors, collectors and revenue agents, see Circulars and Rulings of Department of June 20, 1865, and Aug. 24, 1865. (II. Int. Rev. Rec., pp. 84–146. Series 2, Nos. 1, 2, 3, 4.)

Judge Smalley of the United States Circuit Court has rendered a decision at Buffalo, that a United States assessor has no right to review any assessment made by him, and which has been transmitted to the collector and paid; and that the assessor has no authority under the law to require any man to appear for examination in regard to such returns, nor to compel him to submit his books for examination, and that the assessors' proceedings in all such cases are a nullity, and without color of law. See review of the extent and effect of this decision. (III. Int. Rev. Rec., pp. 134–150.)

APPEALS TO ASSESSOR.

WITNESSES AT APPEALS.—"The Proviso to Section 19 provides for the rates at which witnesses should be paid when attending the appeals of assessors, and although this is a special provision relating to such cases, yet as the general practice of paying witnesses is universal, there seems to be no violence done in construing Section 19 as applicable to the case of witnesses when summoned under Section 14."

"Any expenses of this character will have to be paid by the collector as disbursing agent under the regulations of June 27, 1865." (Ruling of Commissioners July 26, 1865, Int. Rev. Rec. Vol. II. p. 101, Circular No. 4, Revised in Appendix.)

The bills of assistant assessors are paid by the collectors as disbursing agents, and embrace the per-diem, and the three dollars per hundred persons assessed, and nothing else. If any other items are included in the bills the collectors as disbursing agents are directed to strike out such items and pay the balance only. All claims of assistant assessors other than the persons assessed and the *per diem* are sent to the assessor, and if correct, included in his quarterly account. They are not allowed for services performed on Sundays, unless employed in the superintendence of a distillery in operation on that day. In making charges for persons assessed in any list, each person assessed will be counted but once, although his name may be entered several times on the list. (Circular 22, Revised. No. 4 Revised, Appendix Series 2, No. 2.)

The assistant assessor soon becomes familiar with all the manufacturing establishments, workshops, &c., of his subdivision, with the average amount of their monthly productions, capacity, number of hands employed, state of market, &c.; enabling him with great certainty to estimate the duty. It is also his province, frequently to make personal examination of the different

amount as shall be prescribed by the Commissioner of Internal Revenue, under the direction of the Secretary of the Treasury, with not less than five sureties to be approved by the Solicitor of the Treasury, conditioned that said collector shall faithfully perform the duties of his office according to law, and shall justly and faithfully account for and pay over to the United States, in compliance with the order or regulations of the Secretary of the Treasury, all public moneys which may come into his

---

shops and establishments, and in case of suspected inaccuracies or fraud, to examine in detail the books of the concern. If with courteous and gentlemanly bearing, he performs his duty in the premises (and one destitute of these qualities is not a fit officer) his visits and examinations at the mills and shops of honest tax-payers will never be looked upon with displeasure, or treated in a hostile spirit. There is no more loyal or respectable class in the world than the artisans, artificers and manufacturers of the United States; and so far as the experience of the writer extends, in a district largely engaged in these pursuits, no class seems to be more ready or willing to do their full share to support the burthens of the law. But there are doubtless exceptions; and the utmost energy, industry and firmness are demanded of the assistant assessor, that the dishonest manufacturer may not escape his scrutiny, and the share he should take, equally with others, in the support of the government, be by him fully assumed.

The most important duty of the assistant assessor in preparing and returning his annual list, is of course the income tax. We do not propose in this connection to discuss the requirements of the law in relation to this very important matter of incomes. The rates of tax, the regulations and instructions and decisions pertaining thereto will be hereafter fully considered. But as pertaining to the general duties of an assistant assessor in the matter, we would merely state in this place, that it is his duty to require all persons of lawful age, and all guardians, trustees, executors and administrators of all persons deceased, to make a return of the amount of their income or of the persons whom they represent, in such form as may be prescribed by the commissioner, stating the source from which such income is derived; and in case of refusal, the assistant makes an assessment and adds to the amount the prescribed penalties, as provided in other cases of neglect or refusal to make lists or returns. He also has authority to increase the amount of the list or return of any party making such return, if he is satisfied that the same is understated. In ascertaining the amount he should assess upon delinquents, he has the right to refer to any list of assessment or collection taken under the laws of the respective States, or to any other records or documents, and to the written list, schedule or return required to be delivered to him, if such has been made out; and by any other lawful ways and means to gain the fullest information in the matter, which may aid him in ascertaining and verifying the facts. After his assessment of the income of any individual is made, the assessor, dissatisfied with the return, has, as before stated, plenary power to send for persons, books and papers, and examine witnesses in the matter of false or understated returns.

So much in relation to the official duty of an assistant assessor, in connection with the annual list and returns. When complete, he arranges the same, and divides them into two general lists in alphabetical order; the first exhibiting the name of the residents of his assessment division liable to duty, tax or license, and the object for which they are liable, with the amonnt of the duty or tax payable; and the second exhibiting also in alphabetical order the names of non-residents, with similar statement of enumeration, assessments and values, with the duty or tax due. These general annual lists he returns to the assessor, within thirty days after the term fixed by the act for the completion of this part of the work. (See Instructions, Series 2, No. 1. See Appendix.)

hands or possession; which bond shall be filed in the office of the First Comptroller of the Treasury. And such collector shall, from time to time, renew, strengthen, and increase his official bond, as the Secretary of the Treasury may direct, with such further conditions as the said Commissioner shall prescribe.

Deputy Collectors and their Bonds. Responsibility of Collectors for their Acts.

SEC. 10. *And be it further enacted,* That each collector shall be authorized to appoint, by an instrument of writing under his hand, as many deputies as he may think proper, to be by him compensated for their services, and also to revoke any such appointment, giving such notice thereof as the Commissioner of Internal Revenue shall prescribe; and may require bonds or other securities, and accept the same, from such deputy; and each such deputy shall have the like authority, in every respect, to collect the duties and taxes levied or assessed within the portion of the district assigned to him which is by this act vested in the collector himself; but each collector shall, in every respect, be responsible both to the United States and to individuals, as the case may be, for all moneys collected, and for every act done by any of his deputies whilst acting as such, and for every omission of duty.

Annual Tax. Nature of Return. General Provisions as to Returns.

SEC. 11. *And be it further enacted,* That it shall be the duty of any person, partnership, firm, association, or corporation, made liable to any duty, license, stamp, or tax imposed by law when not otherwise provided for, on or before the first Monday of May in each year, and in other cases before the day of levy, to make a list or return, verified by oath or affirmation, to the assistant assessor of the district where located, of the amount of annual income, the articles or objects charged with a special duty or tax, the quantity of goods, wares, and merchandise made or sold, and charged with a specific or ad valorem duty or tax, the several rates and aggregate amount, according to the respective provisions of this act, and according to the forms and regulations to be prescribed by the Commissioner of Internal Revenue, under the direction of the Secretary of the Treasury, for which such person, partnership, firm, association, or corporation is liable to be assessed.

Regulations of Commissioners binding on all persons. Duties of Assistants.

SEC. 12. *And be it further enacted,* That the instructions, regulations, and directions, as hereinbefore mentioned, shall be binding on each assessor and his assistants, and on each collector and his deputies, and on all other persons, in the performance of the duties enjoined by or under this act; pursuant to which instructions the said assessors shall, on the first Monday of May in each year, and from time to time thereafter, in accordance with this act, direct and cause the several assistant assessors to proceed through every part of their respective districts, and inquire after and concerning all persons being within the assessment districts where they respectively reside, owning, possessing, or having the care or management of any property, goods, wares, and merchandise, articles or objects liable to pay any duty, stamp, or tax, including all persons liable to pay a license or other duty, under the provisions of this act, and to make a list of the owners, and to value and enumerate the said objects of taxation respectively, by reference to any lists of assessment or collection taken under the laws of the respective States, to any other records or documents, to the written list, schedule, or return required to be made out and delivered to the assistant assessor, and by all other lawful ways and means, in the manner prescribed by this act, and in conformity with the regulations and instructions before mentioned.

Same Subject.

SEC. 13. *And be it further enacted,* That if any person liable to pay any duty or tax, or owning, possessing, or having the care or management of property, goods, wares, and merchandise, articles or objects liable to pay any duty, tax, or license, shall fail to make and exhibit a list or return required by law, but shall consent to disclose the particulars of any and all the property, goods, wares, and merchandise, articles and objects liable to pay any duty or tax, or any business or occupation liable to pay any license, as aforesaid, then, and in that case, it shall be the duty of the officer to make such list or return, which being distinctly read, consented to, and signed and verified by oath or affirmation by the person so owning, possessing, or having the care and management as aforesaid, may be received as the list of such person.

Particular Provisions as to Returns. Notices. Examination of Books, &c., by Assessors and Assistants. Oaths and Affirmations as to Lists. Summons on Order of Court, &c. General Power of Assessor and Assistants in case of Fraud.

SEC. 14. *And be it further enacted,* [That in case any person shall be absent from his or her residence or place of business at the time an assistant assessor shall call for the annual list or return, and no annual list or return has been rendered by such person to the assistant assessor as required by law, it shall be the duty of such assistant assessor to leave at such place of residence or business, with some one of suitable age and discretion, if such be present, otherwise to deposit in the nearest post office a note or memorandum, addressed to such person, requiring him or her to render to such assistant assessor the list or return required by law within ten days from the date of such note or memorandum, verified by oath or affirmation. And if any person, on being notified or required as aforesaid, shall refuse or neglect to render such list or return within the time required as aforesaid, or if any person without notice, as aforesaid, shall not deliver a monthly or other list or return at the time required by law, or if any person shall deliver or disclose to any assessor or assistant assessor any list, statement, or return which, in the opinion of the assessor, is false or fraudulent, or contains any understatement or undervaluation, it shall be lawful for the assessor to summon such person, his agent, or other person having possession, custody, or care of books of account containing entries relating to the trade or business of such person, or any other persons he may deem proper, to appear before such assessor and produce such book, at a time and place therein named, and to give testimony or answer interrogatories under oath or affirmation respecting any objects liable to tax as aforesaid, or the lists, statements, or returns thereof, or any trade, business, or profession liable to any tax as aforesaid. And the assessor may summon, as aforesaid, any person residing or found within the State in which his district is situated. And when the person intended to be summoned does not reside and cannot be found within such State, the assessor may enter any collection district where such person may be found, and there make the examination hereinbefore authorized. And to this end he shall there have and may exercise all the power and authority he has or may lawfully exercise in the district for which he is commissioned. The summons authorized by this section shall in all cases be served by an assistant assessor of the district where the person to whom it is directed may be found, by an attested copy delivered to such person in hand or left at his last and usual place of abode, allowing such person at the rate of one day for each twenty-five miles he may be required to travel, computed from the place of service to the place of examination; and the certificate of service signed by such assistant assessor shall be evidence of the facts it states on the hearing of an application for an attachment, and when the summons requires the production of books, it shall be sufficient if such books are described with reasonable certainty. In case any person so summoned shall neglect or refuse to obey such summons, or to give testimony, or to answer interrogatories as required, it shall be lawful for the assessor to apply to the judge of the district court or to a commissioner of the circuit court of the United States, for the district within which the person so summoned resides, for an attachment against such person as for a contempt. It shall be the duty of such judge or commissioner to hear such application, and, if satisfactory proof be made, to issue an attachment, directed to some proper officer, for the arrest of such person, and upon his being brought before him to proceed to a hearing of the case; and upon such hearing the judge or commissioner shall have power to make such order as he shall deem proper, not inconsistent with the provisions of existing laws for the punishment of contempt, to enforce obedience to the requirements of the summons and punish such person for his default or disobedience. It shall be the duty of the assessor or assistant assessor of the district within which such person shall have taxable property to enter into and upon the premises, if it be necessary, of such person so refusing or neglecting, or rendering a false or fraudulent list or return, and to make, according to the best information which he can obtain, including that derived from the evidence elicited by the examination of the assessor, and on his own view and information, such list or return, according to the form prescribed, of the property, goods, wares, and merchandise, and all articles or objects liable to tax, owned or possessed or under the care or management of such person, and assess the tax thereon, including the amount, if any, due for special or income tax; and in case of the return of a false or fraudulent list or valuation, he shall add one hundred per centnm to such tax, and in case of a refusal or neglect, except in cases of sickness or absence, to make a list or return, or to verify the same as aforesaid, he shall add fifty per centum to such tax; and in case of neglect occasioned by sickness or absence as aforesaid, the assessor may allow such further time for making and delivering such list or return as he may judge necessary, not exceeding thirty days; and the amount so added to the tax, shall, in all cases, be collected by the collector at the same time and in the same manner as the tax; and the list or return so made and subscribed by such assessor or assistant assessor shall be taken and reputed as good and sufficient for all legal purposes.]

Penalty for Fraudulent Returns, or for Refusal to Appear and Produce Books, etc.

SEC. 15. *And be it further enacted,* That if any person shall deliver or disclose to any assessor or assistant assessor appointed in pursuance of law any false or fraudulent list, return, account or statement, with intent to defeat or evade the valuation, enumeration, or assessment intended to be made, or if any person who being duly summoned to appear to testify, or to appear and produce such books as aforesaid, shall neglect to appear or to produce said books, he shall, upon conviction thereof before any circuit or district court of the United States, be fined in any sum not exceeding one thousand dollars, or be imprisoned for not exceeding one year, or both, at the discretion of the court, with costs of prosecution.

Taxation of Non-Residents.

SEC. 16. *And be it further enacted,* That whenever there shall be in any assessment district any property, goods, wares, and merchandise, articles or objects, not owned or possessed by, or under the care or management of, any person within such district, and liable to be taxed as aforesaid, and no list of which shall have been transmitted to the assistant assessor, in the manner provided by this act, it shall be the duty of the assistant assessor for such district to enter into and upon the premises where such property is situated, and take such view thereof as may be necessary, and to make lists of the same, according to the form prescribed, which lists being subscribed by the said assessor, shall be taken and reputed as good and sufficient lists of such property, goods, wares, and merchandise, articles or objects as aforesaid, for all legal purposes.

Returns in Districts of Residence, and Transmission of Lists to other Districts.

SEC. 17. *And be it further enacted*, That any owner or person having the care or management of property, goods, wares, and merchandise, articles or objects, not lying or being within the assessment district in which he resides, shall be permitted to make out and deliver the lists thereof required by this act (provided the assessment district in which the said objects of duty or taxation are situated is therein distinctly stated) at the time and in the manner prescribed, to the assistant assessor of the assessment district wherein such person resides. And it shall be the duty of the assistant assessor who receives any such list to transmit the same to the assistant assessor where such objects of taxation are situate, who shall examine such list; and if he approves the same, he shall return it to the assistant assessor from whom he received it, with his approval thereof; and if he fails to approve the same, he shall make such alterations therein and additions thereto as he may deem to be just and proper, and shall then return the said list to the assistant assessor from whom it was received, who shall proceed, in making the assessment of the tax upon the list by him so received, in all respects as if the said list had been made out by himself.

Annual, Monthly and Special Lists. Manner of Making up the same by the Assessor.

SEC. 18. *And be it further enacted*, That the lists aforesaid shall, where not otherwise specially provided for, be taken with reference to the day fixed for that purpose by this act, as aforesaid; and where duties accrue at other and different times, the list shall be taken with reference to the time when said duties become due, and shall be denominated annual, monthly, and special lists. And the assistant assessors, respectively, after collecting the said lists, shall proceed to arrange the same, and to make two general lists—the first of which shall exhibit, in alphabetical order, the names of all persons, firms, companies, or corporations liable to pay any duty, tax, or license under this act, residing within the assessment district, together with the value and assessment or enumeration, as the case may require, of the objects liable to duty or taxation within such districts for which each such person is liable, or for which any firm, company, or corporation is liable, with the amount of duty or tax payable thereon; and the second list shall exhibit, in alphabetical order, the names of all persons residing out of the collection district who own property within the district, together with the value and assessment or enumeration thereof, as the case may be, with the amount of duty or tax payable thereon as aforesaid. The forms of the said general list shall be devised and prescribed by the assessor, under the direction of the Commissioner of Internal Revenue, and lists taken according to such forms shall be made out by the assistant assessors and delivered to the assessor within thirty days after the day fixed by this act as aforesaid, requiring lists from individuals; or where duties, licenses, or taxes accrue at other and different times, the lists shall be delivered from time to time as they become due.

Advertisement of Annual List. Lists Submitted to Inspection. Appeals. Assessor's Office to be Always Open, &c. Increase of List and Notice Thereof. Witnesses on Appeal and Fees Therefor.

SEC. 19. *And be it further enacted*, [That the assessor for each collection district shall give notice by advertisement in one newspaper published in each county within said district, and if there be none published in any county of the district, then in a newspaper published in the collection district adjoining thereto, and shall post notices in at least four public places within each assessment district, and shall mail a copy of such notice to each postmaster in his district, to be posted in his office, stating the time and place within said collection district when and where appeals will be received and determined relative to any erroneous or excessive valuations, assessments or enumerations by the assessor or assistant assessor returned in the annual list, and such notice shall be advertised and posted by the assessor, and mailed as aforesaid, at least ten days before the time appointed for hearing said appeals. And it shall be the duty of the assessor for each collection district, at the time fixed for hearing such appeals, as aforesaid, to submit the proceedings of the assessor and assistant assessor, and the annual lists taken and returned as aforesaid, to the inspection of any and all persons who may apply for that purpose. And such assessor is hereby authorized at any time to hear and determine in a summary way, according to law and right, upon any and all appeals which may be exhibited against the proceedings of the said assessor or assistant assessors, and the office or principal place of business of the said assessor shall be open during the business hours of each day, for the hearing of appeals by parties who shall appear voluntarily before him: *Provided*, That no appeal shall be allowed to any party after he shall have been duly assessed, and the annual list containing the assessment has been transmitted to the collector of the district. And all appeals to the assessor, as aforesaid, shall be made in writing, and shall specify the particular cause, matter, or thing respecting which a decision is requested, and shall, moreover, state the ground or principle of error complained of. And the assessor shall have power to re-examine and determine upon the assessments and valuations, and rectify the same as shall appear just and equitable; but such valuation, assessment or enumeration shall not be increased without a previous notice of at least five days to the party interested to appear and object to the same if he judge proper, which notice shall be in writing and left at the dwelling-house, office, or place of business of the party by such assessor, assistant assessor, or other person, or sent by mail to the nearest or usual post-office address of said party: *Provided further*, That on the hearing of appeals it shall be lawful for the assessor to require by summons the attendance of witnesses and the production of books of account, in the same manner and under the same penalties as are provided in cases of refusal or neglect to furnish lists or returns. The costs for the attendance and mileage of said witnesses shall be taxed by the assessor and paid by the delinquent parties, or by the disbursing agent for the district, on certificate of the assessor, at the rates allowed to witnesses in the district courts of the United States.]

Making Up of Lists by Assessor. Contents of Lists. Transmission of Lists to Other Districts. Special Lists.

SEC. 20. *And be it further enacted*, [That the assessor of each collection district, shall, immediately after the expiration of the time for hearing appeals concerning taxes returned in the annual list, and from time to time, as taxes become liable to be assessed, make out lists containing the sums payable according to law upon every subject of taxation for each collection district; which list shall contain the name of each person residing within the said district, or owning or having the care or superintendence of property lying within the said district, or engaged in any business or pursuit which is liable to any tax, when such person or persons are known, together with the sums payable by each; and where there is any property within any collection district liable to tax, not owned or occupied by or under the superintendence of any person resident therein, there shall be a separate list of such property, specifying the sum payable, and the names of the respective proprietors when known. And the assessor making out any such separate list shall transmit to the assessor of the district where the persons liable to pay such tax reside, or shall have their principal place of business, copies of the list of property held by persons so liable to pay such tax, to the end that the taxes assessed under the provisions of this act may be paid within the collection district where the persons liable to pay the same reside, or may have their principal place of business. And in all other cases the said assessor shall furnish to the collectors of the several collection districts, respectively, within ten days after the time of hearing appeals concerning taxes returned in the annual list, and from time to time thereafter as required, a certified copy of such list or lists for their proper collection districts. And in case it shall be ascertained that the annual list, or any other list, which may have been, or which shall hereafter be, delivered to any collector, is imperfect or incomplete in consequence of the omission of the names of any persons or parties liable to tax or duty, or in consequence of any omission, or understatement, or undervaluation, or false or fraudulent statement contained in any return or returns made by any persons or parties liable to tax, the said assessor may, from time to time, or at any time within two years* from the time of the passage of this act or from the time of the delivery of the list to the collector as aforesaid, enter on any monthly or special list the names of such persons

*This is a new and important provision, and quite necessary for the proper administration of the law: it having been claimed that upon the transmission of the annual or other list to the collector, the assessor was "*functus officio*."

or parties so omitted, together with the amount of tax for which they may have been or shall become liable, and also the names of the persons or parties in respect to whose returns, as aforesaid, there has been or shall be any omission, undervaluation, understatement, or false or fraudulent statement, together with the amounts for which such persons or parties may be liable, over and above the amount for which they may have been, or shall be, assessed upon any return or returns made as aforesaid, and shall certify or return said list to the collector as required by law. And all provisions of law for the ascertainment of liability to any tax, or the assessment or collection thereof, shall be held to apply, as far as may be necessary, to the proceedings herein authorized and directed. And whenever the word "duty" is used in this act, or the acts to which this is an amendment, it shall be construed to mean "tax," whenever such construction shall be necessary in order to effect the purposes of said acts.]

Penalties for Malfeasance on the part of Assessor.

SEC. 21. *And be it further enacted,* That every assessor or assistant assessor who shall enter upon and perform the duties of his office without having taken the oath or affirmation prescribed by this act, or who shall willfully neglect to perform any of the duties prescribed by this act at the time and in the manner herein designated, or who shall knowingly make any false or fraudulent list or valuation or assessment, or shall demand or receive any compensation, fee, or reward other than those provided for herein for the performance of any duty, or shall be guilty of extortion or willful oppression in office, shall, upon conviction thereof in any circuit or district court of the United States having jurisdiction thereof, be subject to a fine of not exceeding one thousand dollars, or to imprisonment for not exceeding one year, or both, at the discretion of the court, and shall be dismissed from office, and shall be forever disqualified from holding any office under the government of the United States. And one-half of the fine so imposed shall be for the use of the United States and the other half for the use of the informer, who shall be ascertained by the judgment of the court*; and the said court shall also render judgment against the said assessor or assistant assessor for the amount of damages sustained in favor of the party injured, to be collected by execution.

Assessors' Compensation. Office Rent. Clerk Hire. Compensation of Assistants. Verification of Accounts. Additional Compensation in Certain Districts. Limit of Same.

SEC. 22. *And be it further enacted,* [That there shall be allowed and paid to the several assessors a salary of fifteen hundred dollars per annum, payable quarterly; and, in addition thereto, where the receipts

*See general provisions hereafter in relation to *informers,* and the mode of ascertaining by general regulations his share in forfeitures. (Section 179 of this act.)

of the collection district shall exceed the sum of one hundred thousand dollars, and shall not exceed the sum of four hundred thousand dollars annually, one-half of one per centum upon the excess of receipts over one hundred thousand dollars. Where the receipts of a collection district shall exceed four hundred thousand dollars, and shall not exceed six hundred thousand, one-fifth of one per centum upon the excess of receipts over four hundred thousand dollars.* Where the receipts shall exceed six hundred thousand dollars, one-tenth of one per centum upon such excess; but the salary of no assessor shall in any case exceed the sum of four thousand dollars. And the several assessors shall be allowed and paid the sums actually and necessarily expended, with the approval of the Commissioner of Internal Revenue, for office rent; but no account for such rent shall be allowed or paid until it shall have been verified in such manner as the Commissioner shall require, and shall have been audited and approved by the proper officer of the Treasury Department. And the several assessors shall be paid, after the account thereof shall have been rendered to and approved by the proper officers of the treasury, their necessary and reasonable charges for clerk hire; but no such account shall be approved unless it shall state the name or names of the clerk or clerks employed and the precise periods of time for which they were respectively employed, and the rate of compensation agreed upon, and shall be accompanied by an affidavit of the assessor stating that such service was actually required by the necessities of his office, and was actually rendered, and also by the affidavit of each clerk, stating that he has rendered the service charged in such account on his behalf, the compensation agreed upon, and that he has not paid, deposited, or assigned, or contracted to pay, deposit, or assign any part of such compensation to the use of any other person, or in any way, directly or indirectly, paid or given, or contracted to pay or give, any reward or compensation for his office or employment, or the emoluments thereof; and the chief clerk of any such assessor is hereby authorized to administer, in the absence of the assessor, such oaths or affirmations as are required by this act. And there shall be allowed and paid to each assistant assessor four dollars for every day actually employed in collecting lists and making valuations, the number of days necessary for that purpose to be certified by the assessor, and three dollars for every hundred persons assessed contained in the tax list, as completed and delivered by him to the assessor, and twenty-five cents for each permit granted for making any tobacco, snuff, or cigars; and assistant assessors may be allowed in the settlement of their accounts such sum as the Commissioner of Internal Revenue may approve, not exceeding three hundred dollars per annum for office rent; but no account for such rent shall be allowed or paid until it shall have been verified in such manner as the Commissioner of Internal Revenue may require, and shall

*In districts where $1,200,000 is annually collected, the assessor's commissions will reach the maximum of $2,500, or with his salary of $1,500, the full maximum of $4,000.

have been audited and approved by the proper officers of the Treasury Department; and assistant assessors, when employed outside of the town in which they reside, in addition to the compensation now allowed by law, shall, during such time so employed, receive one dollar per day; and the said assessors and assistant assessors, respectively, shall be paid, after the account thereof shall have been rendered to and approved by the proper officers of the treasury, their necessary and reasonable charges for stationery and blank books used in the discharge of their duties, and for postage actually paid on letters and documents received and sent, and relating exclusively to official business, and for money actually paid for publishing notices required by this act. *Provided*, That no such account shall be approved unless it shall state the date and the particular item of every such expenditure, and shall be verified by the oath or affirmation of such assessor or assistant assessor; and the compensation herein specified shall be in full for all expenses not otherwise particularly authorized: *Provided further*, That the Commissioner of Internal Revenue may, under such regulations as may be established by the Secretary of the Treasury, after due public notice, receive bids and make contracts for supplying stationery, blank books, and blanks to the assessors, assistant assessors, and collectors in the several collection districts: *Provided further*, That the Secretary of the Treasury shall be, and he is hereby, authorized to fix such additional rates of compensation to be made to assessors and assistant assessors in cases where a collection district embraces more than a single congressional district, and to assessors and assistant assessors, revenue agents, and inspectors in Louisiana, Georgia, South Carolina, Alabama, Florida, Texas, Arkansas, North Carolina, Mississippi, Tennessee, California, Nevada, and Oregon, and the Territories, as may appear to him to be just and equitable, in consequence of the greater cost of living and traveling in those State and Territories, and as may, in his judgment, be necessary to secure the services of competent officers; but the compensation thus allowed shall not exceed the rate of five thousand dollars per annum. Collectors of internal revenue acting as disbursing officers shall be allowed all bills of assistant assessors heretofore paid by them in pursuance of the directions of the Commissioner of Internal Revenue, notwithstanding the assistant assessor did not certify to hours therein, or that two dollars per diem was deducted from his salary or compensation before computation of the tax thereon.*]

Fraud in Appointment of Assistants.

Sec. 23. *And be it further enacted*, That if any assessor shall demand of, or receive directly or indirectly from, any assistant assessor, as a condition of his appointment to or continuance in his said office of as-

*This last provision was inserted into the act for the purpose of indemnifying collectors for bills heretofore paid in good faith, upon a deduction of *two dollars* per diem, instead of one dollar and ninety-three cents, the proper apportionment of the $600 per year not taxable under the section taxing salaries. (See Instructions, Series 2, No. 2, in Appendix.)

sistant assessor, any portion of the compensation herein allowed such assistant assessor, or any other consideration, such assessor so offending shall be summarily dismissed from office, and shall be liable to a fine of not less than five hundred dollars upon conviction of said offence in any district or circuit court of the United States of the district in which such offence may be committed.

Assistant Assessors' Accounts. Approval of Same. Proceedings on Disapproval. Amount wrongfully Approved deducted from Assessor's Pay. Apportionment of Commissions in certain Districts.

SEC. 24. *And be it further enacted*, That assistant assessors shall make out their accounts for pay and charges allowed by law monthly, specifying each item and including the date of each day of service, and shall transmit the same verified by oath or affirmation to the assessor of the district, who shall thereupon examine the same, and, if it appear just and in accordance with law, he shall indorse his approval thereon, but otherwise shall return the same with objections. Any such account so approved may be presented by the assistant assessor to the collector of the district for payment, who shall thereupon pay the same, and, when receipted by the assistant assessor, be allowed therefor upon presentation to the Commissioner of Internal Revenue. Where any account, so transmitted to the assessor, shall be objected to, in whole or in part, the assistant assessor may appeal to the Commissioner of Internal Revenue, whose decision on the case shall be final. And should it appear, at any time, that any assessor has knowingly or negligently approved any account, as aforesaid, allowing any assistant assessor a sum larger than was due according to law, it shall be the duty of the Commissioner of Internal Revenue, upon proper proof thereof, to deduct the sum so allowed from any pay which may be due to such assessor; or the commissioner as aforesaid may direct a suit to be brought in any court of competent jurisdiction against the assessor or assistant assessor in default, for the recovery of the amount knowingly or negligently allowed, as hereinbefore mentioned: *Provided*, [That in calculating the commissions of assessors and collectors of internal revenue in districts whence cotton or distilled spirits are shipped in bond to be sold in another district, one-half the amount of tax received on the quantity of cotton or spirits so shipped, shall be added to the amount on which the commissions of such assessors and collectors are calculated; and a corresponding amount shall be deducted from the amount on which the commissions of the assessors and collectors of the districts to which such cotton or spirits are shipped are calculated.]

Compensation of Collectors. Salary, &c. Commissions. Stationery, Postage, &c.

SEC. 25. *And be it further enacted*, That there shall be allowed to collectors, in full compensation for their services and that of their deputies, a salary of fifteen hundred dollars per annum, to be paid quarterly, and in addition thereto a commission of three per centum upon the first hundred thousand dollars, and a commission of one per centum upon all sums above one hundred thousand dollars and not exceeding four hundred thousand dollars, and a commission of one-half of one per centum on all sums above four hundred thousand dollars and not exceeding one million of dollars, and one-eighth of one per centum on all sums above one million of dollars, such commissions to be computed upon the amounts by them respectively collected and paid over and accounted for under the instructions of the Treasury Department. And there shall be further paid, after the account thereof has been rendered to and approved by the proper officers of the treasury, to each collector his necessary and reasonable charges for advertising, stationery, and blank books used in the performance of his official duties, and for postage actually paid on letters and documents received or sent, and exclusively relating to official business; but no such account shall be approved unless it shall state the date and the particular items of every such expenditure, and shall be verified by the oath or affirmation of the collector: *And provided*, That the Secretary of the Treasury be authorized to make such further allowances, from time to time, as may be reasonable in cases in which, from the territorial extent of the district, or from the amount of internal revenues collected, or from other circumstances, it may seem just to make such allowances.*

Fiscal Year observed in Adjustment of Accounts. Adjustment in case of New Appointments.

SEC. 26. *And be it further enacted*, [That in the adjustment of the accounts of assessors and collectors of internal revenue which shall accrue after the thirtieth of June, eighteen hundred and sixty-four, and in the payment of their compensation for services after that date, the fiscal year of the treasury shall be observed; and where such compensation, or any part of it, shall be by commissions upon assessments or collections, and shall during any year, in consequence of a new appointment, be due to more than one assessor or collector in the same district, such commissions shall be apportioned between such assessors or collectors; but in no case shall a greater amount of the commissions be allowed to two or more assessors or collectors in the same district than is or may be authorized by law to be allowed to one assessor or collector. And the salary and commissions of assessors and collectors heretofore earned and accrued shall be adjusted, allowed, and paid in conformity with the provisions of this section, and not otherwise; but no payment shall be made to assessors or collectors on account of salaries or commissions without the certificate of the Commissioner of Internal Revenue that all reports required by law or regulation have been received, or that a satisfactory explanation has been rendered to him of the cause of the delay.†]

*See Series 2, No. 2, in Appendix.

†This last provision was enacted upon the recommendation of the present

Collector's Triplicate Receipts for Lists.

SEC. 27. *And be it further enacted*, That each collector, on receiving, from time to time, lists and returns from the said assessors, shall subscribe three receipts: one of which shall be made upon a full and correct copy of each list or return, and be delivered by him to, and shall remain with, the assessor of his collection district, and shall be open to the inspection of any person who may apply to inspect the same; and the other two shall be made upon aggregate statements of the lists or returns aforesaid, exhibiting the gross amount of taxes to be collected in his collection district, one of which aggregate statements and receipts shall be transmitted to the Commissioner of Internal Revenue, and the other to the First Comptroller of the Treasury.

(*New Provisions of March* 3, 1865, *and July*, 1866.) *Advertisement of Lists by Collectors. Demand of Payment of Taxes. Distraint by Collectors and Proceedings thereon. Notices to Post-Offices. Estimate of Taxes by Assessor. Proceedings in Case of Banks, &c., failing to Make Returns. Tax a Lien Until Paid. Property Exempt from Distraint. Certificate of Sale to give Title, &c.*

SEC. 28. *And be it further enacted*, [That each of said collectors shall, within twenty days after receiving his annual collection list from the assessors, give notice by advertisement in one newspaper published in each county in his collection district, if there be any, and if not, then in a newspaper of largest circulation published in an adjoining county, and by notifications to be posted in at least four public places in each county in his collection district, that the said taxes have become due and payable, and state the time and place within said county at which he or his deputy will attend to receive the same, which time shall not be less than ten days after the date of such notification, and shall send a copy of such notice by mail to each postmaster in the county, to be posted in his office. And if any person shall neglect to pay, as aforesaid, for more than ten days, it shall be the duty of the collector or his deputy to issue to such person a notice, to be left at his dwelling or usual place of business, or be sent by mail, demanding the payment of said duties or taxes, stating the amount thereof, with a fee of twenty cents for the issuing and service of such notice, and with four cents for each mile actually and necessarily traveled in serving the same. And if such persons shall not pay the duties or taxes, and the fee of twenty cents and mileage as aforesaid, within ten days after the service or the sending by mail of such notice, it shall be the duty of the collector or his deputy to collect the said taxes, and fee of twenty cents and mileage, with a penalty of ten per centum additional upon the amount of duties or taxes. And

Commissioner of Internal Revenue, that greater promptness might be secured in the returns of these revenue officers. Great embarrassment has been felt at the Treasury from this cause, especially in the making up of the account of receipts, &c., at the end of the fiscal year. (See Commissioner Rollins' Annual Report, Dec., 1865.)

with respect to all such taxes as are not included in the annual lists aforesaid, and all taxes the collection of which is not otherwise provided for in this act, it shall be the duty of each collector, in person or by deputy, to give notice and demand payment thereof, in the manner last mentioned, within ten days from and after receiving the list thereof from the assessor, or within twenty days from and after the expiration of the time within which such tax should have been paid; and if the annual or other taxes shall not be paid within ten days from and after such notice and demand, it shall be lawful for such collector, or his deputies, to proceed to collect the said taxes, with ten per centum additional thereto, as aforesaid, by distraint and sale of the goods, chattels, or effects, including stocks, securities, and evidences of debt, of the persons delinquent as aforesaid. And in case of distraint, it shall be the duty of the officer charged with the collection to make, or cause to be made, an account of the goods or effects distrained, a copy of which, signed by the officer making such distraint, shall be left with the owner or possessor of such goods, or effects, or at his or her dwelling or usual place of business, with some person of suitable age and discretion, if any such can be found, with a note of the sum demanded, and the time and place of sale; and the said officer shall forthwith cause a notification to be published in some newspaper within the county wherein said distraint is made, if there is a newspaper published in said county, or to be publicly posted at the post-office, if there be one within five miles, nearest to the residence of the person whose property shall be distrained, and in not less than two other public places, which notice shall specify the articles distrained, and the time and place for the sale thereof, which time shall not be less than ten nor more than twenty days from the date of such notification to the owner or possessor of the property and the publication or posting of such notices as herein provided, and the place proposed for sale shall not be more than five miles distant from the place of making such distraint. And said sale may be adjourned from time to time by said officer, if he shall think it advisable to do so, but not for a time to exceed in all thirty days. And if any person, bank, association, company, or corporation, liable to pay any tax, shall neglect or refuse to pay the same after demand, the amount shall be a lien in favor of the United States from the time it was due until paid, with the interest, penalties, and costs that may accrue in addition thereto, upon all property and rights to property belonging to such person, bank, association, company, or corporation; and the collector, after demand, may levy, or by warrant may authorize a deputy collector to levy, upon all property and rights to property belonging to such person, bank, association, company, or corporation, or on which the said lien exists, for the payment of the sum due as aforesaid, with interest and penalty for non-payment, and also of such further sum as shall be sufficient for the fees, costs, and expenses of such levy. And in all cases of sale, as aforesaid, the certificate of such sale shall transfer to the purchaser all right, title, and interest of such delinquent in and to the property sold; and where such property shall consist of stocks, said certificate shall be notice, when received, to any corporation, company, or association of said transfer, and shall be authority to such corporation, company, or association to record the same on their books and records, in the same manner as if transferred or assigned by the person or party holding the same, in lieu of any original or prior certificates, which shall be void, whether canceled or not. And said certificates, where the subject of sale shall be securities or other evidences of debt, shall be good and valid receipts to the person holding the same, as against any person holding, or claiming to hold, possession of such securities or other evidences of debt. And all persons, and officers of companies or corporations, are required, on demand of a collector or deputy collector about to distrain or having distrained on any property or rights of property, to exhibit all books containing evidence or statements relating to the subject or subjects of distraint, or the property or rights of property liable to distraint for the tax so due as aforesaid: *Provided*, That in any case of distraint for the payment of the taxes aforesaid, the goods, chattels, or effects so distrained shall and may be restored to the owner or possessor, if prior to the sale, payment of the amount due shall be made to the proper officer charged with the collection, together with the fees and other charges; but in case of non-payment, as aforesaid, the said officer shall proceed to sell the said goods, chattels, or effects at public auction, and shall retain from the proceeds of such sale the amount demandable for the use of the United States, and a commission of five per centum thereon for his own use, with the fees and charges for distraint and sale, rendering the overplus, if any there be, to the person who may be entitled to receive the same: *Provided further*, That there shall be exempt from distraint and sale, if belonging to the head of a family, the school books and wearing apparel necessary for such family; also arms for personal use, one cow, two hogs, five sheep and the wool thereof, provided the aggregate market value of said sheep shall not exceed fifty dollars; the necessary food for such cow, hogs and sheep for a period not exceeding thirty days; fuel to an amount not greater in value than twenty-five dollars; provisions to an amount not greater than fifty dollars; household furniture kept for use, to an amount not greater than three hundred dollars; and the books, tools, or implements of a trade or profession to an amount not greater than one hundred dollars shall also be exempt; and the officer making the distraint shall summon three disinterested householders of the vicinity, who shall appraise and set apart to the owner the amount of property herein declared to be exempt.*]

---

*Compare:
1. As to salaries. (Decisions of Commissioner, 96 and 125.)
2. Certificates of. (Circular No. 22, Oct., 1864.)
3. Regulations as to Collections. Decision of June 20, 1865. (Int. Rev. Rec., Vol. III., p. 103.)
4. Money paid to. (Circular 38, Jan., 1866.)
5. Compensation of. (Circular 21, Revised, Series 2, No. 2, in Appendix.)
6. Relative functions of, and other officers. (Circular Ruling, June 21, 1865, Int. Rev. Rec., Vol. II., p. 84.)
7. **Quarterly and monthly accounts of. Series 2, No. 2 in Appendix.)**

Sale of Property for Taxes. Disposition of Surplus. Property may be Purchased in Behalf of the United States. Collector's Account of Sales.

Sec. 29. *And be it further enacted,* [That in all cases where property liable to distraint for taxes under this act may not be divisible, so as to enable the collector by a sale of part thereof to raise the whole amount of the tax, with all costs, charges, and commissions, the whole of such property shall be sold, and the surplus of the proceeds of the sale, after satisfying the tax, costs and charges, shall be paid to the person legally entitled to receive the same; or if he cannot be found, or refuse to receive the same, then such surplus shall be deposited in the treasury of the United States, to be there held for the use of the person legally entitled to receive the same, until he shall make application therefor to the Secretary of the Treasury, who, upon such application, and satisfactory proofs in support thereof, shall, by warrant on the treasury, cause the same to be paid to the applicant. And if any of the property advertised for sale as aforesaid is of a kind subject to tax, and such tax has not been paid, and the amount bid for such property is not equal to the amount of such tax, the collector may purchase the same in behalf of the United States for an amount not exceeding the said tax. And in all cases where property subject to tax, but upon which the tax has not been paid, shall be seized upon distraint, and sold, the amount of such tax shall, after deducting the expenses of such sale, be first appropriated out of the proceeds thereof, to the payment of said tax. And if no assessment of tax has been made upon such property, the collector shall make a return thereof in the form required by law, and the assessor shall assess the tax thereon. And all property so purchased may be sold by said collector, under such regulations as may be prescribed by the Commissioner of Internal Revenue. And the collector shall render a distinct account of all charges incurred in the sale of such property to the Commissioner of Internal Revenue, who shall, by regulation, determine the fees and charges to be allowed in all cases of distraint and other seizures; or where necessary expenses for making such distraint or seizure have been incurred, and in case of sale, the said collector shall pay into the treasury the surplus, if any there be, after defraying such fees and charges.]

Sale of Real Estate by Collector. Particular Provisions in Relation Thereto. Redemption of Land Sold, &c. Record of Sales and Duties of Collector on the Redemption, &c.

Sec. 30. *And be it further enacted,* [That in any case where goods, chattels, or effects sufficient to satisfy the taxes imposed by law upon any person liable to pay the same, shall not be found by the collector or deputy collector whose duty it may be to collect the same, he is hereby authorized to collect the same by seizure and sale of real estate; and the officer making such seizure and sale shall give notice to the person whose estate is proposed to be sold, by giving him in hand, or leaving at his last or usual place of abode, if he has any such within the collection district where said estate is situated, a notice, in writing, stating what particular estate is proposed to be sold, describing the same with reasonable certainty, and the time when and place where said officer proposes to sell the same; which time shall not be less than twenty nor more than forty days from the time of giving said notice. And the said officer shall also cause a notification to the same effect to be published in some newspaper within the county where such seizure is made, if any such there be, and shall also cause a like notice to be posted up at the post-office nearest to the estate to be seized, and in two other public places within the county; and the place of said sale shall not be more than five miles distant from the estate seized, except by special order of the Commissioner of Internal Revenue. At the time and place appointed, the officer making such seizure shall proceed to sell the said estate at public auction, offering the same at the minimum price, including the expense of making such levy, and all charges for advertising and an officer's fee of ten dollars. And in case the real estate so seized, as aforesaid, shall consist of several distinct tracts or parcels, the officer making sale thereof shall offer each tract or parcel for sale separately, and shall, if he deem it advisable, apportion the expenses, charges, and fees, aforesaid, to such several tracts or parcels, or to any of them, in estimating the minimum price aforesaid. And if no person offers for said estate the amount of said minimum price, the officer shall declare the same to be purchased by him for the United States, and shall deposit with the district attorney of the United States a deed thereof, as hereinafter specified and provided; otherwise the same shall be declared to be sold to the highest bidder. And said sale may be adjourned from time to time by said officer for a period not exceeding thirty days in all, if he shall think it advisable so to do. If the amount bid shall not be then and there paid, the officer shall forthwith proceed to again sell said estate in the same manner; and upon any sale and the payment of the purchase money, shall give to the purchaser a certificate of purchase, which shall set forth the real estate purchased, for whose taxes the same was sold, the name of the purchaser, and the price paid therefor; and if the said real estate be not redeemed in the manner and within the time hereinafter provided, then the said collector or deputy collector shall execute to the said purchaser, upon his surrender of said certificate, a deed of the real estate purchased by him as aforesaid, and in accordance with the laws of the State in which such real estate is situate upon the subject of sales of real estate under execution, which said deed shall be *prima facie* evidence of the facts therein stated; and if the proceedings of the officer as set forth have been substantially in accordance with the provisions of this act, shall be considered and operate as a conveyance of all the right, title, and interest the party delinquent had in and to the real estate thus sold at the time the lien of the United States attached thereto. Any person, whose estate may be proceeded against as aforesaid, shall have the right to pay the amount due, together with the costs and charges thereon, to the collector or deputy collector at any time prior to the sale thereof, and all further proceedings shall cease from the time of such payment. The owners of any real estate sold as aforesaid, their heirs, executors, or administrators, or any person having any interest therein, or a lien thereon, or any person in their behalf, shall be permitted to redeem the land sold as aforesaid, or any particular tract thereof, at any time within one year after the sale thereof, upon payment to the purchaser, or, in case he cannot be found in the county in which the land sought to be redeemed is situate, then to the collector of the district in which the land is situate, for the use of the purchaser, his heirs or assigns, the amount paid by the said purchaser and interest thereon at the rate of twenty per centum per annum. And any collector or deputy collector may, for the collection of taxes imposed upon any person or for which any person may be liable by this act, and committed to him for collection, seize and sell the lands of such person situated in any other collection district within the State in which said officer resides; and his proceedings in relation thereto shall have the same effect as if the same were had in his proper collection district. And it shall be the duty of every collector to keep a record of all sales of land made in his collection district, whether by himself or his deputies, or by another collector, in which shall be set forth the tax for which any such sale was made, the dates of seizure and sale, the name of the party assessed, and all proceedings in making said sale, the amount of fees and expenses, the name of the purchaser, and the date of the deed; which record shall be certified by the officer making the sale. And it shall be the duty of any deputy making sale, as aforesaid, to return a statement of all his proceedings to the collector, and to certify the record thereof. And in case of the death or removal of the collector or the expiration of his term of office from any other cause, said record shall be delivered to his successor in office; and a copy of every such record, certified by the collector, shall be evidence in any court of the truth of the facts therein stated. And when any lands sold, as aforesaid, shall be redeemed as hereinbefore provided, the collector shall make an entry of the fact upon the record aforesaid, and the said entry shall be evidence of such redemption. And when any property, personal or real, seized and sold by virtue of the foregoing provisions, shall not be sufficient to satisfy the claim of the United States for which distraint or seizure may be made against any person whose property may be so seized and sold, the collector may, thereafter, and as often as the same may be necessary, proceed to seize and sell, in like manner, any other property liable to seizure of such person until the amount due from him, together with all expenses, shall be fully paid. *Provided,* That the word "county" wherever the same occurs in this act or the acts of which this is amendatory, shall be construed to mean also a parish or any other equivalent subdivision of a State or Territory.]

Taxes Returned Against Non-Residents.

SEC. 31. *And be it further enacted,* That if any collector shall find, upon any list of taxes returned to him for collection, property lying within his district which is charged with any specific or ad valorem tax or duty, but which is not owned, occupied, or superintended by some person known to such collector to reside or to have some place of business within the United States, and upon which the duty or tax has not been paid within the time required by law, such collector shall forthwith take such property into his custody, and shall advertise the same, and the tax charged upon the same, in some newspaper published in his district, if any shall be published therein, otherwise in some newspaper in an adjoining district, for the space of thirty days; and if the taxes thereon, with all charges for advertising, shall not be paid within said thirty days, such collector shall proceed to sell the same, or so much as is necessary, in the manner provided for the sale of other goods distrained for the non-payment of taxes, and out of the proceeds shall satisfy all taxes charged upon such property, with the costs of advertising and selling the same. And like proceedings to those provided in the preceding section for the purchase and resale of property which cannot be sold for the amount of duty or tax due thereon shall be had with regard to property sold under the provisions of this section. And any surplus arising from any sale herein provided for shall be paid into the treasury, for the benefit of the owner of the property. And the Secretary of the Treasury is authorized, in any case where money shall be paid into the treasury for the benefit of any owner of property sold as aforesaid, to repay the same, on proper proof being furnished that the person applying therefor is entitled to receive the same.

Collection of Taxes of Non-Residents.

SEC. 32. *And be it further enacted,* That whenever a collector shall have on any list duly returned to him the name of any person not within his collection district who is liable to tax, or of any person so liable to tax who shall have, in the collection district in which he resides, no sufficient property subject to seizure or distraint from which the money due for tax can be collected, it shall and may be lawful for such collector to transmit a copy or statement containing the name of the person liable to such tax aforesaid, with the amount and nature thereof, duly certified under his hand, to the collector of any district to which said person shall have removed, or in which he shall have property, real or personal, liable to be seized and sold for duty or tax, and the collector of the district to whom the said certified copy or statement shall be transmitted shall proceed to collect the said duty or tax in the same way as if the name of the person and objects of tax contained in the said certified copy or statement were on any list furnished to him by the assessor of his own collection district; and the said collector, upon receiving said certified copy or statement as aforesaid, shall transmit his receipt for it to the collector, sending the same to him.

Collector's Monthly Returns to the Department. Depositaries, &c.

SEC. 33. *And be it further enacted,* That the several collectors shall, at the expiration of each and every month after they shall, respectively, commence their collections, transmit to the Commissioner of Internal Revenue a statement of the collections made by them, respectively, within the month, and pay over monthly, or at such time or times as may be required by the Commissioner of Internal Revenue, the moneys by them respectively collected within the said term, and at such places as may be designated and required by the Commissioner of Internal Revenue; and each of the said collectors shall complete the collection of all sums assigned to him for collection, as aforesaid, shall pay over the same into the treasury, and shall render his accounts to the Treasury Department as often as he may be required. And the Secretary of the Treasury is authorized to designate one or more depositories in each State, for the deposit and safe-keeping of the money collected by virtue of this act; and the receipt of the proper officer of such depository to a collector for the money deposited by him shall be a sufficient voucher for such collector in the settlement of his accounts at the Treasury Department. And the Commissioner of Internal Revenue may, under the direction of the Secretary of the Treasury, prescribe such regulations with reference to such deposits as he may deem necessary.

(Act of June 14, 1866.) An Act to regulate and secure the safekeeping of Public Money intrusted to Disbursing Officers of the United States.* *Be it enacted by the Senate and House of Representatives of the United States of America in Congress assembled,* That from and after the passage of this act it shall be the duty of every disbursing officer of the United States having any public money intrusted to him for disbursement to deposit the same with the Treasurer or some one of the Assistant Treasurers of the United States, and to draw for the same only as may be required for payments to be made by him in pursuance of law; and all transfers from the Treasury of the United States to a disbursing officer shall be by draft or warrant on the Treasury or an Assistant Treasurer of the United States: *Provided,* That in places where there is no Treasurer nor Assistant Treasurer of the United States, the Secretary of the Treasury may, when he deems it essential to the public interest, specially authorize in writing the deposit of such public money in any other public depository, or, in writing, authorize the same to be kept in any other manner, and under such rules and regulations as he may deem most safe and effectual to facilitate the payments to public creditors.

SEC. 2. *And be it further enacted,* That if any disbursing officer of the United States shall deposit any public money intrusted to him

*This important act is incorporated into the text of the law on account of its immediate applicability and pertinency to the internal revenue officers, made disbursing officers.—ED.

in any place or in any manner, except as authorized by law, or shall convert to his own use in any way whatever, or shall loan, with or without interest, or shall for any purpose not prescribed by law withdraw from the Treasurer or any Assistant Treasurer, or any authorized depository, or shall for any purpose not prescribed by law, transfer or apply any portion of the public money intrusted to him, every such act shall be deemed and adjudged an embezzlement of the money so deposited, converted, used, loaned, withdrawn, transferred, or applied, and every such act is hereby declared a felony, and upon conviction thereof shall be punished by imprisonment for a term not less than one year nor more than ten years, or by fine not more than the amount embezzled, nor less than one thousand dollars, or by both such fine and imprisonment, at the discretion of the court.

SEC. 3. *And be it further enacted*, That if any banker, broker, or any person, not an authorized depository of public money, shall knowingly receive from any disbursing officer, or collector of internal revenue, or other agent of the United States, any public money on deposit or by way of a loan or accommodation, with or without interest, or otherwise than in payment of a debt against the United States; or shall use, transfer, convert, appropriate, or apply any portion of the public money for any purpose not prescribed by law; or shall counsel, aid, or abet any disbursing officer or collector of internal revenue or other agent of the United States in so doing, every such act shall be deemed and adjudged an embezzlement of the money so deposited, loaned, transferred, used, converted, appropriated, or applied; and any president, cashier, teller, director, or other officer of any bank or banking association who shall violate any of the provisions of this act shall be deemed and adjudged guilty of embezzlement of public money, and punished as provided in section two of this act.

Collectors Charged with Taxes receipted for. Credited with Payments and Commissions. Taxes of Persons Absconding, Insolvent, &c.

SEC. 34. *And be it further enacted*, [That each collector shall be charged with the whole amount of taxes, whether contained in lists delivered to him by the assessors, respectively, or delivered or transmitted to him by any assistant assessors from time to time, or by other collectors, or by his predecessor in office, and with the additions thereto, with the par value of all stamps deposited with him, and with all moneys collected for passports, penalties, forfeitures, fees, or costs, and he shall be credited with all payments into the treasury made as provided by law, with all stamps returned by him uncanceled to the treasury, and with the amount of taxes contained in the lists transmitted in the manner above provided to other collectors, and by them receipted as aforesaid; and also with the amount of the taxes of such persons as may have absconded, or become insolvent, prior to the day when the tax ought, according to the provisions of law, to have been collected, and with all uncollected taxes transferred by him or by his deputy acting as collector to his successor in office: *Provided,* That it shall be proved to the satisfaction of the Commissioner of Internal Revenue that due diligence was used by the collector, who shall certify the facts to the First Comptroller of the Treasury. And each collector shall also be credited with the amount of all property purchased by him for the use of the United States, provided he shall faithfully account for and pay over the proceeds thereof upon a resale of the same as required by law. In case of the death, resignation or removal of the collector, all lists and accounts of taxes uncollected shall be transferred to his successor in office as soon as such successor shall be appointed and qualified, and it shall be the duty of such successor to collect the same.]

Failure of Collector to Render Accounts. Proceedings thereupon against him.

SEC. 35. *And be it further enacted,* That if any collector shall fail either to collect or to render his account, or to pay over in the manner or within the times hereinbefore provided, it shall be the duty of the First Comptroller of the Treasury, and he is hereby authorized and required, immediately after evidence of such delinquency, to report the same to the Solicitor of the Treasury, who shall issue a warrant of distress against such delinquent collector, directed to the marshal of the district, therein expressing the amount with which the said collector is chargeable, and the sums, if any, which have been paid over by him, so far as the same are ascertainable. And the said marshal shall, himself, or by his deputy, immediately proceed to levy and collect the sum which may remain due, with five per centum thereon, and all the expenses and charges of collection, by distress and sale of the goods and chattels or any personal effects of the delinquent collector, giving at least five days' notice of the time and place of sale, in the manner provided by law for advertising sales of personal property on execution in the State wherein such collector resides. And the bill of sale of the officer of any goods, chattels, or other personal property distrained and sold as aforesaid, shall be conclusive evidence of title to the purchaser, and prima facie evidence of the right of the officer to make such sale, and of the correctness of his proceedings in selling the same. And for want of goods and chattels, or other personal effects of such collector, sufficient to satisfy any warrant of distress, issued pursuant to the preceding section of this act, the lands and real estate of such collector, or so much thereof as may be necessary for satisfying the said warrant, after being advertised for at least three weeks in not less than three public places in the collection district, and in one newspaper printed in the county or district, if any there be, prior to the proposed time of sale, shall be sold at public auction by the marshal or his deputy, who, upon such sale, shall, as such marshal or deputy marshal, make and deliver to the purchaser of the premises so sold a deed of conveyance thereof, to be executed and acknowledged in the manner and form prescribed by the laws of the State in which said lands are situated, which said deed so made shall invest the purchaser with all the title and interest of the defendant or defendants named in said warrant existing at the time of the seizure thereof. And all moneys that may remain of the proceeds of such sale after satisfying the said warrant of distress, and paying the reasonable costs and charges of sale, shall be returned to the proprietor of the lands or real estate sold as aforesaid.

Penalty on Collectors for Extortion and Oppression.

SEC. 36. *And be it further enacted*, That each and every collector, or his deputy,* who shall be guilty of any extortion or willful op-

---

*DEPUTY COLLECTORS.

In case of the sickness or temporary disability of a collector, he may devolve his duties upon one of his deputies, and for the official acts and defaults of the latter, his principal is responsible to the United States.

Upon the death, resignation or removal of a collector from office, the deputies act till the successor is appointed, the oldest deputy discharging the duties of the principal collector; the official bond of the latter being held for such official acts and defaults of such deputies. In case of two deputy collectors appointed the same day, the one residing nearest the residence of the collector shall perform the duties, of the collector, under the circumstances above named, unless the Secretary of the Treasury should designate some other deputy to act in this behalf.

If the deputy has given bond or other security to the collector, for the faithful performance of his duties, the same shall be available to the legal representatives and sureties of the latter (in case such deputy should succeed to the duties of the deceased collector,) for indemnification for loss or injury accruing from his acts.

The aim of all deputy collectors should be, to render the performance of the duties of their somewhat unwelcome mission as little obnoxious as possible, consistent with faithfulness and firmness.

I will add hereto a few practical suggestions as to his official duties:

(a) Upon his appointment he files a bond or other satisfactory security with the collector of the district from whom he derived his appointment. If it is satisfactory to the latter, he receives his commission, and all necessary blanks, stationery, books and instructions from his principal.

(b) He at once gives public notice of his appointment in some newspaper in the county where he resides.

(c) He receives the lists, whether "annual," "monthly," or "special," from his principal, and gives a receipt therefor, in which he expressly contracts to be accountable for the amount of the tax contained on such list.

(d) In anticipation of the issue of the complete annual list, he receives from time to time from his principal, soon after the first of May, lists of issued licenses, accompanied by the licenses; the fees for which, he should immediately collect, and deliver the licenses to the applicants.

(e) He should notify in writing each person, firm or corporation, named in the list he receives to collect, of the amount of the tax in his hands, due from such person, firm or corporation; which notice may be left at the place of business or residence of the party, or be sent by mail; and if the tax is not promptly paid, he should in all cases collect the penalty and other fees, impartially, of all delinquents.

(f) He should keep a book of accounts, charging himself with the gross amount of all lists committed to him.

(g) His collections should, in all cases where feasible, be deposited in some bank, in his name as "deputy collector," and not to his private account.

pression, under color of law, or shall knowingly demand other or greater sums than shall be authorized by law, or shall receive any fee, compensation, or reward, except as herein prescribed, for the performance of any duty, or shall willfully neglect to perform any of the duties enjoined by this act, shall, upon conviction, be subject to a fine of not exceeding one thousand dollars, or to be imprisoned for not exceeding one year, or both, at the discretion of the court, and be dismissed from office, and be forever thereafter incapable of holding any office under the government; and one-half of the fine so imposed shall be for the use of the United States, and the other half for the use of the informer, who shall be ascertained by the judgment of the court; and the said court shall also render judgment against said collector or deputy collector for the amount of damages accruing to the party injured, to be collected by execution. And each and every collector, or his deputies, shall give receipts for all sums by them collected.

Power of Revenue Officers to Enter upon Factories and Distilleries, &c., to Examine into Sources of Revenue, &c.

SEC. 37. *And be it further enacted,* That a collector or deputy collector, assessor, assistant assessor, revenue agent, or inspector, shall

(h) He should make returns to his principal of his collections, monthly, accompanied by an abstract of the list.

(k) If any tax is uncollectable, he should so state, and give his reason in brief; or a statement of any facts going to show the insolvency of the delinquent, or any other facts and circumstances affecting his inability to pay the duty.

(l) He should render all reasonable facilities to persons having business at his office; avoiding the extreme, of taking advantage of every casual error or inadvertence in the time when a tax is due, for the purpose of enforcing a penalty, but firmly insisting upon a full compliance with the law, according to the letter of its requirements, in respect to the prompt payment of the tax.

(m) He should be ever watchful in his scrutiny, that trades, occupations and manufactures, are not carried on without license, and payment of the duty. If he chooses, he can be a most efficient and valuable co-operator with the assessor and his assistants, in seeing to it, that the government is not defrauded out of its rights by the concealments and evasions of any who are liable to taxation, and the inadvertence of others who are ignorant of their obligations.

(n) All penalties collected should be accounted for to their principals, in their monthly returns.

(o) In no case should the deputy collector pay the tax himself to avoid the trouble of seeking some small tax-payer. Cases have occurred, when deputies have committed to them a small tax, perhaps of a few cents, and the cost of collection would be many times the amount of the assessment. He pays it himself; the person liable deems that he is forgotten by the government, and straightway *he* forgets to render further returns.

(p) If required by the collector, he should attend to the sale of stamps, making regular monthly returns of sales to his principal, on or before the tenth of the month.

(q) He should insist that in all cases when possible, payments to him should be made in national currency.

(r) At no time should he allow himself to be in arrears in his payments to the collector, neither should he, under any circumstances, mingle government funds with his own; and the operations of each month should be closed up as far as possible, in the rendition of his accounts, at its close.

be authorized to enter, in the day time, any brewery, distillery, manufactory, building, or place where any property, articles, or objects, subject to duty or taxation under the provisions of this act, are made, produced, or kept, within his district, so far as it may be necessary for the purpose of examining said property, articles, or objects, or inspecting the accounts required by this act from time to time to be made or kept by any manufacturer or producer, relating to such property, articles or objects. And every owner of such brewery, distillery, manufactory, building, or place, or persons having the agency or superintendence of the same, who shall refuse to admit such officer, or to suffer him to examine said property, articles, or objects, or to inspect said accounts, shall, for every such refusal, forfeit and pay the sum of five hundred dollars: *Provided, however,* That when such premises shall be open at night, such officers may enter while so open in the performance of their official duties.

Penalties for Obstructing Revenue Officers. Ditto on Officers for Divulging Secret Operations.

SEC. 38. *And be it further enacted,* That if any person shall forcibly obstruct or hinder any assessor or assistant assessor, or any collector or deputy collector, revenue agent or inspector, in the execution of this act, or of any power and authority hereby vested in him, or shall forcibly rescue, or cause to be rescued, any property, articles, or objects, after the same shall have been seized by him, or shall attempt or endeavor so to do, the person so offending shall, upon conviction thereof, for every such offence, forfeit and pay the sum of five hundred dollars, or double the value of property so rescued, or be imprisoned for a term not exceeding two years, at the discretion of the court: *Provided,* That if any such officer shall divulge to any party, or make known in any manner other than as provided in this act, the operations, style of work or apparatus of any manufacturer or producer visited by him in the discharge of his official duties, he shall be subject to the penalties prescribed in Section 36 of this act.

Collector may devolve his Duties upon a Deputy, in case of Sickness.

SEC. 39. *And be it further enacted,* That in case of the sickness or temporary disability of a collector to discharge such of his duties as cannot under existing laws be discharged by a deputy, they may be devolved by him upon one of his deputies; and for the official acts and defaults of such deputy the collector or his sureties shall be held responsible to the United States.

Oldest Deputy to Act in Certain Cases.

SEC. 40. *And be it further enacted,* That in case a collector shall die, resign, or be removed, the deputies of such collector shall continue to act until his successor is appointed; and the deputy of such collector longest in service at the time immediately preceding shall, until a successor shall be appointed, discharge all the duties of said collector; and for the official acts and defaults of such deputy a remedy shall be had on the official bond of the collector, as in other cases; and of two or more deputy collectors, appointed on the same day, the one residing nearest the residence of the collector at the time of his death, resignation, or removal, shall discharge the said duties until the appointment of a successor: *Provided*, That in case it shall appear to the Secretary of the Treasury that the interest of the government shall so require, he may, by his order, direct said duties to be performed by such other one of the said deputies as he may in such order designate. And any bond or security taken from a deputy by such collector, pursuant to this act, shall be available to his legal representatives and sureties to indemnify them for loss or damage accruing from any act of the deputy so continuing or succeeding to the duties of such collector.

Collectors to Collect Taxes and Sue for Fines, &c., and in name of United States. Employment of Counsel in Suits.

SEC 41. *And be it further enacted*, [That it shall be the duty of the collectors aforesaid, or their deputies, in their respective districts, and they are hereby authorized, to collect all the taxes imposed by law, however the same may be designated, and to prosecute for the recovery of any sum or sums which may be forfeited by virtue of law; and all fines, penalties, and forfeitures which may be incurred or imposed by virtue of law, shall be sued for and recovered, in the name of the United States, in any proper form of action, or by any appropriate form of proceeding, *qui tam*, or otherwise, before any circuit or district court of the United States for the district within which said fine, penalty, or forfeiture may have been incurred, or before any other court of competent jurisdiction. And taxes may be sued for and recovered in the name of the United States, in any proper form of action before any circuit or district court of the United States for the district within which the liability to such tax may have been or shall be incurred, or where the party from whom such tax is due may reside at the time of the commencement of said action. But no such suit shall be commenced unless the Commissioner of Internal Revenue shall authorize or sanction the proceedings: *Provided*, That in case of any suit for penalties or forfeitures brought upon information received from any person, other than a collector, deputy collector, assessor, assistant assessor, revenue agent, or inspector of Internal revenue, the United States shall not be subject to any costs of suit, nor shall the fees of any attorney or counsel employed by any such officer be allowed in the settlement of his account, unless the employment of such attorney or counsel shall be authorized by the Commissioner of Internal Revenue, either express or by general regulations.]

False Swearing deemed Perjury.

SEC. 42. *And be it further enacted*, That if any person, in any case, matter, hearing, or other proceeding in which an oath or affirmation shall be required to be taken or administered under and by virtue of this act, shall, upon the taking of such oath or affirmation, knowingly and willfully swear or affirm falsely, every person so offending shall be deemed guilty of perjury, and shall, on conviction thereof, be subject to the like punishment and penalties now provided by the laws of the United States for the crime of perjury.

Separate Accounts kept at Treasury of Moneys Received from several Districts.

SEC. 43. *And be it further enacted,* That separate accounts shall be kept at the treasury of all moneys received from internal taxes in each of the respective States, Territories, and collection districts; and that separate accounts shall be kept of the amount of each species of tax that shall accrue, so as to exhibit, as far as may be, the amount collected from each source of revenue, with the moneys paid as compensation and for allowances to the collectors and deputy collectors, assessors and assistant assessors, inspectors, and other officers employed in each of the respective States, Territories, and collection districts, an abstract in tabular form of which accounts, it shall be the duty of the Secretary of the Treasury annually, in the month of December, to lay before Congress.

Refunding of Taxes Illegally Collected. Indemnity of Collectors and Other Officers against Costs in Suits. In Second Assessments, and Claim for Remission, the burden of Proof of Good Faith shall be upon Claimant.

SEC. 44. *And be it further enacted,* [That the Commissioner of Internal Revenue, subject to regulations prescribed by the Secretary of the Treasury, shall be, and is hereby, authorized, on appeal to him made, to remit, refund, and pay back all taxes, erroneously or illegally assessed or collected, all penalties collected without authority, and all taxes that shall appear to be unjustly assessed or excessive in amount, or in any manner wrongfully collected, and also repay to collectors or deputy collectors the full amount of such sums of money as shall or may be recovered against them or any of them in any court, for any internal taxes or licenses collected by them, with the costs and expenses of suit, and all damages and costs recovered against assessors, assistant assessors, collectors, deputy collectors, and inspectors, in any suit which shall be brought against them or any of them by reason of anything that shall or may be done in the due performance of their official duties; and all judgments and moneys recovered or received for taxes, costs, forfeitures, and penalties shall be paid to the collector as internal taxes are required to be paid: *Provided,* That where a second assessment may have been made in case of a list, statement, or return which in the opinion of the assessor or assistant assessor was false or fraudulent, or contained any understatement or undervaluation, such assessment shall not be remitted, nor shall taxes collected under such assessment be recovered, refunded, or paid back, unless it is proved that said list, statement, or return was not false or fraudulent, and did not contain any understatement or undervaluation.]

Collectors' Bill of Sale prima facie Evidence of Right to make Sale; and Conclusive as to Regularity.

SEC. 45. *And be it further enacted,* That in all cases of distraint and sale of goods or chattels for non-payment of taxes, duties, or licenses, as provided for, the bill of sale of such goods or chattels given by the officer making such sale, to the purchaser thereof, shall be prima facie evidence of the right of the officer to make such sale, and conclusive evidence of the regularity of his proceedings in selling the same.

Duty of President of the United States in States, &c., where Law Cannot be Executed.

SEC. 46. *And be it further enacted,* That if, for any cause, at any time after this act goes into operation, the laws of the United States cannot be executed in a State or Territory of the United States, or any part thereof, or within the District of Columbia, it shall be the duty of the President, and he is hereby authorized, to proceed to execute the provisions of this act within the limits of such State or Territory, or part thereof, or District of Columbia, so soon as the authority of the United States therein shall be re-established, and to collect the taxes, duties, and licenses in such States and Territories, under the regulations prescribed in this act, so far as applicable; and where not applicable, the assessment and levy shall be made, and the time and manner of collection regulated, by the instructions and directions of the Commissioner of Internal Revenue, under the direction of the Secretary of the Treasury.

Provisions in relation to Collection of Direct Tax by Revenue Officers under the Act.

SEC. 47. *And be it further enacted,* That the officers who may be appointed under this act, except within those districts within any State or Territory which have been or may be otherwise especially provided for by law, shall be, and hereby are, authorized, in all cases where the payment of such tax shall not have been assumed by the State, to perform all the duties relating to or regarding the assessment and collection of any direct tax imposed or which may be imposed by law.

Seizure by Collector of Goods, Articles, &c., held for the purpose of Fraud. Forfeiture of the Articles. Proceedings in rem. Penalties. Provisions in relation to Perishable Property and Appraisal thereof, and Bonds for Return of Property given up to Owners, &c.

SEC. 48. *And be it further enacted,* [That all goods, wares, merchandise, articles, or objects on which taxes are imposed by the provisions of law, which shall be found in the possession, or custody, or within the control of any person or persons, for the purpose of being sold or removed by such person or persons in fraud of the internal revenue laws, or with design to avoid payment of said taxes, may be seized by the collector or deputy collector of the proper district, or by such other collector or deputy collector as may be specially authorized by the Commissioner of Internal Revenue for that purpose, and the same shall be forfeited to the United States; and also all raw materials found in the possession of any person or persons intending to manufacture the same into articles of a kind subject to tax, for the purpose of fraudulent selling such manufactured articles, or with design to evade the payment of said tax, and also all tools, implements, instruments, and personal property whatsoever, in the place or building, or within any yard or enclosure where such articles or such raw materials shall be found, may also be seized by any collector or deputy collector, as aforesaid, and the same shall be forfeited as aforesaid; and the proceedings to enforce said forfeiture shall be in the nature of a proceeding in rem in the circuit or district court of the United States for the district where such seizure is made, or in any other court of competent jurisdiction. And any person who shall have in his custody or possession any such goods, wares, merchandise, articles, or objects subject to tax as aforesaid, for the purpose of selling the same with the design of avoiding payment of the taxes imposed thereon, shall be liable to a penalty of five hundred dollars, or not less than double the amount of taxes fraudulently attempted to be evaded, to be recovered in any court of competent jurisdiction; and the goods, wares, merchandise, articles, or objects which shall be so seized by any collector or deputy collector may, at the option of the collector, be delivered to the marshal of said district, and remain in the care and custody of said marshal, and under his control until he shall obtain possession by process of law, and the costs of seizure made before process issues shall be taxable by the court: *Provided*, That when the property so seized may be liable to perish or become greatly reduced in price or value by keeping, or when it cannot be kept without great expense, the owner thereof, the collector, or the marshal of the district, may apply to the assessor of the district to examine said property; and if, in the opinion of said assessor, it shall be necessary that the said property should be sold to prevent such waste or expense, he shall appraise the same; and the owner thereupon shall have said property returned to him upon giving bond in such form as may be prescribed by the Commissioner of Internal Revenue, and in an amount equal to the appraised value, with such sureties as the said assessor shall deem good and sufficient, to abide the final order, decree, or judgment of the court having cognizance of the case, and to pay the amount of said appraised value to the collector, marshal, or otherwise, as he may be ordered and directed by the court, which bond shall be filed by said assessor with the United States district attorney for the district in which said proceeding in rem may be commenced: *Provided further*, That in case said bond shall have been executed and the property returned before seizure thereof, by virtue of the process aforesaid, the marshal shall give notice of the pendency of proceedings in court, to the parties executing said bond, by personal service or publication and in manner and form as the court may direct, and the court shall thereupon have jurisdiction of said matter and parties in the same manner as if such property had been seized by virtue of the process aforesaid. But if said owner shall refuse or neglect to give said bond the assessor shall issue to the collector or marshal aforesaid an order to sell the same; and the said collector or marshal shall thereupon advertise and sell the said property at public auction in the same manner as goods may be sold on final execution in said district; and the proceeds of the sale, after deducting the reasonable costs of the seizure and sale, shall be paid to the court aforesaid, to abide its final order, decree or judgment.]

Provisions in relation to Returns, Lists, &c., and Imposition of Fines, apply to all Persons and Corporations. Additions to Fines herein made to be Cumulative.

SEC. 49. *And be it further enacted,* That all the provisions hereinafter made for the delivery of returns, lists, statements, and valuations, and for additions to the duty in case of false or fraudulent lists or returns, or in case of undervaluation or understatement on lists or returns, or in case of refusal or neglect to deliver lists or returns, and for the imposition of fines, penalties, and forfeitures, shall be held and taken to apply to all persons, associations, corporations, or companies liable to pay duty or tax; and any additions to duties, fines, penalties, or forfeitures hereinafter imposed for failure to perform any duty required to be performed, shall be held and taken to be additional to those hereinbefore provided.

Act of March 2, 1833, for Removal of Suits to apply to Internal Revenue Cases. Officers of Internal Revenue to be "Revenue Officers" under said Act.

SEC. 50. *And be it further enacted,* That the provisions of the act entitled "An act further to provide for the collection of duties or imports," approved March second, one thousand eight hundred and thirty-three, now in force, shall be taken and deemed as extending to and embracing all cases arising under the laws for the collection of internal duties, stamp duties, licenses, or taxes, which have been or may be hereafter enacted; and all persons duly authorized to assess, receive, or collect such taxes under such laws are hereby declared to be and to have been revenue officers within the true intent and meaning of the said act, and entitled to all the exemptions, immunities, benefits, rights, and privileges therein enumerated or conferred.*

* By the 68th Section of the Act of 1866 (the act just enacted), this section is expressly repealed; but as it is in such repealing section referred to with a saving clause for cases to which it has heretofore been applicable, and under which cases have been removed, &c., it is here retained. (See the Section [68], *infra.*)

Jurisdiction of Circuit Court of the United States and General Provisions under Statute of 1833.

(SEC. 2. Act of March 2, 1833.) *And be it further enacted,* That the jurisdiction of the circuit courts of the United States shall extend to all cases, in law or equity, arising under the revenue laws of the United States for which other provisions are not already made by law; and if any person shall receive any injury to his person or property for or on account of any act by him done, under any law of the United States, for the protection of the revenue or the collection of duties on imports, he shall be entitled to maintain suit for damage therefor in the circuit court of the United States in the district wherein the party doing the injury may reside, or shall be found. And all property taken or detained by any officer or other person under authority of any revenue law of the United States shall be irrepleviable, and shall be deemed to be in the custody of the law, and subject only to the orders and decrees of the courts of the United States having jurisdiction thereof. And if any person shall dispossess or rescue, or attempt to dispossess or rescue, any property so taken or detained as aforesaid, or shall aid or assist therein, such person shall be deemed guilty of a misdemeanor, and shall be liable to such punishment as is provided by the twenty-second section of the act for the punishment of certain crimes against the United States, approved the thirtieth day of April, anno domini one thousand seven hundred and ninety, for the willful obstruction or resistance of officers in the service of process.

Removal of Actions in State Courts and Proceedings thereupon.

(SEC. 3. Act of March 2, 1833.) *And be it further enacted,* That in any case where suit or prosecution shall be commenced in a court of any State against any officer of the United States, or other person, for or on account of any act done under the revenue laws of the United States, or under color thereof, or for, or on account of any right, authority, or title, set up or claimed by such officer or other person under any such law of the United States, it shall be lawful for the defendant in such suit or prosecution, at any time before trial, upon a petition to the circuit court of the United States, in and for the district in which the defendant shall have been served with process, setting forth the nature of said suit or prosecution, and verifying the said petition by affidavit, together with a certificate signed by an attorney or counsellor-at-law of some court of record of the State in which such suit shall have been commenced, or of the United States, setting forth that, as counsel for the petitioner, he has examined the proceedings against him, and has carefully inquired into all the matters set forth in the petition, and that he believes the same to be true; which petition, affidavit, and certificate shall be presented to the said circuit court, if in session, and if not, to the clerk thereof, at his office, and shall be filed in said office, and the cause shall thereupon be entered on the docket of said court, and shall be thereafter proceeded in as a cause originally commenced in that court; and it shall be the duty of the clerk of said court, if the suit were commenced in the court below by summons, to issue a writ of *certiorari* to the State court, requiring said court to send to the said circuit court the record and proceedings in said cause; or if it were commenced by *capias*, he shall issue a writ of *habeas corpus cum causa*, a duplicate of which said writ shall be delivered to the clerk of the State court, or left at his office by the marshal of the district, or his deputy, or some person duly authorized thereto; and thereupon it shall be the duty of the said State court to stay all further proceedings in such cause, and the said suit or prosecution, upon delivery of such process, or leaving the same as aforesaid, shall be deemed and taken to be moved to the said circuit court, and any further proceedings, trial or judgment therein in the State court shall be wholly null and void; and if the defendant in any such suit be in actual custody on mesne process therein, it shall be the duty of the marshal, by virtue of the writ of *habeas corpus cum causa*, to take the body of the defendant into his custody, to be dealt with in the said cause according to the rules of law and the order of the circuit court, or of any judge thereof, in vacation. And all attachments made, and all bail and other security given upon such suit, or prosecution, shall be and continue in like force and effect as if the same suit or prosecution had proceeded to final judgment and execution in the State court; and if, upon the removal of any such suit, or prosecution, it shall be made to appear to the said circuit court that no copy of the record and proceedings therein, in the State court, can be obtained, it shall be lawful for said circuit court to allow and require the plaintiff to proceed *de novo*, and to file a declaration of his cause of action, and the parties may thereupon proceed as in actions originally brought in said circuit court; and on failure of so proceeding, judgment of *non pros.* may be rendered against the plaintiff, with costs for the defendant.

Record to be Supplied, &c.

(Sec. 4. Act of March 3, 1865.) *And be it further enacted*, That in any case in which any party is, or may be by law, entitled to copies of the record and proceedings in any suit or prosecution in any State court to be used in any court of the United States, if the clerk of said State court shall, upon demand, and the payment or tender of the legal fees, refuse or neglect to deliver to such party certified copies of such record and proceedings, the court of the United States in which such record and proceedings may be needed, on proof, by affidavit, that the clerk of such State court has refused or neglected to deliver copies thereof, on demand as aforesaid, may direct and allow such record to be supplied by affidavit, or otherwise, as the circumstances of the case may require and allow; and thereupon, such proceeding, trial, and judgment may be had in the said court of the United States, and all such processes awarded, as if certified copies of such records and proceedings had been regularly before the said court.

Section 16, Act of August 6, 1846, applied to Revenue Officers.

SEC. 51. *And be it further enacted,* That the provisions of the sixteenth section of the act approved August sixth, eighteen hundred and forty-six, entitled "An act to provide for the better organization of the treasury, and for the collection, safe-keeping, transfer, and disbursement of the public revenue," are hereby applied to, and shall be construed to include, all officers of the internal revenue charged with the safe-keeping, transfer, or disbursement of the public moneys arising therefrom, and to all other persons having actual charge, custody, or control of moneys or accounts arising from the administration of the internal revenue.

*Entries of Public Moneys received under Revenue Acts to be duly made. Penalties for improper use or deposit of Public Moneys. Embezzlement. Evidence under Charge of, &c.**

(SEC. 16. Adopted August 6, 1846.) *And be it further enacted,* That all officers and other persons charged by this act, or any other act, with the safe-keeping, transfer, and disbursement of the public moneys, other than those connected with the Post Office Department, are hereby required to keep an accurate entry of each sum received, and of each payment or transfer; and that if any one of the said officers, or of those connected with the Post Office Department, shall convert to his own use, in any way whatever, or shall use, by way of investment in any kind of property or merchandise, or shall loan, with or without interest, or shall deposit in any bank, or shall exchange for other funds, except as allowed by this act, any portion of the public moneys intrusted to him for safe-keeping, disbursement, transfer, or for any other purpose, every such act shall be deemed and adjudged to be an embezzlement of so much of the said moneys as shall be thus taken, converted, invested, used, loaned, deposited, or exchanged, which is hereby declared to be a felony; and any failure to pay over or to produce the public moneys intrusted to such person shall be held and taken to be *prima facie* evidence of such embezzlement; and if any officer charged with the disbursements of public moneys shall accept, or receive, or transmit to the Treasury Department to be allowed in his favor, any receipt or voucher from a creditor of the United States, without having paid to such creditor, in such funds as the said officer may have received for disbursement, or such other funds as he may be authorized by this act to take in exchange, the full amount specified in such receipt or voucher, every such act shall be deemed to be a conversion by such officer to his own use of the amount specified in such receipt or voucher; and any officer or agent of the United States, and all persons advising or participating in such act, being convicted thereof before any court of

* See act of June 14, 1866, *supra.*

the United States of competent jurisdiction, shall be sentenced to imprisonment for a term of not less than six months nor more than ten years, and to a fine equal to the amount of the money embezzled. And upon the trial of any indictment against any person for embezzling public money under the provisions of this act, it shall be sufficient evidence, for the purpose of showing a balance against such person, to produce a transcript from the books and proceedings of the treasury, as required in civil cases, under the provisions of the act entitled "An act to provide more effectually for the settlement of accounts between the United States and receivers of public money," approved March third, one thousand seven hundred and ninety-seven; and the provisions of this act shall be so construed as to apply to all persons charged with the safe-keeping, transfer, or disbursement of the public money, whether such persons be indicted as receivers or depositaries of the same; and the refusal of such person, whether in or out of office, to pay any draft, order, or warrant which may be drawn upon him by the proper officer of the Treasury Department, for any public money in his hands belonging to the United States, no matter in what capacity the same may have been received or may be held, or to transfer or disburse any such money promptly, upon the legal requirement of any authorized officer of the United States, shall be deemed and taken, upon the trial of any indictment against such person for embezzlement, as *prima facie* evidence of such embezzlement.

Act of March 3, 1797, *General Provisions.*

(Sec. 1. Act of March 3, 1797.) *Be it enacted by the Senate and House of Representatives of the United States of America in Congress assembled,* That when any revenue officer, or other person accountable for public money, shall neglect or refuse to pay into the treasury the sum or balance reported to be due to the United States upon the adjustment of his account, it shall be the duty of the Comptroller, and he is hereby required, to institute suit for the recovery of the same, adding to the sum stated to be due on such account the commissions of the delinquent, which shall be forfeited in every instance where suit is commenced and judgment obtained thereon, and an interest of six per cent. per annum, from the time of receiving the money, until it shall be repaid into the treasury.

Evidence in Cases of Delinquency.

(Sec. 2. Act of March 3, 1797.) *And be it further enacted,* That in every case of delinquency, where suit has been or shall be instituted, a transcript from the books and proceedings of the treasury, certified by the Register, and authenticated under the seal of the department, shall be admitted as evidence, and the court trying the cause shall be thereupon authorized to grant judgment and award execution accordingly. And all copies of bonds, contracts, or other papers relating to or connected with the settlement of any account between the United States and an individual, when certified by the Register to be true copies of the originals on file, and authenticated under the seal of the department, as aforesaid, may be annexed to such transcripts, and shall have equal validity and be entitled to the same degree of credit which would be due to the original papers if produced and authenticated in court: *Provided*, That where suit is brought upon a bond, or other sealed instrument, and the defendant shall plead "*non est factum*," or upon motion to the court, such plea or motion being verified by the oath or affirmation of the defendant, it shall be lawful for the court to take the same into consideration and (if it shall appear to be necessary for the attainment of justice) to require the production of the original bond, contract, or other paper specified in such affidavit.

Rendition of Judgment.

(SEC. 3. Act of March 3, 1797.) *And be it further enacted*, That where suit shall be instituted against any person or persons indebted to the United States, as aforesaid, it shall be the duty of the court where the same may be pending to grant judgment at the return term, upon motion, unless the defendant shall, in open court, (the United States attorney being present,) make oath or affirmation that he is equitably entitled to credits which had been, previous to the commencement of the suit, submitted to the consideration of the accounting officers of the treasury, and rejected; specifying each particular claim so rejected in the affidavit, and that he cannot then come safely to trial. Oath or affirmation to this effect being made, subscribed, and filed, if the court be thereupon satisfied, a continuance until the next succeeding term may be granted; but not otherwise, unless as provided in the preceding section.

Conditions of Claim for Credits by Revenue Officers, &c.

(SEC. 4. Act of March 3, 1797.) *And be it further enacted*, That in suits between the United States and individuals no claim for a credit shall be admitted upon trial but such as shall appear to have been presented to the accounting officers of the treasury for their examination, and by them disallowed, in whole or in part, unless it should be proved to the satisfaction of the court that the defendant is, at the time of trial, in possession of vouchers not before in his power to procure, and that he was prevented from exhibiting a claim for such credit at the treasury by absence from the United States or some unavoidable accident.

Priority of United States in cases of Insolvency.

(SEC. 5. Act of March 3, 1797.) *And be it further enacted*, That where any revenue officer, or other person hereafter becoming indebted to the United States by bond or otherwise, shall become insolvent, or where the estate of any deceased debtor, in the hands of executors or administrators, shall be insufficient to pay all the debts due from the deceased, the debt due to the United States shall be first satisfied, and the priority hereby established shall be deemed to extend as well to cases in which a debtor not having sufficient property to pay all his debts shall make a voluntary assignment thereof, or in which the estate and effects of an absconding, concealed, or absent debtor shall be attached by process of law, as to cases in which an act of legal bankruptcy shall be committed.

Costs of Execution may be executed in any State.

(SEC. 6. Act of March 3, 1797.) *And be it further enacted,* That all writs of execution upon any judgment obtained for the use of the United States in any of the courts of the United States in one State may run and be executed in any other State, or in any of the Territories of the United States, but shall be issued from and made returnable to the court where the judgment was obtained, any law to the contrary notwithstanding.

Prior legal Remedies not to be Impaired.

(SEC. 7. Act of March 3, 1797.) *And be it further enacted,* That nothing in this act shall be construed to repeal, take away, or impair any legal remedy or remedies for the recovery of debts now due, or hereafter to be due, to the United States, in law or equity, from any person or persons whatsoever, which remedy or remedies might be used if this act was not in force.

Oaths may be administered by Revenue Officers.

SEC. 52. *And be it further enacted,* That all assessors and their assistants, all collectors and their deputies, revenue agents and all inspectors, are hereby authorized to administer oaths and take evidence touching any part of the administration of this law with which they are respectively charged, or where such oaths and evidence are by law authorized to be taken; and any perjury therein shall be punished in the like manner, and to the same degree, as in the case of perjury committed in proceedings in the courts of the United States.

[Sections 53, 54, 55, 56, 57, of the act of 1864, repealed.*]

Inspection of Oil, Tobacco and Cigars. Form of Oath. Penalty for Obstruction in the Duties.

SEC. 58. *And be it further enacted,* That there shall be appointed by the Secretary of the Treasury, in every collection district where the same may be necessary, one or more inspectors† of spirits, refined coal oil or other oil, tobacco, cigars, and other articles, who shall take an oath faithfully to perform their duties, in such form as the Commissioner of Internal Revenue shall prescribe, and who shall be entitled to receive

* They pertained to "spirits, ale, beer and porter," for which new and elaborate provisions are hereinafter provided.—ED.

† See Appendix for full instructions to inspectors of cigars, &c., most of which are still applicable.

such fees as may be fixed and prescribed by said Commissioner, to be paid by the owner or manufacturer of the articles inspected, gauged or proved. And any manufacturer of spirits, refined coal oil or other oil, tobacco, cigars, or other articles which may by law be required to be inspected, who shall refuse to admit an inspector upon his premises, so far as it may be necessary for the performance of his duties, or who shall obstruct an inspector in the performance of his duties, shall forfeit the sum of one hundred dollars, to be recovered in the manner provided for other penalties imposed by this act.

[Section 59 of the act of 1864 repealed.]

Distillers and Refiners of Oil may erect Warehouses. Tax paid before Renewal.

SEC. 60. *And be it further enacted*, That the owner or owners of any distillery or oil refinery may provide, at his or their own expense, a warehouse, in conformity with such regulations as the Secretary of the Treasury may prescribe: and such warehouse, when approved by the collector, is hereby declared a bonded warehouse of the United States, and shall be used only for storing distilled spirits, or refined coal oil, or naphtha, and to be under the custody of the collector or his deputy. And the duty on the spirits, coal oil, or naphtha stored in such warehouse shall be paid before it is removed from such warehouse, unless removed in pursuance of law.

Distilled Spirits, Oil, Naphtha, &c., may be removed without payment of Tax under Bonds. Transfer to other Warehouses. Reinspection and Allowance for Leakage. Bonded Goods at risk of Owner. Withdrawal of Goods from Warehouse, &c.

SEC 61. *And be it further enacted*, That all distilled spirits, and all distilled or refined coal oil, distillate, benzine or benzole, and naphtha, upon which an excise duty is imposed by law, may, after being inspected, gauged, proved, and marked by the inspector according to the provisions of this act, be removed, without payment of the duty, under such rules and regulations, and upon the execution of such transportation bonds or other security as the Secretary of the Treasury may prescribe. The said spirits, oil, or naphtha so removed shall be transferred directly from the distillery or refinery to a bonded warehouse, established in conformity with law and treasury regulations, and may be transported from such warehouse to any one other bonded warehouse used for the storage of distilled spirits, coal oil, or naphtha. And after the arrival of such distilled spirits, coal oil, or naphtha at the bonded warehouse within the district of the assessor to which it has been transferred, it shall be again inspected, and the duty shall be assessed and paid on any deficiency or reduction of the number of proof gallons beyond such allowance for leakage as may be established by the regulations of the Commissioner of Internal Revenue, received at the warehouse, from the number of proof gallons as stated in the bond given at the place of shipment. And any distilled spirits, coal oil, or naphtha in the public warehouses shall be subject to the same rules and regulations, and be chargeable with the same costs and expenses in all respects, to which imported goods deposited in public store or bonded warehouse may be subject; and shall be in charge of a proper officer, to be designated by the Secretary of the Treasury, who, with the owner and proprietor of the warehouse, shall have the joint custody of all the distilled spirits, oil, or naphtha so stored in said warehouse, which shall be at the risk of the owner of the said spirits, oil, or naphtha. And all labor on the same shall be performed by the owner or proprietor of the warehouse, under the supervision of the officer in charge of the same, and at the expense of said owner or proprietor of the warehouse; and the same fees shall be paid for exports as are charged to exporters for like services in the custom-house. And no drawback shall in any case be allowed on any distilled spirits, coal oil, or naphtha, upon which an excise duty shall have been paid, either before or after it shall have been placed in a bonded warehouse: *Provided*, That any distilled spirits, coal oil, or naphtha may be withdrawn from the bonded warehouse after payment, to the collector of internal revenue for the district in which the warehouse is situated, of the duty imposed by law, or may be removed without payment of the duty for the purpose of being exported, or for the purpose of being redistilled or canned for export, after the quantity and proof of the spirits, oil, or naphtha to be removed has been ascertained and inspected according to the provisions of law, under such rules and regulations and the execution of such bond or other security as the Secretary of the Treasury may prescribe. And any spirits, oil, or naphtha so removed for distillation shall be returned to the warehouse and shall be again inspected, and the duty shall be paid to the said collector on any deficiency or reduction beyond the allowance for loss by redistillation established by the Commissioner of Internal Revenue, in the number of proof gallons received at the warehouse for the purpose of being exported, as aforesaid. And nothing in this section shall be construed to prevent the manufacture for exportation, without payment of duty, of medicines, preparations, compositions, perfumery, cosmetics, cordials, and other liquors manufactured wholly or in part of domestic spirits, as provided for in this act.

[Sections 62, 63, 64, 65, 66, 67, 68, 69, 70, of the act of 1864, are repealed.*]

Substitution of Special Tax for Licenses. New Provisions of Act of 1866.†

SEC. 71. *And be it further enacted*, [That no person, firm, company, or corporation shall be engaged in, prosecute, or carry on any

* These related to distilleries and breweries, for which new provisions are hereinafter substituted, and substantially a new system established, with more stringent regulations to prevent fraud.

† It will be perceived that a "special tax" has been substituted for the term "license" in former laws. It had been heretofore held by respectable, consti-

trade, business, or profession, hereinafter mentioned and described, until he or they shall have paid a special tax therefor in the manner hereinafter provided.]

Registration of Persons formerly Licensed.

SEC. 72. *And be it further enacted*, [That every person, firm, company, or corporation engaged in any trade, business, or profession, on which a special tax is imposed by law, shall register with the assistant assessor of the assessment district, first, his or their name or style, and in case of a firm or company, the names of the several persons constituting such firm or company, and their places of residence; second, the trade, business, or profession, and the place where such trade, business, or profession is to be carried on; third, if a rectifier, the number of barrels he designs to rectify; if a peddler, whether he designs to travel on foot or with one, two, or more horses or mules; if an innkeeper, the yearly rental value of the house and property to be occupied for said purpose. All of which facts shall be returned duly certified by such assistant assessor, to both the assessor and collector of the district; and the special tax shall be paid to the collector or deputy collector of the district as hereinafter provided for such trade, business, or profession, who shall give a receipt therefor.]

Penalties for Non-Payment of Special Tax.

SEC. 73. *And be it further enacted*, [That any one who shall exercise or carry on any trade, business, or profession, or do any act hereinafter mentioned, for the exercising, carrying on, or doing of which a special tax is imposed by law, without payment thereof as in that behalf required, shall, for every such offence, besides being liable to the payment of the tax, be subject to imprisonment for a term not exceeding two years, or a fine not exceeding five hundred dollars, or both, and such fine shall be distributed between the United States and the informer, if there be any, as provided by law.]

---

tutional lawyers, that a license issued under the authority of the United States, (notwithstanding the express provisions of the revenue law, that "no license hereinbefore provided for shall, if granted, be held or construed to exempt any person carrying on the trade, business or profession specified in said license, from any penalty or punishment provided by the law of any State, for carrying on such trade, business, or profession within such State, or in any manner to authorize the commencement or continuance of such trade, business, or profession, contrary to the laws of such State, or in places prohibited by municipal law," (Sec. 78,) *ex vi termini* gave some *authority*, *permission*, and *liberty* to carry on the business named in such license, in contravention of merely State and municipal enactments and regulations. To avoid any such unfounded construction to be given to the term "license," and for other reasons, the special tax herein provided for, has been adopted by Congress.

It does not become the editor of this volume to comment upon the effect of this change of phraseology, and its apparent supererogatory character. It certainly will avoid one technical legal point, and abundant cavils of State right theorists.

Receipts for Payment of Special Tax a Substitute for Licenses. Provisions as to Place where Business is to be Carried on. Production of Receipt on Demand. Seizure of Goods, &c., of Peddlers not Producing Receipt, &c.*

SEC. 74. *And be it further enacted*, [That the receipt for the payment of any special tax shall contain and set forth the purpose, trade, business, or profession for which such tax is paid, and the name and place of abode of the person or persons paying the same; if by a rectifier, the quantity of spirits intended to be rectified; if by a peddler, whether for traveling on foot, or with one, or two, or more horses or mules, the time for which payment is made, the date or time of payment, and (except in the case of auctioneers, produce brokers, commercial brokers, patent-right dealers, photographers, builders, insurance agents, insurance brokers, and peddlers) the place at which the trade, business, or profession for which the tax is paid shall be carried on: *Provided*, that the payment of the special tax herein imposed shall not exempt from an additional special tax the person or persons, (except lawyers, physicians, surgeons, dentists, cattle brokers, horse dealers, peddlers, produce brokers, commercial brokers, patent-right dealers, photographers, builders, insurance agents, insurance brokers, and auctioneers,) or firm, company, or corporation doing business in any other place than that stated; but nothing herein contained shall require a special tax for the storage of goods, wares, or merchandise in other places than the place of business, nor for the sale by manufacturers or producers of their own goods, wares, and merchandise, at the place of production or manufacture, and at their principal office or place of business, provided no goods, wares, or merchandise shall be kept, except as samples, at said office or place of business. And every person exercising or carrying on any trade, business, or profession, or doing any act for which a special tax is imposed shall, on demand of any officer of internal revenue, produce and exhibit the receipt for payment of the tax, and unless he shall do so may be taken and deemed not to have paid such tax. And in case any peddler shall refuse to exhibit his or her receipt, as aforesaid, when demanded by any officer of internal revenue, said officer may seize the horse, or mule, wagon, and contents, or pack, bundle, or basket of any person so refusing, and the assessor of the district in which the seizure has occurred may, on ten days' notice, published in any newspaper in the district, or served personally on the peddler, or at his dwelling-house, require such peddler to show cause, if any he has, why the horses, or mules, wagon, and contents, pack, bundle, or basket so seized shall not be forfeited; and in

---

*In reciting and commenting upon former decisions and rulings, under this Section, it has not been deemed necessary by the editor to substitute the new term, "special tax," for the term "license," contained in former laws, under which the decisions and rulings have been made.

(Some of these decisions and rulings have been adopted by Congress, in the text of the present act, and some have been modified: but they are retained, both as illustrative of former provisions, and suggestive of the reasons for changes and modifications in the act as just enacted.)

case no sufficient cause is shown, the assessor may direct a forfeiture, and issue an order to the collector or to any deputy collector of the district, for the sale of the property so forfeited; and the same, after payment of the expenses of the proceedings, shall be paid to the collector for the use of the United States. And all such special taxes shall become due on the first day of May in each year, or on commencing any trade, business, or profession upon which such tax is by law imposed. In the former case the tax shall be reckoned for the year, and in the latter case, proportionately for that part of the year from the first day of the month in which the liability to a special tax commenced to the first day of May following.*]

Transfer of Business, on Death, &c., of Persons who have Paid the Special Tax, and Conditions of such Transfer.

SEC. 75. *And be it further enacted,* [That upon the death of any person having paid the special tax for any trade, business, or profession, it may and shall be lawful for the executors or administrators, or the wife or child, or the legal representatives of such deceased person to occupy the house or premises, and in like manner to exercise or carry on, for the residue of the term for which the tax shall have been paid, the same trade, business, or profession as the deceased before exercised or carried on, in or upon the same houses or premises, without payment of any additional tax. And in case of the removal of any person or persons

---

*SPECIAL TAX.

"All licenses expire by limitation April 30, in each year. Applications for renewal of licenses should be made previous to their expiration. It is the duty of all persons requiring license to file such application, whether notified or not; and default therein renders them liable to the penalties for carrying on business without license. The name and private residence of the applicant must be stated in the first space of the blank; and if for a partnership, the name and residence of each member must be stated. If change of residence is contemplated, the place, if known, to which they will remove, ought to be given.

As the license for "wholesale dealers" is based upon their sales for the preceding year, that is to say, from May of one year to May of the following year, the amount of such sales must in all cases be stated, and it is competent for the assistant assessor to cause such statement to be verified by affidavit, for which an appropriate blank is provided.

If wholesale dealers intend to effect any change or alteration in their business during the ensuing year, either by reduction of capital, dissolution of partnership, or other causes, they should make it known to the assistant assessor at the time of filing the application; and if such change will, in his judgment, obviously reduce their sales below those of the preceding year, as rendered, proper allowance may be made by him, and the assessment completed accordingly. Merchants will save themselves much annoyance by frankly furnishing all necessary information in regard to their business, as it is only by being placed in possession of all the facts in a case, that the officer of the revenue is enabled efficiently to discharge his duty, and avoid making erroneous assessments.

The officer is bound in honor to reveal nothing in relation to the affairs of a tax-payer, that he may learn in the performance of his duties. (See Int. Rev. Rec., Vol. III., pp. 155, 156, 131. Appendix, Series 2, No. 4.

from the house or premises for which any trade, business, or profession was taxed, it shall be lawful for the person or persons so removing to any other place to carry on the trade, business, or profession specified in the tax receipt at the place to which such person or persons may remove without payment of any additional tax: *Provided*, That all cases of death, change or removal as aforesaid, shall be registered with the assistant assessor and with the collector, together with the name or names of the person or persons making such change or removal, or successor to any person deceased, under regulations to be prescribed by the Commissioner of Internal Revenue.]

Provisions when More than One Business is Carried on by the Same Person.

SEC. 76. *And be it further enacted*, [That in every case where more than one of the pursuits, employments, or occupations, hereinafter described, shall be pursued or carried on in the same place by the same person at the same time, except as hereinafter provided, the tax shall be paid for each according to the rates severally prescribed: *Provided*, That in cities and towns having a less population than six thousand persons according to the last preceding census, one special tax shall be held to embrace the business of land warrant brokers, claim agents, and real estate agents, upon payment of the highest rate of tax applicable to either one of said pursuits.]

Provisions in Relation to Auctioneers.

SEC. 77. *And be it further enacted*, [That no auctioneer shall by virtue of having paid the special tax as an auctioneer sell any goods or other property at private sale, nor shall he employ any other person to act as auctioneer in his behalf, except in his own store or warehouse or in his presence; and any auctioneer who shall sell goods or commodities otherwise than by auction without having paid the special tax imposed upon such business, shall be subject and liable to the penalty imposed upon persons dealing in, or retailing, trading, or selling goods or commodities without payment of the special tax for exercising or carrying on such trade or business; and where goods or commodities are the property of any person or persons taxed to deal in or retail, or trade in or sell the same, it shall and may be lawful for any person exercising or carrying on the trade or business of an auctioneer to sell such goods or commodities for and on behalf of such person or persons in said house or premises.]

Business carried on in Copartnership Requires but one Special Tax, except, &c.

SEC. 78. *And be it further enacted*, [That any number of persons, except lawyers, conveyancers, claim agents, patent agents, physicians, surgeons, dentists, cattle brokers, horse dealers, and peddlers, doing business in copartnership at any one place, shall be required to pay but one special tax for such copartnership.]

Provisions as to Particular Occupations.

SEC. 79. *And be it further enacted,* [That a special tax shall be and hereby is imposed as follows, that is to say:

One. [Banks chartered or organized under a general law with a capital not exceeding fifty thousand dollars, and bankers* using or employ-

---

*I. BANKERS AND BROKERS.

A banker's license should be assessed upon the even thousands of capital, omitting fractions. National banks should take licenses as well as others.

By the statute of 1862, bankers paid for a license $100. A banker was defined as one "who keeps a place of business where credits are opened in favor of any person, firm or corporation, by the deposit or collection of money or currency, and the same or any part thereof shall be paid out or remitted upon the draft, check, or order of such creditor, but not to include incorporated banks or other banks legally authorized to issue notes as circulation, nor agents for the sale of merchandise for account of producers or manufacturers." (Law of 1862, § 64, ¶ 1.)

A *broker*, by the same statute, paid $50 for a license, and was defined to be one "whose business is to purchase or sell stocks, coined money, bank notes, or other securities for themselves or others, or who deals in exchanges relating to money." (*Ibidem*, § 64, ¶ 13.)

Under this statute, a variety of decisions were made; but it was decided in October, 1862, "that it was impossible to lay down an arbitrary rule as a test, whether a man's business was that of banker or broker, and assessors must exercise their best judgment." This was of course unsatisfactory enough.

In *Ruling No.* 55, (Boutwell's Manual, p. 309,) it was decided that incorporated banks (not *those* liable to banker's license) buying and selling coin or exchange, are required to take a broker's license, and that if an individual receives money on deposit for persons other than those for whom he sells produce or merchandise, he must take out a license as a banker, in addition to his license as broker. That a person who invests his own property may or may not be a broker, according to circumstances. That banks frequently selling coin must take broker's license; and that a bank agent who is supplied with the bills of the bank for the purpose of discounting notes, becomes a broker thereby. (Boutwell's Manual, pp. 309, 310.)

The law was thus left in a distressing state of uncertainty, and the license taxes on each business were frequently evaded. (See Decisions Nos. 43 and 91.) In the former of those decisions it was ruled that banks might draw and sell drafts against funds accumulated in other places without making themselves liable to broker's license, but dealing in exchanges relating to money, subjects them to the broker's license; and it was ruled in decision No. 91 that where banks bought and sold drafts whenever presented or called for, they were subjected to a broker's license; and generally that when incorporated banks do the business of a broker, they must take license as such.

No changes were made in the amendatory act of March, 1863, to affect this question of the liability of bankers and brokers to the license tax,—but amendments were made by the act of June 30, 1864, in relation to the *licenses* of both bankers and brokers; and more especially by Section 99 of that revision of the law, providing for a tax upon the sales of merchandise of brokers and bankers doing business as brokers, which rendered the proper definitions of both, and their relative liabilities, a matter of the utmost consequence.

The provisions in relation to banker's licenses, were as follows:

Bankers using or employing a capital not exceeding the sum of fifty thousand dollars shall pay one hundred dollars for each license; when using or employing a capital exceeding fifty thousand dollars, for every additional thousand dollars in excess of fifty thousand dollars, two dollars. Every person, firm, or company, and every incorporated or other bank, having a place of business where credits are opened by the deposit or collection of money or currency,

ing a capital not exceeding the sum of fifty thousand dollars, shall pay one hundred dollars; when exceeding fifty thousand dollars, for every additional thousand dollars in excess of fifty thousand dollars, two dollars. Every incorporated or other bank, and every person, firm or company having a place of business where credits are opened by the deposit or collection of money or currency, subject to be paid or remitted upon draft, check, or order, or where money is advanced or loaned on stocks, bonds, bullion, bills of exchange, or promissory notes, or where stocks, bonds, bullion, bills of exchange, or promissory notes are received for

---

subject to be paid or remitted upon draft, check, or order, or where money is advanced or loaned on stocks, bonds, bullion, bills of exchange, or promissory notes, or where stocks, bonds, bullion, bills of exchange, or promissory notes, are received for discount or sale, shall be regarded a banker under this act: *Provided,* That any savings bank having no capital stock, and whose business is confined to receiving deposits and loaning the same for the benefit of its depositors, and which does no other business of banking, shall not be liable to pay for a license as a banker.

And as to brokers' licenses it was enacted: "Brokers shall pay fifty dollars for each license. Every person, firm, or company, except such as hold a license as a banker, whose business it is as a broker to negotiate purchases or sales of stocks, exchange, bullion, coined money, bank notes, promissory notes or other securities, for themselves or others, shall be regarded as a broker under this act: *Provided, That any person holding a license as a banker shall not be required to take out a license as a broker.*" While Section 99 provided, "That all brokers and bankers doing business as brokers, shall be subject to pay the following duties and rates of duty upon the sales of merchandise, produce, gold and silver bullion, foreign exchange, uncurrent money, promissory notes, stocks, bonds, or other securities, as hereinafter mentioned, and shall be subject to all the provisions, where not inapplicable thereto, for the returns, assessment, collection of the duties, and liens and penalties as are prescribed for the persons, firms, companies, or corporations, owning or possessing, or having the management of railroads, steamboats, and ferry-boats, that is to say: Upon all sales of merchandise, produce, or other goods, one-eighth of one per centum; upon all sales and contracts for sales of stocks and bonds, one-twentieth of one per centum on the par value thereof; and of foreign exchange, promissory notes, or other securities, one-twentieth of one per centum on the amount of such sales, and upon any sales or contracts for the sale of gold and silver bullion and coin, one-tenth of one per centum on the amouut of such sales or contracts: *Provided,* That any person, firm, or company, not being licensed as a broker, or banker, or wholesale or retail dealer, who shall sell ar offer to sell any merchandise, produce, or gold and silver bullion, foreign exchange, uncurrent money, promissory notes, stocks, bonds, or other securities, not bona fide at the time his own property, and actually on hand, shall be liable in addition to all other penalties provided in such cases, to pay fifty per centum in addition to the foregoing duties and rates of duty."

The importance of this section, and the large amount involved in the proper enforcement of the law, made it a most interesting question to both brokers and bankers, as to the capacity in which either were acting when they made or effected the taxable sales.

These questions arose, among others:

1. When is a bank to be considered as doing business as a broker, in order to subject it to the tax under Section 99?

2. How is the question to be considered in connection with the proviso to paragraph 9, of Section 79, in relation to the license of the broker, "That any person holding a license as a banker, shall not be required to take out a license as a broker?"—and,

discount or for sale, shall be regarded as a bank or as a banker: *Provided*, That any savings bank having no capital stock, and whose business is confined to receiving deposits and loaning or investing the same for the benefit of its depositors, and which does no other business of banking, shall not be subject to this tax.

Two. Wholesale dealers whose annual sales do not exceed fifty thousand dollars, shall pay fifty dollars; and if their annual sales ex-

---

3. Is a broker liable to tax under Section 99, when he sells his own property?

Much controversy has arisen in determining these questions, and we can only refer to some of the decisions and rulings that have been made.

1. "Where a banker has taken out a broker's license under the old law, he should be allowed a ratable proportion of the amount paid for such license, in determining the amount now due for a banker's license." (Rulings No. 4, Boutwell, 2d Ed., 133.)

2. "When brokers in stocks or bonds, receive any part of their commissions on sales of United States securities from the parties *selling* such stocks or bonds, they are liable to tax." (Rulings No. 20, Boutwell, 2d Ed., 135.)

3. "Government vouchers are considered as securities; and any person who makes a business of negotiating purchases or sales of such securities for others, must take a broker's license *unless licensed as a banker*." (Rulings No. 114, Boutwell, 2d Ed., 147.)

4. Parties who engage in broker's business since July, 1864, (the time when the law of June 30, 1864, took effect,) and take a banker's license, are exempt from broker's license." (Rulings No. 66, *ibidem*, p. 141.)

5. A person or firm can purchase on their own account, and with their own funds, and sell in the same way, without license and without being liable to tax on such sales. A person who loans money on stocks, bonds or specie, cannot sell the same on account of the borrower without paying tax, under Section 99 or proviso thereto, nor can one bank sell for another without paying tax on sales. (Ruling Dec. 14, 1864. I. Int. Rev. Rec., p. 75. *Ibidem*, p. 109.)

See also Department Circular No. 46, in Appendix. Opinion of Attorney General, May 4, 1866, in Appendix. Cited III. Int. Rev. Rec., p. 155.

6. "Sales made by brokers for themselves are subject to the same duty as those made for others." (United States *vs* Cutting and *al.* Opinion of United States Sup. Court, 1866. Amendment to ¶ 9 of § 79, act of 1864.)

7. "Banks which sell gold or government securities or account for their dealers and correspondents for a commission, are liable to tax on such sales." (Int. Rev. Rec., Dec. 23, 1865.)

8. "So long as a broker's sales are limited to his own securities, his transactions do not become those of a broker; but when, in addition to such sales, he negotiates sales of securities for others, he engages in the business of a broker, and becomes a *banker*, doing business as a broker." A broker, and a banker doing business as a broker, stand precisely on the same footing in the statute. (See United States *vs.* Fish and *al.* Cited in opinion of Atty. Gen., as above. Courtney, Dist. Atty., *arguendo*. Clark *vs.* United States. N. Y. Tribune, June 6, 1866.)

We may close this note with the remark, that the intention of the law is to tax certain transactions, sales, &c.; no matter who effects them, (whether bankers or brokers.) Where bankers do business as brokers they are liable to the tax as brokers. The change of name does not, under the proviso, protect them in evasion.

II. WHOLESALE DEALERS.

The wholesale dealer should make return of the gross amount of his sales, with no deduction for "cash discounts," &c. (Ruling March 30, 1866. III. Int. Rev. Rec., 132.)

Under the original law, a wholesale was distinguished from a retail dealer

ceed fifty thousand dollars, for every additional thousand dollars in excess of fifty thousand dollars, they shall pay one dollar; and the amount of all sales within the year beyond fifty thousand dollars shall be returned monthly to the assistant assessor, and the tax on sales in excess of fifty thousand dollars shall be assessed by the assessors, and paid monthly, as other monthly taxes are assessed and paid. Every person shall be regarded as a wholesale dealer whose business it is, for himself or on commission, to sell or offer to sell any goods, wares, or merchandise of foreign or domestic production, not including wines, spirits, or malt liquors, whose annual sales exceed twenty-five thousand dollars. And the payment of the special tax as a wholesale dealer shall not exempt any such person acting as a commercial broker from the payment of the special tax imposed upon commercial brokers: *Provided*, That no person paying the special tax as a wholesale dealer in liquors shall be required to pay an additional special tax on accouut of the sale of other goods, wares, or merchandise on the same premises. *And provided further*, That, in estimating the amount of sales for the purposes of this section, any sales made, by or through another wholesale dealer on commission shall not be again estimated and included as sold by the party for whom the sale was made.

Three. Retail dealers shall pay ten dollars. Every person whose business or occupation it is to sell or offer for sale any goods, wares, or merchandise of foreign or domestic production, not including spirits,

---

by the character of the sales, whether in unbroken or broken packages. Now the distinction arises solely from the amount of sales.

All persons whose licenses depend upon the amount of their sales should be required when applying for license, to make return of the sales of the previous year. If it shall be found that the sales are in excess of the amount for which the license tax has previously been assessed, an assessment should be made for the deficiency at once, and returned to the collector upon the next monthly list. The assessor should judge of the amount of sales, and not be governed entirely by the dealer's returns. If it appears probable that loss will ensue if the tax is not assessed before the end of the year, the assessment may be made sooner. When a wholesale dealer has recently commenced business he may be allowed to estimate his probable sales for the coming year. (The provision of the present statute in relation to monthly returns to the assistant assessor will not be forgotten.)

Whenever a licensed retail dealer is found to have made sales exceeding $25,000, he should be reassessed as a wholesale dealer from the date of his first license. The collector should indorse upon his license the amount of reassessment paid.

Whenever a license under which a certain limited amount of business only can be transacted is transferred to another person, the collector at the time of making the transfer should enter upon the license the amount of business then already done thereunder, and such license so transferred will cover transactions in the hands of the second or subsequent holder equal to the said limited amount, *less* the amount or amounts so entered, and no more. (Series 2, No. 4.)

III. RETAIL DEALERS.

(a) Carpenters, masons, painters, barbers, &c., who furnish materials, require a license as retail dealers, when the amount of their annual receipts reaches $1,000 per year. (b) Nurserymen should also be licensed, if their

wines, ale, beer, or other malt liquors, and whose annual sales exceed one thousand and do not exceed twenty-five thousand dollars, shall be regarded as a retail dealer.

Four. Wholesale dealers in liquors whose annual sales do not exceed fifty thousand dollars shall pay one hundred dollars, and if exceeding fifty thousand dollars, for every additional one thousand dollars in excess of fifty thousand dollars, they shall pay one dollar, and such excess shall be assessed and paid in the same manner as required of wholesale dealers. Every person who shall sell or offer for sale any distilled spirits, fermented liquors, or wines of any kind in quantities of more than three gallons at one time to the same purchaser, or whose annual sales, including sales of other merchandise, shall exceed twenty-five thousand dollars, shall be regarded as a wholesale dealer in liquors.

---

sales are above $1,000 annually. (c) A manufacturer, who receives at his factory for sale, other goods than those manufactured by himself, must also take out a dealer's license, if he sells of such goods to an amount of $1,000 annually. (d) There are certain manufactures that are exempt from ad valorem or other tax; but they require a dealer's license, either wholesale or retail, depending upon the amount of their sales. (e) A tanner may sell at his tannery the wool taken from the pelts he tans, without a dealer's license. (f) Farmers, selling their own produce from their wagons, &c., require no license; but if they have a store or stall for sale of such produce, they must be licensed. If they make a business of raising trees for sale, they also require license. For selling the milk of their own cows, they need no license; but if they purchase milk to sell with their own milk, or take milk to market for their neighbors, they require license. If a farmer hires a pasture, and stocks the same with cows, in order to sell the milk, he will not be regarded in the light of selling the product of his own farm, but must be licensed. (g) The selling of wheat or other grain by a farmer, the product of his own farm, does not require a dealer's license; but if he converts his grain into flour or meal, he cannot sell the latter without a license; so if he disposes of his hay or other products from a specified stand in town or city. (In all these cases the provision that the yearly sales should amount to at least $1,000, will not be overlooked.) (h) It is no breach of the law, for a farmer or other person, killing a beef for his own use to sell a portion to his neighbor, and he is not required to take license. (i) Persons selling from boats or vessels, must take out license as dealers, either wholesale or retail, according to amount of sales. (k) Farmers who produce annually butter, cheese, sugar, charcoal, &c., in excess of $1,000 at one place, should take license as manufacturers. They may, however, sell all the products of their own farms in the manner of peddlers without peddlers' license. (l) Where a person sells fruit trees or other agricultural products in the manner of a broker, that is to say, without the actual possession of the goods which he sells, but sells by sample through representation, or takes orders, &c., he is liable, in respect to the amount of his sales, either as produce or commercial brokers. The mere delivery of trees by a nurseryman to the order of his agent, would not subject the agent having a commercial or produce broker's license to a dealer's license in addition. In such case the nurseryman would alone be liable as a dealer on all sales of produce, whether made through brokers or otherwise. (II. Int. Rev. Rec., p. 120.)

IV. WHOLESALE DEALERS IN LIQUORS

may sell liquors at retail, and both wholesale and retail dealers in liquors may sell other merchandise and may sell liquors to be drank on the premises, without additional tax. (Series 2, No. 4.)

Five. Retail dealers in liquors shall pay twenty-five dollars. Every person who shall sell or offer for sale, foreign or domestic spirits, wines, ale, beer, or other malt liquors in quantities of three gallons or less, and whose annual sales, including all sales of other merchandise, do not exceed twenty-five thousand dollars, shall be regarded as a retail dealer in liquors.

Six. Lottery ticket dealers shall pay one hundred dollars. Every person, association, firm, or corporation who shall make, sell, or offer to sell lottery tickets or fractional parts thereof, or any token, certificate, or device representing or intending to represent a lottery ticket or any fractional part thereof, or any policy of numbers in any lottery, or shall manage any lottery, or prepare schemes of lotteries, or superintend the drawing of any lottery, shall be deemed a lottery ticket dealer: *Provided*, That the manager of any lottery shall give bond in the sum of one thousand dollars that the person paying such tax shall not sell any tickets or supplementary ticket of such lottery which has not been duly stamped according to law, and that he will pay the tax imposed by law upon the gross receipts of his sales.

Seven. Horse dealers shall pay ten dollars. Any person whose business it is to buy or sell horses or mules shall be regarded a horse dealer under this act: *Provided*, That one special tax having been paid, no additional tax shall be imposed upon any horse dealer for keeping a livery stable, nor upon any livery stable keeper for dealing in horses.

Eight. Livery stable keepers shall pay ten dollars. Any person whose business it is to keep horses for hire, or to let, or to keep, feed, or board horses for others, shall be regarded as a livery stable keeper.

Nine. Brokers shall pay fifty dollars. Every person, firm, or com-

---

V. RETAIL DEALERS IN LIQUORS.

If the sales of a retail dealer in liquors exceed $25,000, or if he sells in quantities of more than three gallons at one time to the same purchaser, he should be reassessed as a wholesale dealer in liquors. The collector should enter the amount of reassessment paid him upon the license.

If a party taxed as retail liquor dealer wishes to retire from the business, he may sell his stock to another person without taking a wholesale liquor dealer's license. (Int. Rev. Rec., Sept. 9, 1864.)

But if he sells to several different persons, at private sale, in quantities exceeding three gallons, he becomes liable to tax as wholesale dealer in liquor. (Series 2, No. 4.)

When spirituous liquors are medicated or mixed with foreign substances, but to so slight a degree that they are still used as beverages and are sold as such, a liquor dealer's license will be required by the seller. When the medication or admixture is carried to such an extent that the liquor is no longer susceptible of being used as a beverage, a liquor dealer's license will not be required. (*Ibidem.*)

VI. LOTTERY TICKET DEALERS.

It will be perceived that this paragraph has been modified to cover cases of those who, in New York City and elsewhere, had attempted to evade the law.

IX. BROKERS.

(See note I., Bankers.)

pany, whose business it is to negotiate purchases or sales of stocks, bonds, exchange, bullion, coined money, bank notes, promissory notes, or other securities, for themselves or others, shall be regarded as a broker: *Provided*, That any person having paid the special tax as a banker shall not be required to pay the special tax as a broker.

Ten. Pawnbrokers using or employing a capital of not exceeding fifty thousand dollars shall pay fifty dollars; and when using or employing a capital exceeding fifty thousand dollars, for every additional thousand dollars in excess of fifty thousand dollars, shall pay two dollars. Every person whose business or occupation it is to take or receive, by way of pledge, pawn, or exchange, any goods, wares, or merchandise, or any kind of personal property whatever, as security for the repayment of money lent thereon, shall be deemed a pawnbroker.

Eleven. Land warrant brokers shall pay twenty-five dollars. Any person shall be regarded as a land-warrant broker who makes a business of buying and selling land-warrants, or of furnishing them to settlers or other persons.

Twelve. Cattle brokers, whose annual sales do not exceed ten thousand dollars, shall pay ten dollars; and if exceeding the sum of ten thousand dollars, one dollar for each additional thousand dollars, and such excess shall be assessed and paid in the same manner as required of wholesale dealers.* Any person whose business it is to buy or sell, or deal in cattle, hogs, or sheep, shall be considered as a cattle broker.

Thirteen. Produce brokers, whose annual sales do not exceed the sum of ten thousand dollars, shall pay ten dollars. Every person other than one having paid the special tax as a commercial broker or cattle broker, or wholesale or retail dealer, or peddler, whose occupation it is to buy or sell agricultural or farm products, and whose annual sales do not exceed ten thousand dollars, shall be regarded as a produce broker.

XII. CATTLE BROKERS.

If a farmer buys cattle merely with a view to grazing or feeding, or to raise stock, and thus preparing to sell them to butchers or to others, he would not be liable to this license. II. Int. Rev. Rec., Oct., 1864.

It would be otherwise if he makes it a business to buy cattle, using the farm as a temporary depot for the cattle. (I. Int. Rev. Rec., p. 117.)

XIII. PRODUCE BROKERS.

If a produce broker's sales exceed $10,000 annually, he should be treated as a commercial broker or a dealer, as the case may be.

Licensed peddlers may buy up produce to sell again as peddlers, without license as produce brokers. Produce brokers cannot peddle produce from house to house without licenses as peddlers.

Original or unbroken packages or pieces, are held to be packages or pieces sold just as they come from the manufacturer, wholesale dealer, or importer, without being broken or divided.

Every person other than one holding a license as a broker, wholesale or retail dealer, who buys or sells agricultural products, must have a produce broker's license. (Ruling, vide I. Int. Rev. Rec., p. 116.)

---

* The returns to be made monthly, etc.

Fourteen. Commercial brokers shall pay twenty dollars. Any person or firm whose business it is, as a broker, to negotiate sales or purchases of goods, wares, or merchandise, or to negotiate freights and other business for the owners of vessels, or for the shippers, or consignors, or consignees of freight carried by vessels, shall be regarded a commercial broker.

Fifteen. Custom-house brokers shall pay ten dollars. Every person whose occupation it is, as the agent of others, to arrange entries and other custom-house papers, or transact business at any port of entry relating to the importation or exportation of goods, wares, or merchandise, shall be regarded a custom-house broker.

Sixteen. Distillers shall pay one hundred dollars. Every person, firm, or corporation who distills or manufactures spirits, or who brews or makes mash wort or wash for distillation or the production of spirits, shall be deemed a distiller under this act: *Provided*, That distillers of apples, grapes, or peaches, distilling or manufacturing fifty and less than one hundred and fifty barrels per year from the same, shall pay fifty dollars; and those distilling or manufacturing less than fifty barrels per year from the same shall pay twenty dollars: *And provided, further*, That no tax shall be imposed for any still, stills, or other apparatus used by druggists and chemists for the recovery of alcohol for pharmaceutical and chemical or scientific purposes which has been used in those processes.

XIV. COMMERCIAL BROKERS.

Persons traveling about the country as the agent of manufacturers and dealers, seeking orders, &c., in original packages, are regarded as commercial brokers within the meaning of the law. (Decision 159, subsequently modified, *vide.*)

Persons traveling about the country as the agents of manufacturers or dealers, seeking orders for goods as agents of one person or firm only, such as salaried clerks or men hired by the month, should not be required to take licenses as commercial brokers.

All parts of Decision No. 159 inconsistent with the above are revoked.

The liability of peddlers and commercial brokers to license tax depends upon the acts done, and is not affected by the fact that the party is employed by others and is acting merely as an agent.

When a produce broker, having license as such, sells more than $10,000 worth of produce, he becomes subject to a commercial broker's license. The new license begins when that point is reached, and ratably assessed to following May. (Comm. Oct. 10, 1865.)

A commercial broker is supposed to travel in the transaction of his business. If he has a dealer's license, and does not travel, he needs no extra license. (II. Int. Rev. Rec., 156.)

Traveling agents for manufacturers of grave-stones are to be considered as commercial brokers. (*Ibidem*, p. 197.)

XVI. DISTILLERS.

Distillers may sell their liquors at the distillery in large or small quantities, either to be drank on the premises or not, without other license. The same privilege is allowed to brewers and rectifiers. Distillers, brewers and rectifiers may also deliver their liquors to their regular customers about the country, without license as peddlers. (Series 2, No. 4.)

Seventeen. Brewers shall pay one hundred dollars. Every person, firm, or corporation who manufactures fermented liquors of any name or description, for sale, from malt, wholly or in part, or from any substitute therefor, shall be deemed a brewer: *Provided*, That any person, firm, or corporation who manufactures less than five hundred barrels per year shall pay the sum of fifty dollars.

Eighteen. Rectifiers who shall rectify any quantity of spirituous liquors, not exceeding five hundred barrels, packages, or casks, containing not more than forty gallons to each barrel, package, or cask, shall pay twenty-five dollars, and twenty-five dollars additional for each additional five hundred such barrels, packages, or casks, or any fractional part thereof. Every person, firm, or corporation who rectifies, purifies, or refines distilled spirits or wines by any process, or who by mixing distilled spirits or wine with any materials manufactures any spurious imitation, or compound liquors for sale under the name of whisky, gin, rum, wine, "spirits," "wine bitters," or any other name, shall be regarded as a rectifier.

Nineteen. Coal oil distillers, and distillers of burning fluid and camphene, shall pay fifty dollars. Any person, firm, or corporation who shall refine, produce, or distill petroleum or rock oil, or oil made of coal, asphaltum, shale, peat, or other bituminous substances, or shall manufacture illuminating oil, shall be regarded as a coal oil distiller.

Twenty. Keepers of hotels, inns, or taverns shall be classified and rated according to the yearly rental, or, if not rented, according to the estimated yearly rental of the house and property intended to be so occupied, as follows, to wit: When the rent or valuation of the yearly rental of said house and property shall be two hundred dollars, or less, they shall pay ten dollars; and if exceeding two hundred dollars, for any additional one hundred dollars or fractional part thereof in excess of two hundred dollars, five dollars: *Provided*, that a payment of such special tax shall be construed to permit the person so keeping a hotel, inn, or tavern to furnish the necessary food for the animals of such travelers or sojourners without the payment of an additional special tax as a livery stable keeper. Every place where food and lodging are provided

---

XVII. BREWERS

Cannot manufacture spirituous liquors under their license as brewers.

XX. HOTELS.

(a) If the keeper of a hotel sells spirits or fermented liquors, to be drank on the premises, or keeps a billiard table or tables in the building, he must take the appropriate additional licenses therefor. (b) Steamers or vessels upon the waters of the United States, on board of which passengers and travelers are provided with food and lodging, are required to pay a license fee. (c) If there be fraud or collusion in the return of actual rent to the assessor, there is a penalty imposed, equal to double the amount of license fee required. (d) When a hotel-keeper owns his building, the proper yearly rental is fixed and established by the assessor at its proper value; but if leased, at not less than the actual rent agreed to be paid by the lessee. (e) If a "furnished hotel" is leased, it would seem that the rent agreed to be paid for both house

for and furnished to travelers and for pay, shall be regarded as a hotel, inn, or tavern: *Provided*, That keepers of hotels, taverns, and eating-houses in which liquors are sold by retail, to be drank upon the premises, shall pay an additional tax of twenty-five dollars. The yearly rental shall be fixed and established by the assessor of the proper district at its proper value; but if rented, at not less than the actual rent agreed on by the parties. All steamers and vessels upon waters of the United States on board of which passengers or travelers are provided with food or lodgings, shall be subject to and required to pay twenty-five dollars: *Provided*, That any person who shall make false or fraudulent returns concerning the actual rent mentioned in this paragraph shall be subject to a penalty therefor of double the amount of the tax.

Twenty-one. Keepers of eating-houses shall pay ten dollars. Every place where food or refreshments of any kind, not including spirits, wines, ale, beer, or other malt liquors, are provided for casual visitors and sold for consumption therein, shall be regarded as an eating-house. But the keeper of an eating-house having paid the tax therefor, shall not be required to pay a special tax as a confectioner, anything in this act to the contrary notwithstanding; and keepers of hotels, inns, taverns, and eating-houses, having paid the special tax therefor, shall not be required to pay additional tax for selling tobacco, snuff, or cigars on the same premises, anything in this act to the contrary notwithstanding.

Twenty-two. Confectioners shall pay ten dollars. Every person who sells at retail confectionery, sweetmeats, comfits, or other confects, in any building, shall be regarded as a confectioner. But wholesale and retail dealers, having paid the special tax therefor, shall not be required to pay the special tax as a confectioner, anything in this act to the contrary notwithstanding.

Twenty-three. Claim agents and agents for procuring patents shall pay ten dollars. Every person whose business it is to prosecute claims in any of the executive departments of the federal government, or procure patents, shall be deemed a claim or patent agent, as the case may be.

Twenty-four. Patent-right dealers shall pay ten dollars. Every person whose business it is to sell, or offer for sale, patent rights, shall be regarded as a patent-right dealer.

Twenty-five. Real-estate agents shall pay ten dollars. Every person whose business it is to sell or offer for sale real estate for others, or to rent houses, stores, or other buildings or real estate, or to collect rent for others, except lawyers paying a special tax as such, shall be regarded as a real-estate agent.

---

and furniture should be the basis of license grade and tax. (f) A tobacconist's license is not required of a regularly licensed hotel.

Hotel-keepers may feed the horses of their guests without livery stable keeper's license. (Series 2, No. 4.) This is specially provided for in the present statute.

Twenty-six. Conveyancers shall pay ten dollars. Every person, other than one having paid the special tax as a lawyer or claim agent, whose business it is to draw deeds, bonds, mortgages, wills, writs, or other legal papers, or to examine titles to real estate, shall be regarded as a conveyancer.

Twenty-seven. Intelligence-office keepers shall pay ten dollars. Every person whose business it is to find or furnish places of employment for others, or to find or furnish servants upon application in writing or otherwise, receiving compensation therefor, shall be regarded as an intelligence-office keeper.

Twenty-eight. Insurance agents shall pay ten dollars. Any person who shall act as agent of any fire, marine, life, mutual, or other insurance company or companies, or any person who shall negotiate or procure insurance for which he receives any commission or other compensation, shall be regarded as an insurance agent: *Provided*, That if the annual receipts of any person as such agent shall not exceed one hundred dollars, he shall pay five dollars only: *And provided further*, That no special tax shall be imposed upon any person for selling tickets or contracts of insurance against injury to persons while traveling by land or water.

Twenty-nine. Foreign insurance agents shall pay fifty dollars. Every person who shall act as agent of any foreign fire, marine, life, mutual, or other insurance company or companies shall be regarded as a foreign insurance agent.

Thirty. Auctioneers whose annual sales do not exceed ten thousand dollars shall pay ten dollars, and if exceeding ten thousand dollars shall pay twenty dollars. Every person shall be deemed an auctioneer whose business it is to offer property at public sale to the highest or best bidder: *Provided*, That the provisions of this paragraph shall not apply to judicial or executive officers making auction sales by virtue of any judgment or decree of any court, nor public sales made by or for executors or administrators, or guardians of any estate held by them as such.

XXVI. CONVEYANCERS.

(a) Surveyors, who draft the deeds of lands surveyed by them, must take a conveyancer's license. As any amount of business of this kind requires a license, it would seem that magistrates, &c., in the country, who draft deeds, wills, &c., no matter how few, should be licensed as conveyancers. But each case must depend upon its own facts, and assistants must use their best discretion.

It may be remarked generally, however, that a person should hold himself out by words, or advertisement, or acts, as ready to do business in this line, before he would be liable to tax.

XXX. AUCTIONEERS.

The sales which a wholesale dealer makes through brokers and auctioneers are to be included in the amount of annual sales upon which the license of such dealer is based, and the license of the wholesale dealer does not release the brokers and auctioneers through whom he makes his sales, from their liability to taxation under Sections 98 and 99 of the act of June 30, 1864. (II. Int. Rev. Rec., 44. Commissioner's Decision, Aug. 4, 1865.)

(a) Judicial officers, sheriffs, constables, &c., and executors and administra-

Thirty-one. Manufacturers shall pay ten dollars. Any person, firm, or corporation who shall manufacture by hand or machinery any goods, wares, or merchandise, not otherwise provided for, exceeding annually the sum of one thousand dollars, or shall be engaged in the manufacture or preparation for sale of any articles or compounds, or shall put up for sale in packages with his own name or trade-mark thereon, any articles or compounds, shall be regarded as a manufacturer.

Thirty-two. Peddlers shall be classified and rated as follows, to wit: When traveling with more than two horses, or mules, the first class, and shall pay fifty dollars; when traveling with two horses, or mules, the second class, and shall pay twenty-five dollars; when traveling with one horse, or mule, the third class, and shall pay fifteen dollars; when traveling on foot, or by public conveyance, the fourth class, and shall pay ten dollars. Any person, except persons peddling only charcoal, newspapers, Bibles, magazines, religious tracts, or the products of his farm or garden, who sells or offers to sell, at retail, goods, wares, or other commodities, traveling from place to place, in the town, or through the country, shall be regarded a peddler: *Provided*, That any peddler who sells, or offers to sell, distilled spirits, fermented liquors, or wines, dry goods, foreign or domestic, by one or more original packages or pieces, at one time, to the same person or persons, or who peddles jewelry, shall pay fifty dollars: *Provided further*, That manufacturers and producers of agricultural tools and implements, garden seeds, fruit and ornamen-

---

tors selling under a decree of court, do not require license. (b) An auctioneer's license formerly covered sales only in the district where his license was applied for. But by the act of June 30, 1864, they were not so restricted. The license should, however, be taken out in the district where he has his office or principal place of business. They cannot have offices or places of business in more than one district under one license. The necessity of this ruling will be manifest when we come to treat of the tax upon their monthly sales.

XXXII. PEDDLERS.

Gold or silver watches are not considered "jewelry," within the law. (d) Manufacturers and producers of agricultural tools and implements, garden seeds, stoves and hollow ware, brooms, wooden ware, and powder, delivering or selling at wholesale any of said articles, by themselves or their authorized agents, at places other than at the place of manufacture, shall not be required for any sale thus made, to take out any additional license therefor. (e) Peddlers cannot sell as part of their stock, wine, spirits or malt liquors. (f) Dealers in ice, milk, confectioners, grocers, bakers and butchers, may deliver from their carts or wagons, what had been previously purchased or contracted for without a peddler's license, provided they have license as "dealers." They must not, however, sell or deliver articles in quantities not previously ordered; if so, they do require a peddler's license. (g) We have before stated that farmers may sell the products of their own farms, without a dealer's license. They may also sell such products "from house to house," without being subject to a peddler's license. (h) A patent-right dealer cannot sell his patent machines, &c., while traveling from place to place, unless licensed as a peddler. (i) The application for this license is made at the place of residence of the applicant, and the license authorizes him to travel all over the United States.

Persons who travel about the country soliciting orders for books, maps, &c., but who do not deliver or receive pay for the same, are not thereby liable to license duty. If, however, such persons deliver and receive pay for such

tal trees, stoves, and hollow-ware, brooms, wooden-ware, charcoal, and gunpowder, delivering and selling at wholesale any of said articles, by themselves or their authorized agents, at places other than the place of manufacture, shall not therefor be required to pay any special tax: *Provided further*, That persons who sell shell or other fish, or both, trundling from place to place, and not from any shop or stand, shall be required to pay five dollars only; and no special tax shall be imposed for selling shell or other fish from hand-carts or wheelbarrows.

Thirty-three. Apothecaries shall pay ten dollars. Every person who keeps a shop or building where medicines are compounded or prepared according to prescriptions of physicians, or where medicines are sold, shall be regarded as an apothecary. But wholesale and retail dealers, who have paid the special tax therefor, shall not be required to pay a tax as an apothecary, nor shall apothecaries who have paid the special tax be required to pay the tax as retail dealers in liquor in consequence of selling alcohol, or of selling or of dispensing, upon physicians' prescriptions, the wines and spirits officinal in the United States and other national pharmacopœias, in quantities not exceeding half a pint of either at any one time, nor exceeding in aggregate cost value the sum of three hundred dollars per annum.

Thirty-four. Photographers shall pay ten dollars. Any person who makes for sale photographs, ambrotypes, daguerreotypes, or pictures, by the action of light, shall be regarded a photographer.

Thirty-five. Tobacconists shall pay ten dollars. Any person, firm, or corporation whose business it is to manufacture cigars, snuff, or tobacco in any form, shall be regarded as a tobacconist.

Thirty-six. Butchers shall pay ten dollars. Every person whose business it is to sell butchers' meat at retail, shall be regarded as a butcher: *Provided*, That no butcher having paid the special tax therefor, shall be required to pay the special tax as a retail dealer on account of selling other articles at the same store, stall, or premises: *Provided*

---

books, &c., either at or subsequent to the time of subscription, they will require license as peddlers. The same is true of persons delivering books on orders or subscriptions taken by others. (Ruling, July 13, 1865.)

Every person traveling as a peddler must be able to show that they have paid the proper tax. Such license, under the former law, could not be taken out in the name of a manufacturer, &c., to be used by the employe. (Ruling June 3, 1865.)

XXXVI. BUTCHERS.

Persons engaged in the business of selling butchers' meat at wholesale, or beef by the quarter or side, are not considered in the law as butchers, but as dealers.

"No license is required for butchering as such. Selling meat at retail (which is understood as selling to consumers only) requires the seller to have license. If he sells no more than a thousand dollars' worth from a shop or stand, he needs but a five dollar license; if more, a ten dollar license. If he sells at wholesale, (*i. e.*, to parties who propose to sell again,) he requires a dealer's license, wholesale or retail, based on amount of sales." (Commr. June 16, 1866.)

This paragraph (36) relates only to persons selling butchers' meat at retail.

further, That butchers who sell butchers' meat exclusively by themselves or agents, traveling from place to place, and not from any shop or stand, shall be required to pay five dollars only, any existing law to the contrary notwithstanding.

Thirty-seven. Proprietors of theaters, museums, and concert halls, shall pay one hundred dollars. Every edifice used for the purpose of dramatic or operatic or other representations, plays, or performances, for admission to which entrance money is received, not including halls rented or used occasionally for concerts or theatrical representations, shall be regarded as a theater: *Provided*, That when any such edifice is under lease at the passage of this act, the tax shall be paid by the lessee, unless otherwise stipulated between the parties to said lease.

Thirty-eight. The proprietor or proprietors of circuses shall pay one hundred dollars. Every building, tent, space, or area where feats of horsemanship or acrobatic sports or theatrical performances are exhibited, shall be regarded as a circus: *Provided*, That no special tax paid in one State shall exempt exhibitions from the tax in another State. And but one special tax shall be imposed for exhibitions within any one State.

Thirty-nine. Jugglers shall pay twenty dollars. Every person who performs by sleight-of-hand shall be regarded as a juggler. The proprietors or agents of all other public exhibitions or shows for money, not enumerated in this section, shall pay ten dollars: *Provided*, That a special tax paid in one State shall not exempt exhibitions from the tax in another State. And but one special tax shall be required for exhibitions within any one State.

Forty. Proprietors of bowling alleys and billiard rooms shall pay ten dollars for each alley or table. Every place or building where bowls are thrown or billiards played, and open to the public with or without price, shall be regarded as a bowling alley or billiard room, respectively.

Forty-one. Proprietors of gift enterprises shall pay one hundred and fifty dollars. Every person, firm, or corporation who shall sell or offer for sale any real estate or article of merchandise of any description whatsoever, or any ticket of admission to any exhibition or performance, with a promise, express or implied, to give or bestow, or in any manner hold out the promise of gift or bestowal of any article or thing for

---

Butchers paying ten dollars may retail other merchandise than meat at the same store, but may not peddle meat without paying a peddler's license. Butchers with carts, paying five dollars, may peddle meat or fish, but cannot sell other articles. (Int. Rev. Rec., Sept. 21, 1865.)

Butchers whose sales do not exceed one thousand dollars annually are entitled to license upon payment of five dollars. Butchers who sell butchers' meat exclusively by themselves or agents, traveling from place to place, are entitled to license upon payment of five dollars, regardless of the amount sold. (Series 2, No. 4.)

Persons who sell meat at wholesale are wholesale or retail dealers according to the amount of their annual sales. By selling at wholesale in this connection is meant selling to be sold again.

and in consideration of the purchase by any person of any other article or thing, shall be regarded as a proprietor of a gift enterprise: *Provided,* That no such proprietor, in consequence of being thus taxed, shall be exempt from paying any other tax imposed by law, and the special tax herein required shall be in addition thereto.

Forty-two. Owners of stallions and jacks shall pay ten dollars. Every person who keeps a horse or a jack for the use of mares, requiring or receiving pay therefor, shall be regarded as the owner thereof, and shall furnish a statement to the assessor or assistant assessor, which shall contain a brief description of the animal, its age, and place or places where used or to be used: *Provided,* That all accounts, notes, or demands for the use of any such horse or jack, the owner or keeper thereof not having paid the tax as aforesaid, shall be void.

Forty-three. Lawyers shall pay ten dollars. Every person who for fee or reward shall prosecute or defend causes in any court of record or other judicial tribunal of the United States, or of any of the States, or whose business it is to give legal advice in relation to any cause or matter whatever, shall be deemed to be a lawyer.

Forty-four. Physicians, surgeons, and dentists shall pay ten dollars. Every person (except apothecaries) whose business it is, for fee and reward, to prescribe remedies or perform surgical operations for the cure of any bodily disease or ailing, shall be deemed a physician, surgeon, or dentist.

Forty-five. Architects and civil engineers shall pay ten dollars. Every person whose business it is to plan, design, or superintend the construction of buildings, or ships, or of roads, or bridges, or canals, or railroads, shall be regarded as an architect and civil engineer, under this act: *Provided,* That this shall not include a practical carpenter who labors on a building.

Forty-six. Builders and contractors shall pay ten dollars. Every

---

XLIII. LAWYERS

do not need a conveyancer's license, and there is no partnership license; but they can have as many offices as they choose under one license.

They cannot do the business of a claim agent or commercial broker without license therefor; but they may collect rents, &c., for clients, as incident to professional services under the lawyer's license.

XLIV. SURGEONS AND PHYSICIANS.

Veterinary surgeons are equally liable as other surgeons to the proper license (special tax). (Ruling May 4, 1866.)

XLV. BUILDERS AND CONTRACTORS.

Builders and contractors are not subject to license tax in any year in which they do not construct on contract, nor unless their contracts are in excess of $2,500. If a builder commences business in March, and makes a contract amounting to $100,000, he should take license for the balance of the year, and the tax is to be estimated as follows: The lowest rate of license being $25 per annum, the proportion for two months is $4 1-6, to which is to be added one dollar for each thousand dollars in the contract in excess of $25,000. The same law and rulings are applicable to sub-contractors. (Series 2, No. 4.)

person whose business it is to construct buildings, or ships, or bridges, or canals, or railroads, by contract, whose receipts from building contracts exceed two thousand five hundred dollars in any one year, shall be regarded as a builder and contractor under this act.

Forty-seven. Plumbers and gas-fitters shall pay ten dollars. Every person, firm, or corporation, whose business it is to fit, furnish, or sell plumbing materials, gas-pipes, gas-burners, or other gas-fixtures, shall be regarded a plumber and gas-fitter, within the meaning of this act.

Forty-eight. Assayers, assaying gold and silver, or either, of a value not exceeding in one year two hundred and fifty thousand dollars, shall pay one hundred dollars, and two hundred dollars when the value exceeds two hundred and fifty thousand dollars and does not exceed five hundred thousand dollars, and five hundred dollars when the value exceeds five hundred thousand dollars. Any person or persons or corporation whose business or occupation it is to separate gold and silver from other metals or mineral substances with which such gold or silver, or both, are alloyed, combined, or united, or to ascertain or determine the quantity of gold or silver in any alloy or combination with other metals, shall be deemed an assayer.

Forty-nine. Miners shall pay ten dollars. Every person, firm, or company, who shall employ others in the business of mining for coal, or for gold, silver, copper, lead, iron, zinc, spelter, or other minerals, not having paid the tax therefor, as a manufacturer, and no other, shall be regarded as a miner: *Provided*, That this shall not apply to any miner whose receipts as such shall not exceed, annually, one thousand dollars.

Fifty. Express carriers and agents shall pay ten dollars. Every person, firm, or company, engaged in the carrying or delivery of money, valuable papers, or any articles for pay, or doing an express business, whose gross receipts therefrom exceed the sum of one thousand dollars per annum, shall be regarded as an express carrier: *Provided*, That but one special tax of ten dollars shall be imposed upon any one person, firm, or company, in respect to all the business to be done by such person, firm, or company, on a continuous route, and the payment of such tax shall cover all business done upon such route by such person, firm, or company, anywhere in the United States; and such tax shall be required only from the principal in such business, and not from any subordinate: *Provided further*, That persons owning or employing not more than one vehicle shall not be required to pay such tax.

Fifty-one. Grinders of coffee or spices shall pay one hundred dollars. Any person who manufactures or prepares for use and sale, by grinding or other process, coffee, spices, or mustard, or adulterated coffee, spices, or mustard, or any article or compound intended for use

---

XLVII. MINERS.

A miner may employ *one* person in the business of mining for coal, silver, &c., without license. (Series 2, No. 4.)

XLIX. GRINDERS OF COFFEE AND SPICES.

This is a new provision of the present act.

in the adulteration of or as substitutes for coffee, spices, or mustard, shall be regarded as a grinder of coffee or spices: *Provided*, That any person who shall roast coffee for use and sale shall be required to pay the special tax herein imposed upon grinders of coffee or spices.]

When Special Tax shall not be Assessed. Re-assessments upon Amount of Sales. Existing Licenses not to be Impaired.

SEC. 80. *And be it further enacted*, [That the special tax shall not be imposed upon apothecaries, confectioners, butchers, keepers of eating-houses, hotels, inns, or taverns, or retail dealers, except retail dealers in spirituous and malt liquors when their annual gross receipts shall not exceed the sum of one thousand dollars, any provision of law to the contrary notwithstanding; the amount of such annual receipts to be ascertained or estimated in such manner as the Commissioner of Internal Revenue shall prescribe, as well as the amount of all other annual sales or receipts where the tax is graduated by the amount of sales or receipts; and where the amount of the tax has been increased by law above the amount paid by any person, firm or company, or has been understated or underestimated, such person, firm, or company shall be again assessed, and pay the amount of such increase: *Provided*, That when any person, before the passage of this act, has been assessed for a license, the amount thus assessed being equal to the tax herein imposed for the business covered by such license, no special tax shall be assessed until the expiration of the period for which such license was assessed.]

Cases in which the Special Tax is not imposed. Payment of a Special Tax shall not Legalize a Trade or Business prohibited by State or Municipal Laws.

SEC. 81. *And be it further enacted*, [That nothing contained in the preceding sections of this act shall be construed to impose a special tax upon vintners who sell wine of their own growth at the place where the same is made; nor upon apothecaries as to wines or spirituous liquors which they use exclusively in the preparation or making up of medicines; nor shall physicians be taxed for keeping on hand medicines solely for the purpose of making up their own prescriptions for their own patients; nor shall farmers be taxed as manufacturers or producers for making butter or cheese with milk from their own cows, or for any

---

SECS. 80, 81. By the modifications of these sections of the present act, apothecaries, confectioners, butchers, eating-houses, hotels, inns, or taverns, tobacconists, and retail dealers, other than of liquors, are not taxed unless their gross receipts exceed one thousand dollars.

It is also provided that when by former acts a license has been issued for an amount equal to the special tax herein imposed, no special tax shall be assessed until the expiration of such license.

Also, that farmers shall not be taxed as manufacturers or producers for making butter or cheese with milk from their own cows, or for any other farm products.

It is not supposed, however, that this provision is to apply to *cheese or butter factories*. (But quere.) See decision of Department, III. Int. Rev. Rec., 3, 12, 140.

other farm products: *Provided,* That the payment of any tax imposed by law shall not be held or construed to exempt any person carrying on any trade, business, or profession from any penalty or punishment provided by the laws of any State for carrying on such trade, business, or profession within such State, or in any manner to authorize the commencement or continuance of such trade, business, or profession contrary to the laws of such State, or in places prohibited by municipal law; nor shall the payment of any tax herein provided be held or construed to prohibit or prevent any State from placing a duty or tax for State or other purposes on any trade, business, or profession upon which a tax is imposed by law.]*

Manufactures, Articles and Products. Specific and ad valorem Duty. Sworn Statement of proposed Business and Returns.†

SEC. 82. *And be it further enacted,* That every individual, partnership, firm, association, or corporation, (and any word or words in this act indicating or referring to person or persons shall be taken to mean and include partnerships, firms, associations, or corporations, when not otherwise designated or manifestly incompatible with the in-

---

* Vide previous note on page 59.

†MANUFACTURERS.

The wide ramifications of manufacturing industry in the United States, and the minute "division of labor" in every department of mechanical skill, has given rise, necessarily, to many perplexing questions as to what constitutes a manufacture in itself, subject to taxation under this and the following sections of the law. That under any excise system, which imposed duties upon manufactured articles, there would be, unavoidably, a frequent duplication of taxation, is apparent. It necessarily exists, where the object to be attained is to levy duties as equally as possible upon each branch of manufacture. But the difficulty has been to ascertain at what stage of the processes, or "what shape should the 'article' assume" to render it taxable.

The *first* decision promulgated by the Department after the law of 1862 took effect, was, "that each particular manufacture is taxed for its value, though materials used in its production are in themselves manufactures, on which a duty has previously been paid." (Commissioner's Decision No. 1, Oct., 1862. 1st Ed. Boutwell's Manual, p. 220.)

An operative in a machine shop may make an article complete in itself, which if manufactured for sale by another person as a specialty, would be subject to taxation; but the operative here, merely furnishes the article that it may be incorporated into a finished machine or article of which it constitutes a component part, and it escapes taxation, until the finished machine of the employer is ready for market.

But this rule is not a general one. If the operative in the case supposed should make *nails* or *screws* which were to be used in the same establishment in the manufacture of an article of furniture, they would be subject to taxation as nails or screws, at the proper rate, while the finished article of furniture would pay a duty on its entire value, regardless of the fact that the nails or screws incorporated into it had been duly assessed. The general rule has been stated thus: "Whatever is made for sale in such a state or condition that it finds purchasers or has a demand in the market, is regarded as a manufacture and is subject to taxation, unless specially exempted. (Boutwell's Tax-payer's Manual, "Ruling 136." Int. Rev. Rec., Vol. III., pp. 94, 95. Appendix, tit. "Manufacturers." Boutwell's Tax-payer's Manual, "Rulings 119 to 229.")

If a manufacturer, having his place of business in Springfield, furnishes matent thereof,) shall comply with the following requirements, that is to say:

First. Before commencing, or, if already commenced, before continuing, any manufacture liable to be assessed under the provisions of this act, and which shall not be differently provided for elsewhere, every person shall furnish, without previous demand therefor, to the assistant assessor a statement, subscribed and sworn to, or affirmed, setting forth the place where the manufacture is to be carried on, and the principal place of business for sales, the name of the manufactured article, the

---

terial (steel forgings, for instance,) to another manufacturer in Hartford, to be more completely finished and adapted to an article manufactured and made ready for market in the factory of the former, the parts will not be subject to taxation in Hartford, but the employer will comply with the law when he pays a tax upon the finished article. The maker of the parts will be considered in the light of an employee. But it would be otherwise if the latter made similar articles for general sale, in his Hartford factory. (Int. Rev. Rec., Vol. III.)

The taxes levied, either specifically or ad valorem, upon manufactured products, (not including distilled spirits, fermented liquors, tobacco or cigars under the term,) constitute one of the most productive sources of internal revenue. This is especially true of the Northern and Middle States of the Union. For the fiscal year ending June 30, 1865, the aggregate revenue from all sources amounted to $211,129,529, of which sum $104,379,609 was collected from manufactures and productions. Various changes and modifications have been made in the rate of tax, and mode of assessment, in each amended law; and the rulings and decisions of the Commissioners in the construction of the provisions of the tax, have been labored and exhaustive. Many of the more important rulings, so far as they apply to the present law, and in construction of the provisions of taxation upon particular articles not exempt from duty, will be found in the appendix, (carefully collated,) or under specific heads in the body of this work, and the reader is referred to them. The labor of correctly assessing these taxes has been greatly lessened, by a simplification in the provisions of the statute, and greater distinctness in its language. (e. g.) Great difficulty has arisen from the mode of ascertaining the proper valuation of manufactured goods subject to ad valorem rates, from doubts and some uncertainty as to the time, place and manner of making such valuation; and more especially as former statutes have allowed certain "deductions" from assessable values, (either from estimated values when goods were shipped for foreign ports, or consigned to others than agents for sale, or used by the manufacturer in other productions, and when actually sold,) to ascertain what "deductions" were authorized by the letter and spirit of the statute.

This difficulty no longer exists. All deductions from sales of manufactured goods are banished from the law, upon the recommendation of the present able and experienced Commissioner, Mr. Rollins; and goods removed, consigned or consumed by the manufacturer are valued at the precise average market value of like goods at the time when the same became liable to duty. (See Section 86, law of 1864. Annual Report of Commissioner Rollins, Dec., 1865. Commissioner's Decisions, No. 69, Jan., 1863. Treasury Circular No. 34, Aug. 2, 1865. Commissioners' Decision No. 144, Sept. 21, 1864.)

The law of June 30, 1864, also provided that on all repairs of engines, cars, carriages, *or other articles*, when such repairs increased the value of the articles so repaired ten per centum, or over, a duty should be levied. The present statute repeals this provision, and the vexed and annoying matter of "repairs" will cease to cumber the statutes, and the volumes of rulings and decisions. (See Report of Revenue Commissioners, pp. 37, 38.)

The Commissioners say, "taxes of this character are taxes upon prudence and economy, and their existence upon the statute book can only be justified by imperative necessity."

proposed market for the same, whether foreign or domestic, and generally the kind and quality manufactured or proposed to be manufactured.

Second. He shall within ten days after the first day of each and every month, or on or before a day prescribed by the Commissioner of Internal Revenue, make return under oath or affirmation of the products and sales or delivery of such manufacture in form and detail as may be required, from time to time, by the Commissioner of Internal Revenue.

Third. All such returns, statements, descriptions, memoranda, oaths, and affirmations shall be in form, scope, and detail as may be prescribed, from time to time, by the Commissioner of Internal Revenue.

The following examples strikingly illustrate the difficulty and annoyance of interpreting and enforcing the tax upon repairs: thus, a worker in iron or tin makes a stove in one hour, upon which he pays a six per cent. manufacturing tax, and the next hour repairs a stove, on which, if the repairs exceed ten per cent of the value, he is required to pay a tax of three and six-tenths per cent. A blacksmith in like manner makes a taxable article, and then in like manner repairs one just like it. Neither of these persons can reasonably be expected to keep separate accounts of these transactions, upon which the rates of tax differ. Furthermore, the tax on repairs must necessarily depend entirely upon the workman's own estimate of the value of the article before the repair, as it is not taxable unless its value is increased ten per cent. by the repair; and the assessor, or assistant, cannot, and should not, be present as a spy to appraise all articles repaired.

Again: if the worker in wood repairs a wheelbarrow worth one dollar, by adding ten cents to its value, it is taxable, but if he repairs a carriage or piano worth five hundred dollars, no tax accrues unless he adds fifty dollars to its value. The tax, with this limitation, therefore, is generally favorable to articles of luxury, and bears stringently upon articles of necessity.

Again: by the present limitation of the tax on manufactures and repairs, to such manufactures and repairs, as together exceed the rate of six hundred dollars a year, (or fifty dollars a month,) and a tax on the difference when the same exceeds the rate of six hundred dollars, and does not exceed the rate of one thousand dollars, a new calculation must often be made after it is ascertained that the repairs have increased the value ten per cent. Thus if the manufactures and repairs amount to eighty dollars, which amount is less than the rate of one thousand dollars per year, (estimated monthly,) than the tax is upon the excess of fifty dollars, namely, thirty dollars. The tax upon this excess, namely, thirty dollars, is to be apportioned at different rates of tax, in the proportion which the amount of repairs bears to the amount of manufactures.

It is, moreover, often found practically impossible to assess a tax on repairs upon the principles of the present law. Thus, for example, a wheelwright repairs a carriage to the amount of three per cent., and knows nothing more about it. The owner or his agent then passes it to another tradesman, blacksmith, trimmer, or painter, neither of whom knows what the extent of entire repairs may be, nor the value of the carriage before the repairs. The result is, that the repair, however extensive, must go untaxed, or the owner must be taxed. By the strict construction of the present law, it is doubtful whether an owner can be taxed as a manufacturer, unless he furnishes materials in whole or in part, and whether the subject of repair furnished by the owner is in itself a material for the repair. For it is the "repair" which is by the law made a manufacture. But whether this be the case or not, it is the universal testimony of all revenue assessors and collectors that all taxes which are intermittent, occasional, or exceptional, like this on repairs, should be avoided, inasmuch as the tax is not understood by the tax-payers, is difficult of collection,

Duties payable Monthly. Tax a Lien. Lien of Manufacturer.

SEC. 83. *And be it further enacted,* That upon the amounts, quantities, and values of produce, goods, wares, merchandise, and articles produced or manufactured, and sold or delivered, hereinafter enumerated, the manufacturer or producer thereof, whether manufactured or produced for himself or for others, shall pay to the collector of internal revenue within his district, monthly, within ten days from the twentieth day of each month,* or on or before a day to be prescribed by the Commissioner of Internal Revenue, the duties on such products or manufactures. And for neglect to pay such duties within said ten days, the amount of such duties, with the additions hereinbefore prescribed, may be levied upon the real and personal property of any such producer or manufacturer. And such duties and additions, and whatever shall be the expenses of levy, shall be a lien from the day prescribed by the Commissioner for their payment aforesaid, in favor of the United States, upon the said real and personal property of such producer or manufacturer; and such lien may be enforced by distraint, as provided in this act. And in all cases of goods manufactured or produced in whole or in part upon commission, or where the material is furnished by one party and manufactured by another, if the manufacturer shall be required to pay under this act the tax hereby imposed, such person or persons so paying the same shall be entitled to collect the amount thereof of the owner or owners, and shall have a lien for the amount thus paid upon the produced or manufactured goods.

Proceedings for Neglect or Refusal to pay Tax. Duties and Powers of Collector.

SEC. 84. *And be it further enacted,* That for neglect or refusal to pay the duties provided by law on manufactured articles, or articles produced as aforesaid, the goods, wares, and merchandise manufactured or produced and unsold by or not passed out of the possession of such manufacturer or producer shall be forfeited to the United States, and may

---

tends to render the law odious and inquisitorial, and requires more labor and expense on the part of the government to collect it than is compensated by any revenue accruing therefrom.

The revenue derived from this source during the fiscal year, 1865, was as follows:

From repairs of engines, carriages, cars, &c., ...	$294,437 15
From repairs of ships, steamboats, and other vessels, .	36,835 61
Making the whole reduction of the revenue by the repeal of this section, assuming as a basis the returns of 1865,	331,272 76

(Report of Commissioners, pp. 38, 39.)

* But compare section 12, act of 1866, *infra*. Heretofore the assessors have been required to return to the collector the monthly list on or before the 20th of each month. But now he has, by the 12th section, till the *last* day of the month to make his returns to the collector.

be sold or disposed of for the benefit of the same, in manner as shall be prescribed by the Commissioner of Internal Revenue, under the direction of the Secretary of the Treasury. In such case the collector or deputy collector may take possession of said articles, and may maintain such possession in the premises and buildings where they may have been manufactured, or deposited, or may be. He shall summon, giving notice of not less than two nor more than ten days, the parties in possession of said goods, enjoining them to appear before the assessor or assistant assessor, at a day and hour in such summons fixed, then and there to show cause, if any there be, why, for such neglect or refusal, such articles should not be declared forfeited to the United States. The manufacturers or producers thereof shall be deemed to be the parties interested, if the articles shall be, at the time of taking such possession, upon the premises where manufactured or produced; if they shall at such time have been removed from the place of manufacture or production, the parties interested shall be deemed to be the persons or parties in whose custody or possession the articles shall be found. Such summons shall be served upon such parties in person, or by leaving a copy thereof at the place of abode or business of the party to whom the same may be directed. In case no such party or place can be found, which fact shall be determined by the collector's return on the summons, such notice, in the nature of a summons, shall be given by advertisement for the term of three weeks in one newspaper in the county nearest to the place of such sale. If at or before such hearing such duties shall not have been paid, and the assessor or assistant assessor shall adjudge the summons and notice, service and return of the same to be sufficient, the said articles shall be by him declared forfeit, and shall be sold, disposed of, or turned over by the collector to the use of any department of the government as may be directed by the Secretary of the Treasury, who may require of any officer of the government into whose possession the same may be turned over the proper voucher therefor; and the proceeds of sale of said articles, if any there be after deducting the duties and additions thereon, together with the fees, costs, and expenses of all proceedings incident to the seizure and sale, to be determined by said Commissioner, shall be refunded and paid to the owner, or, if he cannot be found, to the manufacturer or producer in whose custody the articles were when seized, as the said Commissioner may deem just, by draft on the same or some other collector; or if the said articles are turned over without sale to the use of any department of the government, the excess of the value of said articles, after deducting the amount of the duties, additions, fees, costs, and expenses accrued thereon when turned over as aforesaid, shall be refunded and paid by the said department to the owner, or, if he cannot be found, to the manufacturer or producer in whose custody or possession the said articles were when seized as aforesaid. The Commissioner of Internal Revenue, with the approval of the Secretary of the Treasury, may review any such case of forfeiture and do justice in the premises. If the forfeiture shall have been wrongly declared, and sale made, the Secretary is hereby authorized, in case the specific articles cannot be restored to the party aggrieved in as good order and condition as when seized, to make up to such party in money his loss and damage from the contingent fund of his department. Immediate notice of any seizure of manufactured articles or products shall be given to the Commissioner of Internal Revenue by the collector or deputy collector, who shall also make return of his proceedings to the said Commissioner after he shall have sold or otherwise disposed of the articles or products so forfeited; and the assessor or assistant assessor shall also make return of his proceedings relating to such forfeiture to the said Commissioner. And any violation of, or refusal to comply with, the provisions of the eighty-second section of this act, shall be good cause for seizure and forfeiture, substantially in manner as detailed in this section; but before forfeiture shall be declared by virtue of the provisions of this section, the amount of duties which may be due from the person whose manufactures or products are seized, shall first be ascertained in the manner prescribed in the eighty-fifth section of this act; and such violation or refusal to comply shall further make any party so violating or refusing to comply liable to a fine or penalty of five hundred dollars, to be recovered in manner and form as provided in this act. Articles which the collector may adjudge perishable may be sold or disposed of before declaration of forfeiture. Said sales shall be made at public auction, and notice thereof shall be given as the said Commissioner shall prescribe.

Assistant Assessors in certain cases to Assume and Estimate Tax.

SEC. 85. *And be it further enacted*, That in case of the manufacture and sale or production and sale, consumption or delivery of any goods, wares, merchandise, or articles as hereinafter mentioned, without compliance on the part of the party manufacturing or producing the same with all the requirements and regulations prescribed by law in relation thereto, the assistant assessor may, upon such information as he may have, assume and estimate the amount and value of such manufactures or products, and upon such assumed amount assess the duties and add thereto fifty per centum; and said duties shall be collected in like manner as in case the provisions of this act in relation thereto had been complied with, and to such articles all the foregoing provisions for liens, fines, penalties, and forfeitures shall in like manner apply.

Form of Manufacturers' Return, and what it shall Contain.

SEC. 86. *And be it further enacted*, [That any person, firm, company, or corporation, manufacturing or producing goods, wares, and merchandise, sold or removed for consumption or use, upon which taxes are imposed by law, shall, in their return of the value and quantity, render an account of the full amount of actual sales made by the manufacturer, producer, or agent* thereof, and shall state whether any part,

* An Agent is defined to be "any person, not a purchaser, who receives the property of another to be sold and accounted for to the owner." (Circular No.

and if so what part, of said goods, wares, and merchandise has been consumed or used by the owner, owners, or agent, or used for the production of another manufacture or product, together with the market value of the same at the time of such use or consumption; whether such goods, wares, and merchandise were shipped for a foreign port or consigned to auction or commission merchants, other than agents, for sale; and shall make a return according to the value at the place of shipment, when shipped for a foreign port, or according to the value at the place of manufacture or production, when removed for use or consumption, or consigned to others than agents of the manufacturer or producer. The value and quantity of the goods, wares, and merchandise required to be stated as aforesaid shall be estimated by the actual sales made by the manufacturer, or by his agent. And where such goods, wares, and merchandise have been removed for consumption or for delivery to others, or placed on shipboard, or are no longer within the custody or control of the manufacturer or his agent, not being in his factory, store or warehouse, the value shall be estimated at the average of the market value of the like goods, wares, and merchandise at the time when the same became liable to tax.]

Statements and Returns, Bonds, Permits, &c., of Manufacturers of Tobacco.

SEC. 87. *And be it further enacted*, [That any person, firm, company, or corporation who may now be engaged in the manufacture of tobacco, snuff, or cigars, or who shall hereafter commence or engage in such manufacture, before commencing, or, if already commenced, before continuing, such manufacture for which they may be liable to be assessed under the provisions of law, shall, in addition to a compliance with all other provisions of law, furnish to the assessor or assistant assessor a statement, subscribed under oath or affirmation, accurately setting forth the place, and, if in a city, the street and number of the street where the manufacturing is, or is to be, carried on, the name and description of the manufactured article, and, if the same shall be manufactured for or to be sold and delivered to any other person or party, the name and residence and business or occupation of the person or party for whom the said article is to be manufactured or to whom it is to be delivered, and generally the kind and quality manufactured or proposed to be manufactured; and shall give a bond to the United States, with one or more sureties to be approved by the collector of the district, in the sum of three thousand dollars for each cutting machine for use, in the sum of one thousand dollars for each screw-press kept for use for

---

34, August 2, 1865.) This is now held to include commission merchants who sell *usually* the goods consigned to them. They may sell in their own name, but when they guarantee the sales, under del credere commission or otherwise, the goods will not be taxed till the account of such sales is rendered to the manufacturer, &c. There has been some diversity of ruling on this point, but the above seems now to be the true definition of agent.

making plug or pressed tobacco, in the sum of five thousand dollars for each hydraulic press kept for use, in the sum of one thousand dollars for each snuff mull kept for use, and in the sum of one hundred dollars for each person employed by said person, firm, company, or corporation in making cigars, conditioned that he will comply with all the requirements of law in regard to the manufacture of tobacco, snuff, or cigars; that he will not employ others to manufacture cigars who have not obtained the requisite permit for making cigars; that he will not engage in any attempt, by himself or by collusion with others, to defraud the government of any tax on any manufacture of tobacco, snuff, or cigars; that he will render truly and correctly all the returns, statements, and inventories prescribed for manufacturers of tobacco, snuff and cigars; that whenever he shall add to the number of cutting machines, presses, snuff mulls, or cigar-makers, used or employed by him, he will immediately give notice thereof to the collector who holds the bond, that he will pay to the collector of the district all the taxes which may or should be assessed and due on any tobacco, snuff, or cigars so manufactured, and that he will not knowingly sell, purchase, or receive for sale any such tobacco, snuff, or cigars, which have not been inspected, branded or stamped as required by law, or upon which the tax has not been paid if it has accrued or become payable. And the said bond may be renewed or changed from time to time, in regard to the sureties or amount thereof, according to the discretion of the collector, under the instructions of the Commissioner of Internal Revenue. And every person, firm, company, or corporation aforesaid shall exhibit, whenever demanded by any officer of internal revenue, a certificate from the collector, who is hereby authorized and directed to issue the same, setting forth the kind and number of machines, presses, snuff mulls, and number of cigar-makers for which the bond has been given. And any person, firm, or corporation manufacturing tobacco, snuff, or cigars of any description without first furnishing the bond in the cases herein required, shall be subject to a fine of three hundred dollars, and in addition thereto, upon conviction thereof, shall be liable to imprisonment for a term not exceeding one year, at the discretion of the court.]

Record of "Permits" to be kept by Assistant Assessor and returned to Assessor.

SEC. 88. *And be it further enacted,* [That it shall be the duty of the assistant assessor of each district to keep a record, in a book or books to be provided for the purpose, to be open to the inspection of any person upon reasonable request, of the name of any and every person, firm, company, or corporation who may be engaged in the manufacture of tobacco, snuff, or cigars in his district, together with the place where such manufacture is carried on, and place of residence of the person or persons engaged therein, and the assistant assessor shall enter in said record, under the name of each manufacturer, an abstract of his monthly returns; and each assessor shall keep a similar record for the entire district.]

Further Provisions in relation to the Manufacture of Tobacco. Forfeiture for Frauds, &c.

SEC. 89. *And be it further enacted,* [That in all cases where tobacco, snuff, or cigars, of any description, are manufactured, in whole or in part, upon commission or shares, or where the material from which any such articles are made, or are to be made, is furnished by one party and manufactured by another, or where the material is furnished or sold by one party with an understanding or contract with another, that the manufactured article is to be received in payment therefor or any part thereof, the tax imposed by law thereon may be assessed upon the party for whom the same was made, or to whom the same was delivered, as aforesaid, or upon the person or party who made the same, as the assessor shall deem best for the collection of the revenue. And in case of fraud, on the part of either of said parties, in respect to said manufacture, or of any collusion on their part with intent to defraud the revenue, such material and manufactured articles shall be liable to forfeiture; and such articles shall be liable to be assessed the highest rates of tax imposed by law upon any article of like kind.]

Inventories and Returns of Tobacco Manufacturers. Books and Accounts to be kept. Penalties for Fraud. Removals to Warehouses. Bonds and Security.

SEC. 90. *And be it further enacted,* [That any person, firm, company, or corporation, now or hereafter engaged in the manufacture of tobacco, snuff, or cigars of any description whatsoever, shall be, and hereby is, required to make out and deliver to the assistant assessor of the assessment district a true statement or inventory of the quantity of each of the different kinds of tobacco, snuff-flour, snuff, cigars, tin-foil, licorice and stems held or owned by him or them on the first day of January of each year, or at the time of commencing business under this act, setting forth what portion of said goods was manufactured or produced by him or them, and what was purchased from others, whether chewing, smoking, fine-cut, shorts, pressed, plug, snuff-flour or prepared snuff, or cigars, which statement or inventory shall be verified by the oath or affirmation of such person or persons, and be in manner and form as prescribed by the Commissioner of Internal Revenue; and every such person, company, or corporation shall keep in book form an accurate account of all the articles aforesaid thereafter purchased by him or them, the quantity of tobacco, snuff, snuff-flour, or cigars, of whatever description, manufactured, sold consumed, or removed for consumption or sale, or removed from the place of manufacture; and he or they shall, on or before the tenth day of each month, furnish to the assistant assessor of the district a true and accurate abstract of all such purchases, and sales or removals, which abstract shall be verified by oath or affirmation; and in case of refusal or neglect to deliver the inventory, or keep the account, or furnish the abstract aforesaid, he or they shall forfeit the sum of five hundred dollars, to be recovered with costs of suit. And it shall be the duty of any manufacturer or vender of tin-foil or other material used in manufacturing tobacco, snuff, or cigars, on demand of any officer of internal revenue, to render to such officer a correct statement, verified by oath or affirmation, of the quantity and amount of tin-foil or other materials sold or delivered to any person or persons named in such demand; and in case of refusal or neglect to render such statement, or of cause to believe such statement to be incorrect or fraudulent, the assessor of the district may cause an examination of persons, books, and papers to be made in the same manner as provided in the fourteenth section of this act. And all the provisions of law relating to manufacturers generally, so far as applicable and not inconsistent herewith, shall be held to apply to the manufacture of tobacco, snuff and cigars: *Provided*, The tax imposed upon the manufacturer of tobacco, snuff, or cigars, shall be held to accrue upon the sale or removal from the place of manufacture, unless removed to a bonded warehouse: *Provided further*, That manufactured tobacco, snuff, or cigars, whether of domestic manufacture or imported, may be transferred, without payment of the tax, to a bonded warehouse established in conformity with law and treasury regulations, under such rules and regulations and upon the execution of such transportation bonds or other security as may be prescribed by the Commissioner of Internal Revenue, subject to the approval of the Secretary of the Treasury, said bonds or other security to be taken by the collector of the district from which such removal is made; and may be transported from such a warehouse to any other bonded warehouse established as aforesaid, and may be withdrawn from bonded warehouse for consumption on payment of the tax, or removed for export to a foreign country without payment of tax, in conformity with the provisions of law relating to the removal of distilled spirits, all the rules, regulations and conditions of which, so far as applicable, shall apply to tobacco, snuff, or cigars, in bonded warehouse. And no drawback shall in any case be allowed upon any manufactured tobacco, snuff, or cigars.]

General Provisions in relation to Inspection of Tobacco and Cigars. Boxing and Stamping. Duties of Inspectors. Stamp Accounts.

SEC. 91. *And be it further enacted*, [That all manufactured tobacco, snuff, or cigars, shall, before the same is used or removed for consumption, be inspected by an inspector appointed under the provisions of law, who shall mark or affix a stamp upon the box or other package containing such tobacco, snuff, or cigars, in a manner to be prescribed by the Commissioner of Internal Revenue, denoting the kind, quantity, or number contained in each package, with the date of inspection and the name of the inspector, and the collection district. The fees of such inspector shall in all cases be paid by the owner of the manufactured tobacco, snuff, or cigars, so inspected. And any person who shall affix upon any box or other package containing such tobacco, snuff, or cigars, any mark or stamp which shall be false or fraudulent in any of the particulars before recited in this section, or shall, with intent to defraud the United States, or to cause the same to be defrauded, change in any manner such stamp or mark, or such box or package so marked or stamped, shall be liable to a fine of not less than fifty dollars or to imprisonment, not exceeding two years for every such offence. And all cigars manufactured after the passage of this act shall be packed in boxes or paper packages. And any manufactured tobacco, snuff, and cigars, whether of domestic manufacture or imported, which shall be sold or pass out of the hands of the manufacturer or importer, except into a bonded warehouse, without the inspection marks or stamps affixed, unless otherwise provided, shall be forfeited, and may be seized wherever found, and shall be sold, and the proceeds of such sale shall be distributed between the United States and the informer, if there be any, as provided by law. The Commissioner of Internal Revenue shall keep an account of all stamps delivered to the several inspectors; and said inspectors shall also keep an account of all stamps by them used or placed upon boxes containing cigars, and of all tobacco, snuff, and cigars inspected, and the name of the person, firm, or company for whom the same were so inspected, and shall return to the assessor of the district a separate and distinct account of the same, and also return to the said Commissioner, on demand, all stamps not otherwise accounted for, and shall give a bond for a faithful performance of all the duties to which he may be assigned, and to return or account for all stamps which may be placed in his hands.]

Penalties for Fraud in the Sale and Removal of Manufactured Tobacco and Cigars. Do. for knowingly Receiving or Purchasing Fraudulently. Accounts of Manufacturers. Further Duties of Inspectors, &c.

SEC. 92. *And be it further enacted,* [That if any person other than the manufacturer shall sell, or consign, or remove for sale, or part with the possession of any manufactured tobacco, snuff, or cigars upon which the taxes imposed by law have not been paid, with the knowledge thereof, such person shall be liable to a penalty of one hundred dollars for each offence. And any person who shall purchase or receive for sale any such tobacco, snuff, or cigars, which has not been inspected, branded, or stamped as required by law, or upon which the tax has not been paid, if it has accrued or become payable, with knowledge thereof, such person shall be liable to a penalty of fifty dollars, for each and every offence. And any person who shall purchase or receive for sale any such tobacco, snuff, or cigars, from any manufacturer who has not paid the special tax, shall be liable for each and every offence to a penalty of one hundred dollars, and, in addition thereto, a forfeiture of all the articles, as aforesaid, so purchased or received, or the full value thereof. And every person, before making any cigars after the passage of this act, shall apply for and procure from the assistant assessor of the district in which he resides, a permit authorizing such persons to carry on the trade of cigar making, for which permit he shall pay said assistant assessor the sum of twenty-five cents. And every person employed or working at the business of cigar making in any other district than that in which he or she is a resident shall, before making any cigars in such other district, present said permit to the assistant assessor of the district where so employed or working, and procure the indorsement of said assistant assessor thereon, authorizing said business in said district, for which indorsement the assistant assessor shall be entitled to receive from the applicant the sum of ten cents. And it shall be the duty of every assistant assessor, upon application of any person residing in his district, to furnish a permit, or to indorse upon the permit of the applicant, if resident in another district, authority to pursue the trade of cigar making within the proper district of such assistant assessor; and said assistant assessor shall keep a record of all permits granted or indorsed by him, showing the date of each permit, the name, residence, and place of employment of the party named therein, the name and district of the officer who originally granted the same, or who may have made any subsequent indorsements thereon, and the name or names of the party or parties by whom the person named in such permit is employed, or, if working for himself, stating such fact; and every person making cigars shall keep an accurate account in a book of all the cigars made by him, for whom, and their kind or quality; and, if made for any other person, shall state in said account the name of the person for whom the same were made, and his place of business, and shall, on the first Monday of every month, deliver to the assistant assessor of the district a copy of such account, verified by oath or affirmation that the same is true and correct. And if any person shall make any cigars without procuring such permit, or the proper indorsements thereon, or neglect to keep such account in book form, he shall be punished by a fine of five dollars for each day he shall so offend, or by imprisonment for such time as the court may order for each day's offence, not exceeding thirty days in the whole, upon any one conviction. And if any person making cigars shall fail to make the return herein required, or shall make a false return, he shall be punished by a fine not exceeding one hundred dollars, or by imprisonment not exceeding thirty days. And any person may apply to the assistant assessor or inspector of the district to have any cigars of his own manufacture counted; and on receiving a certificate of the number, for which such fee as may be prescribed by the Commissioner of Internal Revenue shall be paid by the owner thereof, may sell and deliver such cigars to any purchaser, in the presence of said assistant assessor or inspector, in bulk or unpacked, without payment of the tax. A copy of the certificate shall be retained by the assistant assessor, or by the inspector, who shall return the same to the assessor of the district. The purchaser shall pack such cigars in boxes or paper packages, and have the same inspected and marked or stamped according to the provisions of law, and shall make a return of the same, as inspected, to the assistant assessor of the district, and, wherein the same were manufactured, and unless removed to a bonded warehouse, shall pay the taxes on such cigars within fifteen days after purchasing them, to the collector of the district wherein they were manufactured, and before the same have been removed from the store or building of such purchaser, or from his possession; and if such purchaser shall neglect for more than fifteen days to pack and have such cigars duly inspected, and to pay the taxes thereon according to law, he shall be fined not exceeding five hundred dollars, and be imprisoned not exceeding six months, at the discretion of the court, and the cigars may be seized by the collector and shall be forfeited to the United States. And if any person, firm, company, or corporation shall employ or procure any person to make any cigars, who has not the permit or the endorsement thereon required by this act, he shall be punished by a fine of ten dollars for each day he shall so employ such person, or by imprisonment not exceeding ten days. And if any person shall be found making cigars without such permit, or the indorsement thereon, the collector of the district may seize any cigars, or tobacco for making cigars, which may be found in possession of such person, and the same shall be forfeited to the United States and sold; and the proceeds of such sale shall be distributed between the United States and the informer, if there be any, as provided by law.]

Amount of Manufactured Articles Exempt upon certain Rates. Tax upon Removal of Goods. Naphtha, &c., Exempt.

Sec. 93. *And be it further enacted,* [That all goods, wares, and merchandise, or articles manufactured or made, or produced, (except refined petroleum, refined coal oil, cotton, gold and silver, spirituous and malt liquors, manufactured tobacco, snuff, and cigars) by any person or firm, where the product shall not exceed the rate of one thousand dollars per annum, and shall be made or produced by the labor of such person or firm, or by his or their family,* shall be and are hereby exempt from

*1. It has, however, been decided that although a small manufacturer may employ an apprentice, journeyman, or any other subordinate employe; yet if he does not make to exceed $600 in a year, he is exempt from tax, if he personally superintends the work, and has the general oversight of the business.

2. A custom began to obtain among some manufacturers to return their goods at a stated value, and afterwards charging the tax as a separate and distinct item to the account of the purchaser. There are many objections to this course. It imposes the tax as a direct tax on the consumer, which the law intends should be imposed upon the manufacturer. It also directly defrauds the government of a portion of its dues. The law imposes the tax upon the sale value of the goods, which necessarily includes the tax as a part of such value. A return upon any such basis is a short return, and does not give the full amount of the tax actually due. (e. g.) If the manufacturer proposes to realize ninety-five cents for an article, and the tax is five per cent., he should make his sale price one dollar. A. has broadcloth which he could afford to sell for $4.75 per yard, if he could evade the payment of the tax. He makes his bill as follows:

D. C. bought of A. 100 yards cloth, at $4.75, ...	$475 00
Excise tax, 5 per cent., ...	23 75
	$498 75

But the bill would be made correctly as follows:

D. C. bought of A. 100 yards cloth, at $5, ...	$500 00

tax; where the product shall exceed such rate and not exceed the rate of three thousand dollars,* the tax shall be levied, assessed, and collected only upon the excess above the rate of one thousand dollars per annum; and in all other cases the whole annual product, including any business or transaction where one party has been furnished with materials or any part thereof, and employed by another party to manufacture, make, or finish the goods, wares and merchandise, or articles, paying or promising to pay therefor, and to whom the same are returned when so made and finished, shall be assessed and the tax paid thereon by the producer or manufacturer: *Provided*, That whenever a producer or manufacturer shall use or consume, or shall remove for consumption or use, any articles, goods, wares, or merchandise, which, if removed for sale, would be liable to taxation, he shall be assessed for the tax upon the articles, goods, wares, or merchandise so used, or so removed for consumption or use. But naphtha the product of the distillation of petroleum, and other similar bituminous substances when used or consumed for fuel or cleaning, shall be exempt from tax.]

Tax on Raw Cotton. Mode of ascertaining Weight. No Drawback Allowed in certain cases.

(SECTION 1. Law of 1866.) *Be it enacted by the Senate and House of Representatives of the United States of America in Congress assembled*, [That on and after the first day of August, eighteen hundred and sixty-six, in lieu of the *taxes* on unmanufactured cotton, as provided in "An act to provide internal revenue to support the government, to pay interest on the public debt, and for other purposes," approved June thirtieth, eighteen hundred and sixty-four, as amended by

A. makes his return to the assessor as $500, the amount to be taxed, or at five per cent., a tax of $25, and the net sum remaining with the manufacturer will be $475. Now if the first form of bill is rendered the tax would be assessed on the $498.75. But this would make the tax $24,93¾, which ought to be $25, and leave the manufacturer $473,81¼, instead of $475, the net amount which he desires to realize; so that neither the government nor the manufacturer gets what he intended.

3. It was provided by the amendments of March 3, 1865, that no duty imposed by any previous act, which has become due, or of which return has been or ought to be made, shall be remitted or released by this act, (amendment), but the same shall be collected and paid. For instance, when duties accrue in the month of March, 1865, a return of the same is not required until after April 1, when the provisions of the amended rate of duty take effect. Now if the manufacturer makes a sale on the 1st day of March, the duty upon the article accrues and becomes fixed; the obligation to return such duty also becomes fixed, although he is not bound to make an actual return until or after April 1; and the same is true of sales made on any other day of the month. The tax due is to be determined by the law in force at the time when the tax or duty accrues. When however the tax accrues on or after April 1, the rate is to be determined by the amended law (i. e.) when of the goods made in March, none are sold, consumed, used or removed for consumption during that month, no tax accrues till after April 1. The same rule will of course apply to any amended statute. (See Section 66.)

* This is an entirely new and important modification of former acts.

the act of March third, eighteen hundred and sixty-five, there shall be paid by the producer, owner, or holder, upon all cotton produced within the United States, and upon which no tax has been levied, paid, or collected, a tax of three cents per pound, as hereinafter provided; and the weight of such cotton shall be ascertained by deducting four per centum for tare from the gross weight of each bale or package; and such tax shall be and remain a lien thereon, in the possession of any person whomsoever, from the time when *this law takes effect, or* such cotton is produced as aforesaid until the same shall have been paid; and no drawback shall, in any case, be allowed on raw or unmanufactured cotton of any tax paid thereon when exported in the raw or unmanufactured condition. But no tax shall be imposed upon any cotton imported from other countries, and on which an import duty shall have been paid.]

Mode of Assessment upon Cotton. Tax when Payable. Mode of Inspection and Marking.

(Sec. 2. Act of July, 1866.) *And be it further enacted,* [That the aforesaid tax upon cotton shall be levied by the assessor on the producer, owner, or holder thereof. And said tax shall be paid to the collector of internal revenue within and for the collection district in which said cotton shall have been produced, and before the same shall have been removed therefrom, except where otherwise provided in this act: and every collector to whom any tax upon cotton shall be paid shall mark the bales or other packages upon which the tax shall have been paid, in such manner as may clearly indicate the payment thereof, and shall give to the owner or other person having charge of such cotton a permit for the removal of the same, stating therein the amount and payment of the tax, the time and place of payment, and the weight and marks upon the bales and packages, so that the same may be fully identified; and it shall be the duty of every such collector to keep clear and sufficient records of all such cotton inspected or marked, and of all marks and identifications thereof, and of all permits for the removal of the same, and of all his transactions relating thereto, and he shall make full returns thereof, monthly, to the Commissioner of Internal Revenue.]

Special Officers designated in certain Cotton Districts. Provision for Expenses of.

(Sec. 3. Act of July, 1866.) *And be it further enacted,* [That the Commissioner of Internal Revenue is hereby authorized to designate one or more places in each collection district where an assessor or an assistant assessor and a collector or deputy collector shall be located, and where cotton may be brought for the purpose of being weighed and appropriately marked: *Provided,* That it shall be the duty of the assessor or assistant assessor and the collector or deputy collector to assess and cause to be properly marked the cotton wherever it may be in said district, provided their necessary traveling expenses to and from said designated place, for that purpose, be paid by the owners thereof.]

Removal of Cotton upon Permits. Transportation Bonds. Delivery of to the Collector of District to which removed, &c.

(SEC. 4. Act of July, 1866.) *And be it further enacted*, [That all cotton having been weighed and marked as herein provided, and for which permits shall have been duly obtained of the assessor, may be removed from the district in which it has been produced to any one other district, without prepayment of the tax due thereon, upon the execution of such transportation bonds or other security and in accordance with such regulations as shall be prescribed by the Commissioner of Internal Revenue, subject to the approval of the Secretary of the Treasury. The said cotton so removed shall be delivered to the collector of internal revenue or his deputy forthwith upon its arrival at its point of destination, and shall remain subject to his control until the taxes thereon, and any necessary charges of custody thereof, shall have been paid, but nothing herein contained shall authorize any delay of the payment of said taxes for more than ninety days from the date of the permits; and when cotton shall have been weighed and marked for which a permit shall have been granted without prepayment of the tax, it shall be the duty of the assessor granting such permit to give immediate notice of such permit to the collector of internal revenue for the district to which said cotton is to be transported, and he shall also transmit therewith a statement of the taxes due thereon, and of the bonds or other securities for the payment thereof, and he shall make full returns and statements of the same to the Commissioner of Internal Revenue.]

Removal or Transportation of Cotton not Inspected and Marked, Unlawful. Penalties for Fraud in this matter, &c.

(SEC. 5. Act of July, 1866.) *And be it further enacted*, [That it shall be unlawful from and after the first day of September, eighteen hundred and sixty-six, for the owner, master, supercargo, agent, or other person having charge of any vessel, or for any railroad company, or other transportation company, or for any common carrier, or other person, to convey, or attempt to convey, or transport any cotton—the growth or produce of the United States—from any point in the district in which it shall have been produced, unless each bale or package thereof shall have attached to or accompanying it the proper marks or evidence of the payment of the revenue tax and a permit of the collector for such removal, or the permit of the assessor, as hereinbefore provided, under regulations of the Commissioner of Internal Revenue, subject to the approval of the Secretary of the Treasury, or to convey or transport any cotton from any State in which cotton is produced to any port or place in the United States, without a certificate from the collector of internal revenue of the district from which it was brought, and such other evidence as the Commissioner of Internal Revenue, subject to the approval of the Secretary of the Treasury, may prescribe, that the tax has been paid thereon, or the permit of the assessor, as hereinbefore provided, and such certificate and evidence as aforesaid shall be furnished to the collector of the district to which it is transported, and his permit obtained before landing, discharging, or delivering such cotton at the place to which it is transported as aforesaid. And any person or persons who shall violate the provisions of this act in this respect, or who shall convey, or attempt to convey from any State in which cotton is produced to any port or place without the United States, any cotton upon which the tax has not been paid, shall be liable to a penalty of one hundred dollars for each bale of cotton so conveyed or transported, or attempted to be conveyed or transported, or to imprisonment for not more than one year, or both; and all vessels and vehicles employed in such conveyance or transportation shall be liable to seizure and forfeiture, by proceedings in any court of the United States having competent jurisdiction. And all cotton so shipped or attempted to be shipped or transported, without payment of the tax, or the execution of such transportation bonds or other security, as provided in this act, shall be forfeited to the United States, and the proceeds thereof distributed according to the statute in like cases provided.]

Drawback on Articles made entirely of Cotton,—Rate of Allowance.

(Sec. 6. Act of July, 1866.) *And be it further enacted,* [That upon articles manufactured exclusively from cotton, when exported, there shall be allowed as a drawback an amount equal to the internal tax which shall have been assessed and paid upon such articles in their finished condition, and in addition thereto a drawback or allowance of as many cents per pound upon the pound of cotton cloth, yarn, thread, or knit fabrics, manufactured exclusively from cotton and exported, as shall have been assessed and paid in the form of an internal tax upon the raw cotton entering into the manufacture of said cloth or other article, the amount of such allowance or drawback to be ascertained in such manner as may be prescribed by the Commissioner of Internal Revenue, under the direction of the Secretary of the Treasury; and so much of section one hundred and seventy-one of the act of June thirty, eighteen hundred and sixty-four, "To provide internal revenue to support the government, to pay interest on the public debt, and for other purposes," as now provides for a drawback on manufactured cotton, is hereby repealed.]

Returns required of the Manufacturers of Cotton. Particular Provisions in relation thereto. Penalties for false statements and fraud herein.

(Sec. 7. Act of July, 1866.) *And be it further enacted,* [That it shall be the duty of every person, firm, or corporation, manufacturing cotton for any purpose whatever, in any district where cotton is produced, to return to the assessor or assistant assessor of the district in which such manufacture is carried on, a true statement in writing, signed by him, and verified by his oath or affirmation, on or before the tenth day of each month; and the first statement so rendered shall be on or before the tenth day of August, eighteen hundred and sixty-six, and shall state the quantity of cotton which such manufacturer had on hand and unmanufactured, or in process of manufacture, on the first day of said month; and each subsequent statement shall show the whole quantity in pounds, gross weight, of cotton purchased or obtained, and the whole quantity consumed by him in any business or process of manufacture during the last preceding calendar month, and the quantity and character of the goods manufactured therefrom; and every such manufacturer or consumer shall keep a book, in which he shall enter the quantity, in pounds, of cotton which he has on hand on the first day of August, eighteen hundred and sixty-six, and each quantity or lot purchased or obtained by him thereafter; the time when and the party or parties from whom the same was obtained; the quantity of said cotton, if any, which is the growth of the collection district where the same is manufactured; the quantity, if any, which has not been weighed and marked by any officer herein authorized to weigh and mark the same; the quantity, if any, upon which the tax had not been paid, so far as can be ascertained, before the manufacture thereof; and also the quantities used or disposed of by him from time to time in any process of manufacture or otherwise, and the quantity and character of the product thereof, which book shall, at all times during business hours, be open to the inspection of the assessor, assistant assessors, collector or deputy collectors of the district, inspectors, or of revenue agents; and such manufacturer shall pay monthly to the collector, within the time prescribed by law, the tax herein specified, subject to no deductions, on all cotton so consumed by him in any manufacture, and on which no excise tax has previously been paid; and every such manufacturer or person whose duty it is so to do, who shall neglect or refuse to make such returns to the assessor, or to keep such book, or who shall make false or fraudulent returns, or make false entries in such book, or procure the same to be so done, in addition to the payment of the tax to be assessed thereon, shall forfeit to the United States all cotton and all products of cotton in his possession, and shall be liable to a penalty of not less than one thousand nor more than five thousand dollars, to be recovered with costs of suit, or to imprisonment not exceeding two years, in the discretion of the court; and any person or persons who shall make any false oath or affirmation in relation to any matter or thing herein required shall be guilty of perjury, and shall be subject to the punishment prescribed by existing statutes for that offence: *Provided*, That nothing herein contained shall be construed in any manner to affect the liability of any person for any tax imposed by law on the goods manufactured from such cotton.]

General Provision of Law applicable to Cotton.

(Sec. 8. Act of July, 1866.) *And be it further enacted*, [That the provisions of the act of June thirty, eighteen hundred and sixty-four, as amended by the act of March third, eighteen hundred and sixty-five, relating to the assessment of taxes and enforcing the collection of the same, and all proceedings and remedies relating thereto, shall apply to the assessment and collection of the tax, fines, and penalties imposed by, and not inconsistent with, the provisions of the preceding sections of this act; and the Commissioner of Internal Revenue, subject to the approval of the Secretary of the Treasury, shall make all necessary rules and regulations for ascertaining the weight of all cotton to be assessed, and for appropriately marking the same, and generally for carrying into effect the foregoing provisions. And the Secretary of the Treasury is authorized to appoint all necessary inspectors, weighers, and markers of cotton, whose compensation shall be determined by the Commissioner of Internal Revenue, and paid in the same manner as inspectors of tobacco are paid.]

(Sec. 9. Act of July, 1866.) *And be it further enacted,* [That the act entitled "An act to provide internal revenue to support the government, to pay interest on the public debt, and for other purposes," approved June thirty, eighteen hundred and sixty-four, as amended by the act of March third, eighteen hundred and sixty-five, be, and the same is hereby, amended as follows, viz:]*

Specific and ad valorem Taxes upon Articles, Goods, Wares and Merchandise.

Sec. 94. *And be it further enacted,* [That upon the articles, goods, wares, and merchandise hereinafter mentioned, except where otherwise provided, which shall be produced and sold, or be manufactured or made and sold, or be consumed or used by the manufacturer or producer thereof, or removed for consumption or use, or for delivery to others than agents of the manufacturer or producer within the United States or Territories thereof, there shall be assessed, collected, and paid the following taxes, to be paid by the producer or manufacturer thereof, that is to say:

On Candles, of whatever material made, a tax of five per centum ad valorem.

On Gas,† illuminating, made of coal wholly or in part, or any other material, when the product shall not be above two hundred thousand cubic feet per month, a tax of ten cents per one thousand cubic feet; when the product shall be above two and not exceeding five hundred thousand cubic feet per month, a tax of fifteen cents per one thousand cubic feet; when the product shall be above five hundred thousand and not exceeding five millions of cubic feet per month, a tax of twenty cents per one thousand cubic feet; when the product shall be above

*The preliminary only of Section 9 is retained. Its specific amendments are incorporated into the various sections of the law of June 30, 1864, as amended March 3, 1865, and fully incorporated into this volume. (See preface to this volume.)

†"Any substance in the elastic æriform state applied for the purpose of illumination is embraced within the meaning and scope of the law, and rendered liable to taxation." (Commr., Apr. 6, 1866, III. Int. Rev. Rec., 132.)

five millions, a tax of twenty-five cents per one thousand cubic feet. And the general average of the monthly product for the year preceding the return required by law shall determine the rate of tax herein imposed. And where any gas-works have not been in operation for the next year preceding the return as aforesaid, then the rate shall be determined by the estimated average of the monthly product: *Provided*, that the product required to be returned by law by any gas company shall be understood to be, in addition to the gas consumed by said company or other party, the product charged in the bills actually rendered by the gas company during the month preceding the return; and until the thirtieth day of April, 1867, all gas companies whose price is fixed by law are authorized to add the tax herein imposed to the price per thousand feet on gas sold, and all such companies which have heretofore contracted to furnish gas to municipal corporations are in like manner, and for the same period, authorized to add such tax to such contract price: *Provided further*, That all gas furnished for lighting street lamps or for other purposes, and not measured, and all gas made for and used by any hotel, inn, tavern, and private dwelling-house, shall be subject to tax, whatever the amount of product, and may be estimated; and if the returns in any case shall be understated or underestimated, it shall be the duty of the assistant assessor of the district to increase the same as he shall deem just and proper: *And provided further*, That gas companies located within the corporate limits of any city or town, whether in the same district or otherwise, or so located as to compete with each other, shall pay the rate of tax imposed by law upon the company having the largest production: *And provided further*, That coal tar and ammoniacal liquor produced in the manufacture of illuminating gas, and the products of the re-distillation of coal tar, and the products of the manufacture of ammoniacal liquor thus produced, shall be exempt from tax.

On illuminating, lubricating, or other MINERAL OILS, marking not less than thirty-six nor more than fifty-nine degrees Baume's hydrometer, the product of the distillation, re-distillation, or refining of crude petroleum, twenty cents per gallon; and all such oils between the specific gravity, by Baume's test, of thirty-six and fifty-nine degrees, inclusive, shall be deemed refined illuminating oil, and any person or persons who, for the purpose of sale or consumption, shall mix any of the heavier paraffine oils with such illuminating oils, or with naphtha, or either one with the other, shall be deemed manufacturers of illuminating oil, and taxed as such, and said oil thus mixed, either with or without further distillation, shall be subject to a tax of twenty cents per gallon, if after said mixing or distillation the product marks, by Baume's hydrometer, between said points of thirty-six and fifty-nine degrees, inclusive.

On illuminating, lubricating, or other mineral OILS,* marking not less than thirty-six nor more than fifty-nine degrees Baume's hydrometer, the

* See decision No. 165, III. Int. Rev. Rec., 28.

exclusive product of the refining of crude oil produced by a single distillation of coal, shale, asphaltum, peat, or other bituminous substances, not otherwise provided for, ten cents per gallon.

On oil, naphtha, benzine, benzole, or gasoline, marking more than fifty-nine degrees Baume's hydrometer, the product of the distillation, re-distillation, or refining of crude petroleum, or of crude oil produced by a single distillation of coal, shale, peat, asphaltum, or other bituminous substances, a tax of ten cents per gallon: *Provided*, That distillers and refiners of illuminating, lubricating, or other mineral oil, naphtha, benzine, benzole, or gasoline, shall be subject to all the provisions of law applicable to distillers of spirits, with regard to special taxes, bonds, returns, assessments, removing to and withdrawing from warehouses, liens, penalties, forfeitures, drawbacks, and all other provisions designed for the purpose of ascertaining the quantity distilled, and securing the payment of taxes, so far as the same may, in the judgment of the Commissioner of Internal Revenue, and under regulations prescribed by him, be deemed necessary for that purpose: *And provided further*, That distillers and refiners of coal or mineral oil, whose product shall not exceed twenty-five barrels per day, on a monthly average, shall not be required to make returns oftener than once in thirty days.

On SPIRITS OF TURPENTINE,* ten cents per gallon.

On COFFEE,† roasted or ground, on all ground spices and dry mustard, and upon all articles intended for use as substitutes for or as adulterations of coffee, spices, or mustard, and upon all compounds and mixtures prepared for sale, or intended for use and sale as coffee, spices, or mustard, or as substitutes therefor, one cent per pound: *Provided*, That the exemption of one thousand dollars in annual value of product manufactured shall not apply to any of the above-specified articles, mentioned in this paragraph.

On MOLASSES produced from the sugar-cane, and not from sorghum or imphee, a tax of three cents per gallon.

On syrup‡ of molasses or sugar-cane juice, when removed from the plantation, concentrated molasses or melado, and cistern bottoms, of sugar produced from the sugar-cane and not made from sorghum or imphee, a tax of three-fourths of one cent per pound.

On SUGAR not above number twelve Dutch standard in color, produced from the sugar-cane and not from sorghum or imphee, other than those produced by the refiner, a tax of one cent per pound.

On sugars above number twelve and not above number eighteen Dutch standard in color, produced directly from the sugar-cane and not from sorghum or imphee, a tax of one and one-half cent per pound.

---

* See decision No. 165, III. Int. Rev. Rec., 28.

† "There is no provision of law for deducting from the amount of a mixture that is ground and sold as coffee the amount of taxed materials that enter into and form a part of such mixture." (Commr., Mar. 12, 1866, III. Int. Rev. Rec., 101.)

‡ Syrups used in drinks are a taxable manufacture. (Commr., Apr. 9, 1866, III. Int. Rev. Rec., 124.)

On sugar above number eighteen Dutch standard in color, produced directly from the sugar-cane and not from sorghum or imphee, a tax of two cents per pound.

On the gross amount of the sales of sugar refiners, including all the products of their manufactories or refineries, a tax of two and one-half of one per centum ad valorem: *Provided,* That every person shall be regarded as a sugar-refiner, and pay the taxes required by law, whose business it is to advance the quality and value of sugar upon which a tax or duty has been paid, by melting and recrystallization, or by liquoring, claying, or other washing process, or by any other chemical or mechanical means, or who shall by boiling or other process advance the quality or value of molasses, concentrated molasses, or melado, upon which a tax or duty has been paid.

On Sugar Candy and all Confectionery made wholly or in part of sugar, valued at not exceeding twenty cents per pound, including the tax, a tax of two cents per pound; exceeding twenty and not exceeding forty cents per pound including the tax, a tax of four cents per pound; when exceeding forty cents per pound including the tax, or sold by the box, package, or otherwise than by the pound, a tax of ten per centum ad valorem.

On Chocolate and cocoa prepared, a tax of one and a half cent per pound.

On Gun Cotton, a tax of five per centum ad valorem.

On Gunpowder, and all explosive substances used for mining, blasting, artillery, or sporting purposes, not otherwise provided for, when valued at thirty-eight cents per pound or less, including the tax, a tax of five per centum ad valorem; and when valued at above thirty-eight cents per pound including the tax, a tax of ten cents per pound.

On Varnish or Japan, made wholly or in part of gum copal, or other gums or substances, a tax of five per centum ad valorem.

On Glue and Gelatine of all descriptions, in the solid state, a tax of one cent per pound.

On glue and cement, made wholly or in part of glue, sold in the liquid state, a tax of forty cents per gallon.

On Pins, solid head or other, a tax of five per centum ad valorem.

On Photographs, ambrotypes, daguerreotypes, or other pictures taken by the action of light, and not hereinafter exempted from tax, a tax of five per centum ad valorem.

On Screws, commonly called wood screws, a tax of ten per centum ad valorem.

On Clocks and timepieces, and on clock movements, when sold without being cased a tax of five per centum ad valorem.

On all Soaps* valued at above three cents per pound, not perfumed, and on salt-water soap made of cocoa-nut oil, a tax of five mills per pound.

On all Perfumed Soaps, a tax of three cents per pound.

---

* See III. Int. Rev. Rec., 85, 140.

On all Uncompounded Chemical Productions not otherwise provided for, a tax of five per centum ad valorem.

On Essential Oils* of all descriptions, a tax of five per centum ad valorem.

On all Furniture†, or other articles made of wood, sold in the rough or unfinished, not otherwise provided for, a tax of five per centum ad valorem: *Provided*, That all furniture, or other articles made of wood, previously assessed, and a tax paid thereon, shall be assessed a tax of five per centum ad valorem upon the increased value‡ only thereof when sold in a finished condition.

---

* See decision 165, III. Int. Rev. Rec., 28.

† Parties who buy furniture in the "white" and paint and finish it, and have sale-rooms in the same building where they make sales, cannot claim deduction for expense of sales. (III. Int Rev. Rec., 125, Ruling of Commr.)

‡ INCREASED VALUES.

Probably no section of the law has given rise to more difficulty of construction, and upon which there has been a greater number of rulings and decisions, than this; it may be added, that no section has given greater dissatisfaction to manufacturers, or has caused greater want of uniformity of assessment in different districts. The vexed questions arising out of the use of this term, "increased values," were first brought prominently to the attention of Commissioner Boutwell, in the matter of the manufacture of clothing under a proviso to Section 75, of the law of 1862; and after hearing able arguments upon the subject, a very able opinion was given by him in December of that year. The language of the proviso to Section 75, was, "That on all cloths, dyed, printed, bleached, manufactured into other fabrics or otherwise prepared, on which a duty or tax shall have been paid, before the same were so dyed, &c., the said duty or tax (of three per cent. as the law then was) shall be assessed only upon the *increased* value thereof." It was plausibly argued by counsel in that case, that if clothing was a manufacture, independent of the fact that the *cloth* of which it was composed had already been subject to a tax as cloth, that under this proviso to Section 75, the tax should only be assessed upon the "increased value;" that is to say, that the manufacturer of clothing should be allowed to deduct the value of the cloth before it was cut up, before he was assessed upon the clothing. But a conclusive answer to this was made by the Commissioner, viz.: that the proviso treats of cloths as fabrics, and provides for a tax on the increased value of such cloths "as fabrics," when they have been subjected to the process of dyeing, &c., and that in the language of commerce and trade, cloth is a fabric, but a coat is not." (See Decision of Commissioners, Dec. 1, 1862, also Decision of October, 1862. Act of Amendment, March 5, 1863, Section 30.)

This last cited decision provided a mode of ascertaining the increased value of certain cloths, &c., and required assessors to procure returns of the sales of such cloth so dyed, &c., and from the price per yard to deduct the estimated value of the increased work, &c., upon the goods, assessing the tax upon the difference. (Decision No. 85, March, 1863.)

It will be perceived that the present Section 95, adopted in the act of June 30, 1864, extends the principle of increased value to "any manufactured articles, goods, wares, or merchandise, and makes them, if not otherwise specially provided for, liable to an additional tax, from the fact that they have been increased in value by being more completely finished or fitted for use; or to use the language of the statute, "the increasing of values shall be deemed 'manufacturing,'" and any person engaged therein shall be liable to all the provisions of the law for the collection of internal duties relating to manufactures, or to licenses, returns, payment of taxes, liens, fines, penalties and forfeitures."

On SALT, a tax of three cents per one hundred pounds.

On SCALES, PUMPS, GARDEN ENGINES, and HYDRAULIC RAMS, a tax of three per centum ad valorem.

On TIN WARE of all descriptions, not otherwise provided for, a tax of five per centum ad valorem.

On all IRON,* not otherwise provided for, advanced beyond muck-bar, blooms, slabs, or loops, and not advanced beyond bars, and band, hoop, and sheet iron, not thinner than number eighteen wire-gauge, and plate iron not less than one-eighth of an inch in thickness, a tax of three dollars per ton: *Provided*, That a ton shall, for all the purposes of this act, be deemed and taken to be two thousand pounds.

If the goods are increased in value by being polished, painted, varnished, waxed, oiled, gilded, electrotyped, galvanized, plated, framed, ground, pressed, colored, dyed, trimmed and ornamented, without changing the original character or purpose for which the same were intended to be used, they are subject to an ad valorem duty upon the amount of such increased value; to be ascertained by deducting from the value of the finished article when sold or removed for sale, delivery or consumption, the cost or value of the original article to the person, firm, or company, liable to the duty imposed upon such increased value thereof.

Construing this section in connection with the general principle of the excise law, that each particular manufacture is taxed for its value, though materials used in its production are in themselves manufactures, on which a duty has previously been paid, and it will be manifest that the principle extends to the whole range of manufactured productions, "not otherwise provided for," and that the questions will be almost as multitudinous as the subjects of taxation.

We have incorporated into the Appendix a variety of decisions and rulings illustrative of the vexed subject, and the reader is referred thereto. (Decision 164. See Appendix. III. Int. Rev. Rec., pp. 95, 100, 102.)

It will not be forgotten in this connection that whatever is made for sale, in such a state or condition that it finds purchasers, or has a demand in the market, and is recognized and known to the trade as a manufacture in itself, distinct from anything else, is subject to taxation unless specially exempted. This matter of tax upon the increase of value and upon articles independent of themselves and incorporated with other manufactures, is well illustrated in a ruling of Commissioner Rollins, of date November, 1864, in relation to the tax on carriages. He says:—

1. A carriage would not be taxable on its "increased value," because of its different parts, made by separate manufacturers, having paid a previous tax.

2. A carriage sold before being lined, trimmed or painted, if the tax had been assessed and paid upon it in that state, would be taxable on its increased value, when afterwards it is lined trimmed or painted.

3. If a manufacturer makes all the different parts of a carriage, (if he ever does,) carriage-making being his business; making the entire running gear as well as the body, and lining, trimming and painting, furnishing and fitting the carriage for use, sale or consumption, he is to be assessed on the entire value of such carriage as shown by its sale, subject to the usual "deductions."

4. He is also liable to pay tax on the axles, boxes, nuts, washers, nails, screws, handles, leather, &c., provided he make all these materials just as if he sold them to be wrought into a carriage at the hands of another builder, or just as he would expect to pay an excise tax thereon, if he had to purchase them of a dozen different manufacturers.

It will be manifest that any other rule would aggregate all manufacturing into collossal establishments, to the prejudice or ruin of small artisans.

* For a variety of interesting decisions and rulings in relation to manufactures, &c., of iron, see III. Int. Rev. Rec., pp. 116, 13, 67, 71, 188.

On band, hoop and sheet iron, thinner than number eighteen wire-guage, plate iron less than one-eighth of an inch in thickness, and cut nails and spikes, not including nails, tacks, brads, or finishing nails, usually put up and sold in papers, whether in papers or otherwise, a tax of five dollars per ton: *Provided*, That rods, bands, hoops, sheets, plates, spikes, and nails, not including such as are usually put up in papers as before mentioned, manufactured from iron upon which the tax of three dollars has been levied and paid, shall be subject only to a tax of two dollars per ton in addition thereto, anything in this act to the contrary notwithstanding.

On STEEL made directly from muck-bar, blooms, slabs, or loops, a tax of three dollars per ton.

On STOVES and HOLLOW WARE in all conditions, whether rough, tinned, or enameled, and castings of iron, not otherwise provided for, a tax of three dollars per ton.

On TUBES made of wrought iron, a tax of five dollars per ton.

On steam, locomotive, and marine ENGINES, including the boilers, and on railroad cars, a tax of five per centum ad valorem: *Provided*, That when the boilers, tubes, wheels, tire, axles, bells, shafts, cranks, wrists, or head-lights of such engines, or cars, shall have been once assessed, and a tax previously paid thereon, the amount so paid shall be deducted from the taxes on the finished engine or cars.

On BOILERS of all kinds, water tanks, sugar tanks, oil stills, sewing machines, lathes, tools, planes, planing machines, shafting and gearing, a tax of five per centum ad valorem.

On RAILINGS, GATES, FENCES, FURNITURE, and STATUARY MADE OF IRON, a tax of five per centum ad valorem.

On COPPER AND BRASS TUBES, nails, or rivets, sheet lead, and lead pipes and shot, a tax of five per centum ad valorem.

On goat, calf, kid, sheep, horse, hog, and dog SKINS, tanned or dressed in the rough, a tax of five per centum ad valorem.

On goat, calf, kid, sheep, horse, hog, and dog skins, curried or finished, a tax of five per centum ad valorem: *Provided*, That all goat, calf, kid, sheep, horse, hog, and dog skins upon which duties or taxes have been actually paid, shall be assessed on the increased value only when curried or finished.

On patent, enameled, and JAPANNED LEATHER and skins of every description, a tax of five per centum ad valorem: *Provided*, That when a tax or duty has been paid on the leather in the rough, the tax shall be assessed and paid only on the increased value.

On oil-dressed leather, a tax of five per centum ad valorem.

On leather of all descriptions, tanned or partially tanned, in the rough, a tax of five per centum ad valorem.

On leather of all descriptions, curried or finished, a tax of five per centum ad valorem: *Provided*, That all leather in the rough upon which duties or taxes have been actually paid shall be assessed on the increased value only when curried or finished.

On all LIQUORS known or denominated as wine, not made from

grapes, currants, rhubarb, or berries, produced by being rectified or mixed with other spirits, or into which any matter whatever may be infused to be sold as wine, or by any other name, and not otherwise provided for in this act, a tax of fifty cents per gallon : *Provided,* That the return, assessment, collection, and the time of collection of the taxes on such wines, shall be subject to the regulations of the Commissioner of Internal Revenue. And any person who shall willingly and knowingly sell or offer for sale any such wine made after the passage of this act, upon which the tax herein imposed has not been paid, or which has been fraudulently evaded, shall, upon conviction thereof, be subject to a fine of five hundred dollars or to imprisonment not exceeding two years, at the discretion of the court.

On CLOTH and all textile or knitted or felted articles, or fabrics of cotton, wool, or other materials, before the same has been dyed, printed, or bleached, and on all cloth painted, enameled, shirred, tarred, varnished, or oiled, a tax of five per centum ad valorem.

On THREAD AND TWINE, a tax of five per centum ad valorem.

On ARTICLES OF CLOTHING manufactured or produced for sale by weaving, knitting, or felting; on silk hats, bonnets, and hoop-skirts; on articles manufactured or produced for sale as constituent parts of clothing, or for trimming, or ornamenting the same, and on articles of wearing apparel manufactured or produced for sale from India-rubber, gutta-percha, or from fur, or fur skins dressed with the fur on, a tax of five per centum ad valorem: *Provided,* That on all articles made of fur the value of which shall not exceed twenty dollars, a tax of two per centum only shall be paid.

On BOOTS, SHOES, and SHOE-STRINGS a tax of two per centum ad valorem; to be paid by every person making, manufacturing, or producing for sale boots or shoes, or furnishing the materials or any part thereof, and employing others to make, manufacture, or produce them: *Provided,* That any boot or shoemaker making boots or shoes to order as custom work only, and not for general sale, and whose work, exclusive of the materials, does not exceed annually in value one thousand dollars, shall be exempt from this tax.

On CLOTHING, gloves, mittens, moccasins, caps, felt hats, and other articles of dress for the wear of men, women, and children, not otherwise assessed and taxed, a tax of two per centum ad valorem, to be paid by every person making, manufacturing, or producing for sale clothing, gloves, mittens, moccasins, caps, felt hats, and other articles of dress, or furnishing the materials or any part thereof, and employing others to make, manufacture, or produce them: *Provided,* That any tailor, or any maker of gloves, mittens, moccasins, caps, felt hats, or other articles of dress to order as custom work only, and not for general sale, and whose work, exclusive of the materials, does not exceed annually in value one thousand dollars, shall be exempt from this tax; and articles of dress made or trimmed by milliners or dressmakers for the wear of women and children shall also be exempt from this tax: *Provided,* That the branching into sprays, branches, or wreaths of artificial flowers, on which an impost or internal tax has already been paid, shall not be considered a manufacture within the meaning of this act.*

On Paper not otherwise herein provided for, a tax of three per centum ad valorem.†

On all Manufactures not otherwise provided for, of cotton, wool, silk, worsted, hemp, jute, India-rubber, gutta-percha, wood, glass, pottery-ware, leather, paper, iron, steel, lead, tin, copper, zinc, brass, gold, silver, horn, ivory, bone, bristles, wholly or in part, or of other materials, a tax of five per centum ad valorem: *Provided*, That on all cloths or articles dyed, printed, or bleached, on which a tax or duty shall have been paid before the same were so dyed, printed, or bleached, the said tax of five per centum shall be assessed only upon the increased value thereof: *And provided further*, That any cloth or fabrics or articles, as aforesaid, when made of thread, yarn, or warps, imported, or upon which an internal tax shall have been assessed and paid, shall be assessed and pay a tax on the increased value only thereof; and when made wholly by the same manufacturer shall be subject to a tax only of five per centum ad valorem: *And provided further*, That brown earthen and common or gray stone-ware shall be subject to a tax of two and one-half per cent ad valorem, and no more.

On all Diamonds, Emeralds, Precious Stones and imitations thereof, and all other jewelry, a tax of five per centum ad valorem: *Provided*, That when diamonds, emeralds, precious stones or imitations thereof, imported from foreign countries, and upon which import duties have been paid, shall be set or reset in gold or any other material, the tax shall be assessed and paid only upon the value of the settings.

On Bullion in lump, ingot, bar, or otherwise, a tax of one-half of one per centum ad valorem, to be paid by the assayer of the same, who shall stamp the product of the assay as the Commissioner of Internal Revenue, under the direction of the Secretary of the Treasury, may prescribe by general regulations. And all sales, transfers, exchanges, transportation, and exportation of gold or silver assayed at any mint of the United States, or by any private assayer, unless stamped as prescribed by general regulations, as aforesaid, are hereby declared unlawful; and every person or corporation who shall sell, transfer, transport, exchange, export or deal in the same, shall be subject to a penalty of one thousand dollars for each offence, and to a fine not exceeding that sum, and to imprisonment for a term not exceeding two years nor less than six months. No jeweller, worker or artificer in gold or silver shall use either of those metals except it shall have first been stamped as aforesaid, as required by this act. No person or corporation shall export or cause to be exported from the United States any gold or silver in its natural state, not coined, assayed, or stamped, as aforesaid; and for every violation of this paragraph every offender shall be subject to the penalties herein provided: *Provided*, That nothing herein contained

* See last note.

† Probably no subject gave rise to more discussion and examination in Congress than this. (See report of Revenue Commission.)

shall apply to the re-working of old gold or silver in lump, ingot, or bar, as aforesaid.

On Snuff, manufactured of tobacco or any substitute for tobacco, ground, dry, or damp, pickled, scented, or otherwise, of all descriptions, when prepared for use or sale, a tax of forty cents per pound.

On cavendish, plug, twist, and all other kinds of manufactured Tobacco, not herein otherwise provided for, a tax of forty cents per pound.

On Tobacco twisted by hand, or reduced from leaf into a condition to be consumed without the use of any machine or instrument, and without being pressed, sweetened, or otherwise prepared, and on fine-cut shorts, a tax of thirty cents per pound.

On Fine-cut Chewing Tobacco, whether manufactured with the stems in or not, or however sold, whether loose, in bulk, or in rolls, packages, papers, wrappers, or boxes, a tax of forty cents per pound.

On Smoking Tobacco, sweetened, stemmed, or butted, a tax of forty cents per pound.

On Smoking Tobacco of all Kinds, not sweetened, nor stemmed, nor butted, including that made of stems, or in part of stems, and imitations thereof, a tax of fifteen cents per pound.

On Cigarettes, or small cigars, made of tobacco, inclosed in a wrapper, or binder, and not over three and a half inches in length, and on cigars made with twisted heads, and on cheroots, and on cigars known as short-sixes, the market value of which is not over eight dollars per thousand, a tax of two dollars per thousand.

On all Cheroots, Cigarettes, and Cigars, the market value of which is over eight dollars and not over twelve dollars per thousand, a tax of four dollars per thousand. On all cheroots, cigarettes, and cigars, the market value of which is over twelve dollars per thousand, a tax of four dollars per thousand, and in addition thereto twenty per cent. ad valorem on the market value thereof.

And the Commissioner of Internal Revenue, with the approval of the Secretary of the Treasury, may prescribe such regulations for the inspection and valuation of cigars, cheroots, and cigarettes, and the collection of the tax thereon, as shall, in his judgment, be most effective for the prevention of inequalities and frauds in the payment of such tax. And, in addition to other regulations, it shall be the duty of the inspector or assessor who appraises any cigars, cigarettes, or cheroots, to examine the manufacturer thereof, or his agent, under oath, which oath shall be administered by the inspecting and appraising officer, and reduced to writing, and signed by such manufacturer or his agent, with a view to ascertaining whether such manufacturer has any interest, direct or indirect, in any sale that has been made, or any resale to be made of said cigars, cigarettes, or cheroots, by the concealment of which he seeks to obtain a false, fraudulent, or deceptive appraisement.

Tax on Increased Value and mode of ascertaining the same.

Sec. 95. *And be it further enacted*, That whenever any manufactured articles, goods, wares, or merchandise on which an excise or impost duty has been paid, and which are not specially provided for, are increased in value by being polished, painted, varnished, waxed, oiled, gilded, electrotyped, galvanized, plated, framed, ground, pressed, colored, dyed, trimmed, ornamented, or otherwise more completely finished or fitted for use or sale, without changing the original character or purposes for which the same are intended to be used, there shall be levied, collected, and paid a tax of five per centum ad valorem upon the amount of such increased value, to be ascertained by deducting from the value of the finished article when sold, or removed for sale, delivery, or consumption, the cost or value of the original article to the person, firm, or company liable to the duty imposed upon the increased value thereof. The increasing of values in the manner aforesaid shall be deemed manufacturing, and any person, firm, company, or corporation engaged therein shall be liable to all the provisions of law for the collection of internal duties relating to manufacturers as to licenses, returns, payment of taxes, liens, fines, penalties, and forfeitures.

Exempt Articles (*under former Law.*)

SEC. 96. *And be it further enacted,* That newspapers, boards, shingles, laths, and other lumber, staves, hoops, shooks, headings, and timber partially wrought and unfinished for chairs, tubs, pails, hubs, spokes, felloes, snaths, lasts, shovel and fork handles, matchwood, umbrella stretchers, alcohol made or manufactured of spirits or materials upon which the duties imposed by law shall have been paid, bone dust, plaster or gypsum, malt, burning fluid, printers' ink, flax prepared for textile or felting purposes until actually woven, marble and slate or other building stones in block, rough and unwrought, charcoal, coke, all flour and meal made from grain, bread and breadstuffs, butter, cheese, concentrated milk, cider, and cider vinegar, and sugar or molasses made from other articles than the sugar-cane, paraffine, whale and fish oil, value of the bullion used in the manufacture of silver-ware, silver bullion rolled or prepared for plater's use exclusively, and cut tapes and small wares used in the manufacture of hoop-skirts, shall be, and hereby are, exempt from duty. And also all goods, wares, and merchandise, and articles made or manufactured from materials which have been subject to and upon which internal duties have been actually paid, or materials imported upon which duties have been paid or upon which no duties have been imposed by law, where the increased value* of such goods, wares, or merchandise, and articles so made or manufactured, shall not exceed the amount of five per centum ad valorem, shall be, and hereby are, exempt from duty.

---

* Assistant assessors will be cautious not to confound the provisions of Section 95, with those of Section 96. "The increase in value of manufactures by any of the processes specified in Section 95, is subject to taxation without reference to the ratio of percentage of increase, and is a different subject-matter from that contemplated in Section 96. Under Section 95 the increased value may amount to only one per cent., and be taxable; but under the processes of

Goods purchased by Government Free of Duty.

(SEC. 17. Act of March 3, 1865.) *And be it further enacted,* That the privilege of purchasing supplies of goods imported from foreign countries for the use of the United States, duty free, which now does or hereafter shall exist by provision of law, shall be extended, under such regulations as the Secretary of the Treasury may prescribe, to all articles of domestic production which are subject to tax by the provisions of this act.

Manufacturers under Contracts made prior to Act, allowed to Add Prices equivalent to Additional Tax imposed.

SEC. 97. *And be it further enacted,* That every person, firm, or corporation, who shall have made any contract prior to the passage of this act, and without other provision therein for the payment of duties imposed by law enacted subsequent thereto, upon articles to be delivered under such contract, is hereby authorized and empowered to add to the price thereof so much money as will be equivalent to the duty so subsequently imposed on said articles, and not previously paid by the vendee, and shall be entitled by virtue hereof to be paid and to sue for and recover the same accordingly: *Provided,* That where the United States is the purchaser under such prior contract, the certificate of the proper officer of the department by which the contract was made, showing, according to regulations to be prescribed by the Secretary of the Treasury, the articles so purchased by the United States, and liable to such subsequent duty, shall be taken and received, so far as the same is

---

finishing, &c., contemplated in Section 96, the increase in value must exceed five per cent., or no tax is required." (Boutwell's Manual, Decision 176.)

For mode of determining the increased value, consult Decision 164 of Nov., 1865, and for a variety of illustrations of, upon particular articles, viz:

Salt. (Int. Rev. Rec., Vol. I., p. 75.)
Tarred Paper. (*Ibidem.*)
Sails and Tents. (*Ibidem,* p. 100.)
Articles Dyed. (*Ibidem.*)
Tassels. (*Ibidem,* p. 168, 180.)
Imported Cloths. (*Ibidem,* pp. 163, 180.)
General Principles. (*Ibidem,* pp. 96, 149.)

See also Int. Rev. Rec., Vol. II., pp. 29, 196, 54, 92, 108, 156, 172.

Ruling: "You represent that a manufacturer of spool thread buys yarn in the hank in a brown state, but which is spun specially for the manufacturer of spool thread; that he then dresses, sizes, and otherwise finishes the yarn, and manufactures it into thread, which is wound upon spools, and completed for market. You wish to know whether the thread should be taxed on 'increased value' under Sections 94 and 95. In answer I have to say, that from your statement it appears that the yarn in question was spun specially for the purpose of making spool thread, and that an import duty had been paid on it; this office is of opinion, therefore, that when it is more completely finished and fitted for use in the form of thread, it is liable to duty on 'increased value,' under Section 95." (Ruling March 15, 1866. III. Int. Rev. Rec., p. 117.)

The painting of window sashes is taxable as increased value. Otherwise with setting in of glass. (Commissioner's Letter, Dec. 22, 1864.)

applicable, in discharge of such subsequent duties on articles so contracted to be delivered to the United States and actually delivered according to such contract.

Tax on Auction Sales. Returns. Penalties for Delinquency.

SEC. 98. *And be it further enacted,* [That there shall be levied and collected and paid monthly on all sales of real estate, goods, wares, merchandise articles, or things at auction, including all sales of stocks, bonds, and other securities, a duty of one-tenth of one per centum on the gross amount of such sales: *Provided,* That no tax shall be levied under the provisions of this section upon any sales by or for judicial or executive officers making auction sales by virtue of a judgment or decree of any court, nor to public sales made by guardians, executors, or administrators.]

Tax on Sales of Brokers, Banks and Bankers. Contracts of Sale to be Stamped. Particulars of Memoranda of Sales.

SEC. 99. *And be it further enacted,* [That there shall be paid on all sales made by brokers, banks, or bankers, whether made for the benefit of others or on their own account, the following taxes, that is to say: Upon all sales and contracts for the sale of stocks, bonds, gold and silver bullion and coin, promissory notes or other securities, a tax at the rate of one cent for every hundred dollars of the amount of such sales or contracts; and on all sales and contracts for sale negotiated and made by any person, firm or company not paying a special tax as a broker, bank or banker, of any gold or silver bullion, coin, promissory notes, stocks, bonds, or other securities, not his or their own property, there shall be paid a tax at the rate of five cents for every hundred dollars of the amount of such sales or contracts; and on every sale and contract for sale, as aforesaid, there shall be made and delivered by the seller to the buyer a bill or memorandum of such sale or contract, on which there shall be affixed a lawful stamp or stamps in value equal to the amount of tax on such sale, to be determined by the rates of tax before mentioned; and in computing the amount of the stamp tax in any case herein provided for, any fractional part of one hundred dollars of value or amount on which tax is computed shall be accounted as one hundred dollars. And every bill or memorandum of sale or contract of sale, before mentioned, shall show the date thereof, the name of the seller, the amount of the sale or contract, and the matter or thing to which it refers. And any person or persons liable to pay the tax as herein provided, or any one who acts in the matter as agent or broker for such person or persons, who shall make any such sale or contract, or who shall, in pursuance of any sale or contract, deliver or receive any stocks, bonds, bullion, coin, promissory notes, or other securities, without a bill or memorandum thereof as herein required, or who shall deliver or receive such bill or memorandum without having the proper stamps affixed thereto, shall forfeit and pay to the United States a penalty of five hundred dollars for each and every offence where the tax so evaded, or attempted to be evaded, does not exceed one hundred dollars, and a penalty of one thousand dollars when such tax shall exceed one hundred dollars, which may be recovered with costs in any court of the United States of competent jurisdiction, at any time within one year after the liability to such penalty shall have been incurred; and the penalty recovered shall be awarded and distributed by the court between the United States and the informer, if there be any, as provided by law, who, in the judgment of the court, shall have first given the information of the violation of the law for which recovery is had: *Provided,* That where it shall appear that the omission to affix the proper stamp was not with intent to evade the provisions of this section, said penalty shall not be incurred. And the provisions of law in relation to stamp duties in Schedule B of this act shall apply to the stamp taxes herein imposed upon sales and contracts of sales made by brokers, banks or bankers, and others as aforesaid. And there shall be paid monthly on all sales by commercial brokers of any goods, wares, or merchandise, a tax of one-twentieth of one per centum upon the amount of such sales; and on or before the tenth day of each month, every commercial broker shall make a list or return to the assistant assessor of the district of the gross amount of such sales as aforesaid for the preceding month, in form and manner as may be prescribed by the Commissioner of Internal Revenue: *Provided,* That in estimating sales of goods, wares, and merchandise for the purposes of this section, any sales made by or through another broker upon which a tax has been paid, shall not be estimated and included as sold by the broker for whom the sale was made.]

Taxes on Watches, Carriages, &c. Schedule A.

SEC. 100. *And be it further enacted,* [That there shall be levied, annually, on every carriage, gold watch, and billiard table, and on all gold or silver plate, the tax or sums of money set down in figures against the same, respectively, or otherwise specified and set forth in Schedule A, hereto annexed, to be paid by the person or persons owning, possessing, or keeping the same, on the first day in May, in each year, and the same shall be and remain a lien thereon until paid.]

SCHEDULE A.

Carriage, phæton, carryall, rockaway, or other like carriage, and any coach, hackney coach, omnibus, or four-wheeled carriage, the body of which rests upon springs of any description, which may be kept for use, for hire, or for passengers, and which shall not be used exclusively in husbandry or for the transportation of merchandise, valued at exceeding three hundred dollars and not above five hundred dollars each, including harness used therewith, six dollars, ...	$6 00
Carriages of like description, valued above five hundred dollars each, ten dollars, ...	10 00

On gold watches, composed wholly or in part of gold or gilt, kept for use, valued at one hundred dollars or less, each, one dollar, ... $1 00

On gold watches, composed wholly or in part of gold or gilt, kept for use, valued at above one hundred dollars, each, two dollars, 2 00

Billiard tables, kept for use, each, ten dollars, ... 10 00

Provided, That billiard tables kept for hire, and upon which a special tax has been imposed, shall not be required to pay the tax on billiard tables kept for use, as aforesaid, anything herein contained to the contrary notwithstanding.

On plate, of gold, kept for use, per ounce troy, fifty cents, . . $0 50

On plate, of silver, kept for use, per ounce troy, five cents, . . 0 05

Provided, That silver spoons or plate of silver used by one family to an amount not exceeding forty ounces troy belonging to any one person, plate belonging to religious societies, and souvenirs and keepsakes actually given and received as such and not kept for use; also, all premiums awarded as a token of merit by any agricultural society, corporation, or association of persons, for any purpose whatever, shall be exempt from tax.

[Sections 101 and 102, containing the provisions in relation to cattle slaughtered, are by this law repealed.]

Railroads, Steamboats, Canals, Stage Coaches. Tax on Receipts. Provision as to addition to Rates of Fare equal to Tax till 1867, *&c.**

Sec. 103. *And be it further enacted,* [That every person, firm, company, or corporation owning or possessing or having the care or management of any railroad, canal, steamboat, ship, barge, canal-boat,

---

* CANALS.

Canal boats are included in the term vessels, and if used for the transport of passengers, furnishing food and lodgings, they require license. (I. Int. Rev. Rec., 35. See I. Int. Rev. Rec., 166, for Letters of Secretary of Treasury, in relation to liability of canal boats to tonnage duty, &c., and fees for their admeasurement.)

TAX UPON RAILROADS, &c.

The tax has been modified in the different acts. By the original act of 1862, railroads and steamboats, using steam, were subject to a duty of three per cent. upon the gross amount of all the receipts of such companies, for the transportation of passengers. Under this law it was ruled that the returns should be made from their principal office or place of business, and that the receipt for transportation of troops should be subject, as well as from any other class of passengers. (Decision No. 26.) Also that the returns for receipts from passengers should include all sums received for lodging, use of berths, state-rooms, &c. (Decision No. 73.) The act provided that if other than steam power was used, as in case of ferry boats propelled by steam or horse power, the duty should be one and one-half per cent. on gross receipt for transportation of passengers. (Estee's Tax Law, p. 63.) These companies were authorized by this act to add the tax to the rate of fare of passengers. (Proviso, Sec. 80, Law of 1862.)

An amendment in case of ferry boats was adopted in March, 1863, imposing a duty upon all their gross receipts; but it was confined to them, and the railroad and steamboat duty was not changed.

or other vessel, or any stage coach or other vehicle, except hacks or carriages not running on continuous routes, engaged or employed in the business of transporting passengers for hire, or in transporting the mails of the United States upon contracts made prior to August first, eighteen hundred and sixty-six, shall be subject to and pay a tax of two and one-half per centum of the gross receipts from passengers and mails of such railroad, canal, steamboat, ship, barge, canal-boat, or other vessel, or such stage coach or other vehicle: *Provided*, That the tax hereby imposed shall not be assessed upon receipts for the transportation of persons or mails between the United States and any foreign port; but such tax shall be assessed upon the transportation of persons from a port within the United States through a foreign territory to a port within the United States, and shall be assessed upon and collected from persons, firms, companies, or corporations within the United States, receiving hire or pay for such transportation of persons or mails; and so much of section one hundred and nine as requires returns to be made of receipts hereby exempted from tax when derived from transporting property for hire is hereby repealed: *Provided also*, That any person or persons, firms, companies, or corporations owning, possessing, or having the care or management of any toll-road, ferry, or bridge, authorized by law to receive toll for the transit of passengers, beasts, carriages, teams, and freight of any description, over such toll-road, ferry, or bridge, shall be subject to and pay a tax of three per centum of the gross amount of all their receipts of every description; but when the gross receipts of any such bridge or toll-road, for and during any term of twelve consecutive calendar months, shall not exceed the amount necessarily expended during said term to keep such bridge or road in repair, no tax shall be assessed upon such receipts during the month next following any such term: *Provided further*, That all such persons, companies, and corporations shall, until the 30th day of April, 1867, have the right to add the tax imposed hereby to their rates of fare when-

---

By the act of June 30, 1864, as amended March 3, 1865, the tax imposed upon railroads, steamboats, ferry boats and bridges, was made two and one-half per cent. upon the gross receipts of the companies owning the same, (including of course, receipts for freight as well as passengers), and also upon stage-coaches, or other vehicles engaged in the business of transporting passengers or United States Mail, with a proviso that vehicles used in the transportation of silver ores from the mines to the place where reduced or worked, should be exempt; and the receipts of all persons, &c., receiving not exceeding $1,000 per annum; also providing that the duty should not be chargeable upon steamers and vessels plying between the United States and foreign ports. Upon ferries and bridges receiving tolls for *passengers and freight*, the duty was fixed at three per cent. on gross receipts, unless in case the receipts were less than the expenses of repairs, in which the gross receipts were exempt. All these companies were by this act authorized to add the tax to the rates of fare. (Law of June 30, 1864, Sec. 103.)

By Section 10 of the amendatory act of March, 1865, persons and companies subject to the duty of two and one-half per cent. were authorized to add one cent in lieu of a fraction arising from the amount of addition to rate of fare by Section 103, and it will be seen that this provision is retained after great opposition in the present *act*.

ever their liability thereto may commence, any limitations which may exist by law or by agreement with any person or company which may have paid or be liable to pay such fare to the contrary notwithstanding; and whenever the addition to any fare shall amount only to the fraction of one cent, any person, or company liable to the tax of two and one-half per centum may add to such fare one cent in lieu of such fraction, and such person, or company, shall keep for sale at convenient points tickets in packages of twenty and multiples of twenty, to the price of which only an amount equal to the revenue tax shall be added: *And provided further*, That no tax under the foregoing provisions of this section shall be assessed upon any person, firm, company, or corporation whose gross receipts do not exceed one thousand dollars per annum: *And provided further*, That all boats, barges, and flats not used for carrying passengers, nor propelled by steam or sails, which are floated or towed by tug-boats or horses, and used exclusively for carrying coal, oil, minerals, or agricultural products to market, shall be required hereafter, in lieu of enrollment fees or tonnage tax, to pay an annual special tax, for each and every such boat of a capacity exceeding twenty-five tons, and not exceeding one hundred tons, five dollars; and when exceeding one hundred tons, as aforesaid, shall be required to pay ten dollars; and said tax shall be assessed and collected as other special taxes provided for in this act.]

Tax on Express Companies' Receipts.

SEC. 104. *And be it further enacted*, That any person, firm, company, or corporation carrying on or doing an express business, shall be subject to and pay a duty of three per centum on the gross amount of all the receipts of such express business.*

A clause in the amendatory *tariff* act of March 3, 1865, exempts the receipts of vessels paying tonnage duties from the tax imposed in Section 103, of the revenue act of June 30, 1864; and it was sought to evade the payment of the tax last named, on the part of ferry boats and other craft, by making an *unnecessary* enrollment. (For rulings, correspondence, &c., upon this matter, *vide* II. Int. Rev. Rec., 116. Letters of Secretary Chase, June 22, 1864. Commissioner Orton, September 12, 1865. Letter of Assistant Secretary Hartley, September 15, 1865.)

By the present statute, Section 103, it will be perceived that hacks and carriages, not running on a continuous route, are made exempt from this tax upon gross receipts; also that the tax should be assessed upon the fares, &c., for transportation of persons from a port within the United States, *through a foreign country*, to another port in the United States, and be collected from the persons, corporations, &c., within the United States, receiving the pay or hire for such transportation. It is also provided, (and as such, is amendatory of this section), that certain boats, barges and flats, conveying coal, oil, minerals or agricultural productions, shall in lieu of tonnage fees, pay annual special taxes for their boats, &c., as recited in the text. This will avoid the vexed question of the tonnage duty above alluded to.

*EXPRESS BUSINESS.

(See Int. Rev. Rec., Vol. I., pp. 148, 90, 82.)

*Tax on Gross Receipts of Insurance Premiums, and nature of Returns.**

SEC. 105. *And be it further enacted,* That there shall be levied, collected, and paid a duty of one and a half of one per centum upon the gross receipts of premiums, or assessments for insurance from loss or damage by fire or by the perils of the sea, made by every insurance company, whether inland or marine or fire insurance company, and by every association or individual engaged in the business of insurance against loss or damage by fire, or by the perils of the sea; and by every person, firm, company, or corporation, who shall issue tickets or contracts of insurance against injury to persons while traveling by land or water; and a like duty shall be paid by the agent of any foreign insurance company having an office or doing business within the United States; and that in the account or return to be rendered, they shall state the amount insured, renewed, or continued, the gross amount of premiums received and assessments collected, and the duties by law accruing thereon.

Tax on Passports.† Receipts of Collector therefor.

SEC. 106. *And be it further enacted,* That for every passport issued from the office of the Secretary of State there shall be paid the sum of five dollars; which amount may be paid to any collector appointed under this act, and his receipt therefor shall be forwarded with the application for such passport to the office of the Secretary of State, or any agent appointed by him, to be transmitted to the Commissioner of Internal Revenue, there to be charged to the account of such collector. And the collectors shall account for all moneys received for passports in the manner hereinbefore provided, and a like amount shall be paid for every passport issued by any minister or consul of the United States, who shall account therefor to the treasury.

Tax on Receipts of Telegraph Companies.

SEC. 107. *And be it further enacted,* [That any person, firm, company, or corporation owning or possessing or having the care or management of any telegraphic line by which telegraphic despatches or messages are received or transmitted, shall be subject to and pay a tax

---

* INSURANCE COMPANIES.

(For various rulings under former and present provisions of law, see Decisions Nos. 29, 30, 31, 35, 65. Circular No. 16.)

As to the same, see the Commissioner's Decisions No. 139, Aug., 1864. (I. Int. Rev. Rec., pp. 9, 27, 82, 156, 172.) Agents and brokers for, (II. Int. Rev. Rec., 147, 204.) Gross receipts of, (II. Int. Rev. Rec., 108.) Payment of tax by, (II. Int. Rev. Rec., 68, 89.) Stock dividends, (II. Int. Rev. Rec., 61.) Monthly returns, (II. Int. Rev. Rec., 45.)

†PASSPORTS

Issued by State governments are illegal and void, and in no case recognized by the Department of State. (Letter of Secretary Seward, May 12, 1866.)

of three per centum on the gross amount of all receipts of such person, firm, company, or corporation.]

Theaters, Operas, Circuses and Museums.

SEC. 108. *And be it further enacted,* That any person, firm or corporation, or the manager or agent thereof, owning, conducting, or having the care or management of any theater, opera, circus, museum, or other public exhibition of dramatic or operatic representations, plays, performances, musical entertainments, feats of horsemanship, acrobatic sports, or other shows which are opened to the public for pay, but not including occasional concerts, school exhibitions, lectures, or exhibitions of works of art, shall be subject to and pay a duty of two per centum on the gross amount of all receipts derived by such person, firm, company, or corporation from such representations, plays, performances, exhibitions, shows, or musical entertainments.

Returns of the Companies heretofore named. What they shall show. Inspection of their Books, &c.

SEC. 109. *And be it further enacted,* That any person, firm, company, or corporation owning or possessing, or having the care or management of any railroad, canal, steamboat, ship, barge, canal boat, or other vessel, or any ferry, toll road or bridge, as enumerated and described in section one hundred and three of this act; or carrying on or doing an express business; or engaged in the business of insurance, as hereinbefore described; or owning or having the care and management of any telegraph line, or owning, possessing, leasing, or having the control or management of any circus, theater, opera, or museum, shall, within twenty days after the end of each and every month, make a list or return in duplicate to the assistant assessor of the district, stating the gross amount of their receipts, respectively, for the month next preceding, which return shall be verified by the oath or affirmation of such owner, possessor, manager, agent, or other proper officer, in the manner and form to be prescribed from time to time by the Commissioner of Internal Revenue; and shall also pay to the collector the full amount of duties which have accrued on such receipts for the month aforesaid. And in case of neglect or refusal to make said lists or return for the space of ten days after such return should have been made as aforesaid, the assessor or assistant assessor shall proceed to estimate the amount received and the duties payable thereon, and shall add thereto ten per centum as hereinbefore provided in other cases of delinquency to make return for purposes of assessment; and for the purpose of making such assessment, or of ascertaining the correctness of any such return, the books of any such person, firm, company, or corporation shall be subject to the inspection of the assessor or assistant assessor on his demand or request therefor. And in case of neglect or refusal to pay the duties, with the addition aforesaid, when the same have been ascertained, for the space of ten days after the same shall have become payable, the owner, possessor, or person having the management as aforesaid, shall pay, in addition, ten per centum on the amount of such duties and addition; and for any attempt knowingly to evade the payment of such duties, the said owner, possessor, or person having the care or management as aforesaid, shall be liable to pay a penalty of one thousand dollars for every such attempt, to be recovered as provided in this act for the recovery of penalties. And all provisions of this act in relation to liens and collections by distraint, not incompatible herewith, shall apply to this section and the objects therein embraced: [*Provided*, That no return shall be required of receipts not subject to tax.]

*Banks and Banking. Taxes of in detail.**

SEC. 110. *And be it further enacted*, [That there shall be levied, collected, and paid a tax of one twenty-fourth of one per centum each month upon the average amount of the deposits of money, subject to payment by check or draft, or represented by certificates of deposit or otherwise, whether payable on demand or at some future day, with any person, bank, association, company, or corporation engaged in the business of banking; and a tax of one twenty-fourth of one per centum each month, as aforesaid, upon the capital of any bank, association, company, or corporation, and on the capital employed by any person in the business of banking beyond the average amount invested in United States bonds; and a tax of one-twelfth of one per centum each month upon the average amount of circulation issued by any bank, association, corporation, company, or person, including as circulation all certified checks and all notes and other obligations calculated or intended to cir-

---

*TAX UPON BANKS.

When the capital of a bank is transferred to a national bank, the outstanding circulation should be returned as from the old bank until in accordance with this section the bank shall deposit in the treasury of the United States, in lawful money, the amount of such outstanding circulation. (Decision 152, January, 1865.)

In making the deduction from the taxable capital which is authorized by law, the term "bonds," must be literally construed as covering only those government securities which are publicly known under such designation. For a schedule of the same (see Decision 140, Appendix.)

For circular in relation to the returns under sections 110, 120, 121 and 122, (see Appendix, Circular No. 16; see also Circular No. 23, October, 1864, in Appendix.)

The *original* bank return will be filed in the assessor's office; the duplicate returned to the Department with the tax due. (See modified instructions of Circular 23 in Circular 26, December 24, 1864.)

Ruling: "The working or employed capital of a bank comprehends the authorized capital, together with the surplus fund. In neither sections, 79 nor 110, (act of 1864), is the term "authorized capital" used, nor any indication that the license or tax is to be limited to that amount and thus leave the large surplus which is actually *employed* as capital untaxed." (Boutwell, "Rulings No. 1," p. 132.) This ruling has, however, been questioned.

Ruling: "The particular manner in which bank capital is invested, does not effect its liability to taxation. If invested in real estate, it is as much capital as gold, stocks, &c. Returns should be made on such real estate, estimating

culate or to be used as money, but not including that in the vault of the bank, or redeemed and on deposit for said bank; and an additional tax of one-sixth of one per centum, each month, upon the average amount of such circulation issued as aforesaid, beyond the amount of ninety per centum of the capital of any such bank, association, corporation, company, or person. And a true and accurate return of the amount of circulation, of deposit and of capital, as aforesaid, and of the amount of notes of persons, State banks or State banking associations paid out by them for the previous month, shall be made and rendered monthly by each of such banks, associations, corporations, companies, or persons to the assessor of the district in which any such bank, association, corporation, or company may be located, or in which such person has his place of business, with a declaration annexed thereto, and the oath or affirmation of such person, or of the president or cashier of such bank, association, corporation, or company, in such form and manner as may be prescribed by the Commissioner of Internal Revenue, that the same contains a true and faithful statement of the amounts subject to tax as aforesaid; and for any refusal or neglect to make or to render return and payment as required by law, any such bank, association, corporation, company, or person so in default, shall be subject to and pay a penalty of two hundred dollars, besides the additional penalty and forfeitures in other cases provided by law; and the amount of circulation, deposit, and capital, and notes of persons, State banks and banking associations paid out, as aforesaid, in default of the proper return, shall be estimated by the assessor or asistant assessor of the district as aforesaid, upon the best information he can obtain; and every such penalty may be recovered for the use of the United States in any court of competent jurisdiction. And in the case of banks with branches, the tax herein provided for shall be assessed upon the circulation of each branch, severally, and the amount of capital of each branch shall be considered to be the amount al-

---

it at its actual value at the time of making return." (Boutwell's "Rulings No. 6, p. 133.)

All bank dividends, declared payable after July 1, 1864, are taxable under section 120, act of 1864. Any portion, however, of a surplus dividend, which arises from a "reduction of capital," should not be held taxable. (Boutwell's "Rulings No. 11.")

In estimating the "average amount of circulation," in excess of ninety per cent. of capital, the amount of authorized capital and surplus fund, should be taken as the basis of calculation. (Boutwell's "Rulings No. 12." Compare Decision 29, January, 1864.)

By Circular No. 36, of October, 1865, it was ruled in relation to the "tax on capital and deposits of savings banks and institutions for savings," that the proviso to the 110th section of the act of June 30, 1864, exempting "savings banks having no capital stock, and whose business is confined to receiving deposits and loaning the same on interest for the benefit of the depositors only," &c., having been stricken out, this class of banks is subject to the general provisions of the act of June 30, 1864, and the returns should conform to the 110th section. (See act of March 3, 1865.) This Circular gave rise to great complaint and some judicial decisions. Hence the provisions of the present statute, greatly relieving this class of institutions.

"Whenever a corporation which is required to withhold five per cent. of the dividends declared, declares a dividend of more than the 'net gain since prior

lotted to such branch; and so much of an act entitled "An act to provide ways and means for the support of the government," approved March third, eighteen hundred and sixty-three, as imposes any tax on banks, their circulation, capital, or deposits, other than is herein provided, is hereby repealed: *Provided*, That this section shall not apply to associations which are taxed under and by virtue of the act "to provide a national currency secured by a pledge of United States bonds, and to provide for the circulation and redemption thereof." And the deposits in associations or companies known as Provident Institutions, Savings Banks, Savings Funds, or Savings Institutions, having no capital stock and doing no other business than receiving deposits to be loaned or invested for the sole benefit of the parties making such deposits, without profit or compensation to the association or company, shall be exempt from tax on so much of their deposits as they have invested in securities of the United States, and on all deposits less than five hundred dollars made in the name of any one person; and the returns required to be made by such Provident Institutions and Savings Banks after July, eighteen hundred and sixty-six, shall be made on the first Monday of January and July of each year, in such form and manner as may be prescribed by the Commissioner of Internal Revenue.]

Particular Provisions for the Taxation of Gross Receipts of Lotteries. Penalties for False Returns of Companies, Frauds, &c.

SEC. 111. *And be it further enacted*, That every individual partnership, firm, and association, being proprietors, managers, or agents of lotteries, [and all lottery ticket dealers,] shall pay a tax of five per centum

---

dividend,' the amount taken from the surplus fund to complete it would be the difference between the *whole* amount of dividend and net gains since," prior one. (Letter of Commissioner, July 18, 1865.)

"When a State bank is converted into a national bank during any given month, the tax on capital and deposits should be returned to the date of the transfer of the same to a national bank, and on circulation for an entire month." (Letter of Commissioner, July 19, 1865.)

States possess the power to authorize the taxation of the shares of those national banks in the hands of stockholders whose capital is wholly invested in stocks and bonds of the United States. (Van Allen and als. *vs.* Board of Assessors. U. S. Sup. Court. Int. Rev. Rec., April 7, 1866.)

As to the mode of payment by banks and other taxed institutions, to the treasury, (see III. Int. Rev. Rec., p. 36.)

"'Undivided profits' may be classed with 'capital' in the payment of duty for the six months preceding January 1, 1866, and for succeeding terms." (See Letter of Spinner, Treasurer U. S., February 10, 1866, cited in III. Int. Rev., p. 52.)

Return of average deposits in national banks, (Treasurer Spinner, February 13, 1866, III. Int. Rev., p. 52.)

It has been ruled that when a manufacturing corporation receives the earnings of the operatives on deposit, and issues *pass books*, with statement of amount deposited and withdrawn, and of accrued interest allowed, that the ordinary rules applicable to savings banks and the taxation of the same will be enforced. (Letter of Commissioner, Dec. 6, 1865. III. Int. Rev. Rec., p. 93.)

on the gross amount of the receipts from the said business; and all persons making such sales shall, within ten days after the first day of each and every month, make and render a list or return in duplicate to the assistant assessor of the gross amount of such sales, made as aforesaid, with the amount of duty which has accrued or should accrue thereon; which list shall have annexed thereto a declaration, under oath or affirmation, in such form and signed by such officer, agent, or clerk, as may be prescribed by the Commissioner of Internal Revenue, that the same is true and correct, and the said proprietors, managers, and agents shall on or before the twentieth day of each and every month, as aforesaid, pay the collector or deputy collector of the proper district the amount of the duty or tax as aforesaid. And in default of making such lists or returns, the said proprietors, managers, and agents, and all other persons making such sales, shall be subject to and pay a penalty of one thousand dollars, besides the additions, penalties, and forfeitures in other cases provided; and the said proprietors, managers, and agents shall, in default of paying the said duty or tax at the time herein required, be subject to and pay a penalty of one thousand dollars, or be imprisoned not exceeding one year. In all cases of delinquency in making said list, return, or payment, the assessments and collections shall be made in the manner prescribed in the provisions of this act in relation to manufactures, articles, and products: *Provided*, That the managers of any sanitary fair, or of any charitable, benevolent, or religious association, may apply to the collector of the district and present to him proof that the proceeds of any contemplated lottery, raffle, or gift enterprise will be applied to the relief of sick and wounded soldiers, or to some other charitable use, and thereupon the Commissioner shall grant a permit to hold such lottery, raffle, or gift enterprise, and the said sanitary fair, or charitable or benevolent association, shall be exempt from all charge, whether from tax or license, in respect of such lottery, raffle, or gift enterprise: *Provided further*, That nothing in this section contained shall be construed to legalize any lottery.

Lottery Tickets to be Stamped with Name, Date, &c.

SEC. 112. *And be it further enacted*, That each lottery ticket or certificate supplementary thereto shall be legibly stamped at the time of sale with the name of the vendor and the date of such sale, under a penalty of fifty dollars, to be paid by the vendor of each lottery ticket or certificate supplementary thereto sold without being first stamped as aforesaid.*

Penalties for Sale without payment of Special Tax, &c.

SEC. 113. *And be it further enacted*, That in addition to all other penalties and forfeitures now imposed by law for the evasion of license

---

*LOTTERIES.

Gross receipts of, (Int. Rev. Rec., Vol. I., p. 124.) Dealers' licenses, (Int. Rev. Rec., Vol. II., pp. 4, 66.) Receipts of, (Int. Rev. Rec., Vol. II., p. 4,) Dealers of tickets and tax, (Int. Rev. Rec., Vol. II., p. 76.)

fees or other taxes upon the lottery business, any person who shall hereafter sell or dispose of any lottery ticket or certificate supplementary thereto, or any device in the nature thereof, without having first duly obtained a license, as hereinbefore mentioned, shall incur a penalty of five hundred dollars for each and every such offence; and any person who shall purchase, obtain, or receive any lottery ticket or any policy of numbers, tokens, certificate, wager, or device, representing or intended to represent a lottery ticket or fractional part thereof, from any person not having a license to deal in lottery tickets, as provided by law, may recover from such person of whom the same was purchased, obtained, or received, at any time within three years thereafter, before any court of competent jurisdiction, a sum equal to twice the amount paid for the same, with just and legal costs.

Same Subject. Books to be kept by Managers.

(SEC. 13. Act of March 3, 1865.) *And be it further enacted*, That all persons and every person who shall engage or be concerned in the business of a lottery dealer without having first obtained a license so to do, under such rules and regulations as shall be prescribed by the Secretary of the Treasury, shall forfeit and pay a penalty of one thousand dollars, to be assessed by the assessor of the proper district and collected as assessed taxes are collected, subject, nevertheless, to the provisions of law relating to erroneous assessments, and shall, on conviction by any court of competent jurisdiction, suffer imprisonment for a period not exceeding a year, at the discretion of the court. And it shall be the duty of all managers and proprietors, and their agents, to keep, or cause to be kept, just and true books of account, wherein all their transactions shall be plainly and legibly set forth, which books of account shall at all reasonable times and hours be subject to the inspection of the assessor, assistant assessor, revenue agent, and inspector of the proper district; and any manager, proprietor, agent, or vendor under this act, who shall refuse or prohibit such inspection of his or their books, as aforesaid, shall pay a penalty of one thousand dollars, or suffer imprisonment for a term not exceeding one year, for every such offence.

Tax payable on Advertisements. Quarterly Returns of. How Verified. Estimate of Assistant Assessor on neglect or refusal to make Returns. General Provisions in relation to Returns of. Amounts Exempt.*

SEC. 114. *And be it further enacted*, That there shall be levied, collected, and paid by any person or persons, firm, or company, publishing any newspaper, magazine, review, or other literary, scientific, or

---

*ADVERTISEMENTS.

"Trow's City Directory is liable to tax as a printed book, (this was under the laws of 1864,) and the advertisements contained in this publication are subject to a tax of 3 per cent., the same as that of any other periodical." (Commissioners' Decision, Oct. 3, 1865. II. Int. Rev. Rec., p. 125.)

news publication issued periodically [or otherwise, or publishing any guide, almanac, catalogue, directory, or any other paper or book,] on the gross receipts for all advertisements, or all matters for the insertion of which in said newspaper or other publication, as aforesaid, or in extras, supplements, sheets, or fly-leaves accompanying the same, pay is required or received, a duty of three per centum; and the person or persons, firm, or company, owning, possessing, or having the care or management of any and every such newspaper or other publication as aforesaid, shall make a list or return on the first day of January, April, July, and October of each year, containing the gross amount of receipts as aforesaid, and the amount of duties which have accrued thereon, and render the same in duplicate to the assistant assessor of the district where such newspaper, magazine, review, or other literary or news publication is or may be published; which list or return shall have annexed a declaration, under oath or affirmation, to be made according to the manner and form which may be from time to time prescribed by the Commissioner of Internal Revenue, of the owner, possessor, or person having the care or management of such newspaper, magazine, review, or other publication, as aforesaid, that the same is true and correct; and shall also, quarterly, within ten days after the time of making said list or return, pay to the collector or deputy collector of the district the full amount of said duties. And in case of neglect or refusal to comply with any of the provisions contained in this section, or to make and render said list or return, for the space of ten days after the time when said list or return ought to have been made, as aforesaid, the assistant assessors of the respective districts shall proceed to estimate the duties as heretofore provided in other cases of delinquency; and in case of neglect or refusal to pay the duties, as aforesaid, for the space of ten days after said duties become due and payable, and have been demanded, said owner, possessor, or person or persons having the care or management of said newspapers or publications, as aforesaid, shall pay, in addition thereto, a penalty of ten per centum on the amount due. And in case of fraud or evasion, whereby the revenue is attempted to be defrauded, or the duty withheld, said owners, possessors, or person or persons having the care or management of said newspapers or other publications, as aforesaid, shall forfeit and pay a penalty of one thousand dollars for each offence, or for any sum fraudulently unaccounted for. And all provisions in this act in relation to returns, additions, penalties, forfeitures, liens, assessments, and collection, not incompatible herewith, shall apply to this section and the objects herein embraced: *Provided,* That in all cases where the rate or price of advertising is fixed by any law of the United States, State, or Territory, it shall be lawful for the company, person or persons, publishing said advertisements, to add the duty or tax imposed by this act to the price of said advertisements, any law to the contrary notwithstanding; and that the receipts for advertisements to the amount of six hundred dollars annually, by any person or persons, firm, or company, publishing any newspaper, magazine, review, or other literary, scientific, or news publication, issued periodically, shall be exempt from duty: *And provided further*, That all newspapers whose average circulation does not exceed two thousand copies shall be exempted from all taxes for advertisements.

Commissioner to Determine when certain Returns shall be Made and Taxes Paid.

SEC. 115. *And be it further enacted*, That whenever by this act any license,* duty, or tax of any description has been imposed on any person or corporate body, or property of any person, or incorporated or unincorporated company, having more than one place of business, it shall be lawful for the Commissioner of Internal Revenue to prescribe and determine in what district such tax shall be assessed and collected, and to what officer thereof the official notices required in that behalf shall be given, and of whom payment of such tax shall be demanded: *Provided*, That all taxes on manufactures, manufacturing companies, and manufacturing corporations, shall be assessed and the tax collected in the district within which the place of manufacture is located, unless otherwise provided.

The Assessment of the Income Tax. Rates of Taxation. Deduction for Taxes withheld by Banks. Tax to be levied for Previous Calendar Year. United States Securities included. The $600 Deductions, &c. Profits and Loss on Real Estate, &c., &c.†

(SEC. 116. Act of March 3, 1865.) *And be it further enacted*, That there shall be levied, collected, and paid annually upon the an-

*The term "Special Tax" should be substituted here. Probably a clerical omission of the Committee. See also pp. 120–121.

† "Income tax should be returned in the district where the parties are resident on May 1st. In case of removals out of the district after that date, the correct practice would seem to be to forward the return for collection to the district to which the party has removed. It should be borne in mind by tax-payers that the omission of an assessor, from any cause, to notify a party of liability, or to demand a return of any kind, will not operate to discharge a delinquent tax-payer from the penalties prescribed by law for his delinquency. Ignorance of the law will not excuse a failure to comply with its provisions, for the reason that every person is presumed to know the law of the society in which he lives; and is bound to obey it. Hence persons desiring to avoid fines and annoyance, should allow no time to pass, without their income returns being duly made and forwarded to the assistant assessor.

All persons having charge of estates in the capacity of guardians, trustees, executors, administrators, or otherwise, are required to furnish proper income returns of the minors, or other persons, derived from the trust estate; and no deduction of $600 can be allowed to such minor or beneficiary, except on the express statement, under oath, of the guardian or trustee, that the minor or beneficiary is in receipt of no other income from which the amount of $600 may be deducted.

Every failure to make prompt and proper return of income, subjects the party so failing to return, to assessment and a penalty of twenty-five per cent. on the amount of the tax. As soon as the assessment list is completed, notice of the fact will be advertised by the assessor for ten days, in a newspaper to be published in the county, notifying all persons of the time and place where

nual gains, profits, and income of every person residing in the United States, or of any citizen of the United States residing abroad, whether derived from any kind of property, rents, interests, dividends or salaries, or from any profession, trade, employment, or vocation, carried on in the United States or elsewhere, or from any other source whatever, a duty of five per centum on the excess over six hundred dollars and not exceeding five thousand dollars, and a duty of ten per centum on the excess over five thousand dollars; [and a like tax shall be levied, collected and paid annually upon the gains, profits and income of every business, trade, or profession carried on in the United States by persons residing without the United States not citizens thereof;] and in ascertaining the income of any person liable to an income tax, the amount of income received from institutions whose officers, as required by law, withhold a per centum of the dividends made by such institutions and pay the same to the Commissioner of Internal Revenue, or other officer authorized to receive the same, shall be included; and the amount so withheld shall be deducted from the tax which otherwise would be assessed upon such person. And the duty herein provided for shall be assessed, collected, and paid upon the gains, profits, and income for the year ending the thirty-first day of December next preceding the time for levying, collecting, and paying said duty: *Provided*, That income de-

---

said assessor will sit to hear appeals. At such time all claims for excessive or erroneous assessment, must be presented to the assessor for correction or reduction. The list will be open to the inspection of all persons applying to inspect the same; such claims must, however, be presented within the time specified in the advertised notice, in order to entitle them to consideration, as no appeal can be allowed after the list shall have been transmitted to the collector.

All appeals from assessments must be in writing, specifying the particular matter respecting which a decision is requested, and must also state the ground or principle of error complained of. (Int. Rev. Rec., Vol. III., No. 21, p. 155. "Instructions," *infra.*, Series 2, No. 4.)

The following letter has been addressed to Assessor Stewart, of Baltimore, by the Commissioner of Internal Revenue.

WASHINGTON, Thursday, June 7, 1866.

SIR: Your letter of 24th May has been received. In reply I have to say that, under the regulations lately adopted by this office, gains derived from, and losses incurred by, the purchase and sale of stocks, regarded as gains and losses in business, and without reference to the time during which the stocks are held. Interest and dividends derived from stocks are regarded as income derived from fixed investments, without reference to the time during which such stocks are held. But when gains derived from the sales of stocks involve interest received or accrued, such gains may be regarded as derived from business alone. Salaries, except where specially provided for by statute, are regarded as income from business. The value of property used in business, less the amount of insurance, may be deducted when lost from the gains and profits of the business.

The fact that a person returns a gain or claims a loss upon the purchase and sale of stocks, does not necessarily imply that he does a business which requires or has required the license of a broker. The liability to be taxed for such license should be determined upon its own merits, and is an independent question.

E. A. ROLLINS, Commissioner.

rived from interest upon notes, bonds, and other securities of the United States, and also all premiums upon gold and coupons, shall be included in estimating incomes under this section: *Provided further*, That only one deduction of six hundred dollars shall be made from the aggregate incomes of all the members of any family, composed of parents and minor children, or husband and wife: *And provided further*, That net profits realized by sales of real estate purchased within the year, for which income is estimated, shall be chargeable as income; and losses on sales of real estate purchased within the year, for which income is estimated, shall be deducted from the income of such year.

Deductions for State Taxes. Ditto on Salaries. Homestead Rents. Particular Deductions.

SEC. 117. *And be it further enacted*, That in estimating the annual gains, profits, and income of any person, all national, State, county, and municipal taxes, paid within the year, shall be deducted from the gains, profits, or income of the person who has actually paid the same, whether owner, tenant, or mortgagor; also the salary or pay received for services in the civil, military, naval, or other service of the United States, including senators, representatives, and delegates in Congress, above the rate of six hundred dollars per annum; also the amount paid by any person for the rent of the homestead used or occupied by himself or his family, and the rental value of any homestead used or occupied by any person or by his family, in his own right or in the right of his wife, shall not be included and assessed as part of the income of such person. In estimating the annual gains, profits, or income of any person, the interest received or accrued upon all notes, bonds, and mortgages, or other forms of indebtedness bearing interest, whether paid or not, if good and collectable, less the interest paid by or due from said person, shall be included and assessed as part of the income of such person for each year; and also all income or gains derived from the purchase and sale of stocks or other property, real or personal, and of live stock, and the amount of live stock, sugar, wool, butter, cheese, pork, beef, mutton, or other meats, hay and grain, or other vegetable or other productions, being the growth or produce of the estate of such person sold, not including any part thereof unsold or on hand during the year next preceding the thirty-first of December, until the same shall be sold, shall be included and assessed as part of the income of such person for each year, and his share of the gains and profits of all companies, whether incorporated or partnership, shall be included in estimating the annual gains, profits, or income of any person entitled to the same, whether divided or otherwise. In estimating deductions from income, as aforesaid, when any person rents buildings, lands, or other property, or hires labor to cultivate land, or to conduct any other business from which such income is actually derived, or pays interest upon any actual incumbrance thereon, the amount actually paid for such rent, labor, or interest, shall be deducted; and also the amout paid out for usual or ordinary repairs, not exceeding the average paid out for such purposes for the preceding five years, shall be deducted, but no deduction shall be made for any amount paid out for new buildings, permanent improvements, or betterments; made to increase the value of any property or estate: *Provided,* That in cases where the salary or other compensation paid to any person in the employment or service of the United States shall not exceed the rate of six hundred dollars per annum, or shall be by fees, or uncertain or irregular in the amount or in the time during which the same shall have accrued or been earned, such salary or other compensation shall be included in estimating the annual gains, profits, or income of the person to whom the same shall have been paid, in such manner as the Commissioner of Internal Revenue, under the direction of the Secretary of the Treasury, may prescribe.

Who shall make Returns. Guardians' and Trustees' Returns. Verification of Returns. Penalties for Neglect or Refusal to make. Declarations under Oath. Appeal to Assessor.

SEC. 118. *And be it further enacted,* That it shall be the duty of all persons of lawful age to make and render a list or return, in such form and manner as may be prescribed by the Commissioner of Internal Revenue, to the assistant assessor of the district in which they reside, of the amount of their income, gains, and profits, as aforesaid; and all guardians and trustees, whether as executors, administrators, or in any other fiduciary capacity, shall make and render a list or return, as aforesaid, to the assistant assessor of the district in which such guardian or trustee resides, of the amount of income, gains, and profits of any minor or person for whom they act as guardian or trustee; and the assistant assessor shall require every list or return to be verified by the oath or affirmation of the party rendering it, and may increase the amount of any list or return, if he has reason to believe that the same is understated; and in case any person, guardian, or trustee shall neglect or refuse to make and render such list or return, or shall render a false or fraudulent list or return, it shall be the duty of the assessor or the assistant assessor to make such list, according to the best information he can obtain, by the examination of such person, and his books and accounts, or any other evidence, and to add twenty-five per centum as a penalty to the amount of the duty due on such list in all cases of willful neglect or refusal to make and render a list or return, and, in all cases of a false or fraudulent list or return having been rendered, to add one hundred per centum, as a penalty, to the amount of duty ascertained to be due, the duty and the additions thereto as penalty to be assessed and collected in the manner provided for in other cases of willful neglect or refusal to render a list or return, or of rendering a false and fraudulent return: *Provided,* That any party, in his or her own behalf, or as guardian or trustee, shall be permitted to declare, under oath or affirmation, the form and manner of which shall be prescribed by the Commissioner of Internal Revenue, that he or she, or his or her ward or beneficiary, was not possessed of an income of six hundred dollars, liable to be assessed according to the provisions of this act; or may declare that he or she has been assessed and paid an income duty elsewhere in the same year, under authority of the United States, upon his or her gains and profits, as prescribed by law; and if the assistant assessor shall be satisfied of the truth of the declaration, shall thereupon be exempt from income duty in said district; or if the list or return of any party shall have been increased by the assistant assessor, such party may exhibit his books and accounts, and be permitted to prove and declare, under oath or affirmation, the amount of annual income liable to be assessed; but such oaths and evidence shall not be considered as conclusive of the facts, and no deductions claimed in such cases shall be made or allowed until approved by the assistant assessor. Any person feeling aggrieved by the decision of the assistant assessor in such cases, may appeal to the assessor of the district, and his decision thereon, unless reversed by the Commissioner of Internal Revenue, shall be final, and the form, time, and manner of proceedings shall be subject to rules and regulations to be prescribed by the Commissioner of Internal Revenue.

*The same Subject. When Income Tax Payable. Penalties for Non-payment after Notice and Demand. Amount of Tax a Lien. Warrants for Collection. Certificates to vest Title, &c., &c.**

SEC. 119. *And be it further enacted,* [That the taxes on incomes herein imposed shall be levied on the first day of May, and be due and

---

*INCOMES.

The internal revenue tax upon incomes was imposed by the act of 1862, and with various changes and modifications, has assumed its present form. It is one of the most important sources of revenue, having produced in the year ending June 30, 1863, only including actual collections for ten months, $455,-741; in the following year, $14,919,279, (together with $28,929,312, imposed under the joint resolution of July 4, 1864,) while in the fiscal year ending June 30, 1865, it produced as estimated something over $58,000,000. The system was adopted upon the basis of the English statute of 1797, devised by Mr. Pitt to meet a desperate emergency in the finances, arising from the enormous expense of subsidizing continental Europe in the struggle of "legitimacy" and monarchical conservatism, with the overshadowing power of French republicanism. After exhausting almost every conceivable subject of assessment, he originated the idea of laying a tax upon the "assessed value of houses, windows, &c.," under the name of "the assessed taxes bill." In the first year of its operation, it subjected him to a great and unexpected unpopularity, and he was even mobbed in the streets of London, while he was pressing the bill through Parliament. In the year following its enactment, it being found that, instead of seven millions sterling, (the amount which the "assessed taxes bill" was estimated to produce,) less than half the amount had been realized, the name of the system was changed, and its basis essentially modified, and it was introduced into Parliament as "the income tax." The chief objections urged against the former bill, were, that in the first place, it was based upon the presumption of expenditure, (income,) founded upon the assessed taxes, and secondly, "that the expenditure was a *passed one.*" The new bill obviated these objections in part by providing that the statement of income should proceed from the person himself, and the assessment be made upon such state-

payable on or before the thirtieth day of June, in each year, until and including the year eighteen hundred and seventy, and no longer; and to any sum or sums annually due and unpaid after the thirtieth of June, as aforesaid, and for ten days after notice and demand thereof by the collector, there shall be levied in addition thereto the sum of ten per centum on the amount of duties unpaid, as a penalty, except from the estates of deceased and insolvent persons.*]

---

ment, as under the system of adopted here; the commissioner (assessor) having power in certain cases to make arbitrary assessments. This bill also met with great opposition in both houses of Parliament, and it was urged that the result of a system of direct taxation of this character would eventually drain the resources of the nation. It was also eloquently urged, that the bill involved what was deemed to be a revolutionary principle that "all property belonged to the State;" that it led to inconvenient and unjust disclosures of property, especially in the case of mercantile men, and involved gross inequalities. The second bill however, became a law, and in spite of the fierce hostility it encountered from the capitalists, land-holders and non-exempt classes of England, it was not extinguished until after the peace of Amiens in 1802. The following year, it was renewed in the shape of a "property tax;" incomes under $300 annually being exempt as before. In 1806 upon the raising of the tax to ten per cent. it was limited to continue in force, only during the pending war with the French Emperor. Peace did not, however, permanently come till 1816; during nearly the whole of which period, the nation with no little chafing, bore "the galling burden," as it was styled, "upon the industry and resources of the people." After the peace of 1816, it was attempted to retain one-half of the tax; yet the hostility became too formidable. and the principle became established that an "income tax was a war tax," and could only be justified by the existence of war, and its extraordinary necessities, or as was remarked by Mr. Wilberforce, "war and income taxes were wedded together." In 1842 it was again introduced by Mr. Peel, then Premier, in order to procure immediate relief to the finances, and "give an opportunity for the reduced duties to recover their productiveness," the tax however to expire by limitation in 1845. He succeeded in carrying the measure, and subject to occasional changes of rate and amount, (the tax is an annual enactment in England,) it continued till 1856, when it was doubled to provide extraordinary revenue for the expenses of the war of the Crimea. Upon the termination of the war in 1857, it was feared by those who were opposed to the tax, and had insisted upon the recognized principle, that an income tax was a war tax only, that it would be continued at the war rate in time of profound peace; but their fears proved groundless, and the rate was reduced to seven pence in the pound, or less than one-fifth of the average rate in this country under the foregoing sections. A commission was however raised to give the matter of income taxation a thorough investigation, but their labors, although exhaustive and exceedingly valuable, and shedding great light upon the politico-economic aspects of the system, seem to have had but little influence upon subject legislation. The tax is retained as a convenient and powerful aid to the chancellor of the exchequer, in adjusting any deficiency in his annual budget. It is interesting to observe that as in England, each annual change in this tax is accompanied with a limitation for its existence; but it will probably remain upon the statute book for many years to come, unpopular though it may be deemed, as a fruitful and not oppressive source of revenue, and a powerful aid to the credit of the government.—Ed.] (See letter of Prof. Goldwin Smith, communicated to Albany Evening Journal, March 26, 1866.

---

* The real amendment here by the present Congress was the striking out all after the words "insolvent persons."

Tax on the Dividends of Banks, Trust Companies, &c. Tax to be Withheld by Officers. General Provisions for Returns and Penalties.

SEC. 120. *And be it further enacted,* [That there shall be levied and collected a tax of five per centum on all dividends in scrip or money thereafter declared due, wherever and whenever the same shall be payable, to stockholders, policy-holders, or depositors, or parties

---

Report of Revenue Commissioners' "Income." Report of Commissioner Rollins, December, 1865. Springfield Republican, May 16, 1866.)

Frequent complaints are made of the injustice of not allowing the losses in business to be offset by the income from permanent investments. But it should be considered that the law imposes the tax upon incomes from various specific sources; and again, a loss of a portion of the capital of the tax-payer only affects him to the extent of the amount of tax he is called on to pay. If he has made nothing from the "sources of his income" he pays no tax upon such part of his capital. (e. g.) If A. is worth $250,000 and invested $125,000 of this property in a branch of business which produced him nothing, or in which he made a loss in 1864, he surely cannot say he has no income, if he received from the remaining $125,000 his regular dividends and interest. He pays less income tax than he would have done had he not engaged in the unprofitable business. He remains a rich man still, although he has unfortunately sunk a portion of his capital. [There is no part of the income tax provisions, which probably gives greater dissatisfaction than this. But is there good ground for this dissatisfaction? Doubtless the language of the law is somewhat indistinct. It is, "Annual gains, profits and income," whether derived from any kind of property, &c., *or* "from any employment carried on," &c. Tax-payers do not properly make the distinction between "capital" and the "gains and profits" of capital. The law does not tax capital, but the income of capital, it does not tax "business or employment," but the gains and profits of such business or employment. When a person is engaged in divers kinds of business, the balance of gain in the aggregate, is his "income." If but a portion of his capital is engaged in such business, and the business shows a loss, he still has an "income" from such portion of the unemployed but invested capital as grew out of the dividends, &c., of such investment. Shall the loss sustained on the unprofitable moiety of his capital be borne by the government, or himself? Shall he be allowed to say, "My income shall depend upon, and be estimated by the status of my capital,"? The government does not keep a "profit and loss" account with "capital," but rather with the income of capital. But it is a matter, as good, honest Sir Roger de Coverly has it, of which "much may be said on both sides of the question." Much confusion will be avoided by ever remembering that the tax is not upon property or capital, but upon its annual accretions.—ED.]

Upon the completion of the "income list" by the assistant assessors of the several subdivisions, it is forwarded to the assessor of the district. After being carefully revised by him, he makes a corrected copy of the same, and advertises when and where he will hear appeals. The list remains in his office open to public inspection. All claims for reduction or erroneous assessment must be duly presented to him. Appeals must be in writing, which must state the ground of appeal, and in what respect it is claimed that the true principle of the law has not been followed in the assessment. Parties can appear by counsel.

When improper deductions have been made or knowingly approved by assessors, such errors cannot be corrected after the tax has been paid. In this regard, the officer is *functus officio*. But see the new provisions of present law remedying this. But when parties have understated any items or amounts of income, the amounts so understated may be increased by the assessor whenever he may discover the fact, and a reassessment may be

whatsoever, including non-residents, whether citizens or aliens, as part of the earnings, income, or gains of any bank, trust company, savings institution, and of any fire, marine, life, inland insurance company, either stock or mutual, under whatever name or style known or called, in the United States or Territories, whether specially incorporated or existing under general laws, and on all undistributed sums, or sums made or added during the year to their surplus or contingent fund; and said banks, trust companies, savings institutions, and insurance companies shall pay the said tax, and are hereby authorized to deduct and withhold from all payments made on account of any dividends or sums of money that may be due and payable as aforesaid the said tax of five per centum. And a list or return shall be made and rendered to the assessor or assistant assessor on or before the tenth day of the month following that in which any dividend or sums of money become due or payable as aforesaid, and said list or return shall contain a true and faithful account of the amount of taxes as aforesaid; and there shall be annexed thereto a declaration of the president, cashier, or treasurer of the bank, trust company, savings institution, or insurance company, under oath or affirmation, in form and manner as may be prescribed by the Commissioner of Internal Revenue, that the same contains a true and

---

made as provided in the law, and in case of fraud the parties will be held liable to prosecution. If a tax-payer makes a return which is subsequently discovered to be false and fraudulent, he cannot escape his obligations to the government. And we would here remark, in conclusion of this branch of the revenue law, that a new system, of this wide-sweep of details, and so materially modified by the amendments to former statutes, must necessarily give rise to conflicting opinions on the part of the public. There are in the United States many thousands of assistant assessors, who, for the time being, are in their particular subdivision "the law upon this subject." An appeal to the district assessor is often difficult and inconvenient, and sometimes well-nigh impossible; while an appeal to the department at Washington must necessarily be expensive and dilatory. The general desire on the part of the vast majority of tax-payers to pay all they are assessed, without complaint, has been fully exemplified. They demand, however, most properly and reasonably, that, as far as may be, "all may be treated alike," and they then open their purses to the collector in his annual visitation without murmur; rather with hearty good will, in contributing their mite, though it may be, to sustain the hands of those who protect and vindicate the integrity of "the best government the world has ever seen." There are doubtless many cases of erroneous and fraudulent returns; but this is inevitable under any system and under all circumstances. Human nature must greatly change, before we shall find, that patriotism is more universal than selfishness. It is, however, due to the hundreds of thousands of tax-payers, that we should add, that the cases of fraudulent returns of income are far less frequent, than erroneous returns made up ignorantly, but with honest intentions.

Assessors should instruct their assistants to call personally upon those who have not returned their income on the first Monday in May. If any person is not at home, the notice on the back of form 24 should be filled out, and the blank left. This being done, it becomes the duty of the tax-payer to seek the assistant assessor and deliver his return. (Letter of Commissioner Rollins, April 26, 1866.)

"Mere depreciation in value of property cannot be taken into the account in estimating income unless the property is actually disposed of and loss realized."—(Ruling April 16, 1866. III. Int. Rev. Record, p. 151.)

faithful account of the taxes as aforesaid. And for any default in the making or rendering of such list or return, with such declaration annexed, the bank, trust company, savings institution, or insurance company, making such default, shall forfeit as a penalty the sum of one thousand dollars; and in case of any default in making or rendering said list or return, or of any default in the payment of the tax as required, or any part thereof, the assessment and collection of the tax and penalty shall be in accordance with the general provisions of law in other cases of neglect and refusal: *Provided*, That the tax upon the dividends of life insurance companies shall not be deemed due until such dividends are payable, nor shall the portion of premiums returned by mutual life insurance companies to their policy-holders, nor the annual or semi-annual interest allowed or paid to the depositors in savings banks or savings institutions, be considered as dividends.]

Provisions when Banks Neglect to make Returns of Dividends.

SEC. 121. *And be it further enacted*, That any bank legally authorized to issue notes as circulation which shall neglect or omit to make dividends or additions to its surplus or contingent fund as often as once in

---

UNDIVIDED PROFITS.—"In reply to yours of 27th inst. that by the terms of Section 117 of the Act of 1864, the gains and profits of all companies, whether incorporated or partnership, are to be included in estimating the annual gains, profits or income of any person entitled to the same, whether divided or otherwise. Profits of a gas company, therefore, which have been carried to construction account, should be returned as 'income' by the stockholders. It would appear from Decision 110 of Boutwell, p. 275, 2d Ed., 1863, that the undistributed earnings of a corporation, made subsequently to September, 1862, should have been returned as income by the stockholders for the various years in which the same occurred."—(Ruling April 30, 1866. Cited Int. Rev. Rec., Vol. III., p. 164.)

Money received by the guardian of minor children from a railroad company in settlement of damages for loss of life of father of minors while traveling in the cars of the company, are neither to be taxed as legacy or income. Damages in actions of Tort are not income. (Ruling March 30, 1866. III. Int. Rev. Record, p. 118.)

The value of advances of personal estate made to children since the passage of the Internal Revenue Laws is taxed as income. (Ruling April 17, 1866. III. Int. Rev. Rec., p. 140.)

The sums paid by Life Insurance Companies is not liable to income or legacy tax. (Comm'r. April 23, 1866. Cited III. Int. Rev. Rec., p. 140.)

Income derived from foreign sources should be taxed under Section 116. (Ibidem.)

If a person should fail to make his income returns for 1862, 1863 and 1864, he may be assessed with penalty in 1865 for the omitted years. (Ibidem, p. 151.)

GUARDIANS, ETC.—" A guardian residing abroad should return the income of his ward in the district where the ward resides. But a guardian not residing abroad should return the income of his ward in the district where such guardian resides." (Ruling May 18, 1866. III. Int. Rev. Record, p. 172.

It will not be forgotten that persons not naturalized (aliens,) residing here are not entitled to the $1000 deduction. The same rule applies to citizens residing abroad. The pay "on their entire income."—(See Instructions, Series 2, No. 4, in Appendix.

six months, shall make a list or return in duplicate, under oath or affirmation of the president or cashier, to the assessor or assistant assessor of the district in which it is located, on the first day of January and July in each year, or within thirty days thereafter, of the amount of profits which have accrued or been earned and received by said bank during the six months next preceding said first days of January and July; and shall present one of said lists or returns and pay to the collector of the district a duty of five per centum on such profits, and in

---

We add an extract from the luminous and able speech of Hon. Justin S. Morrill, Chairman of the Committee of Ways and Means, made May 7, 1866, in the House of Representatives, upon introducing the present Act. To his eminently practical and distinguished ability the country is indebted in a great degree for the wise amendments to the Internal Revenue System, and the approximate equality in its distribution of burdens upon the various industrial and other interests of the community.

"The Committee of Ways and Means have proposed some modifications of the Income Law, but have not reached the conclusion, while the industrial employments must remain to a considerable extent heavily burdened, that it can be wholly dispensed with. By its terms as originally passed it was to expire in 1870, and thus a temporary character was put upon its face. In our great emergency it contributed, not to be returned again with interest, a larger amount than the richest banker in Europe would have loaned us even at 60 per cent. discount. Our loyal people paid the Income Tax of 1863 in June of $20,740,451, and then (estimated upon the same lists,) they were called upon in four months to pay another Income Tax (under Joint Resolution of July 4,) and they responded by contributing $28,929,312. Again in 1864 their Income Tax foots up $59,000,000. I point to these facts not only as a proud evidence of their patriotism and wealth, but as a proud evidence of their strict integrity of character. Strong as the temptation might be for evasive returns, sore as they might be in consequence of the swift pursuit and the continuous exactions of the tax gatherers, they even paid more in 1863 upon the second call than the first. Their country was in need, and even the greed for gain could not tempt the American people to defraud their government. The law left it almost to the conscience of each man as to how much he should pay, and all seemed to vie with each other as to who should pay the most. I question whether any people ever paid a tax more honestly and accurately, and I question still more whether any free people ever imposed upon themselves, through their chosen representatives, taxes so thick and fast.

If our Income Tax should be contemplated as a part of the permanent policy of the country, it is not to be denied that it would need various and perhaps fundamental amendments.

The objections to such laws are sufficiently obvious:

1. They are inquisitorial of necessity in their character, and Americans, like people elsewhere, though not averse to a knowledge of the secrets of others, are quite unwilling to disclose their own. Among commercial men such disclosures may be disastrous.

2. The temptation to make understatements and lend to their statements the sanction of an oath, tends to sap and mine public morals, until men begin to excuse themselves for their own wrong-doing, because it being so common that to do otherwise would be to fail in an average smartness.

3. When we take into consideration the sources from which income is derived, the habitudes of the different persons who pay the tax, the difficulty of apportioning it so that each will have paid in just proportion to every other person, leaving each relatively in the same condition, the perplexities become almost insurmountable."

The most important change effected in the present Act was the raising the sum exempt from tax to $1000, instead of $600 as in the Act of June 30, 1864.

case of default to make such list or return and payment within the thirty days, as aforesaid, shall be subject to the provisions of the foregoing section of this act: *Provided*, That when any dividend is made which includes any part of the surplus or contingent fund of any bank, trust company, savings institution, insurance or railroad company, which has been assessed and the duty paid thereon, the amount of duty so paid on that portion of the surplus or contingent fund may be deducted from the duty on such dividend.

Tax on Dividends and Interest on Bonds of Railroads, Canals, Turnpikes, &c. Nature of Returns, &c.

SEC. 122. *And be it further enacted*, [That any railroad, canal, turnpike, canal navigation, or slack-water company, indebted for any money for which bonds or other evidence of indebtedness have been issued, payable in one or more years after date, upon which interest is stipulated to be paid, or coupons representing the interest, or any such company that may have declared any dividend in scrip, or money due or payable to its stockholders, including non-residents, whether citizens or aliens, as part of the earnings, profits, income, or gains of such company, and all profits of such company carried to the account of any fund, or used for construction, shall be subject to and pay a tax of five per centum on the amount of all such interest, or coupons, dividends, or profits, whenever and wherever the same shall be payable; and to whatsoever parties, or person, the same may be payable, including non-residents whether citizens or aliens; and said companies are hereby authorized to deduct and withhold from all payments, on account of any interest, or coupons and dividends due and payable as aforesaid, the tax of five per centum; and the payment of the amount of said tax so deducted from the interest, or coupons, or dividends, and certified, by the president or treasurer of said company, shall discharge said company from that amount of the dividend, or interest, or coupon, on the bonds or other evidences of their indebtedness so held by any person or party whatever, except where said companies may have contracted otherwise. And a list or return shall be made and rendered to the assessor or assistant assessor on or before the tenth day of the month following that in which said interest, coupons, or dividends become due and payable, and as often as every six months; and said list or return shall contain a true and faithful account of the amount of the tax, and there shall be annexed thereto a declaration of the president or treasurer of the company, under oath or affirmation, in form and manner as may be prescribed by the Commissioner of Internal Revenue, that the same contains a true and faithful account of said tax. And for any default in making or rendering such list or return, with the declaration annexed, or of the payment of the tax as aforesaid, the company making such default shall forfeit as a penalty the sum of one thousand dollars; and in case of any default in making or rendering said list or return, or of the payment of the tax, or any part thereof, as aforesaid, the assessment and collection of the duty and penalty shall be made according to the provisions of law in other cases of neglect or refusal: *Provided*, That whenever any of the companies mentioned in this section shall be unable to pay the interest on their indebtedness, and shall in fact fail to pay such interest, that in such cases the tax levied by this section shall not be paid to the United States until said company resume the payment of interest on their indebtedness.]

Tax on the Salaries of Officers in Service of United States. Withholding of by Disbursing Officers.

SEC. 123. *And be it further enacted*, [That there shall be levied, collected, and paid on all salaries of officers, or payments for services to persons in the civil, military, naval, or other employment or service of the United States, including senators and representatives and delegates in Congress, when exceeding the rate of six hundred dollars per annum, a tax of five per centum on the excess above the said six hundred dollars, and a tax of ten per centum on the excess over five thousand dollars; and it shall be the duty of all paymasters and all disbursing officers, under the government of the United States, or persons in the employ thereof, when making any payment to any officers or persons as aforesaid, or upon settling and adjusting the accounts of such officers or persons, to deduct and withhold the aforesaid tax and they shall, at the same time, make a certificate stating the name of the officer or person from whom such deduction was made, and the amount thereof, which shall be transmitted to the office of the Commissioner of Internal Revenue, and entered as part of the internal tax; and the pay-roll, receipts, or account of officers or persons paying such tax, as aforesaid, shall be made to exhibit the fact of such payment. And it shall be the duty of the several Auditors of the Treasury Department, when auditing the accounts of any paymaster or disbursing officer, or any officer withholding his salary from moneys received by him, or when settling or adjusting the accounts of any such officer, to require evidence that the taxes mentioned in this section have been deducted and paid over to the Commissioner of Internal Revenue, or other officer authorized to receive the same: *Provided*, That payments of prize money shall be regarded as income from salaries, and the tax thereon shall be adjusted and collected in like manner: *Provided further*; That this section shall not apply to payments made to mechanics or laborers employed upon public works.]

Legacies and Distributive Shares. General and Particular Provisions. Nature of the Returns, &c.*

SEC. 124. *And be it further enacted*, That any person or persons having in charge or trust, as administrators, executors, or trustees, any

---

*LEGACIES.

When the personal estate of a testator is not sufficient to pay the legacies named in his will, so that it becomes necessary to obtain license from the pro-

legacies or distributive shares arising from personal property, where the whole amount of such personal property, as aforesaid, shall exceed the sum of one thousand dollars in actual value, passing, after the passage of this act, from any person possessed of such property, either by will or by the intestate laws of any State or Territory, or any personal property or interest therein, transferred by deed, grant, bargain, sale, or gift, made or intended to take effect in possession or enjoyment after the death of the grantor or bargainor, to any person or persons, or to any body or bodies politic or corporate, in trust or otherwise, shall be, and hereby are, made subject to a duty or tax, to be paid to the United States, as follows, that is to say:

---

bate court, and sell real estate to make up the deficiency, it does not avoid the liability to the legacy tax, but the tax should be assessed upon the full amount of the legacies. (Decision of Commissioner Lewis, March 3, 1865.)

Contra opinion of Judge Leavitt, United States Circuit Court of Ohio.

Commissioner Orton, however, decided to abide by the decision of the Ohio Circuit Court. (*Vide* Int. Rev. Rec., Jan. 21, 1865.)

Unless the value of personal property remaining after the payment of debts and charges of administration exceed $1000, no legacy tax can be assessed. (Int. Rev. Rec., Sept. 2, 1865.)

If such remainder does exceed $1,000 in actual value, *each* legacy or distributive share, (except when the wife or husband of the decedent receives the same,) is liable to the legacy tax. (Letter of Commissioner, Sept. 19, 1865; and see also the provisions of present law as to minors, p. 135.)

You state the following case: "A testator died, leaving a widow and one son, and bequeathed to the executrix certain personal property, in trust. The income of such property is to be paid to the widow during her life, unless she shall again marry, in which case such income is to be divided equally between her and her son.

At her decease the income is thereafter to be paid to the son during his life, and at his death the whole property is to pass to his children; or in case he shall have no children, then to such persons as he shall indicate in his will. If, however, the widow shall outlive the son, he leaving no children, then the whole property is to be hers absolutely," &c.

"You inquire if in view of the uncertainty existing as to the parties in whom the absolute title to the property will finally vest, any legacy tax can be assessed?"

I reply: "that the government cannot be permitted to suffer detriment, through any peculiarity in the terms of wills."

"In this case the possible marriage of the widow must be left out of consideration. The widow must be considered as taking the entire income of such estate during her life. She is liable, however, to no tax on the legacy. The son's interest will be found by deducting the value of the widow's life interest; the tax due is at the rate of one per cent., and should be paid out of the trust fund, which constitutes the legacy." (Letter of Commissioner, Sept. 14, 1865.)

Legacies are held to pass from the testator at the instant of her decease. This is in conformity with the ruling of my predecessors. (Letter of Commissioner Rollins, Dec. 23, 1865.)

"A.," of Nashua, N. H., made a will, containing, among others, the following items:

"8. I give to my mother, Mrs. ———, the use of $2,000 during her lifetime, or as much more as it may take to make her comfortable, and after her decease, it is my wish that what she has got left should be equally divided between my said wife and my niece, Mrs. ———."

"9. I give my house on Oak Street, Nashua, one-half to my said wife, and

First. Where the person or persons entitled to any beneficial interest in such property shall be the lineal issue or lineal ancestor, brother or sister, to the person who died possessed of such property, as aforesaid, at the rate of one dollar for each and every hundred dollars of the clear value of such interest in such property.

Second. Where the person or persons entitled to any beneficial interest in such property shall be a descendant of a brother or sister of the person who died possessed, as aforesaid, at the rate of two dollars for each and every hundred dollars of the clear value of such interest.

Third. Where the person or persons entitled to any beneficial interest in such property shall be a brother or sister of the father or mother,

---

the other to my said niece, it being expressly understood that my said mother shall have the privilege of living with my wife if she wishes.

"10. I do hereby give and bequeath all other property of which I may be possessed or in any wise interested, to be equally divided between my said wife and my said niece in equal proportions, on the express condition, that they shall not have the privilege of disposing of the same during life, but may do so by will."

Under the date of Dec. 27, 1865, the Deputy Commissioner replies:

"1. The estate of A. should be treated as having passed under the will.

"2. The eighth item should be treated as an unconditional legacy, and is subject to a legacy tax of one per centum.

"3. Under the ninth item, the half of the Oak Street property given to the niece, is subject to a succession tax of two per centum, and the half given to the wife is exempt from tax.

"4. The residuary legatees (item ten) have to all intents but a life interest. The wife is liable to *no* tax in respect to her share thereof. The annual income of the niece from the one-half of the residuary estate should be treated as an annuity. Her expectation of life should be found from the tables of mortality, and the present worth of the said annuity for the said number of years should be assessed at the rate of two per cent." (Letter of Commissioner, 1865.)

The expense of an appraisal, when one is necessary, may be charged in a bill of expenses, and by the assessor, against the Government. (Int. Rev. Rec., Vol. III., p. 108.)

A duplicate copy of the legacy return has heretofore been entered by the assessor upon a special list; but in practice in most districts the return and assessment is entered upon the regular monthly list. As the tax is a lien upon the property, it would seem that no difficulty can possibly arise from a short delay, and no danger that the tax can be evaded.

For instructions as to taxing legacies, distributive shares and succession, (see Appendix. Department series 2, No. 3.)

No legacy taxes accrue where a person died before the 18th July, 1862, and no succession taxes where a person died before the 1st July, 1864; but where a person succeeds in possession to real estate, after June 30, 1864, which has been enjoyed by a life-tenant, the succession tax accrues whether the predecessor died before or after June 30, 1864.

The office does not perceive any essential difference between the requirements of Section 3, of the act of 1862, and those of Section 124, of the act of 1864, except as to the rate of tax. The property is held to *pass* in either case upon the death of the decedent. (Letter of Commissioner, March 6, 1866.)

"You say, a gentleman dies possessed of considerable estate in realty, which he leaves in entire control of his executors to manage and receive the rents and profits thereof for ten years, and at the expiration of that time, if not sooner sold by him, then to sell the same and divide the proceeds among the

or a descendant of a brother or sister of the father or mother, of the person who died possessed, as aforesaid, at the rate of four dollars for each and every hundred dollars of the clear value of such interest.

Fourth. Where the person or persons entitled to any beneficial interest in such property shall be a brother or sister of the grandfather or grandmother, or a descendant of the brother or sister of the grandfather or grandmother, of the person who died possessed, as aforesaid, at the rate of five dollars for each and every hundred dollars of the clear value of such interest.

Fifth. Where the person or persons entitled to any beneficial interest in such property shall be in any other degree of collateral consan-

---

testator's children. When and how are we to assess succession tax in such cases?

"I reply, that if the executor receives all the estate until sold and the children none, the executor should make returns of the present worth of his interest, and when the estate is sold and divided, he should make return for each heir, of what is now a remainder of reversion in expectancy." (Int. Rev. Rec., April 7, 1866.)

A testator died in 1845, and by his will gave to his widow the "improvement" of all his real estate during her life. He also gave to his children certain pecuniary legacies and directed the executor at the death of the widow to "convert all his real estate into money by a sale thereof," and appropriate all the proceeds of the sale to the payment of such legacies.

The widow died in September, 1865. The executor is about to make sale of real estate and enquires whether any tax is to be paid. The only question, it would seem, is whether this is a case falling within Section 138, where the real estate can be regarded as "under any trust for the sale thereof." It was not devised in trust to the executor, and no other interest or power in, or over it, was given to him by will except said power to sell. Is the term "trust" in that section to be restricted to its technical signification, or shall it be taken in its enlarged and popular use. The provision that the duty may be paid by the "Executor," &c., as distinguished from the "trustees," seems to furnish some reason for the last construction.

My impression however, as expressed to the executor, is that this is not a "trust" in contemplation of that section, and that no tax can properly be claimed. As numerous similar cases may arise, a ruling is much to be desired by the assessors. (Assessor Esty to Commissioner, March 2, 1866.)

Reply: "You state the case of heirs who are entitled, under a will, to the proceeds of certain real estate, after the death of the widow, which death occurred in 1865; and you inquire whether the executor must pay a tax on the proceeds so distributed.

"Referring to Sections 127 and 138, act of 1864, I am of the opinion that such tax should be paid by the 'executor.'" (Letter of Commissioner, May 11, 1866.)

Gifts of personal property made for the purpose of evading the legacy tax are subject to income tax. (Int. Rev. Rec., April 28, 1866.)

"Also 'advances' of personal property to children." (Int. Rev. Rec., May 5 and June 2, 1866.)

A legacy given in trust "for the erection of a suitable monument over the graves of my parents in the cemetery," is not liable to a legacy tax. (Letter of Commissioner, February 8, 1866.)

Where children come into possession of real estate subject to a dower or life estate, they should pay on the value of the estate of *which they come into possession*, and will be *further liable upon the decease* of life tenant, to the succession tax upon the value to which they shall *then* succeed in possession. (Section 137, Law of 1864.)

guinity than is hereinbefore stated, or shall be a stranger in blood to the person who died possessed, as aforesaid, or shall be a body politic or corporate, at the rate of six dollars for each and every hundred dollars of the clear value of such interest: *Provided*, That all legacies or property passing by will, or by the laws of any State or Territory, to husband or wife of the person who died possessed, as aforesaid, shall be exempt from tax or duty: [*Provided further*, That any legacy or share of personal property passing, as aforesaid, to a minor child of the person who died possessed, as aforesaid, shall be exempt from taxation under this section, unless such legacy or share shall exceed the sum of one thousand dollars, in which case the excess only above that sum shall be liable to such taxation or duty.]

The Same Subject, continued.

Sec. 125. *And be it further enacted*, That the tax aforesaid [shall be due and payable whenever the party interested in such legacy or distributive share or property or interest aforesaid shall become entitled to the possession or enjoyment thereof, or to the beneficial interest in the profits accruing therefrom, and the same] shall be a lien and charge upon the property of every person who may die as aforesaid, for twenty years, or until the same shall, within that period, be fully paid to and discharged by the United States; [and every administrator, executor, or trustee, having in charge or trust any legacy or distributive share, as aforesaid shall give notice thereof in writing to the assessor or assistant assessor of the district where the deceased, grantor, or bargainer last resided, within thirty days after he shall have taken charge of said trust;] and every executor, administrator, or trustee, before payment and distribution to the legatees or any parties entitled to beneficial interest therein, shall pay to the collector or deputy collector of the district of which the deceased person was a resident, the amount of the duty or tax assessed upon such legacy or distributive share, and shall also make and render to the assessor or assistant assessor of the said district a schedule, list, or statement, in duplicate, of the amount of such legacy or distributive share, together with the amount of duty which has accrued or shall accrue thereon, verified by his oath or affirmation, to be administered and certified thereon by some magistrate or officer having lawful power to administer such oaths, in such form and manner as may be prescribed by the Commissioner of Internal Revenue, which schedule, list, or statement shall contain the names of each and every person entitled to any beneficial interest therein, together with the clear value of such interest, the duplicate of which schedule, list, or statement shall be by him immediately delivered, and the tax thereon paid to such collector; and upon such payment and delivery of such schedule, list, or statement, said collector or deputy collector shall grant to such person paying such duty or tax a receipt or receipts for the same in duplicate, which shall be prepared as hereinafter provided. Such receipt or receipts, duly signed and delivered by such collector or deputy collector, shall be sufficient evidence to entitle such executor, administrator, or trustee, to be credited and allowed such payment by every tribunal which, by the laws of any State or Territory, is, or may be, empowered to decide upon and settle the accounts of executors and administrators. And in case such executor, administrator, or trustee, shall refuse or neglect to pay the aforesaid duty or tax to the collector or deputy collector, as aforesaid, within the time hereinbefore provided, or shall neglect or refuse to deliver to said collector or deputy collector the duplicate of the schedule, list, or statement of such legacies, property, or personal estate, under oath, as aforesaid, or shall neglect or refuse to deliver the schedule, list, or statement of such legacies, property, or personal estate, under oath, as aforesaid, or shall deliver to said assessor or assistant assessor a false schedule or statement of such legacies, property, or personal estate, or give the names and relationship of the persons entitled to beneficial interests therein untruly, or shall not truly and correctly set forth and state therein the clear value of such beneficial interest, or where no administration upon such property or personal estate shall have been granted or allowed under existing laws, the assistant assessor shall make out such lists and valuations as in other cases of neglect or refusal, and shall assess the duty thereon; [and in case of willful neglect, refusal or false statement by such executor, administrator or trustee as aforesaid, he shall be liable to a penalty of not exceeding one thousand dollars, to be recovered with costs of suit. Any tax paid under the provisions of Sections 124 and 125 shall be deducted from the particular legacy or distributive share on account of which the same is charged] and the collector shall commence appropriate proceedings before any court of the United States, in the name of the United States, against such person or persons as may have the actual or constructive custody or possession of such property or personal estate, or any part thereof, and shall subject such property or personal estate, or any portion of the same, to be sold upon the judgment or decree of such court, and from the proceeds of such sale the amount of such tax or duty, together with all costs and expenses of every description to be allowed by such court, shall be first paid, and the balance, if any, deposited according to the order of such court, to be paid under its direction to such person or persons as shall establish title to the same. The deed or deeds, or any proper conveyance of such property or personal estate, or any portion thereof, so sold under such judgment or decree, executed by the officer lawfully charged with carrying the same into effect, shall vest in the purchaser thereof all the title of the delinquent to the property or personal estate sold under and by virtue of such judgment or decree, and shall release every other portion of such property or personal estate from the lien or charge thereon created by this act. And every person or persons who shall have in his possession, charge, or custody, any record, file, or paper containing or supposed to contain any information concerning such property or personal estate, as aforesaid, passing from any person who may die, as aforesaid, shall exhibit the same at the request of the assessor or assistant assessor of the district, and to any law officer of the United States, in the performance of his duty under this act, his deputy or agent, who may desire to examine the same. And if any such person, having in his possession, charge, or custody, any such records, files, or papers, shall refuse or neglect to exhibit the same on request, as aforesaid, he shall forfeit and pay the sum of five hundred dollars: *Provided*, In all legal controversies where such deed or title shall be the subject of judicial investigation the recital in said deed shall be prima facie evidence of its truth, and that the requirements of the law had been complied with by the officers of the government.

*Definition of Terms used, in the provisions as to Succession Taxes.**

SEC. 126. *And be it further enacted*, That for the purposes of this act the term "real estate" shall include all lands, tenements, and hereditaments, corporeal and incorporeal; that the term "succession" shall denote the devolution of title to any real estate; and that the term

---

*SUCCESSIONS.

In practice it has been found convenient for the assessors of the district to file in the office of the register of probate courts, or surrogate's or orphan's courts, the proper blanks for the returns and schedules required by these provisions of the statutes, that the attention of all executors, administrators, &c., may be called to their duties in this behalf at an early stage of the settlement of the estate of the testate or intestate estate they represent. (Vide note to section in relation to duties of assessors and assistants. See series II. No. 3, in appendix.)

When the successor is the husband of the predecessor he is to be considered as a stranger in blood. (Int. Rev. Rec., Vol. III., p. 101.)

A deed of trust for security of a marriage settlement is held to confer upon the grantee a succession, and is subject to the highest rate of duty, when the successor (trustee) is a "stranger in blood."

The succession tax must be assessed in the place where the property lies, either to a resident or non-resident. The successor is taxable as soon as he comes in possession, and although the tax cannot be demanded of executors or administrators unless they are trustees or guardians, where minors are concerned, it is fair to presume they would act as agents of such minors and pay the tax in their behalf, rather than that it should be recovered by distraint. If a widow's dower is to be set off *immediately*, it will be proper for the assessor to wait therefor, before assessing the other successions. If assessors or assistants know of any estate lying in other districts than their own, to which any successor has become such in possession since the 30th of June, 1864, they should acquaint the assessors of these districts of the facts. (Letter of Commissioner, November 16, 1864.)

A successor is not liable to succession taxes until he comes into possession; and when he comes into possession of a *part* of a succession he is liable on that part only until the change in his succession determines; when he is liable to the tax on the increased value. When a successor is beneficially entitled to the income from lands only, (in other words has a life estate only,) the tax is assessable on the present worth of an annuity, of value equal to that of said income, for a term of years equal to the number of years in the annuitant's expectation of life, as determined by the tables of mortality. (Letter of Commissioner, February 21, 1865.)

In cases when dower is not assigned but the widow enjoys the estate in common with her children, it will be easy to estimate the entire value of the estate; subtract the value of such fraction thereof as constitutes the dower,

"person" shall be held to include persons, body corporate, company, or association.

Same Subject. Nature and Character of Taxable Successions.

SEC. 127. *And be it further enacted,* That every past or future disposition of real estate by will, deed, or laws of descent, by reason whereof any person shall become beneficially entitled, in possession or expectancy, to any real estate, or the income thereof, upon the death of any person dying after the passage of this act, shall be deemed to confer, on the person entitled by reason of any such disposition, a "succession;" and the term "successor" shall denote the person so entitled, and the term "predecessor" shall denote the grantor, testator, ancestor, or other person from whom the interest of the successor has been or shall be derived.

Same Subject.

SEC. 128. *And be it further enacted,* That where any real estate shall, at or after the passing of this act, be subject to any charge, estate,

---

and assess the tax on the remainder. On the decease of the widow the children would be liable to further tax under Section 128, law of 1864, on the increase of benefit. (Letter of Commissioner, March 1, 1865.)

No deduction can be made from successions on account of costs and attorney fees in proceedings for partition of real estate. (Int. Rev. Rec., Sept. 16, 1865.)

The assistant assessor should secure returns of successions, as soon as possible after the successors become such in actual possession. But when no probable loss would accrue to the government from reasonable delay, it would be well for assistant assessors to defer requiring returns of successions on embarrassed or insolvent estates, till the prospective interest of the heirs-at-law and other successors shall be approximately ascertained.

The assessment should if possible be made in the district where the property is situated. The tax cannot properly be demanded of the executor or administrator, but only of the successor when he comes into possession. (Boutwell's Manual, 2d Ed., p. 168.)

There is no provision for reimbursing assessors for the expense of an independent appraisal of real estate for the purpose of assessing the succession tax, if the assessment made "does not exceed the duty assessable" according to the return made to the assessor. But when the amount of independent assessment *does* exceed the duty assessable according to the return, the assessment for expenses should be included upon the list, and the entire assessment paid over to the government, and "expenses" charged in a regular bill against the government. (Int. Rev. Rec., April 7, 1866.)

When children come into possession of real estate subject to a dower or life interest, they should pay on the value of the estate of which *they* come into possession, and will be further liable upon the decease of life tenant to the succession tax upon the value to which they shall *then* succeed in possession. (Section 137.)

When the "widow's thirds" are set off by metes and bounds, the children should of course pay immediately the succession tax upon the other two-thirds. Where no division is made as above, the value of the entire interest diminished by the present value of the dower, would be assessed immediately against the children. (Ruling April 17, 1866. III. Int. Rev. Rec., p. 172.)

A conveyance of real property by husband to wife through a third party, is considered, for all purposes of the law, a conveyance directly to the wife, or equitable grantee. Such a conveyance, without consideration, constitutes a succession, but the wife is not liable to succession tax. No stamp is required on such a conveyance. (Ruling. III. Int Rev. Rec., p. 172.)

or interest, determinable by the death of any person, or at any period ascertainable only by reference to death, the increase of benefit accruing to any person upon the extinction or determination of such charge, estate, or interest, shall be deemed to be a succession accruing to the person then entitled, beneficially, to the real estate or the income thereof.

Same Subject.

SEC. 129. *And be it further enacted,* That where any persons, after the passing of this act, shall take any succession jointly, they shall pay the duty chargeable thereon by this act in proportion to their respective interests in the succession; and any beneficial interest in such succession, accruing to any of them by survivorship, shall be deemed to be a new succession, derived from the predecessor from whom the joint title shall have been derived.

Same Subject.

SEC. 130. *And be it further enacted,* That where any disposition of real estate shall be accompanied by the reservation or assurance of, or contract for, any benefit to the grantor, or any other person, for any term of life, or for any period ascertainable only by reference to death, such disposition shall be deemed to confer at the time appointed for the determination of such benefit an increase of beneficial interest in such real estate, as a succession equal in annual value to the yearly amount or yearly value of the benefit so reserved, assured, or contracted for, on the person in whose favor such disposition shall be made.

Same Subject.

SEC. 131. *And be it further enacted,* That where any disposition of real estate shall purport to take effect presently, or under such circumstances as not to confer succession, but, by the effect or in consequence of any engagement, secret trust, or arrangement capable of being enforced in a court of law or equity, the beneficial ownership of such real estate shall not, bona fide, pass according to the terms of such disposition, but shall, in fact, be reserved to the grantor or other person for some period ascertainable only by reference to death, the person shall be deemed, for the purposes of this act, to acquire the real estate so passing as a succession derived from the person making the disposition as the predecessor.

Same Subject. Conveyance without valuable or adequate Consideration, deemed to confer a Succession.

SEC. 132. *And be it further enacted,* That if any person shall, by deed of gift or other assurance of title, made without valuable and adequate consideration, and purporting to vest the estate either immediately or in the future, whether or not accompanied by the possesison, convey any real estate to any person, such disposition shall be held and taken to confer upon the grantee a succession within the meaning of this act.

Same Subject. Rates of Tax.

SEC. 133. *And be it further enacted,* That there shall be levied and paid to the United States in respect of every such succession as aforesaid, according to the value thereof, the following duties, that is to say:

Where the successor shall be the lineal issue or lineal ancestor of the predecessor, a duty at the rate of one dollar per centum upon such value.

Where the successor shall be a brother or sister, or a descendant of a brother or sister of the predecessor, a duty at the rate of two dollars per centum upon such value.

Where the successor shall be a brother or sister of the father or mother, or a descendant of a brother or sister of the father or mother of the predecessor, a duty at the rate of four dollars per centum upon such value.

Where the successor shall be a brother or sister of the grandfather or grandmother, or a descendant of the brother or sister of the grandfather or grandmother of the predecessor, a duty at the rate of five dollars per centum upon such value.

Where the successor shall be in any other degree of collateral consanguinity to the predecessor than is hereinbefore described, or shall be a stranger in blood to him, a duty at the rate of six dollars per centum upon such value: *Provided,* That no duty shall be levied in respect of any succession vesting before or subsequent to the passage of this act, where the successor shall be the wife of the predecessor.

Tax on Successions, when Interest has Passed to Others.

SEC. 134. *And be it further enacted,* That where the interest of any successor in any real estate shall, before he shall have become entitled thereto in possession, have passed by reason of death to any other successor or successors, then one duty only shall be paid in respect of such interest, and shall be due from the successor who shall first become entitled thereto in possession; but such duty shall be at the highest rate which, if every such successor had been subject to duty, would have been payable by any one of them.

Particular Provisions on Same Subject.

SEC. 135. *And be it further enacted,* That wherever, after the passing of this act, any succession shall, before the successor shall have become entitled thereto in possession, have become vested by alienation, or by any title not conferring a new succession, in any other person, then the duty payable in respect thereof shall be paid at the same rate and time as the same would have been payable if no such alienation had been made or derivative title created; and where the title to any succession shall be accelerated by the surrender or extinction of any prior interests, then the duty thereon shall be payable at the time of such surrender or extinction of prior title.

Same Subject. Trusts, &c.

SEC. 136. *And be it further enacted,* That where real estate shall become subject to a trust for any charitable or public purposes, under any past or future disposition, which, if made in favor of an individual, would confer on him a succession, there shall be payable in respect of such real estate, upon its becoming subject to such trusts, a duty at the rate of six per centum upon the amount or principal value of such real estate.

Same Subject. Where Tax shall be Assessed.

SEC. 137. *And be it further enacted*, That the duty imposed by this act [shall be assessed in the collection district where the estate is situate, and] shall be paid at the time when the successor, or any person in his right or on his behalf, shall become entitled in possession to his succession, or to the receipt of the income and profits thereof, except that if there shall be any prior charge, estate, or interest, not created by the successor himself upon or in the succession, by reason whereof the successor shall not be presently entitled to the full enjoyment or value thereof, the duty, in respect of the increased value accruing upon the determination of such charge, estate, or interest, shall, if not previously paid, compounded for, or commuted, be paid at the time of such determination.

Same Subject. Penalties for not Giving proper Notices.

SEC. 138. *And be it further enacted*, That the interest of any successor in moneys to arise from the sale of real estate under any trust for the sale thereof shall be deemed to be a succession chargeable with duty under this act, and the said duty shall be paid by the trustee, executor, or other person having control of the funds. [And every such person having in charge or trust any disposition of real estate or interest therein subject to tax under this act, shall give notice thereof in writing to the assessor or assistant assessor of the district where the estate is situate within thirty days from the time when he shall have taken charge of such trust, and prior to any distribution of said real estate, together with a description and value thereof, and the names of the persons interested therein; and for willful neglect or refusal so to do shall be liable to a penalty of not exceeding five hundred dollars, to be recovered with costs of suit.]

Same Subject. Trusts for Investment.

SEC. 139. *And be it further enacted*, That the interest of any successor in personal property, subject to any trust for the investment thereof in the purchase of real estate to which the successor would be absolutely entitled, shall be chargeable with duty under this act as a succession, and the tax shall be payable by the trustee, executor, or other person having control of the funds.

Same Subject. No Allowance for Contingencies, &c.

SEC. 140. *And be it further enacted*, That, in estimating the value of a succession, no allowance shall be made in respect of any contingent encumbrance thereon; but in the event of such incumbrance taking effect as an actual burden on the interest of the successor, he shall be entitled to a return of a proportionate amount of the duty so paid by him in respect of the amount or value of the incumbrance when taking effect.

Same Subject. Refunding and Defeat of the Succession.

SEC. 141. *And be it further enacted,* That, in estimating the value of a succession, no allowance shall be made in respect of any contingency upon the happening of which the real estate may pass to some other person; but in the event of the same so passing, the successor shall be entitled to a return of so much of the duty paid by him as will reduce the same to the amount which would have been payable by him if such duty had been assessed in respect of the actual duration or extent of his interest: *Provided,* That if the estate of the successor shall be defeated, in whole or in part, by its application to the payment of the debts of the predecessor, the executor, administrator, or trustee so applying it shall pay out of the proceeds of the sale thereof the amount so refunded: *And provided also,* That if the estate of the successor shall be defeated, in whole or in part, by any person claiming title from and under the predecessor, such person shall be chargeable with the amount of duty so refunded, and such amounts shall be collected in the manner herein provided for the collection of duties.

Same Subject. Refunding of Tax by Secretary of Treasury, in certain cases.

SEC. 142. *And be it further enacted,* That where a successor shall not have obtained the whole of his succession at the time of the duty becoming payable, he shall be chargeable only with duty on the value thereof from time to time obtained by him; and whenever any duty shall have been paid on account of any succession, and it shall afterwards be proved, to the satisfaction of the Secretary of the Treasury, that such duty, not being due from the person paying the same, was paid by mistake, or was paid in respect of real estate, which the successor shall have been unable to recover, or of which he shall have been evicted or deprived by any superior title, or that for any other reason it ought to be refunded, the Secretary of the Treasury shall thereupon refund the same to the person entitled thereto, by draught drawn on any collector of internal revenue.

Commissioner may Compound Taxes and Enlarge Time for Payment in Special Cases.

SEC. 143. *And be it further enacted,* That where, in the opinion of the Commissioner of Internal Revenue, any succession shall be of such a nature, or so disposed or circumstanced, that the value thereof shall not be fairly ascertainable under any of the preceding directions, or where, from the complication of circumstances affecting the value of a succession, or affecting the assessment or recovery of the duty thereon, the Commissioner shall think it expedient to exercise this present authority, it shall be lawful for him to compound the duty payable on the succession upon such terms as he shall think fit, and to give discharges to the successor, upon payment of duty according to such composition; and it shall be lawful for him, in any special cases in which he may think it expedient so to do, to enlarge the time for payment of any duty.

Commissioner may Commute Tax on Succession in certain cases.

SEC. 144. *And be it further enacted,* That it shall be lawful for the Commissioner, in his discretion, upon application made by any person who shall be entitled to a succession in expectancy, to commute the duty presumptively payable in respect of such succession for a certain sum to be presently paid, and for assessing the amount which shall be so payable he shall cause a present value to be set upon such presumptive duty, regard being had to the contingencies affecting the liability to such duty, and the interest of money involved in such calculation being reckoned at the rate for the time being allowed by the Commissioner in respect of duties paid in advance, and upon the receipt of such certain sum he shall give discharges to the successor accordingly.

Tax on Successions. A Lien for Five Years.

SEC. 145. *And be it further enacted,* That the duty imposed by this act shall be a first charge on the interest of the successor, and of all persons claiming in his right, in all the real estate in respect whereof such duty shall be assessed for five years [from the time when such tax shall have become due and payable], unless sooner paid.

Separate Tracts of Land may be separately Assessed.

SEC. 146. *And be it further enacted,* That the Commissioner shall, at the request of any successor, or any person claiming in his right, cause to be made so many separate assessments of the duty payable in respect of the interest of the successor in any separate tracts of real estate, or in defined portions of the same tract, as shall be reasonably required; and in such cases the respective tracts shall be chargeable only with the amount of duty separately assessed in respect thereof.

Returns to be made to the Assessor or Assistant Assessor. Assessment on Information in certain cases.

SEC. 147. *And be it further enacted,* [That any person liable to pay a tax in respect to any succession shall give notice to the assessor or assistant assessor of his liability to such tax, within thirty days from the time when he shall become entitled in possession to such succession or to the receipt of the income and profits thereof, and shall at the same time deliver to the assessor or assistant assessor a full and true account of said succession, for the tax whereon he shall be accountable, and of the value of the real estate involved, and of the deductions claimed by him, together with the names of the successor and predecessor and their relation to each other, and all such other particulars as shall be necessary or proper for enabling the assessor or assistant assessor fully and correctly to ascertain the taxes due; and the assessor or assistant assessor, if satisfied with such account and estimate as originally delivered, or with any amendments that may be made therein upon his requisition, may assess the succession tax on the footing of such account and estimate; but it shall be lawful for the assessor or assistant assessor, if dissatisfied with such account, or if no account and estimate shall be delivered to him, to assess the tax on the best information he can obtain, subject to appeal as hereinafter provided; and if the tax so assessed shall exceed the tax assessable according to the return made to the assessor or assistant assessor, and with which he shall have been dissatisfied, or if no account and estimate has been delivered, and if no appeal shall be taken against such assessment, then it shall be in the discretion of the assessor, having regard to the merits of each case, to assess the whole or any part of the expenses incident to the taking of such assessment, in addition to such tax; and if there shall be an appeal against such last-mentioned assessment, then the payment of such expenses shall be in the discretion of the Commissioner of Internal Revenue.]

Penalty for Neglect to make Returns or pay Tax, on Succession.

SEC. 148. *And be it further enacted,* [That if any person required to give any such notice or deliver such account, as aforesaid, shall willfully neglect to do so within the time required by law, he shall be liable to pay the United States a sum equal to ten per centum upon the amount of tax payable by him; and if any person liable to pay any tax in respect of his succession shall, after such tax shall have been finally ascertained, willfully neglect to do so within ten days after being notified, he shall also be liable to pay to the United States a sum equal to ten per centum upon the amount of tax so unpaid, at the same time and in the same manner as the tax to be collected.]

Appeals to the Assessor and to the Commissioner.

SEC. 149. *And be it further enacted,* That it shall be lawful for any party, liable to pay duty in respect of his succession, who shall be dissatisfied with the assessment of the assistant assessor, within thirty days after the date of such assessment, to appeal to the assessor from such assessment, who shall decide on such appeal, and give notice thereof to such party, who, if still dissatisfied, may, within twenty days after notice as aforesaid, appeal from such decision to the Commissioner of Internal Revenue, and furnish a statement of the grounds of such appeal to the Commissioner, whose decision upon the case, as presented by the statements of the assessor or assistant assessor and such party shall be final.

[SEC. 150 is repealed by this act.]

Stamp Taxes. When Provisions in Relation to Stamp Tax shall take effect, &c.

SEC. 151. *And be it further enacted,* That all laws in force at the time of the passage of this act in relation to stamp duties shall continue in force until the first day of August, eighteen hundred and sixty-four; and on and after the first day of August, eighteen hundred and sixty-four, there shall be levied, collected, and paid, for and in respect of the several instruments, matters, and things mentioned and described in the schedule (marked B) hereunto annexed, or for or in respect of the vellum, parchment, or paper upon which such instruments, matters, or things, or any of them, shall be written or printed, by any person or persons, or party who shall make, sign, or issue the same, or for whose use or benefit the same shall be made, signed, or issued, the several duties or sums of money set down in figures against the same, respectively, or otherwise specified or set forth in said schedule.*

---

*STAMPS.

I am indebted mainly to the valuable "Digest of Rulings" of Mr. Boutwell, for the following resumé of decision upon the stamp duties:

1. Deeds of partition or releases are not subject to stamps.
2. Assignments of government land warrants require a five cent stamp, as agreements.
3. Indorsement of payment of interest on a bond, &c., requires no stamp, although in the form of a receipt.
4. Receipts given by railroad and express companies must be stamped.
5. The stamp duty on letters of administration covers all subsequent papers in the settlement of the estate.
6. Photographs must be stamped at retail price.
7. The receipt of a charitable institution need not be stamped. No debt was due from the donor.
8. A school teacher's qualification certificate should be stamped (five cent stamp.)
9. Bills of lading, &c., for transportation of goods require a two cent stamp. Duplicates same as originals.
10. Memorandum checks, drawn by a cashier on his own cash, require no stamp.
11. Stamp-duty on a lease, when value is not ascertained, must be for the largest amount reserved in the lease.
12. When coupon-bonds are stamped the coupons are exempt.
13. Bonds or other official papers, issued by municipal corporations, are exempt.
14. Either party to an instrument may affix the stamp *before* execution.
15. Each copy of an indenture requires a stamp.
16. A conveyance without consideration requires no stamp. (Vide chapter—Successions.)
17. The assignment of bonds or mortgages requires stamps of equal value to the instrument assigned.
18. Certificates of deposit should be stamped.
19. "Notices to quit" are exempt. So with acknowledgment to deeds, &c.,—also all criminal process. United States leases and indentures are also exempt, otherwise with affidavit of disability.
20. The lease for a part of a year should be proportional to the annual retail value.
21. A discharge of a mortgage is exempt. So with power of attorney and other pension and "back pay" papers.
22. If a party sends a note or other paper to a bank, with a request that it be stamped, the party affixing it acts as the agent of the sender.
23. Deeds of "confirmation" are exempt. Also petitions for naturalization.
24. "The deed of a pew is merely a conveyance of personal property, and is subject to a stamp duty of five cents only."

Instruments not to be Recorded till Stamped.

SEC. 152. *And be it further enacted,* [That it shall not be lawful to record any instrument, document, or paper required by law to be stamped unless a stamp or stamps of the proper amount shall have been affixed and canceled in the manner required by law, and the record of any such instrument upon which the proper stamp or stamps aforesaid shall not have been affixed and canceled as aforesaid shall be utterly void, and shall not be used in evidence.]

No Instrument Invalid if proper amount of Stamps are Affixed.

SEC. 153. *And be it further enacted,* That no instrument, document, writing, or paper of any description, required by law to be stamped, shall be deemed or held invalid and of no effect for the want of the particular kind or description of stamp designated for and denoting the duty charged on any such instrument, document, writing, or paper, provided a legal stamp or stamps, denoting a duty of equal amount, shall have been duly affixed and used thereon: *Provided,* That the provisions of this section shall not apply to any stamp appropriated to denote the duty charged on proprietary articles, or articles enumerated in Schedule C.

Certain Papers &c., of Municipal Corporations exempt from Stamp Tax.

SEC. 154. *And be it further enacted,* [That all official instruments, documents, and papers issued by the officers of the United States Government, or by the officers of any State, county, town, or other munic-

---

25. An "original summons" requires a stamp. If more than one person is named defendant and more than one summons is issued, it would seem that each should be stamped.

26. It is a general principle that instruments are to be stamped according to their legal effect.

27. Marriage certificates should be stamped; marriage licenses are exempt.

28. Letters of attorney made in the United States and sent to an attorney abroad, where the powers are to be executed, do not require a stamp.

29. In fire and marine insurance policies the stamp duty is determined by the amount of the *premium* paid. This is sometimes in *money*, sometimes by *note*. If the latter and for a fixed sum, it must be regarded as a part of the premium, whether on demand or "on time," or even if it is understood that its payment is not to be called on, except in case of loss. If the note is merely liable to assessment, or security for such assessment, it should not be recorded as "premium."

30. The stamp duty upon "letters of administration" must be appropriate to the value of the estate to be administered upon. If the administrator has no control over the real estate (as he generally has not, except for the payment of debts or legacies), the stamp duty is regulated by the value of the personal estate.

31. Letters of administration to procure prize money, back pay, pensions, &c., are subject to stamp duty. They are not within the exemption claim of Section 160, Act of June 30, 1864.

32. Where receipts given to parties who deposit valuables with banks for safe-keeping contain guaranties for the value of the same, such guaranties are held to be subject to stamp duty, as agreements or contracts.

ipal corporation, shall be, and hereby are, exempt from taxation: *Provided,* That it is the intent hereby to exempt from liability to taxation such State, county, or other municipal corporation, in the exercise only of functions strictly belonging to them in their ordinary governmental and municipal capacity.]

Penalties for Forging and Counterfeiting Stamps.

SEC. 155. *And be it further enacted,* [That if any person shall forge or counterfeit, or cause or procure to be forged or counterfeited, any stamp, die, plate, or other instrument, or any part of any stamp, die, plate, or other instrument, which shall have been provided, or may hereafter be provided, made, or used in pursuance of this act, or shall forge, counterfeit, or resemble, or cause or procure to be forged, counterfeited, or resembled, the impression, or any part of the impression, of any such stamp, die, plate, or other instrument, as aforesaid, upon any vellum, parchment, or paper, or shall stamp or mark, or cause or procure to be stamped or marked, any vellum, parchment, or paper, with any such forged or counterfeited stamp, die, plate, or other instrument, or part of any stamp, die, plate or other instrument, as aforesaid, with intent to defraud the United States of any of the taxes hereby imposed, or any part thereof, or if any person shall utter, or sell, or expose to sale, any vellum, parchment, paper, article, or thing, having thereupon the impression of any such counterfeited stamp, die, plate, or other instrument, or any part of any stamp, die, plate, or other instrument, or any such forged, counterfeited, or resembled impression, or part of impression, as aforesaid, knowing the same to be forged, counterfeited, or resembled; or if any person shall knowingly use or permit the use of any stamp, die, plate, or other instrument, which shall have been so provided, made, or used, as aforesaid, with intent to defraud the United States; or if any person shall fraudulently cut, tear, or remove, or cause or procure to be cut, torn, or removed, the impression of any stamp, die, plate, or other instrument, which shall have been provided, made, or used, in pursuance of this act, from any vellum, parchment, or paper, or any instrument or writing charged or chargeable with any of the taxes imposed by law; or if any person shall fraudulently use, join, fix, or place, or cause to be used, joined, fixed, or placed to, with, or upon any vellum, parchment, paper, or any instrument or writing charged or chargeable with any of the taxes hereby imposed, any adhesive stamp, or the impression of any stamps die, plate, or other instrument, which shall have been provided, made, or used in pursuance of law, and which shall have been cut, torn, or removed from any other vellum, parchment, or paper, or any instrument or writing charged or chargeable with any of the taxes imposed by law; or if any person shall willfully remove or cause to be removed, alter or cause to be altered, the canceling or defacing marks on any adhesive stamp, with intent to use the same or cause the use of the same after it shall have been once used, or shall knowingly or willfully sell or buy such washed or restored stamps, or offer the same for sale, or give any person for, or expose the same to use, or knowingly use the same, or prepare the same with intent for the further use thereof, or if any person shall knowingly and without lawful excuse (the proof whereof shall lie on the person accused) have in his possession any washed, restored, or altered stamps, which have been removed from any vellum, parchment, paper, instrument, or writing, then, and in every such case, every person so offending, and every person knowingly and willfully aiding, abetting, or assisting in committing any such offence as aforesaid, shall, on conviction thereof, forfeit the said counterfeit stamps and the articles upon which they are placed, and be punished by fine not exceeding one thousand dollars, or by imprisonment and confinement to hard labor not exceeding five years, or both, at the discretion of the court.]

Mode of Cancellation of Stamps. Penalties for failure to Cancel, &c. Penalty for Forging, &c., Private Stamps.

SEC. 156. *And be it further enacted*, That in any and all cases where an adhesive stamp shall be used for denoting any duty imposed by this act, except as hereinafter provided, the person using or affixing the same shall write thereupon the initials of his name and the date upon which the same shall be attached or used, so that the same may not again be used. And if any person shall fraudulently make use of an adhesive stamp to denote any duty imposed by this act without so effectually canceling and obliterating such stamp, except as before mentioned, he, she, or they shall forfeit the sum of fifty dollars: *Provided*, That any proprietor or proprietors of proprietary articles, or articles subject to stamp duty under Schedule C of this act, shall have the privilege of furnishing, without expense to the United States, in suitable form, to be approved by the Commissioner of Internal Revenue, his or their own dies or designs for stamps to be used thereon, to be made under the direction and to be retained in the possession of the Commissioner of Internal Revenue for his or their separate use, which shall not be duplicated to any other person. That in all cases where such stamp is used, instead of his or their writing the date thereon, the said stamp shall be so affixed on the box, bottle, or package, that in opening the same, or using the contents thereof, the said stamp shall be effectually destroyed; and in default thereof, shall be liable to the same penalty imposed for neglect to affix said stamp as hereinbefore prescribed in this act. Any person who shall fraudulently obtain or use any of the aforesaid stamps or designs therefor, and any person forging, or counterfeiting, or causing or procuring the forging or counterfeiting any representation, likeness, similitude, or colorable imitation of the said last mentioned stamp, or any engraver or printer who shall sell or give away said stamps, or selling the same, or, being a merchant, broker, peddler, or person dealing, in whole or in part, in similar goods, wares, merchandise, manufactures, preparations, or articles, or those designed for similar objects or purposes, shall have knowingly or fraudulently in his, her, or their possession any such forged, counterfeited likeness, similitude, or colorable imitation of the said last-mentioned stamp, shall be deemed guilty of a felony, and, upon conviction thereof, shall be subject to all the penalties, fines, and forfeitures prescribed in the preceding section of this act.

Commissioner may Prescribe other Modes of Cancellation of Stamps.

SEC. 157. *And be it further enacted,* That the Commissioner of Internal Revenue be, and he is hereby, authorized to prescribe such method for the cancellation of stamps, as substitute for, or in addition to the method now prescribed by law, as he may deem expedient and effectual. And he is further authorized in his discretion to make the application of such method imperative upon the manufacturers of proprietary articles, or articles included in Schedule C, and upon stamps of a nominal value exceeding twenty-five cents each.

Penalties for Fraud and Evasion of the Law on this Subject. Mode of Affixing Stamps to lost Instruments, &c. How Instruments inadequately stamped may be used in Evidence.

SEC. 158. *And be it further enacted,* [That any person or persons who shall make, sign, or issue, or who shall cause to be made, signed, or issued, any instrument, document, or paper of any kind or description whatsoever, or shall accept, negotiate, or pay, or cause to be accepted, negotiated, or paid, any bill of exchange, draft, or order or promissory note for the payment of money, without the same being duly stamped, or having thereupon an adhesive stamp for denoting the tax chargeable thereon, and canceled in the manner required by law, with intent to evade the provisions of this act, shall, for every such offence, forfeit the sum of fifty dollars, and such instrument, document, or paper, bill, draft, order, or note, not being stamped according to law, shall be deemed invalid and of no effect: *Provided,* That the title of a purchaser of land by deed duly stamped shall not be defeated or affected by the want of a proper stamp on any deed conveying said land by any person from, through, or under whom his grantor claims or holds title: *And provided further,* That hereafter, in all cases where the party has not affixed to any instrument the stamp required by law thereon, at the time of making or issuing the said instrument, and he or they, or any party having an interest therein, shall be subsequently desirous of affixing such stamp to said instrument, or if said instrument be lost, to a copy thereof, he or they shall appear before the collector of the revenue of the proper district, who shall, upon the payment of the price of the proper stamp required by law, and of a penalty of fifty dollars, and where the whole amount of the tax denoted by the stamp required shall exceed the sum of fifty dollars, on payment also of interest, at the rate of six per centum on said tax from the day on which such stamp ought to have been affixed, affix the proper stamp to such instrument, or copy, and note upon the margin thereof the date of his so doing, and the fact that such penalty has been paid; and the same shall thereupon be deemed and held to be as valid, to all intents and purposes, as if stamped when made or issued: *And provided further*, That where it shall appear to said collector, upon oath or otherwise, to his satisfaction, that any such instrument has not been duly stamped at the time of making or issuing the same, by reason of accident, mistake, inadvertence, or urgent necessity, and without any willful design to defraud the United States of the stamp, or to evade or delay the payment thereof, then and in such case, if such instrument, or if the original be lost, a copy thereof duly certified by the officer having charge of any records in which such original is required to be recorded, or otherwise duly proven to the satisfaction of the collector, shall, within twelve calendar months after the first day of August, 1866, or within twelve calendar months after the making or issuing thereof, be brought to the said collector of revenue to be stamped, and the stamp tax chargeable thereon shall be paid, it shall be lawful for the said collector to remit the penalty aforesaid, and to cause such instrument to be duly stamped; and when the original instrument, or a certified or duly proved copy thereof, as aforesaid, duly stamped so as to entitle the same to be recorded, shall be presented to the clerk, register, recorder, or other officer having charge of the original record, it shall be lawful for such officer, upon the payment of the fee legally chargeable for the recording thereof, to make a new record thereof, or to note upon the original record the fact that the error or omission in the stamping of said original instrument has been corrected, pursuant to law, and the original instrument, or such certified copy or the record thereof, may be used in all courts and places in the same manner and with like effect as if the instrument had been originally stamped: *And provided further*, That in all cases where the party has not affixed the stamp required by law upon any instrument made, signed, or issued, at a time when, and at a place where, no collection district was established, it shall be lawful for him, or them, or any party having an interest therein, to affix the proper stamp thereto, or if the original be lost, to a copy thereof, and the instrument or copy to which the proper stamp has been thus affixed prior to the first day of January, 1867, and the record thereof, shall be as valid, to all intents and purposes, as if stamped by the collector in the manner hereinbefore provided.]

Stamps on Foreign Bills of Exchange.

SEC. 159. *And be it further enacted*, That the acceptor or acceptors of any bill of exchange or order for the payment of any sum of money drawn, or purporting to be drawn, in any foreign country, but payable in the United States, shall, before paying or accepting the same, place thereupon a stamp, indicating the duty upon the same, as the law requires for inland bills of exchange, or promissory notes, and no bill of exchange shall be paid or negotiated without such stamp; and if any person shall pay or negotiate, or offer in payment, or receive or take in payment, any such draft or order, the person or persons so offending shall forfeit the sum of two hundred dollars.

Certain Instruments, Papers, &c., exempt from the Stamp Tax.

SEC. 160. *And be it further enacted*, That no stamp duty shall be required on powers of attorney or any other paper relating to applications for bounties, arrearages of pay, or pensions, or to the receipt thereof from time to time, or upon tickets or contracts of insurance when limited to accidental injury to persons, nor on certificates of the measurement or weight of animals, wood, coal, or hay; nor on deposit notes to mutual insurance companies for insurance upon which policies subject to stamp duties have been or are to be issued; nor on any certificate of the record of a deed or other instrument in writing, or of the acknowledgment or proof thereof by attesting witnesses; nor to any endorsement of a negotiable instrument or on any warrant of attorney, accompanying a bond or note, when such bond or note shall have affixed thereto the stamp or stamps denoting the duty required; and whenever any bond or note shall be secured by a mortgage, but one stamp shall be required to be placed on such papers: *Provided*, That the stamp duty placed thereon shall be the highest rate required for said instruments, or either of them.*

---

* In relation to stamping instruments issued without stamps, or insufficiently stamped, see Appendix, Circular No. 43. (III. Int. Rev. Rec., p. 117.)

"Deeds to a trustee for wife, without consideration, are not liable to stamp duty." (Ruling April 24, 1866. III. Int. Rev. Rec., p. 151. See successions.)

For stamps on insurance receipts, (*vide* Int. Rev. Rec., Vol. III. p. 156.)

It will be seen that by the law as herein amended, that when it shall appear that the omission to affix the proper stamp was not with the intent to evade the law, the penalties imposed shall not be incurred. This follows the English statute, and is a wise provision. (See Edwards on Stamp Act, *passim.*)

The stamping of receipts for payment of money or delivery of goods, which have long been in force, seem to be in our large cities and elsewhere willfully evaded. (See Int. Rev. Rec., Vol. III., p. 169.)

Orders to pay dividends are not powers of attorney, but like draft at sight are subject to the stamp of two cents. (Ex-parte Swan. 1 Deacon, 751.)

It is a question whether a stamp is required on an order or draft when no definite sum is mentioned. (Jones *vs.* Sampson, 2 B and C, 318. Edwards on stamp acts, 150.)

An instrument in which several persons bona fide join, having relation to one honest subject matter, whenever each party possesses a several interest of his own, but one in common with the others, will require a suitable stamp, having reference to the common purpose. (Croft *vs.* Tidbury, 14 C. B., 304. Edwards on Stamp Acts, 27.)

For decisions as to additions and alterations on instruments which do not call for a new stamp; and invalidity when alterations and additions are made, (see Edwards on Stamp Act, Chapter II., *passim.*)

For a variety of decisions in relation to stamps on particular instruments, agreements, deeds, mortgages, bills of exchange and promissory notes, policies, of insurance, charter party, bills of lading, certificates, protests, probate of wills and letters of administration, and proprietary articles, also in relation to pleading, evidence and the punishments and penalties in connection with stamps. (Consult "Edwards on the Stamp Act," New York, 1863, an excellent digest of English decisions.)

The Sale of Stamps. Commission on Sales. Commission on Private Stamps. Allowance for Stamps spoiled. Supply of Stamps to Match Makers on Credit. Provisions therefor.

SEC. 161. *And be it further enacted*, That the Commissioner of Internal Revenue be and is hereby, authorized to sell to and supply collectors, deputy collectors, postmasters, stationers, or any other persons, at his discretion, with adhesive stamps, or stamped paper, vellum, or parchment, as herein provided for, in amounts of not less than fifty dollars, upon the payment, at the time of delivery, of the amount of duties said stamps, stamped paper, vellum, or parchment, so sold or supplied, represent, and may allow, upon the aggregate amount of such stamps, as aforesaid, the sum of not exceeding five per centum as commission to the collectors, postmasters, stationers, or other purchasers; but the cost of any paper, vellum, or parchment shall be paid by the purchaser of such stamped paper, vellum, or parchment, as aforesaid: *Provided*, That any proprietor or proprietors of articles named in Schedule C, who shall furnish his or their own die or design for stamps, to be used especially for his or their own proprietary articles, shall be allowed the following commission, namely: On amounts purchased at one time of not less than fifty nor more than five hundred dollars, five per centum; on amounts over five hundred dollars, ten per centum. The Commissioner of Internal Revenue may from time to time make regulations, upon proper evidence of the facts, for the allowance of such of the stamps issued under the provisions of this act as may have been spoiled, destroyed, or rendered useless or unfit for the purpose intended, or for which the owner may have no use, or which through mistake may have been improperly or unnecessarily used, or where the rates or duties represented thereby have been paid in error, or remitted; and such allowance shall be made either by giving other stamps in lieu of the stamps so allowed for, or by repaying the amount or value, after deducting therefrom, in case of repayment, the sum of five per centum to the owner thereof; but no allowance shall be made in any case until the stamps so spoiled or rendered useless shall have been returned to the Commissioner of Internal Revenue, or until satisfactory proof has been made showing the reason why said stamps cannot be so returned: *Provided*, That the Commissioner of Internal Revenue may, from time to time, furnish, supply, and deliver to any manufacturer of friction or other matches, cigar lights or wax tapers, a suitable quantity of adhesive or other stamps, such as may be prescribed for use in such cases, without prepayment therefor, on a credit not exceeding sixty days, requiring, in advance, such security as he may judge necessary to secure payment therefor to the Treasurer of the United States, within the time prescribed for such payment. And upon all bonds or other securities taken by said Commissioner, under the provisions of this act, suits may be maintained by said Treasurer in the circuit or district court of the United States, in the several districts where any of the persons giving said bonds or other securities reside or may be found, in any appropriate form of action.

Commissioner to Stamp certain Instruments exempt, or Subject to certain Tax.

SEC. 162. *And be it further enacted,* That it shall be lawful for any person to present to the collector of the district, subject to the rules and regulations of the Commissioner of Internal Revenue, any instrument not previously issued or used, and require his opinion whether or not the same is chargeable with any stamp duty; and if the said collector shall be of opinion that such instrument is chargeable with any stamp duty, he shall upon the payment therefor, affix and cancel the proper stamp; and if of the opinion that such instrument is not chargeable with any stamp duty, or is chargeable only with the duty by him designated, he is hereby required to impress thereon a particular stamp, to be provided for that purpose, with such words or device thereon as he shall judge proper, which shall denote that such instrument is not chargeable with any stamp duty, or is chargeable only with the duty denoted by the stamp affixed; and every such instrument upon which the said stamp shall be impressed shall be deemed to be not chargeable, or to be chargeable only with the duty denoted by the stamp so affixed, and shall be received in evidence in all courts of law or equity, notwithstanding any objections made to the same by reason of it being unstamped, or of it being insufficiently stamped.

Legal Stamps to be Affixed before Instruments, &c., are used or read in Evidence.

SEC. 163. *And be it further enacted,* [That hereafter no deed, instrument, document, writing, or paper, required by law to be stamped, which has been signed or issued without being duly stamped, or with a deficient stamp, nor any copy thereof, shall be recorded, or admitted, or used as evidence in any court until a legal stamp or stamps, denoting the amount of tax, shall have been affixed thereto as prescribed by law: *Provided,* That any power of attorney, conveyance, or document of any kind, made or purporting to be made in any foreign country to be used in the United States, shall pay the same tax as is required by law on similar instruments or documents when made or issued in the United States; and the party to whom the same is issued, or by whom it is to be used, shall, before using the same, affix thereon the stamp or stamps indicating the tax required.]

Provisions of the Act applicable to Articles in Schedule "C."

SEC. 164. *And be it further enacted,* That all the provisions of this act relating to dies, stamps, adhesive stamps, and stamp duties shall extend to and include (except where manifestly impracticable) all the articles or objects enumerated in schedule marked C, subject to stamp duties, and apply to the provisions in relation thereto.

Penalties for selling Articles in Schedule "C" without proper Stamps.

SEC. 165. *And be it further enacted,* [That if any person, firm, company, or corporation shall make, prepare, and sell, or remove for consumption or sale, drugs, medicines, preparations, compositions, articles, or things, including perfumery, cosmetics, lucifer or friction matches, cigar lights, or wax tapers, and playing cards, and also including prepared mustards, preserved meats, fish, shell-fish, fruits, vegetables, sauces, syrups, jams, and jellies, when packed or sealed in cans, bottles, or other single packages, whether of domestic manufacture or imported, upon which a duty or tax is imposed by law, as enumerated and mentioned in schedule C, without affixing thereto an adhesive stamp or label denoting the duty before mentioned, he or they shall incur a penalty of fifty dollars for every omission to affix such stamp.]

Penalty for Removing Stamps from Articles in Schedule "C."

SEC. 166. *And be it further enacted,* That every manufacturer or maker of any of the articles for sale mentioned in Schedule C, after the same shall have been so made, and the particulars hereinbefore required as to stamps have been complied with, who shall take off, remove, or detach, or cause, or permit, or suffer to be taken off, or removed, or detached, any stamp, or who shall use any stamp, or any wrapper or cover to which any stamp is affixed, to cover any other article or commodity than that originally contained in such wrapper or cover, with such stamp when first used, with the intent to evade the stamp duties, shall for every such article, respectively, in respect of which any such offense shall be committed, be subject to a penalty of fifty dollars, to be recovered together with the costs thereupon accruing; and every such article or commodity as aforesaid shall also be forfeited.

Forfeiture of Articles upon Attempt to evade Tax.

SEC. 167. *And be it further enacted,* That on and after the passage of this act every maker or manufacturer of any of the articles or commodities mentioned in Schedule C, as aforesaid, who shall sell, expose for sale, send out, remove, or deliver any article or commodity, manufactured as aforesaid, before the duty thereon shall have been fully paid, by affixing thereon the proper stamp, as provided by law, or who shall hide, or conceal, or cause to be hidden or concealed, or who shall remove or convey away, or deposit, or cause to be removed or conveyed away from or deposited in any place, any such article or commodity, to evade the duty chargeable thereon, or any part thereof, shall be subject to a penalty of one hundred dollars, together with the forfeiture of any such article or commodity.

Certain Articles in Schedule "C" may be Manufactured in Bonded Warehouses, and may be removed. Materials used may be removed from one Warehouse to another, &c., &c.

SEC. 168. *And be it further enacted,* That all medicines, preparations, compositions, perfumery, cosmetics, cordials, and other liquors manufactured wholly or in part of domestic spirits, intended for exportation, as provided for by law, in order to be manufactured and sold or removed, without being charged with duty and without having a stamp affixed thereto, shall, under such rules and regulations as the Secretary of the Treasury may prescribe, be made and manufactured in warehouses similarly constructed to those known and designated in treasury regulations as bonded warehouses, class two: *Provided*, That such manufacturer shall first give satisfactory bonds to the collector of internal revenue for the faithful observance of all the provisions of law and the rules and regulations as aforesaid, in amount not less than half of that required by the regulations of the Secretary of the Treasury from persons allowed bonded warehouses. Such goods, when manufactured in such warehouses, may be removed for exportation, under the direction of the proper officer having charge thereof, who shall be designated by the Secretary of the Treasury, without being charged with duty, and without having a stamp affixed thereto. Any manufacturer of the articles aforesaid, or of any of them, having such bonded warehouse, as aforesaid, shall be at liberty, under such rules and regulations as the Secretary of the Treasury may prescribe, to convey therein any materials to be used in such manufacture which are allowed by the provisions of law to be exported free from tax or duty, as well as the necessary materials, implements, packages, vessels, brands, and labels for the preparation, putting up, and export of the said manufactured articles; and every article so used shall be exempted from the payment of stamp and excise duty by such manufacturer. Articles and materials so to be used may be transferred from any bonded warehouse in which the same may be, under such regulations as the Secretary of the Treasury may prescribe, into any bonded warehouse in which such manufacture may be conducted, and may be used in such manufacture, and when so used shall be exempt from stamp and excise duty; and the receipt of the officer in charge, as aforesaid, shall be received as a voucher for the manufacture of such articles. Any materials imported into the United States may, under such rules as the Secretary of the Treasury may prescribe, and under the direction of the proper officer, be removed in original packages from on shipboard, or from the bonded warehouse in which the same may be, into the bonded warehouse in which such manufacture may be carried on, for the purpose of being used in such manufacture, without payment of duties thereon, and may there be used in such manufacture. No article so removed, nor any article manufactured in said bonded warehouse, shall be taken therefrom except for exportation, under the direction of the proper officer having charge thereof, as aforesaid, whose certificate, describing the articles by their marks, or otherwise, the quantity, the date of importation, and name of vessel, with such additional particulars as may from time to time be required, shall be received by the collector of customs in cancellation of the bonds, or return of the amount of foreign import duties. All labor performed and services rendered under these regulations shall be under the supervision of an officer of the customs, and at the expense of the manufacturer.

Matches may be Warehoused and Removed without payment of Tax. No Drawback Allowed.

(SEC. 11. Act of March 3, 1865.) *And be it further enacted*, That lucifer or friction matches, and cigar lights and wax tapers, may be transferred, without payment of duty, directly from the place of manufacture to a bonded warehouse established in conformity with law and treasury regulations, and upon the execution of such transportation bonds or other security as the Secretary of the Treasury may prescribe, said bonds to be taken by the collector in the district from which such removal is made, and may be withdrawn therefrom for consumption after affixing the stamps thereto, as provided by the act to which this act is an amendment, or may be removed therefrom for export to a foreign country without payment of duty or affixing stamps thereto, in conformity with the provisions of the act aforesaid, relating to the removal of distilled spirits, all the rules and regulations and conditions of which, as far as applicable, shall apply to lucifer or friction matches, cigar lights, and wax tapers in bonded warehouse. And no drawback shall in any case be allowed upon any lucifer or friction matches, cigar lights, or wax tapers, upon which any excise duty has been paid, or stamps affixed, either before or after they have been placed in bonded warehouse.

Persons Exposing for sale Articles in Schedule "C" to be deemed Manufacturers. Sale of same in Original Packages, &c.

SEC. 169. *And be it further enacted*, [That any person who shall offer or expose for sale any of the articles named in Schedule C, or in any amendments thereto, whether the articles so offered or exposed are imported or are of foreign or domestic manufacture, shall be deemed the manufacturer thereof, and subject to all the duties, liabilities, and penalties imposed by law in regard to the sale of domestic articles without the use of the proper stamp or stamps denoting the tax paid thereon, and all such articles imported, or of foreign manufacture, shall, in addition to the import duties imposed on the same, be subject to the stamp tax, respectively, prescribed in Schedule C, as aforesaid. *Provided*, That when such imported articles, except playing cards, lucifer or friction matches, cigar lights, and wax tapers shall be sold in the original and unbroken package, in which the bottles or other enclosures were packed by the manufacturer, the person so selling such articles shall not be subject to any penalty on account of the proper stamp.]

Commissioner may furnish Stamps to certain Officers for sale.

SEC. 170. *And be it further enacted*, That in any collection district where, in the judgment of the Commissioner of Internal Revenue, the facilities for the procurement and distribution of stamped vellum, parchment, or paper, and adhesive stamps, are or shall be insufficient, the Commissioner, as aforesaid, is authorized to furnish, supply, and deliver to the collector and to the assessor of any such district, and to any assistant treasurer of the United States, or designated depositary thereof, or any postmaster, a suitable quantity or amount of stamped vellum, parchment, or paper, and adhesive stamps, without pre-payment therefor, and shall allow the highest rate of commissions allowed by law to any other parties purchasing the same, and may in advance require of any such collector, assessor, assistant treasurer of the United States, or postmaster, a bond, with sufficient sureties, to an amount equal to the value of any stamped vellum, parchment, or paper, and adhesive stamps which may be placed in his hands and remain unaccounted for, conditioned for the faithful return, whenever so required, of all quantities or amounts undisposed of, and for the payment, monthly, of all quantities or amounts, sold or not, remaining on hand. And it shall be the duty of such collector to supply his deputies with, or sell to other parties within his district who may make application therefor, stamped vellum, parchment or paper, and adhesive stamps, upon the same terms allowed by law, or under the regulations of the Commissioner of Internal Revenue, who is hereby authorized to make such other regulations, not inconsistent herewith, for the security of the United States and the better accommodation of the public, in relation to the matters hereinbefore mentioned, as he may judge necessary and expedient. And the Secretary of the Treasury may from time to time make such regulations as he may find necessary to insure the safe-keeping or prevent the illegal use of all such stamped vellum, parchment, paper, and adhesive stamps.*

SCHEDULE B.

STAMP DUTIES.

	Duty.
Agreement or contract, other than [domestic and inland bills of lading and] those specified in this schedule; any appraisement of value or damage, or for any other purpose; for every sheet or piece of paper upon which either of the same shall be written, five cents, . .	$0 05
Provided, That if more than one appraisement, agreement, or contract shall be written upon one sheet or piece of paper, five cents for each and every additional appraisement, agreement, or contract.	
Bank check, draft, or order for the payment of any sum of money whatsoever, drawn upon any bank, banker, or trust company, or for any sum exceeding ten dollars drawn upon any other person or persons, companies, or corporations, at sight or on demand, two cents, ...	2
Bill of exchange, (inland,) draft, or order for the payment of any sum of money not exceeding one hundred dollars, otherwise than at sight or on demand, or any promissory note, (except bank notes issued for circulation, and checks made and intended to be forthwith presented, and which shall be presented to a bank or banker for payment,) or any memorandum, check, receipt, or other written or printed evidence of an amount of money to be paid on demand, or at a time designated, for a sum not exceeding one hundred dollars, five cents, ...	5
And for every additional hundred dollars, or fractional part thereof in excess of one hundred dollars, five cents, ...	5

*The Commissioner has lately limited the number of such offices so furnished.

	Duty
BILL OF EXCHANGE, (foreign,) or letter of credit, drawn in but payable out of the United States, if drawn singly, or otherwise than in a set of three or more, according to the custom of merchants and bankers, shall pay the same rates of duty as inland bills of exchange or promissory notes.	
If drawn in sets of three or more: For every bill of each set, where the sum made payable shall not exceed one hundred dollars, or the equivalent thereof, in any foreign currency in which such bills may be expressed, according to the standard of value fixed by the United States, two cents,	$0 02
And for every additional hundred dollars or fractional part thereof in excess of one hundred dollars, two cents,	2
BILL OF LADING or receipt, (other than charter-party,) for any goods, merchandise, or effects, to be exported from a port or place in the United States to any foreign port or place, ten cents,	10
BILL OF SALE by which any ship or vessel, or any part thereof, shall be conveyed to or vested in any other person or persons when the consideration shall not exceed five hundred dollars, fifty cents,	50
Exceeding five hundred and not exceeding one thousand dollars, one dollar,	1 00
Exceeding one thousand dollars for every additional amount of five hundred dollars, or fractional part thereof, fifty cents,	50
BOND.—For indemnifying any person for the payment of any sum of money, where the money ultimately recoverable thereupon is one thousand dollars or less, fifty cents,	50
Where the money ultimately recoverable thereupon exceeds one thousand dollars, for every additional one thousand dollars or fractional part thereof in excess of one thousand dollars, fifty cents,	50
BOND for the due execution or performance of the duties of any office, one dollar,	1 00
BOND of any description, other than such as may be required in legal proceedings, or used in connexion with mortgage deeds, and not otherwise charged in this schedule, twenty-five cents,	25
CERTIFICATE of stock in any incorporated company, twenty-five cents,	25
CERTIFICATE of profits, or any certificate or memorandum showing an interest in the property or accumulations of any incorporated company, if for a sum not less than ten dollars and not exceeding fifty dollars, ten cents,	10
Exceeding fifty dollars and not exceeding one thousand dollars, twenty-five cents,	25
Exceeding one thousand dollars, for every additional one thousand dollars, or fractional part thereof, twenty-five cents,	25
CERTIFICATE.—Any certificate of damage, or otherwise, and all other certificates or documents issued by any port warden, marine surveyor, or other person acting as such, twenty-five cents,	25
CERTIFICATE of deposit of any sum of money in any bank or trust company, or with any banker or person acting as such—	
If for a sum not exceeding one hundred dollars, two cents,	2
For a sum exceeding one hundred dollars, five cents,	5
*CERTIFICATE of any other description than those specified, five cents,	5
CHARTER-PARTY.—Contract or agreement for the charter of any ship, or vessel, or steamer, or any letter, memorandum, or other writing between the captain, master, or owner, or person acting as agent	

*STAMPS.—1. The statute of United States of 1862, Chapter 119, Section 110, does not require a stamp to be affixed to the certificate of a magistrate attesting his record of the conviction in a criminal case, which is taken to the Superior Court on appeal. (Commonwealth *vs.* Hardiman. 9 Allen, 487.)

2. If the original writ in an action is duly stamped, the magistrate's certificate upon depositions taken to be used therein, need not be stamped. (Cardell *vs.* Bridge, 9 Allen, 355.)

Duty.

of any ship or vessel, or steamer, and any other person or persons for or relating to the charter of such ship or vessel, or steamer, or any renewal or transfer thereof, if the registered tonnage of such ship or vessel, or steamer, does not exceed one hundred and fifty tons, one dollar, ... $1 00

Exceeding one hundred and fifty tons and not exceeding three hundred tons, three dollars, ... 3 00

Exceeding three hundred tons and not exceeding six hundred tons, five dollars, ... 5 00

Exceeding six hundred tons, ten dollars, ... 10 00

CONTRACT.—Broker's note, or memorandum, of sale of any goods or merchandise, exchange, real estate, or property of any kind or description, issued by brokers or persons acting as such, for each note or memorandum of sale, ten cents, ... 10

Bills or memorandum of the sale or contract for the sale of stocks, bonds, gold or silver bullion, coin, promissory notes, or other securities, shall pay a stamp tax at the rate provided in section 99.

CONVEYANCE.—Deed, instrument, or writing, whereby any lands, tenements, or other realty sold shall be granted, assigned, transferred, or otherwise conveyed to, or vested in, the purchaser or purchasers, or any other person or persons by his, her, or their direction, when the consideration or value does not exceed five hundred dollars, fifty cents, ... 50

When the consideration exceeds five hundred dollars and does not exceed one thousand dollars, one dollar, ... 1 00

And for every additional five hundred dollars, or fractional part thereof, in excess of one thousand dollars, fifty cents, ... 50

ENTRY of any goods, wares or merchandise at any custom house, either for consumption or warehousing, not exceeding one hundred dollars in value, twenty-five cents, ... 25

Exceeding one hundred dollars and not exceeding five hundred dollars in value, fifty cents, ... 50

Exceeding five hundred dollars in value, one dollar, ... 1 00

ENTRY for the withdrawal of any goods or merchandise from bonded warehouse, fifty cents, ... 50

INSURANCE, (LIFE.)—Policy of insurance, or other instrument, by whatever name the same shall be called, whereby any insurance shall be made upon any life or lives—

When the amount insured shall not exceed one thousand dollars, twenty-five cents, ... 25

Exceeding one thousand dollars and not exceeding five thousand dollars, fifty cents, ... 50

Exceeding five thousand dollars, one dollar, ... 1 00

INSURANCE, (MARINE, INLAND, AND FIRE,)—Each policy of insurance or other instrument, by whatever name the same shall be called, by which insurance shall be made or renewed upon property of any description, whether against perils by the sea or by fire, or other peril of any kind, made by any insurance company, or its agents, or by any other company or person, the premium upon which does not exceed ten dollars, ten cents, ... 10

Exceeding ten and not exceeding fifty dollars, twenty-five cents, . 52

Exceeding fifty dollars, fifty cents, ... 50

LEASE, agreement, memorandum, or contract for the hire, use, or rent of any land, tenement, or portion thereof, where the rent or rental value is three hundred dollars per annum or less, fifty cents, . 50

Where the rent or rental value exceeds the sum of three hundred dollars per annum, for each additional two hundred dollars, or fractional part thereof in excess of three hundred dollars, fifty cents, 50

MANIFEST for custom house entry or clearance of the cargo of any ship, vessel, or steamer for a foreign port—

Duty.

If the registered tonnage of such ship, vessel, or steamer does not exceed three hundred tons, one dollar, ... $1 00

Exceeding three hundred tons and not exceeding six hundred tons, three dollars, ... 3 00

Exceeding six hundred tons, five dollars, ... 5 00

MORTGAGE of lands, estate, or property, real or personal, heritable or movable whatsoever, where the same shall be made as a security for the payment of any definite and certain sum of money lent at the time or previously due and owing or forborne to be paid, being payable; also any conveyance of any lands, estate, or property whatsoever, in trust, to be sold or otherwise converted into money, which shall be intended only as security, and shall be redeemable before the sale or other disposal thereof, either by express stipulation or otherwise; or any personal bond given as security for the payment of any definite or certain sum of money exceeding one hundred dollars, and not exceeding five hundred dollars, fifty cents, 50

Exceeding five hundred dollars and not exceeding one thousand dollars, one dollar, ... 1 00

And for every additional five hundred dollars, or fractional part thereof, in excess of one thousand dollars, fifty cents, ... 50

Upon every assignment or transfer of a mortgage the same stamp tax upon the amount remaining unpaid thereon, as is herein imposed upon a mortgage for the same amount.

Provided, That upon each and every assignment or transfer of a policy of insurance, or the renewal or continuance of any agreement, contract, or charter, by letter or otherwise, a stamp duty shall be required and paid equal to that imposed on the original instrument: *And provided further*, That upon each and every assignment of any lease a stamp duty shall be required and paid equal to that imposed on the original instrument, increased by a stamp duty on the consideration or value of the assignment equal to that imposed upon the conveyance of land for similar consideration or value.

PASSAGE TICKET, by any vessel from a port in the United States to a foreign port, not exceeding thirty-five dollars, fifty cents, . 50

Exceeding thirty-five dollars and not exceeding fifty dollars, one dollar, 1 00

And for every additional fifty dollars, or fractional part thereof, in excess of fifty dollars, one dollar, ... 1 00

POWER OF ATTORNEY for the sale or transfer of any stock, bonds, or scrip, or for the collection of any dividends or interest thereon, twenty-five cents, ... 25

POWER OF ATTORNEY OR PROXY for voting at any election for officers of any incorporated company or society, except religious, charitable, or literary societies, or public cemeteries, ten cents, . 10

POWER OF ATTORNEY to receive or collect rent, twenty-five cents, . 25

POWER OF ATTORNEY to sell and convey real estate, or to rent or lease the same, one dollar, ... 1 00

POWER OF ATTORNEY for any other purpose, fifty cents, . . . 50

PROBATE OF WILL, or letters of administration: Where the estate and effects for or in respect of which such probate or letters of administration applied for shall be sworn or declared not to exceed the value of two thousand dollars, one dollar, ... 1 00

Exceeding two thousand dollars, for every additional thousand dollars, or fractional part thereof, in excess of two thousand dollars, fifty cents, ... 50

PROTEST.—Upon the protest of every note, bill of exchange, acceptance, check or draft, or any marine protest, whether protested by a notary public or by any other officer who may be authorized by the law of any State or States to make such protest, twenty-five cents, ... 25

[Receipts for any sum of money, or for the payment of any debt, ex-

	Duty.
ceeding twenty dollars in amount, not being for the satisfaction of any mortgage or judgment or decree of any court, or by indorsement on any stamped obligation in acknowledgment of its fulfillment, for each receipt, two cents, ...	$0 02
Provided, That when more than one signature is affixed to the same paper, one or more stamps may be affixed thereto representing the whole amount of the stamp required for such signatures; and that the term money, as herein used, shall be held to include drafts and other instruments given for the payment of money.]	
LEGAL DOCUMENTS:	
Writ, or other original process by which any suit is commenced in any court of record, either of law or equity, fifty cents, ...	50
Where the amount claimed in a writ, issued by a court not of record, is one hundred dollars or over, fifty cents, ...	50
Upon every confession of judgment, or cognovit, for one hundred dollars or over, (except in those cases where the tax for the writ of a commencement of suit has been paid,) fifty cents, . . .	50
Writs or other process on appeals from justices' courts or other courts of inferior jurisdiction to a court of record, fifty cents, . .	50
Warrant of distress, when the amount of rent claimed does not exceed one hundred dollars, twenty-five cents, ...	25
When the amount claimed exceeds one hundred dollars, fifty cents,	50
Provided, That no writ, summons, or other process issued by and returnable to a justice of the peace, except as hereinbefore provided, or by any police or municipal court having no larger jurisdiction as to the amount of damages it may render than a justice of the peace in the same State, or issued in any criminal or other suits commenced by the United States or any State, shall be subject to the payment of stamp duties: *And provided further,* That the stamp duties imposed by the foregoing Schedule B on manifests, bills of lading, and passage tickets, shall not apply to steamboats or other vessels plying between ports of the United States and ports in British North America.	
Affidavits in suits or legal proceedings shall be exempt from stamp duty.	

SCHEDULE C.

MEDICINES OR PREPARATIONS.

For and upon every packet, box, bottle, pot, phial, or other enclosure, containing any pills, powders, tinctures, troches, lozenges, sirups, cordials, bitters, anodynes, tonics, plasters, liniments, salves, ointments, pastes, drops, waters, essences, spirits, oils, or other medicinal preparations or compositions whatsoever, made and sold, or removed for consumption and sale, by any person or persons whatever, wherein the person making or preparing the same has, or claims to have, any private formula or occult secret or art for the making or preparing the same, or has or claims to have any exclusive right or title to the making or preparing the same, or which are prepared, uttered, vended, or exposed for sale under any letters patent, or held out or recommended to the public by the makers, venders, or proprietors thereof as proprietary medicines, or as remedies or specifics for any disease, diseases or affections whatever, affecting the human or animal body, as follows: Where such packet, box, bottle, pot, phial, or other enclosure, with its contents, shall not exceed, at retail price, or value, the sum of twenty-five cents, one cent, ...	1
Where such packet, box, bottle, pot, phial, or other inclosure, with its contents, shall exceed the retail price or value of twenty-five cents, and not exceed the retail price or value of fifty cents, two cents,	2

	Duty.
Where such packet, box, bottle, pot, phial, or other enclosure, with its contents, shall exceed the retail price or value of fifty cents, and shall not exceed the retail price or value of seventy-five cents, three cents, ...	$0 03
Where such packet, box, bottle, pot, phial, or other inclosure, with its contents, shall exceed the retail price or value of seventy-five cents and shall not exceed the retail price or value of one dollar, four cents, ...	4
Where such packet, box, bottle, pot, phial, or other enclosure, with its contents, shall exceed the retail price or value of one dollar, for each and every fifty cents or fractional part thereof, over and above the one dollar, as before mentioned, an additional two cents, .	2

PERFUMERY, COSMETICS, PHOTOGRAPHS, MATCHES, AND CARDS.

For and upon every packet, box, bottle, pot, phial, or other inclosure, containing any essence, extract, toilet water, cosmetic hair oil, pomade, hair-dressing, hair-restorative, hair-dye, tooth-wash, dentifrice, tooth-paste, aromatic cachous, or any similar articles, by whatsoever name the same heretofore have been, now are, or may hereafter be called, known, or distinguished, used or applied, or to be used or applied as perfumes or applications to the hair, mouth, or skin, made, prepared, and sold, or removed for consumption and sale in the United States, where such packet, box, bottle, pot, phial, or other enclosure, with its contents, shall not exceed, at the retail price or value, the sum of twenty-five cents, one cent, . . .	1
Where such packet, box, bottle, pot, phial, or other enclosure, with its, contents, shall exceed the retail price or value of twenty-five cents, and shall not exceed the retail price or value of fifty cents, two cents, ...	2
Where such packet, box, bottle, pot, phial, or other enclosure, with its contents, shall exceed the retail price or value of fifty cents, and shall not exceed the retail price or value of seventy-five cents, three cents, ...	3
Where such packet, box, bottle, pot, phial, or other enclosure, with its contents, shall exceed the retail price or value of seventy-five cents, and shall not exceed the retail price or value of one dollar, four cents, ...	4
Where such packet, box, bottle, pot, phial, or other enclosure, with its contents, shall exceed the retail price or value of one dollar, for each and every fifty cents or fractional part thereof over and above the one dollar, as before mentioned, an additional two cents, .	2
*FRICTION MATCHES, or lucifer matches, or other articles made in part of wood, and used for like purposes, in parcels or packages containing one hundred matches or less, for each parcel or package, one cent, ...	1
When in parcels or packages coutaining more than one hundred and not more than two hundred matches, for each parcel or package, two cents, ...	2
And for every additional one hundred matches or fractional part thereof, one cent, ...	1
[For wax tapers, double the rates herein imposed upon friction or lucifer matches; on cigar-lights, made in part of wood, wax, glass, paper, or other materials, in parcels or packages containing twenty-five lights or less in each parcel or package, one cent, . . .	1

* MATCHES.—The stamp tax on matches will yield at the present rate of production the large amount of three and a half millions of revenue for the year. The receipts per annum from this source of revenue, are estimated to approximate hereafter twenty millions of dollars. (See Commissioner's Report, tit. "matches.")

	Duty.
When in parcels or packages containing more than twenty-five and not more than fifty lights, two cents, ...	$0 02
For every additional twenty-five lights or fractional part of that number, one cent additional,]	1
PLAYING CARDS.—For and upon every pack, not exceeding fifty-two cards in number, irrespective of price or value, five cents, . . .	5
For and upon every can, bottle, or other single package, containing meats, fish, shell-fish, fruits, vegetables, sauces, sirups, prepared mustard, jams or jellies contained therein and packed or sealed, made, prepared and sold, or offered for sale, or removed for consumption in the United States, on and after the first day of October, eighteen hundred and sixty-six, when such can, bottle, or other single package with its contents shall not exceed two pounds in weight, the sum of one cent, ...	1
When such can, bottle, or other single package, with its contents, shall exceed two pounds in weight, for every additional pound or fractional part thereof, one cent, ...	1

Allowance and Drawback on Manufactures Exported.

SEC. 171. *And be it further enacted*, That from and after the date on which this act takes effect there shall be an allowance or drawback on all articles on which any internal duty or tax shall have been paid, except raw or unmanufactured cotton, crude petroleum or rock oil, refined coal oil, naphtha, benzine or benzole, distilled spirits, manufactured tobacco, snuff, and cigars of all descriptions, bullion, quicksilver, lucifer or friction matches, cigar lights, and wax tapers, equal in amount to the duty or tax paid thereon, and no more, when exported, the evidence that any such duty or tax has been paid to be furnished to the satisfaction of the Commissioner of Internal Revenue by such person or persons as shall claim the allowance or drawback, and the amount to be ascertained under such regulations as shall, from time to time, be prescribed by the Commissioner of Internal Revenue, under the direction of the Secretary of the Treasury, and the same shall be paid by the warrant of the Secretary of the Treasury on the Treasurer of the United States, out of any money arising from internal duties not otherwise appropriated: *Provided*, That no allowance or drawback shall be made or had for any amount claimed or due less than ten dollars, anything in this act to the contrary notwithstanding: *And provided further*, That any certificate of drawback for goods exported, issued in pursuance of the provisions of law, may, under such regulations as may be prescribed by the Secretary of the Treasury, be received by the collector or his deputy in payment of duties under this act. And the Secretary of the Treasury may make such regulations with regard to the form of said certificates and the issuing thereof as, in his judgment, may be necessary: *And provided further*, That in computing the allowance or drawback upon articles manufactured exclusively of cotton when exported, there shall be allowed, in addition to the five per centum duty which shall have been paid on such articles, a drawback of two cents per pound upon such articles, in all cases where the duty imposed by law upon the cotton used in the manufacture thereof has been previously paid; the amount of said allowance to be ascertained in such a manner as may be prescribed by the Commissioner of Internal Revenue, under the direction of the Secretary of the Treasury: [*Provided also*, That no claim for drawback on any articles of merchandise exported prior to June 30, 1864, shall be allowed unless presented to the Commissioner of Internal Revenue within three months after this amendment takes effect.]*

Penalty for Fraudulent Claim to Drawback.

SEC. 172. *And be it further enacted*, That if any person or persons shall fraudulently claim or seek to obtain an allowance or drawback on goods, wares, or merchandise, on which no internal duty shall have been paid, or shall fraudulently claim any greater allowance or drawback than the duty actually paid, as aforesaid, such person or persons shall forfeit triple the amount wrongfully or fraudulently claimed or sought to be obtained, or the sum of five hundred dollars, at the election of the Secretary of the Treasury, to be recovered as in other cases of forfeiture provided for in the general provisions of this act.

Repeal of certain former Acts.

SEC. 173. *And be it further enacted*, That the following acts of Congress are hereby repealed, to wit: The act of July first, eighteen hundred and sixty-two, entitled "An act to provide internal revenue to support the government and to pay interest on the public debt," except the one hundred and fifteenth and one hundred and nineteenth sections thereof; and excepting, further, all provisions of said act which create the offices of Commissioner of Internal Revenue, assessor, assistant assessor, collector, deputy collector, and inspector, and provide for the appointment and qualification of said officers. Also, the act of July sixteenth, eighteen hundred and sixty-two, entitled "An act to impose an additional duty on sugars produced in the United States." Also, the act of December twenty-fifth, eighteen hundred and sixty-two, entitled "An act to amend an act entitled 'An act to provide internal revenue to support the government and to pay interest on the public debt,' approved July first, eighteen hundred and sixty-two." Also, the act of March third, eighteen hundred and sixty-three, entitled "An act to amend an act entitled 'An act to provide internal revenue to support the government and to pay interest on the public debt,' approved July first, eighteen hundred and sixty-two, and for other purposes," excepting the provisions of said act which create the offices of deputy commissioner and cashier of internal duties and revenue agents, and provide for the appointment and qualification of said officers. Also, the

---

*DRAWBACKS, CLAIMS FOR TAXES, ETC.

For a variety of Rulings and Circulars on this subject, see Decisions 54, 64, 67, (revoked April 1, 1863,); Circular No. 14, regulations as to exported goods; Decision August, 1864; III. Int. Rev. Rec., p. 31; Shipments to Canada, &c., *ibidem*, III., p. 39; Circular 21, revised, *ibidem*, p. 175; Regulations, *ibidem*, Vol. I., pp. 32, 51, 87, 189.

twenty-fourth and twenty-fifth sections of the act of July fourteenth, eighteen hundred and sixty-two, entitled "An act increasing temporarily the duties on imports, and for other purposes." Also, the second section of the act of March third, eighteen hundred and sixty-three, entitled "An act to prevent and punish frauds upon the revenue, to provide for the more certain and speedy collection of claims in favor of the United States, and for other purposes," so far as the same applies to officers of internal revenue. And, also, the act of March seventh, eighteen hundred and sixty-four, entitled "An act to increase the internal revenue, and for other purposes," together with all acts and parts of acts inconsistent herewith: *Provided*, That all the provisions of said acts shall be in force for levying and collecting all taxes, duties and licenses properly assessed or liable to be assessed, or accruing under the provisions of former acts, or drawbacks, the right to which has already accrued or which may hereafter accrue under said acts, and for maintaining and continuing liens, fines, penalties, and forfeitures incurred under and by virtue thereof. And for carrying out and completing all proceedings which have been already commenced or that may be commenced to enforce such fines, penalties, and forfeitures, or criminal proceedings under said acts, and for the punishment of crimes of which any party shall be or has been found guilty. *And provided further*, That no office created by the said acts and continued by this act shall be vacated by reason of any provisions herein contained, but the officers heretofore appointed shall continue to hold the said offices without reappointment: *And provided further*, That whenever the duty imposed by any existing law shall cease in consequence of any limitation therein contained before the respective provisions of this act shall take effect, the same duty shall be, and is hereby, continued until such provisions of this act shall take effect; and where any act is hereby repealed, no duty imposed thereby shall be held to cease, in consequence of such repeal, until the respective corresponding provisions of this act shall take effect: *And provided further*, That all manufactures and productions on which a duty was imposed by either of the acts repealed by this act, which shall be in the possession of the manufacturer or producer, or of his agent or agents, on the day when this act takes effect, the duty imposed by any such former act not having been paid, shall be held and deemed to have been manufactured or produced after such date; and whenever by the terms of this act a duty is imposed upon any articles, goods, wares, or merchandise manufactured or produced, upon which no duty was imposed by either of said former acts, it shall apply to such as were manufactured or produced and not removed from the place of manufacture or production, on the day when this act takes effect: *And provided further*, That no direct tax whatsoever shall be assessed or collected under this or any other act of Congress heretofore passed, until Congress shall enact another law requiring such assessment and collection to be made; but this shall not be construed to repeal or postpone the assessment or collection of the first direct tax levied, or which should be levied, under the act entitled "An act to provide increased revenue from imports, to pay interest on the public debt, and for other purposes," approved August fifth, eighteen hundred and sixty-one, nor in any way to affect the legality of said tax or any process or remedy provided in said acts, or any other acts, for the enforcement or collection of the same in any State or States and Territories and the District of Columbia; but said first tax, and any such process or remedy, shall continue in all respects in force, anything in this act to the contrary notwithstanding.

Mode of Paying Salaries under Direction of Secretary of Treasury. Appropriation.

(Sec. 115, Act of July 1, 1862.) *And be it further enacted,* That the pay of the assessors, assistant assessors, collectors, and deputy collectors, shall be paid out of the accruing internal duties or taxes before the same is paid into the treasury, according to such regulations as the Commissioner of Internal Revenue, under the direction of the Secretary of the Treasury, shall prescribe; and for the purpose of paying the Commissioner of Internal Revenue and clerks, procuring dies, stamps, adhesive stamps, paper, printing forms and regulations, advertising, and any other expenses of carrying this act into effect, the sum of five hundred thousand dollars be, and hereby is, appropriated, or so much thereof as may be necessary.

Commissioner may make Necessary Regulations.

Sec. 174. *And be it further enacted,* That the said Commissioner of Internal Revenue, under the direction of the Secretary of the Treasury, is authorized to make all such regulations, not otherwise provided for, as may become necessary by reason of the alteration of the laws in relation to internal revenue, by virtue of this act.

Section 119 of Act of July 1, 1862, to Remain in Full Force.

Sec. 175. *And be it further enacted,* That the one hundred and nineteenth section of an act entitled "An act to provide internal revenue to support the government and to pay interest on the public debt," approved July first, eighteen hundred and sixty-two, shall remain in full force.

Limitation of Direct Tax.

(Sec. 119, Act of July 1, 1862.) *And be it further enacted,* That so much of an act entitled "An act to provide increased revenue from imports, to pay interest on the public debt, and for other purposes," approved August fifth, eighteen hundred and sixty-one, as imposes a direct tax of twenty millions of dollars on the United States, shall be held to authorize the levy and collection of one tax to that amount; and no other tax shall be levied under and by virtue thereof until the first day of April, eighteen hundred and sixty-five, when the same shall be in full force and effect.

Secretary of the Treasury may establish Regulations for certain cases.

SEC. 176. *And be it further enacted,* That when any tax or duty is imposed by law, and the mode or time of assessment or collection is not therein provided, the same shall be established by regulation of the Secretary of the Treasury.

Collector to mark Bales of Cotton. Cotton from Insurrectionary Districts. Tax a Lien.

SEC. 177. *And be it further enacted,* That every collector to whom any duty upon cotton shall be paid shall mark the bales or other packages upon which the duty shall have been paid, in such manner as may clearly indicate the payment thereof, and shall give to the owner, or other person having charge of such cotton, a permit for the removal of the same, stating therein the amount and payment of the duty, the time and place of payment, the weight and marks upon the bales and packages, so that the same may be fully identified. Whenever any cotton, the product of the United States, shall arrive at any port of the United States from any State in insurrection against the government, the assessor or assistant assessor shall immediately assess the taxes due thereon, and shall, without delay, return the same to the collector or deputy collector of said district, and the said collector or deputy collector shall demand of the owner or other person having charge of such cotton the tax imposed by this act, and assessed thereon, unless evidence of previous payment of such tax shall be produced, under such regulations as the Commissioner of Internal Revenue, by the direction of the Secretary of the Treasury, shall from time to time prescribe; and in case the tax so assessed shall not be paid to such collector within ten days after demand, the collector or deputy collector, as aforesaid, shall institute proceedings for the recovery of the tax, as hereinbefore provided, which said tax shall be a lien upon said cotton from the time when said assessment shall be made: *Provided,* That all cotton sold by or on account of the government of the United States shall be free and exempt from duty at the time of and after the sale thereof, and the same shall be marked free, and the purchaser furnished with such a bill of sale as shall clearly and accurately describe the same, which shall be deemed and taken to be a permit authorizing the sale or removal thereof.*

Consuls exempt from Income Tax in certain cases.

SEC. 178. *And be it further enacted,* That consuls of foreign countries in the United States, who are not citizens thereof, shall be, and hereby are, exempt from any income tax imposed by this act which may be derived from their official emoluments, or from property in such countries: *Provided,* That the governments which such consuls may represent shall extend similar exemption to consuls of the United States.

---

* See the new and full provisions as to tax on cotton, *supra*.

*Suits by Collectors for Recovery of Sums Forfeited. General Regulations as to Share of Informers.**

SEC. 179. *And be it further enacted*, [That, where it is not otherwise provided for, it shall be the duty of the collectors, in their respective districts, and they are hereby authorized, to prosecute for the recovery of any sum or sums that may be forfeited; and all fines, penalties, and forfeitures which may be imposed or incurred shall and may be sued for and recovered, where not otherwise provided, in the name of the United

[* The following Circular of the Treasury Department was issued more than a year ago. New provisions are contained in this statute, but the Circular is still important, and is presented.]

MOIETIES TO INFORMERS, ETC.

TREASURY DEPARTMENT, May 31, 1865.

Section 179 of the internal revenue act, as recently amended, after providing for the recovery by suit of the fines, penalties, and forfeitures incurred or imposed by virtue of the act, proceeds as follows: "And where not otherwise herein provided for, one moiety shall be to the use of the person who shall first inform of the cause, matter, or thing whereby any such fine, penalty, or forfeiture shall have been incurred, and the other moiety to the use of the United States; and where any penalty is paid without suit, or before judgment, and a moiety of the same is claimed by any person as informer, the Secretary of the Treasury, on application to him, under such regulations as he shall prescribe, shall determine whether any claimant is entitled to such moiety, and to whom the same shall be paid."

It is not deemed expedient to prepare, at present, full and formal regulations on this subject. Before so doing, the department desire to have the benefit of experience in regard to applications under the above-cited provision of law; but the character of some of the claims already received and of the evidence relied on for their support demonstrates the propriety of calling attention to the following observations:

1. The moiety allowed to the informer is a specific donation, made for services the nature of which is expressly stated in the law, to which the person rendering such services has a just and legal claim; it cannot without gross perversion be transformed into a fund for rewarding the activity or energy of revenue officers who have not rendered the specified service.

2. The mere intimation of a suspicion based upon no tangible ground does not constitute the person making such intimation an informer within the meaning of the law. Hence the reason for suspicion, and the nature of the information given, should be stated in every application for the informer's moiety.

3. All applications should be made under oath, and should state the particulars as fully as practicable. Any other evidence which applicants may present will be carefully weighed. The Secretary will not think himself justified in awarding a moiety in any case where there is not sufficient evidence to enable him to decide *both* the questions submitted to his judgment: *Whether any claimant is entitled to such moiety?* and *To whom shall it be paid?*

4. It is the duty of all revenue officers to furnish, on application of a claimant, full and truthful statements of the part taken by such claimant in the matter in question, and to certify to the accuracy of copies of papers which such claimant may have filed with them relative to the case in which he claims to be informer. No officer is absolved from the performance of this duty for the reason that he is himself a claimant and therefore an interested party. All exhibitions of undue partiality in these cases, on the part of officers of the revenue, will be punished with the utmost rigor. (H. McCulloch, Secretary of the Treasury.)

(See Int. Rev. Rec., Vol. I., p. 197. *Ibidem*, Vol. II., p. 108. *Ex Parte*, Smith and *al.* U. S. Dist. Court Mass., September 27, 1865.)

States, in any proper form of action, or by any appropriate form of proceeding, before any circuit or district court of the United States for the district within which said fine, penalty, or forfeiture may have been incurred, or before any court of competent jurisdiction. And where not otherwise provided for, such share as the Secretary of the Treasury shall by general regulations provide, not exceeding one moiety nor more than five thousand dollars in any one case shall be to the use of the person, to be ascertained by the court which shall have imposed or decreed any such fine, penalty, or forfeiture, who shall first, inform of the cause, matter, or thing whereby such fine, penalty, or forfeiture shall have been incurred: and when any sum is paid without suit, or before judgment, in lieu of fine, penalty, or forfeiture, and a share of the same is claimed by any person as informer, the Secretary of the Treasury, under general regulations to be by him prescribed, shall determine whether any claimant is entitled to such share as above limited, and to whom the same shall be paid, and shall make payment accordingly. It is hereby declared to be the true intent and meaning of the present and all previous provisions of internal revenue acts granting shares to informers that no right accrues to or is vested in an informer in any case until the fine, penalty, or forfeiture in such case is fixed by judgment or compromise and the amount or proceeds shall have been paid, when the informer shall become entitled to his legal share of the sum adjudged or agreed upon and received: *Provided*, That nothing herein contained shall be construed to limit or affect the power of remitting the whole or any portion of a fine, penalty, or forfeiture conferred on the Secretary of the Treasury by existing laws. The Commissioner of Internal Revenue shall be, and is hereby, authorized and empowered to compromise, under such regulations as the Secretary of the Treasury shall prescribe, any case arising under the internal revenue laws, whether pending in court or otherwise. The several circuit and district courts of the United States shall have jurisdiction of all offences against any of the provisions of this act committed within their several districts. *Provided*, That whenever in any civil action for a penalty the informer may be a witness for the prosecution, the party against whom such penalty is claimed may be and shall be admitted as a witness on his own behalf. Every person who shall receive any money or other valuable thing under a threat of informing or as a consideration for not informing against any violator of this act, shall on conviction thereof be punished by a fine not exceeding two thousand dollars, or by imprisonment not exceeding one year, or both, at the discretion of the court, with cost of prosecution.]

Debts Contracted through the Sale of Articles, with intent to Evade Tax, to be Void.

SEC. 180. *And be it further enacted*, That if any person liable and required to pay any tax upon any article, goods, wares, merchandise, or manufactures, as herein provided, shall sell, or cause or allow the same to be sold, before the tax to which such article, goods, wares, merchandise, or manufacture is legally liable is paid, with intent to avoid such tax, or in fraud of the revenue herein provided, any debt contracted in the sale of such article, goods, wares, merchandise, or manufactures, or any security given therefor, unless the same shall have been bona fide transferred to the hands of an innocent holder, shall be entirely void, and the collection thereof shall not be enforced in any court. And if any such article, goods, wares, merchandise, or manufacture has been paid for, in whole or in part, the sum so paid shall be deemed forfeited, and any person who will sue for the same in an action of debt shall recover of the seller the amount so paid, one-half to his own use and the other half to the use of the United States.

Appropriation under Act of June 30, 1864. *Collectors to act as Disbursing Agents.*

SEC. 181. *And be it further enacted,* That four hundred thousand dollars, or so much thereof as may be necessary for the payment of the expenses incident to carrying into effect the various acts connected with internal revenue which are or may be authorized and payable after the first of July, eighteen hundred and sixty-four, is hereby appropriated for that purpose, payable out of any money in the treasury not otherwise appropriated, to be expended under the direction of the Secretary of the Treasury. And it shall be the duty of the collectors of internal revenue, as the Secretary may direct, to act as disbursing agents to pay the aforesaid expenses, without increased compensation therefor, who shall give good and sufficient bonds for the faithful performance of their duties as such disbursing agents for such sum and in such form as shall be prescribed by the First Comptroller of the Treasury, subject to the approval of the Secretary of the Treasury:* *Provided,* That the aforesaid appropriation shall continue in force to the thirtieth day of June, eighteen hundred and sixty-five, and thereafter the Secretary of the Treasury shall embrace in his annual estimates the amount which, in his opinion, will be required for the expenses of this branch of the public service.

Appropriation under Act of March 3, 1865. *Collectors as Disbursing Agents.*

(SEC. 4. Act of March 3, 1865.) *And be it further enacted,* That so much money as may be necessary for the payment of the lawful expenses incident to carrying into effect the various acts relative to the assessment and collection of the internal revenues after the thirtieth day of June, eighteen hundred and sixty-five, until the first day of July, eighteen hundred and sixty-six, and not otherwise provided for, be, and the same is hereby, appropriated from any money in the treasury not otherwise appropriated. And it shall be the duty of such of the collectors of internal revenue as the Secretary of the Treasury may direct

---

* See Appendix for Circular of instructions to collectors as such disbursing agents.

to act as disbursing agents to pay the aforesaid expenses without increased compensation therefor, and to give good and sufficient bonds and sureties for the faithful performance of their duties as such disbursing agents, in such sum and form as shall be prescribed by the First Comptroller of the Treasury, and approved by the Secretary.

Word "State" to include Territories, &c.

SEC. 182. *And be it further enacted,* That wherever the word State is used in this act, it shall be construed to include the Territories and the District of Columbia, where such construction is necessary to carry out the provisions of this act.

The Revenue Commission.

(SEC. 19. Act of March, 3d, 1865.) *And be it further enacted,* That the Secretary of the Treasury is hereby authorized to appoint a commission, consisting of three persons, to inquire and report, at the earliest practicable moment, upon the subject of raising, by taxation, such revenue as may be necessary in order to supply the wants of the government, having regard to, and including, the sources from which such revenue should be drawn, and the best and most efficient mode of raising the same, and to report the form of a bill; and that such commission have power to inquire into the manner and efficiency of the present and past methods of collecting the internal revenue, and to take testimony in such manner and under such regulations as may be prescribed by the Secretary of the Treasury. And such commissioners shall receive for their services three hundred dollars a month for the time necessarily employed, and their necessary traveling expenses.

Saving provisions in relation to Fines and Penalties under Amendatory Act of 1865.

(SEC. 16. Act of March 3d, 1865.) *And be it further enacted,* That all provisions of any former act inconsistent with the provisions of this act are hereby repealed: *Provided, however,* That no duty imposed by any previous act, which has become due or of which return has been or ought to be made, shall be remitted or released by this act, but the same shall be collected and paid, and all fines and penalties heretofore incurred shall be enforced and collected, and all offences heretofore committed shall be punished as if this act had not been passed; and the Commissioner of Internal Revenue, under the direction of the Secretary of the Treasury, is authorized to make all necessary regulations and to prescribe all necessary forms and proceedings for the collection of such taxes and the enforcement of such fines and penalties for the execution of the provisions of this act.

When Amendatory Act of March 3, 1865, *took effect.*

(SEC. 18. Act of March 3d, 1865.) *And be it further enacted,* That this act shall be in force and effect on and after the first day of April, in the year eighteen hundred and sixty-five, unless otherwise provided by this act; and the licenses herein provided for shall take effect on the first day of May next.

Repeal of certain Sections of Amendatory Act of 1865, (*March* 3.) *Amendment of Sections* 6 *and* 14.

(SEC. 10. Act of July, 1866.) *And be it further enacted*, [That sections two, five, eight, nine, ten, and twelve of the act entitled "An act to amend an act entitled 'An act to provide internal revenue to support the government, to pay interest on the public debt, and for other purposes,' approved June thirtieth, eighteen hundred and sixty-four," approved March third, eighteen hundred and sixty-five, be, and the same are hereby repealed.

That section six of the act of March third, eighteen hundred and sixty-five, entitled "An act to provide internal revenue to support the government, to pay interest on the public debt, and for other purposes," approved June thirty, eighteen hundred and sixty-four, be amended by striking out all after the enacting clause, and inserting in lieu thereof the following: That every national banking association, State bank, or State banking association, shall pay a tax of ten per centum on the amount of notes of any person, State bank, or State banking association, used for circulation and paid out by them after the first day of August, eighteen hundred and sixty-six, and such tax shall be assessed and paid in such manner as shall be prescribed by the Commissioner of Internal Revenue.*

THE TAX ON STATE BANK CIRCULATION. ALSO ON CORPORATIONS AND SAVINGS BANKS.

*While these sheets are passing through the press, the following circular has been received:

TREASURY DEPARTMENT, Office of Internal Revenue,
Washington, July 20, 1866.

"Sections 110, 120, and 122 of the act of June 30, 1864, having been amended by the act of July 13, 1866, so as to provide that the taxes imposed therein are not to be returned and paid to the Commissioner of Internal Revenue after August 1, 1865, assessors will instruct the proper officers of corporations, etc., taxable under those sections, that all returns due from them after July 31, 1866, should be made to the proper assistant assessors, and when any such return is received after that date, will inform the person making the same that payment of the tax is to be made to the collector. Duplicate returns should not be forwarded to this office. The taxes should be assessed on the monthly list and paid to the collecter, as other taxes are paid, instead of being deposited to the credit of the Treasury of the United States.

Section 6, of the act of March 3, 1865, is amended so that every national banking association, State bank, or State banking association, shall pay a tax of ten per cent on the amount of notes of any person, State bank, or State banking association, used for circulation, and paid out by them after the first day of August, 1866, and the tax is to be assessed and paid in such manner as shall be prescribed by the Commissioner of Internal Revenue. It is hereby prescribed that the return of said tax shall be made for the preceding month, on or before the tenth day, and said tax shall be due and payable on or before the last day of each and every month after August, 1866. Until otherwise directed the returns can be made in form No. 67. No tax will be required to

That section fourteen of the same act shall be amended by striking out all after the enacting clause, and inserting in lieu thereof the following: That the capital of any State bank or banking association which has ceased or shall cease to exist, or which has been or shall be converted into a national bank, shall be assumed to be the capital as it existed immediately before such bank ceased to exist or was converted as aforesaid; and whenever the outstanding circulation of any bank, association, corporation, company, or person shall be reduced to an amount not exceeding five centum of the chartered or declared capital existing at the time the same was issued, said circulation shall be free from taxation; and whenever any bank which has ceased to issue notes for circulation shall deposit in the treasury of the United States, in lawful money, the amount of its outstanding circulation, to be redeemed at par under such regulations as the Secretary of the Treasury shall prescribe, it shall be exempt from any tax upon such circulation; and whenever any State bank or banking association has been converted into a national banking association, and such national banking association has assumed the liabilities of such State bank or banking association, including the redemption of its bills, by any agreement or understanding whatever with the representatives of such State bank or banking association, such national banking association shall be held to make the required return and payment on the circulation outstanding, so long as such circulation shall exceed five per centum of the capital before such conversion of such State bank or banking association.

That an act entitled "An act to declare the meaning of certain parts of the internal revenue act, approved June thirty, eighteen hundred and sixty-four, and for other purposes," approved March tenth, eighteen hundred and sixty-six, be amended by striking out sections three, four, and five, of said act, and inserting in lieu thereof the following: That it shall be the duty of all persons required to make returns or lists of income and articles or objects charged with an internal tax, to declare in such returns or lists whether the several rates and amounts therein contained are stated according to their values in legal tender currency, or according to their values in coined money; and in case of neglect or refusal so to declare to the satisfaction of the assistant assessor receiving such returns or lists, such assistant assessor is hereby required to make returns or lists for such persons so neglecting or refusing, as in cases of persons neglecting or refusing to make the returns or lists re-

---

be paid under this provision on account of any circulation paid out prior to August 1, 1866.

The returns required to be made after July, 1866, by associations or companies known as provident institutions, savings banks, safety funds, or savings institutions, having no capital stock and doing no other business than receiving deposits, to be loaned or invested for the sole benefit of the parties making such deposits, without profit or compensation to the association or company, are to be made on the first Monday of January and July of each year. This postpones the returns for liabilities occurring in July, 1866, until January, 1867. E. A. ROLLINS, *Commissioner.*"

See also pp. 117, 118 and 119 of this work.

quired by the acts aforesaid, and to assess the tax thereon, and to add thereto the amount of penalties imposed by law in cases of such neglect or refusal. And whenever the rates and amounts contained in the returns or lists as aforesaid, shall be stated in coined money, it shall be the duty of each assessor receiving the same to reduce such rates and amounts to their equivalent in legal tender currency, according to the value of such coined money in said currency for the time covered by said returns. And the lists required by law to be furnished to collectors by assessors shall in all cases contain the several amounts of taxes or duties assessed, estimated, or valued in legal tender currency only.]*

Articles Exempt under the New Act passed by the Present Congress.

(SEC. 11. Act of July, 1866.)† [*And be it further enacted*, That from and after the passage of this act, the articles and products hereinafter enumerated shall be exempt from internal tax:

Alum; aluminum; aluminous cake, patent alum, sulphate of alumina, and cobalt;

Aniline and aniline colors;

Animal charcoal, or carbon;

Anvils;

Articles manufactured in institutions for the blind, and in institutions for the deaf and dumb, which are sold to aid in their support, or the support of the pupils;

Barrels and casks, other than those used for the reception of fluids;

---

* The unrepealed sections of said act are as follows:

An Act to declare the meaning of certain parts of the Internal Revenue Act, approved June thirty, eighteen hundred and sixty-four, and for other purposes.

Be it enacted by the Senate and House of Representatives of the United States of America in Congress assembled, That in section one hundred and twenty of the act entitled "An act to provide internal revenue to support the government, to pay interest on the public debt, and for other purposes," approved June thirty, eighteen hundred and sixty-four, the words "all dividends in scrip, or money thereafter declared due, and whenever the same shall be payable, to stockholders, policy holders or depositors," are hereby declared to mean all dividends in scrip or money wherever payable, and all stockholders, policy holders, depositors or parties whatsoever, including non-residents, whether citizens or aliens.

SEC. 2. *And be it further enacted*, That in section one hundred and twenty-two of said act the word "stockholders" is hereby declared to mean all persons or parties whatsoever that are or may be stockholders, including non-residents, whether citizens or aliens; and the words "all such interest or coupons, dividends or profits, whenever the same shall be payable," are hereby declared to apply to all such interest or coupons, dividends or profits, wherever the same are or may be payable, and to whatsoever party or person the same are or may be payable, including non-residents, whether citizens or aliens.

† In the official copy of Laws of 1866, which has just been issued from Department, this Section is numbered "10." It should be "11," as herein. The error arose from making two Sections "No. 9," (vide page 48 of said edition.) In this volume the proper numbers are preserved, each Section being one higher in number than the Department edition. This will be noted by the reader, and will give rise to no difficulty of reference.

packing boxes made of wood; and boxes of wood or paper for friction matches, cigar lights, and wax tapers;

Beeswax, crude or unrefined;

Bi-chromate and prussiate of potash;

Bleaching powders;

Blue vitriol;

Borax, and boracic acid;

Brass not more advanced than rods or sheets;

Brick, fire-brick, draining-tiles, cement, drain and sewer pipes, earthen and stone water-pipes, retorts and tiles made of clay;

Bristles;

Brooms made from corn, brush, or palm-leaf;

Building stone of all kinds, including slate, marble, freestone, and soapstone, and rock, and ground gypsum;

Bunting and flags of the United States, and banners made of bunting of domestic manufacture;

Burrstones, millstones, and grindstones, rough or wrought;

Candle wicking;

Chronometers;

Coffins and burial cases;

Copperas;

Copper, lead, and tin, in ingots, pigs, or bars;

Copper and yellow sheathing metal, not more advanced than rods or sheets;

Crates, and grain or farm baskets made of splints;

Crucibles of all kinds;

Crutches and artificial limbs, eyes, and teeth;

Deer-skins, smoked; or not oil dressed;

Feather beds, mattresses, palliasses, bolsters, and pillows;

Fertilizers of all kinds;

Flasks and patterns used by founders;

Flax, and the manufactures thereof;

Flavoring extracts solely for cooking purposes;

German silver in bars or sheets;

Gold leaf and gold foil;

Hemp and jute prepared for textile or felting purposes;

Hulls of ships and other vessels;

Illuminating gas manufactured by educational institutions for their own use exclusively;

India-rubber springs used exclusively for railroad cars;

Iron bridges, and castings for iron bridges;

Iron drain and sewer pipes;

Keys, actions, and strings for musical instruments;

Litharge and orange mineral;

Machines driven by horse power and used exclusively for cutting fire-wood, staves, and shingle bolts, and hand-saws;

Magnesium, calcined magnesia, and carbonate of magnesia;

Malleable iron castings, unfinished;

Manganese;

Masts, spars, ship and vessel blocks, and tree-nail wedges, and deck plugs, cordage, ropes, and cables made of vegetable fibre;

Medicinal and mineral waters, of all kinds, sold in bottles or from fountains, and mead;

Mountings and machinery of telescopes for astronomical purposes;

Mills and machinery for the manufacture of sugar, sirup, and molasses from sorghum, imphee, beets and corn;

Mineral coal of all kinds, and peat;

Monuments of stone of all kinds, not exceeding in value the sum of one hundred dollars: *Provided*, That monuments exceeding the value aforesaid, erected by public or private contributions to commemorate the service of Union soldiers who have fallen in battle, shall be exempt from taxation;

Mouldings for looking-glasses and picture frames;

Muriatic, nitric, and acetic acids;

Nickel, quicksilver, and sodium;

Nitrate of lead;

Oakum;

Original paintings, statues, and groups of statuary and casts made thereof by the artist from the original designs;

Oxide of zinc;

Paints, painters' and paper stainers' colors;

Printing paper of all descriptions, and tarred paper for roofing and other purposes; books, maps, charts, and all printed matter, and book-binding;

Paraffine; paraffine oil, not exceeding in specific gravity thirty-six degrees Baume's hydrometer, a residuum of distillation, or the products thereof: lubricating oil made from crude petroleum, coal, or shale not exceeding in specific gravity thirty-six degrees Baume's hydrometer: *Provided*, That such oil shall be subject to the same inspection as illuminating oil; crude petroleum, and crude oil the product of the first and single distillation of coal, shale, asphaltum, peat, or other bituminous substances;

Photographs or any other sun picture, being copies of engravings or works of art, when the same are sold by the producer at wholesale at a price not exceeding fifteen cents each, or are used for the illustration of books;

Pickles when sold by the gallon and not contained in glass packages;

Pig-iron; muck bar; blooms, slabs, and loops;

Ploughs, cultivators, harrows, straw and hay cutters, planters, seed-drills, horse-rakes, hand-rakes, cotton gins, grain cradles, and winnowing-mills;

Pot and pearl ashes;

Productions of stereotypers, lithographers, engravers, and electrotypers;

Putty;

Quinine, morphine, and other vegetable alkaloids, and phosphorus;

Railroad iron, and railroad iron re-rolled;

Railroad chairs and fish plates; railroad, boat, and ship spikes; axe polls; iron axles; shoes for horses, mules, and oxen; rivets, horseshoe nails, nuts, washers, and bolts; vises, iron chains and anchors; when such articles are made of wrought iron which has previously paid the tax or duty assessed thereon;

Reapers, mowers, threshing machines, and separators; corn shellers and wooden ware; cotton and hay presses;

Repairs of articles of all kinds;

Residuum the product of mineral, vegetable, or animal substances drawn from stills after distillation.

Roman and water cements, and lime;

Roofing slate, slabs, and tiles;

Saleratus, sal soda, caustic soda, crude soda, alumino-silicate of soda; aluminate of soda; bi-carbonate of soda; and silicate of soda;

Sails, tents, awnings, and bags made by sewing from fabrics or other articles upon which a duty or tax has been paid; and bags made of paper;

Saltpetre;

Salts of tin;

Silex used in the manufacture of glass;

Soap, valued at not above three cents per pound;

Spelter;

Spindles and castings of all descriptions made specially for locks, safes, looms, spinning machines, pumps, steam engines, hot air and hot water furnaces, and sewing machines, and not sold or used for any other purposes, and upon which a tax is assessed and paid on the article of which the casting is a part;

Spokes, hubs, bows, and felloes; poles, shafts, arms and wheels not ironed or finished for carriages or wagons; wooden handles for ploughs, and for other agricultural, household, and mechanical tools and implements; and pail and tub ears and handles; and wooden tanks, and cisterns for crude mineral oil;

Starch;

Steel, made from iron advanced beyond muck bar, blooms, slabs or loops, in ingots, bars, rails, made and fitted for railroads, sheet, plate, coil, or wire, hoop-skirt wire covered or uncovered, car wheels, thimble skeins and pipe boxes, and springs, tire and axles made of steel used exclusively for vehicles, cars, or locomotives; and clock springs, faces and hands;

Stoves, composed in part of cast iron and in part of sheet iron, or of soapstone or freestone, with or without cast iron or sheet iron: *Provided*, That the cast and sheet iron shall have paid the tax or duty previously assessed thereon;

Sugar, molasses, or sirup made from beets, corn, sugar maple, or from sorghum, or imphee;

Sulphate of barytes;

Sulphur; flowers of sulphur and sulphur flour;

Tar and crude turpentine;

Tin cans used for preserved meats, fish, shell-fish, fruits, vegetables, jams, jellies; paints, oils and spices;

Umbrellas and parasols, and sticks and frames for the same;

Value of bullion used in the manufacture of wares, watches, and watch-cases, and bullion prepared for the use of platers and watch-makers;

Vegetable, animal, and fish oils of all descriptions, not otherwise provided for, including red oil, oleic acid; and admixtures of the same with paraffine oil, not exceeding in specific gravity thirty-six degrees Baume's hydrometer;

Verdigris;

Vinegar;

White and red lead;

Whiting; Paris white;

Window glass of all kinds;

Wine made of grapes, currants or other fruits, and rhubarb;

Wire made from wire less than number twenty wire gauge, upon which a tax has been assessed and paid as wire; and no manufactured wire shall pay a greater tax than that imposed on number twenty, wire gauge;

Yarn and warp for weaving, braiding, or manufacturing purposes exclusively;

Yeast and baking powders;

Zinc in ingots or sheets;

Provided further, That the exemptions aforesaid shall, in all cases, be confined exclusively to said articles in the state and condition specified in the foregoing enumeration, and shall not extend to articles in any other form, nor to manufactures from said articles.]

Return of Monthly and other Lists.

(Sec. 12. Act of July, 1866.) [*And be it further enacted*, That all lists or returns required to be made monthly, by any person, firm company, corporation, or party whatsoever, liable to tax, shall be made on or before the tenth day of each and every month, and the tax assessed or due thereon shall be certified or returned by the assessor to the collector on or before the last day of each and every month.* And all lists or returns required to be made quarterly, and all other lists or returns, for which no provision is otherwise made, shall be made on or before the tenth day of each and every month in which said list or return is required to be made, or succeeding the time when the tax may be due and liable to be assessed, and the tax thereon shall be certified or returned as herein provided for monthly lists or returns. And the tax

* Heretofore it has been required of assessors that they should return to the collector, on or before the 20th of each month, the monthly list of assessments. As the assistant has had till the 15th of each month to render his own lists to the assessor, the former regulations left him but four or five days for his examination of their lists, copies, &c. The new provision is a great improvement.—Ed.]

shall be due and payable on or before the last day of each and every month; and in case said tax is not paid on or before the last day of each and every month the collector shall add ten per centum thereto; *Provided,* That notice of the time when such tax shall become due and payable shall be given in such manner as shall be prescribed by the Commissioner of Internal Revenue; and if said tax shall not be paid on or before the last day of the month as aforesaid, it shall be the duty of said collector to demand payment thereof, with ten per centum additional thereto in the manner prescribed by law, and if said tax and ten per centum additional are not paid within ten days from and after such demand thereof, it shall be lawful for the collector or his deputy to make distraint therefor as provided by law, and so much of section eighty-three of the act of June thirtieth, eighteen hundred and sixty-four as amended by the act of March third, eighteen hundred and sixty-five, as relates to the time of payment and collection of tax, is hereby repealed; and in all cases of neglect to make such lists or returns, or in case of false and fraudulent returns, the provisions of existing law as amended by this act shall be applicable thereto.]

When Apothecaries shall not be deemed Manufacturers.

(Sec. 13. Act of July, 1866.) [*And be it further enacted,* That apothecaries who manufacture, for their own dispensation and sales to consumers and to physicians, the medicines compounded according to the United States or other national pharmacopœias, or of which the full and proper formula is published in any of the dispensatories now or hitherto in common use among physicians or apothecaries, or in any pharmaceutical journal now issued by any incorporated college of pharmacy, shall not be regarded as manufacturers under this act. But apothecaries and all other persons who manufacture for the dispensing and sales of others, or who make and advertise any article, medicinal or otherwise, simple or compound, with any special proprietary claim to merit, or to special advantage in use or effect, whether such claim be based on the properties, qualities, price, or any other distinctive or distinguishing characteristic, whether real or pretended, of the articles so made and advertised, whether such article be or be not made according to the authorities above cited in this section, shall be regarded as manufacturers under this act.]

When Medicinal Drugs and Medicines shall be exempt from Stamp Tax.

(Sec. 14. Act of July, 1866.) [*And be it further enacted,* That no stamp tax shall be imposed upon any uncompounded medicinal drug or chemical, nor upon any medicine compounded according to the United States or other national pharmacopœia, or of which the full and proper formula is published in any of the dispensatories now or hitherto in common use among physicians or apothecaries, or in any pharmaceutical journal now issued by any incorporated college of pharmacy, when not sold or offered for sale, or advertised under any other name, form, or guise than that under which they may be severally denominated and laid down in said pharmacopœias, dispensatories, or journals as aforesaid; nor upon medicines sold to or for the use of any person, which may be mixed and compounded for said person according to the written receipt or prescription of any physician or surgeon. But nothing in this section shall be construed to exempt from stamp tax and medicinal articles, whether simple or compounded by any rule, authority, or formula, published or unpublished, which are put up in a style or manner similar to that of patent or proprietary medicines in general, or advertised in newspapers or by public handbills for popular sale and use, as having any special proprietary claim to merit, or to any peculiar advantage in mode of preparation, quality, use, or effect, whether such claim be real or pretended.]

Forfeiture of Articles, &c., Concealed to Avoid Tax.

(Sec. 15. Act of July, 1866.) [*And be it further enacted,* That in case any goods or commodities for or in respect whereof any tax is or shall be imposed, or any materials, utensils, or vessels proper or intended to be made use of for or in the making of such goods or commodities shall be removed, or shall be deposited or concealed in any place, with intent to defraud the United States of such tax, or any part thereof, all such goods and commodities, and all such materials, utensils and vessels respectively, shall be forfeited; and in every such case, and in every case where any goods or commodities shall be forfeited under this act, or any other act of Congress relating to the internal revenue, all and singular the casks, vessels, cases or other packages whatsoever, containing, or which shall have contained, such goods or commodities, respectively, and every vessel, boat, cart, carriage, or other conveyance whatsoever, and all horses or other animals, and all things used in the removal or for the deposit or concealment thereof, respectively, shall be forfeited; and every person who shall remove, deposit, or conceal, or be concerned in removing, depositing, or concealing any goods or commodities for in respect whereof any tax is or shall be imposed, with intent to defraud the United States of such tax or any part thereof, shall be liable to a fine or penalty of not exceeding five hundred dollars.]

When Search Warrants may be issued in cases of Suspected Fraud.

(Sec. 16. Act of July, 1866.) [*And be it further enacted,* That the judge of any circuit or district court of the United States, or any commissioner thereof, may issue a search warrant, authorizing any internal revenue officer to search any premises, if such officer shall make oath in writing that he has reason to believe, and does believe, that a fraud upon the revenue has been or is being committed upon or by the use of said premises.]

Penalty for receiving Boxes, Barrels, &c., fraudulently having Inspection Marks. Forfeiture of same and contents.

Sec. 17. Act of July, 1866. [*And be it further enacted,* That in case any person shall sell, give, or purchase or receive any box, barrel, bag, or any vessel, package, wrapper, cover, or envelope of any kind, stamped, branded, or marked in any way, so as to show that the contents or intended contents thereof have been duly inspected, or that the tax or duty thereon has been paid, or that any provision of the internal revenue laws has been complied with, whether such stamping, branding, or marking may have been a duly authorized act or may be false and counterfeit, or otherwise without authority of law, said box, barrel, bag, vessel, package, wrapper, cover, or envelope being empty, or containing anything else than the contents which were therein when said articles had been so lawfully stamped, branded, or marked by an officer of the revenue, such person shall be liable to a penalty of not less than fifty nor more than five hundred dollars. And any person who shall make, manufacture, or produce any box, barrel, bag, vessel, package, wrapper, cover, or envelope, stamped, branded, or marked, as above described, or shall stamp, brand, or mark the same, as hereinbefore recited, shall, upon conviction thereof, be liable to penalty as before provided in this section. And any person who shall violate the foregoing provisions of this section, with intent to defraud the revenue, or to defraud any person, shall, upon conviction thereof, be liable to a fine of not less than one thousand nor more than five thousand dollars, or imprisonment for not less than six months, nor more than five years, or both such fine and imprisonment, at the discretion of the court. And all articles sold, given, purchased, received, made, manufactured, produced, branded, stamped, or marked in violation of the provisions of this section, and all their contents, shall be forfeited to the United States.]

Upon the Sale on Distraint of any Whiskey, &c., requiring brands, stamps, &c., the Officer to affix proper Stamps on the Barrels, &c.

(SEC. 18. Act of July, 1866.) [*And be it further enacted,* That where any whiskey, oil, tobacco, or other articles of manufacture or produce, requiring brands, stamps, or marks of whatever kind to be placed thereon, shall be sold upon distraint, forfeiture, or other process provided by law, the same not having been branded, stamped, or marked as required by law, the officer selling the same shall, upon sale thereof, fix or cause to be affixed the brands, stamps, or marks so required, and deduct the expense thereof from the proceeds of such sale.]

Certain Schools and Colleges exempt from Manufacturers' Tax and Special Tax.

(SEC. 19. Act of July, 1866.) [*And be it further enacted,* That manual labor schools and colleges shall not be required to pay a manufacturer's or special tax while the proceeds of the labor of such institutions are applied exclusively to the support and maintenance of such institutions.]

No Suits in certain cases until after Appeal.

(SEC. 20. Act of July, 1866.) [*And be it further enacted,* That no suit shall be maintained in any court for the recovery of any tax alleged to have been erroneously or illegally assessed or collected, until appeal shall have been duly made to the Commissioner of Internal Revenue according to the provisions of law in that regard and the regulations of the Secretary of the Treasury established in pursuance thereof, and a decision of said Commissioner shall be had thereon, unless such suit shall be brought within six months from the time of said decision, or within six months from the time this act takes effect: *Provided*, That if said decision shall be delayed more than six months from the date of such appeal, then said suit may be brought at any time within twelve months from the date of such appeal.]

Collectors in Charge of Exportations in certain Ports of Entry &c. (*Repeal of Section* 15, *Act of* 1865, *March* 3.)

(SEC. 21. Act of July, 1866.) [*And be it further enacted*, That section fifteen of the act of March three, eighteen hundred and sixty-five, entitled "An act to amend an act entitled 'An act to provide internal revenue to support the government, to pay interest on the public debt, and for other purposes,' approved June thirty, eighteen hundred and sixty-four," be amended by striking out all after the enacting clause, and inserting in lieu thereof the following: That in any port of the United States in which there is more than one collector of internal revenue, the Secretary of the Treasury may designate one of said collectors to have charge of all matters relating to the exportation of articles subject to tax under the laws to provide internal revenue; and at such ports as the Secretary of the Treasury may deem it necessary, there shall be an officer appointed by him to superintend all matters of exportation and drawback, under the direction of the collector, whose compensation therefor shall be prescribed by the Secretary of the Treasury, but shall not exceed, in any case, an annual rate of two thousand dollars, excepting at New York, where the compensation shall be an annual rate of three thousand dollars. And all the books, papers, and documents in the bureau of drawback in the respective ports, relating to the drawback of duties paid under the internal revenue laws, shall be delivered to said collector of internal revenue; and any collector of internal revenue, or superintendent of exports and drawbacks, shall have authority to administer such oaths and certify to such papers as may be necessary under any rules and regulations that may be prescribed under the authority herein conferred.]

Distillers and Brewers. Law of 1866. (*Sections* 22 *to* 62, *inclusive, contain a new and elaborate system in relation to Distilled Spirits, Malt Liquors, &c., and minute provisions to secure proper and honest returns from Distillers and Brewers. They are so carefully drawn as to leave no place for either head-note or annotation.*—ED.)

(SEC. 22. Act of July, 1866.) [*And be it further enacted*, That every person, firm, or corporation, who distills or manufactures spirits or alcohol by continuous distillation from grain, who brews or makes mash, wort, or wash, for distillation or the production of spirits, shall be deemed a distiller, under this act. And the making or keeping by any person of grain, mash, wash, or beer, prepared or fit for distillation, together with the possession by such person of a still or other apparatus capable of use for distilling, upon the same premises, shall be deemed and taken as presumptive evidence that such person is a distiller within the meaning of this act.]

(SEC. 23. Act of July, 1866.) [*And be it further enacted*, That every person, firm, or corporation, who rectifies, purifies, or refines distilled spirits or wines by any process, or who, by mixing distilled spirits or wine with any materials, manufactures any spurious, imitation, or compound liquors for sale, under the name of whiskey, brandy, gin, rum, wine, "spirits," or "wine bitters," or any other name, shall be regarded as a rectifier under this act.]

(SEC. 24. Act of July, 1866.) [*And be it further enacted*, That if any person shall carry on the business of a distiller or rectifier without having paid the special tax, as required by law, he shall for every such offence be liable to a fine of not less than double the tax imposed upon the spirits distilled, or double the special tax due for the spirits rectified by such person or found upon the premises hereinafter mentioned, and to imprisonment for a term not exceeding two years; and all spirituous liquors so distilled or rectified, or owned by such person, or found as hereinafter mentioned, and all materials for making or preparing the same, and all vessels containing the same, and all stills or other apparatus capable of being used for distilling, owned by such person or found upon any premises where such business shall be carried on in violation of this section, shall be forfeited to the United States, and may be seized by the collector or deputy collector of the district within which such offence is committed.]

(SEC. 25. Act of July, 1866.) [*And be it further enacted*, That every person engaged in, or intending to be engaged in, the business of a distiller or rectifier, shall give notice in writing, subscribed by him, to the assessor of the district within which such business is to be carried on, stating the name or style under which, the name or names, and the place or places of residence of the person or persons by whom, and the place where said business is to be carried on, and whether of distilling or rectifying. In case of a distiller, the notice shall also state the kind of stills, boilers, and other implements to be used, the capacity of each, the name or names of the owner or owners of the premises on which the distillery is or is to be situated, and if such premises are leased, the terms of the lease. In case of any change in the location, form, capacity, ownership, agency, or superintendence of such distillery, still, boilers, or other implements, like notice shall be given, as aforesaid, within twenty-four hours, of such change; such person shall also give bond, in form to be prescribed by the Commissioner of Internal Revenue, with sureties approved by the collector of the district, who may approve the same if he shall be satisfied, by affidavits made on said bond, of the sufficiency of said sureties, conditioned that he will comply with all the requirements of the law in relation to distilled spirits. The penal sum of such bond shall not be more than double the amount of the tax on the spirits that can be distilled by such still or stills or other implements during a period of fifteen days; said collector may refuse to approve said bond when, in his judgment, the location of the distillery is such as would enable the distiller to defraud the revenue, and in case of such refusal, the distiller may appeal to the Commissioner of Internal Revenue, whose decision in the matter shall be final. A new bond may be required in case of the death, insolvency, or removal of either of the sureties, or in any other contingency, at the discretion of the collector. Any person failing to give the notice or bond hereinbefore required, or giving a false or fraudulent notice, shall be liable to the fine and forfeitures provided in the last preceding section.]

(SEC. 26. Act of July, 1866.) [*And be it further enacted*, That no person, shall use any still, boiler, or other vessel, for the purpose of distilling in any building or on any premises where beer, lager beer, ale, porter, or other fermented liquors, vinegar, or ether, are manufactured or produced, or where sugars or syrups are refined, or where liquors of any description are retailed, or any other business is carried on, or in any dwelling house; and every person who shall use such still, boiler, or other vessel, for the purpose of distilling, as aforesaid, in any building or other premises where the above specified articles are manufactured, produced, or other business is carried on, or in any dwelling house, or who shall procure the same to be done, shall forfeit such stills, boilers, or other vessels so used, and all the spirits distilled, and pay a fine of one thousand dollars, or be imprisoned for not more than one year, in the discretion of the court; and any person who shall manufacture any still, boiler, or other vessel, to be used for the purpose of distilling, shall, before the same is removed from the place of manufacture, notify the collector where such still, boiler, or other vessel is to be used or sent, and by whom it is to be used, and of its capacity, and the time when the same is to be sent or set up; and no such still, boiler, or other vessel, shall be set up without the permit in writing of the collector for that purpose; and any person who shall set up such still, boiler, or other vessel, without first obtaining a permit from the collector of the district in which such still, boiler, or other vessel is intended to be used, or who shall fail to give such notice, shall pay in either case the sum of five hundred dollars, and shall forfeit the distilling apparatus thus removed or set up in violation of law: *Provided*, That saleratus may be made or manufactured in any building or on any premises where spirits are distilled: *Provided further*, That any boiler used in generating steam or heating water to be used in such distillery may be located in any other building or on any other premises to be connected with such still or boiling tubs, by suitable pipes or other apparatus, or the steam from such boiler in the distillery may be conveyed to other premises to be used for manufacturing or other purposes.]

(SEC. 27. Act of July, 1866.) [*And be it further enacted*, That every rectifier or wholesale dealer in distilled spirits shall enter, daily, in a book or books kept for the purpose, under such rules and regulations as the Commissioner of Internal Revenue may prescribe, the number of proof gallons of spirits purchased or received, of whom purchased and received, and the number of proof gallons sold or delivered; and every rectifier or wholesale dealer who shall neglect or refuse to keep such record shall forfeit all spirits in his possession, together with the apparatus, tools, and implements used, and be subject to a fine of five hundred dollars, or imprisonment for not less than six months nor more than one year, in the discretion of the court. And every rectifier shall mark on each package of five gallons or more of distilled or rectified spirits sold by him, his name and place of business.]

(SEC. 28. Act of July, 1866.) [*And be it further enacted,* That the owner or owners of any distillery shall provide, at his or their own expense, a warehouse suitable for the storage of bonded spirits, of their own manufacture only; or he or they may provide a secure room, in a suitable building, to be used as such warehouse, but no dwelling-house shall be used for such purpose; and no door, window, or other opening shall be made or permitted in the walls thereof, leading to any other room or building used for any other purpose, or into the distillery; and after a bond has been given, as hereinafter provided, such warehouse or room, when approved by the Secretary of the Treasury, on report of the district collector, is hereby declared to be a bonded warehouse of the United States, and shall be used only for the storing of spirits manufactured by the owner, agent, or superintendent of such distillery, and shall be under the custody of the inspector as hereinafter provided; and shall be kept locked up by the proper officer in charge, at all times, except when he shall be present; and the tax on the spirits stored in such warehouse shall be paid before removal from such warehouse, unless removed in pursuance of law. And the owner or owners of such warehouse shall execute a general bond to the United States with two or more sureties, to be approved by the collector; and such bond shall be for not less than the amount of taxes on the spirits to be covered thereby, and in such form, and containing such conditions, as shall be approved by the Secretary of the Treasury, and shall be changed or removed from time to time in regard to the amount and sureties thereof, as the collector with the approval of the Secretary of the Treasury may require.]

(SEC. 29. Act of July, 1866.) [*And be it further enacted,* That general bonded warehouses, for the storage of spirits or other merchandise allowed by law to be placed in bond to secure the payment of the internal revenue tax thereon, or the exportation thereof, may be established under such rules and regulations and upon the execution of such bonds as the Secretary of the Treasury may prescribe, and shall be in the immediate custody of storekeepers who shall be appointed for that purpose, whose compensation shall be paid monthly to the collector of the district by the owners or proprietors of such warehouse, and shall not exceed the rates which may be allowed to storekeepers of bonded warehouses established under the laws and regulations relating to customs: *Provided*, That any article manufactured in a bonded warehouse established under the one hundred and sixty-eighth section of the internal revenue act of June thirtieth, eighteen hundred and sixty-four, and located in any of the Atlantic States, may be removed therefrom for transportation to a customs bonded warehouse at any port on the Pacific coast of the United States, for the purpose only of being exported therefrom, under such rules and regulations, and upon the execution of such bonds or other security as Secretary of the Treasury may prescribe.]

(SEC. 30. Act of July, 1866.) [*And be it further enacted*, That there shall be appointed by the Secretary of the Treasury an inspector for every distillery established according to law, who shall take an oath faithfully to perform his duties; and who shall take an account of all the meal and vegetable productions or other substances to be used for the purpose of producing spirits, when put into the mash tub or otherwise used; and shall inspect, gauge and prove all the spirits distilled, under such rules and regulations as may be prescribed by the Commissioner of Internal Revenue; and shall take charge of the bonded warehouse established for the distillery in conformity to law; and such warehouse shall be in the joint custody of such inspector and the owner thereof, his agent or superintendent; and when any spirits shall be placed in such warehouse, an entry therefor, in such form as shall be prescribed by regulations, shall immediately be made and signed by the owner of said spirits, and shall have indorsed thereon a certificate of the inspector that the spirits mentioned have been duly inspected and received in said warehouse, and such entry and certificate shall be filed with the collector of the district; and said inspector shall not engage in any other business while employed as an inspector; and shall be paid five dollars per day for the time during which he is engaged; and the amount of compensation thus paid for inspection shall be assessed by the assessor upon the distiller, and returned to the collector monthly, for collection; and in addition to the above compensation, such inspector shall receive such fee as may be prescribed by the Commissioner of Internal Revenue for each and every proof gallon of distilled spirits inspected by him and removed to the bonded warehouse, which shall be paid by the distiller or owner of the spirits; but no compensation shall be allowed to such inspector for more than one inspection of such spirits. And in case the duties of such inspector shall be greater at any time than he can perform, upon the joint application of the inspector and the owner of such distillery, the Secretary of the Treasury may appoint an assistant inspector; and upon the refusal of the distiller to join in such application, the collector shall decide as to such necessity; and such assistant inspector shall qualify in the same manner and be subject to the same penalties as the inspector, and he shall be paid in the same manner as the inspector, at a rate not exceeding the sum of three dollars per day while so employed; and in case of disagreement as to the necessity of retaining the services of such assistant, between the owner of the distillery and the inspector, the collector shall decide as to such necessity, and his decision in the matter shall be final. And in case of absence by sickness, or from any other cause, of such inspector or assistant, the collector may designate a person to take temporary charge of such distillery and warehouse, who shall during such absence perform the duties, receive the same rate of pay, and be paid in the same manner, as said inspector or assistant for the time he may be so employed: *Provided*, That the owner, agent, or superintendent of any distillery who shall use, cause or permit to be used, any materials for the purpose of producing spirits, or shall distill or remove any spirits in the absence of the acting inspector or assistant, without permission granted by the collector of the district, shall forfeit and pay double the amount of taxes on the spirits so produced, distilled, or removed, and in addition thereto be liable to a fine of one thousand dollars, to be recovered in the manner provided for other penalties: *Provided further*, That any person who shall ship, transport or remove any spirituous or fermented liquors or wines, under any other than the proper name or brand known to the trade as designating the kind and quality of the contents of the casks or packages containing the same, or who shall cause the same to be done, shall forfeit the same, and shall, on conviction thereof, be subject to and pay a fine of five hundred dollars.]

(SEC. 31. Act of July, 1866.) [*And be it further enacted*, That there shall be appointed by the Secretary of the Treasury, in every collection district where the same may be necessary, one or more general inspectors of spirits, who shall be entitled to receive such fee as may be prescribed by the Commissioner of Internal Revenue for each and every proof gallon gauged and proved by him, to be paid by the owner of the spirits; and any owner, agent, or superintendent of any distillery or bonded warehouse who shall refuse to admit an inspector upon such premises, so far as it may be necessary for the performance of his duties, or who shall obstruct an inspector in the performance of his duties, shall forfeit and pay the sum of five hundred dollars, to be recovered in the manner provided for recovery of other penalties imposed by this act.]

(SEC. 32. Act of July, 1866.) [*And be it further enacted*, That every person making or distilling spirits, or owning any still, boiler, or other vessel used for the purpose of distilling spirits, or having such still, boiler, or other vessel so used under his superintendence, either as agent or owner, or using any such still, boiler, or other vessel, shall from day to day make, or cause to be made, true and exact entry in a book, to be kept in such form as the Commissioner of Internal Revenue may prescribe, of the number of pounds or gallons of materials used for the purpose of producing spirits, the number of gallons of spirits distilled, the number of gallons placed in warehouse, and the proof thereof, and the number of gallons sold, with the proof thereof, and the name and place of business or residence of the person to whom sold; and shall also on the first, eleventh, and twenty-first days of each month, or within five days thereafter, render to the assessor or assistant assessor, an account in duplicate, taken from his books in the particulars hereinbefore recited, and verified by oath, of all the facts occurring after the last day of account preceding. The entries to be made in the books of the distiller, as aforesaid, shall, upon the several days when the returns are made, as provided, be verified by oath or affirmation of the person or persons by whom such entries shall have been made, in the presence of the assessor or assistant assessor, or other proper officer, who shall append thereto his certificate of the execution of the same. The owner, agent, or superintendent of any distillery shall in case the original entries required to be made in his books by this act shall not have been made by himself; subjoin to the certificate of the person by whom they were made the following oath or affirmation: "I do hereby certify that to the best of my knowledge and belief the foregoing entries are just and true, and that I have taken all the means in my power to make them so." Said book shall always be open for the inspection of any assessor, assistant assessor, collector, deputy collector, revenue agents, or inspectors, and any premises where distilling shall be carried on shall be open to said officers or either of them, at all times. Any person who shall violate the provisions of this section shall for every such offence be liable to a fine of five hundred dollars. Any person who shall render an account under the provisions of this section which shall be false or fraudulent, shall be liable to a fine of not less than five hundred dollars, or to imprisonment not less than six months.]

(Sec. 33. Act of July, 1866.) [*And be it further enacted*, That there shall be levied, collected, and paid on all distilled spirits upon which no tax has been paid according to law, a tax of two dollars on each and every proof gallon to be paid by the distiller, owner, or any person having possession thereof; and the tax shall be a lien on the spirits distilled, on the distillery used for distilling the same, with the stills, vessels, fixtures, and tools therein, and on the interest of said distiller in the lot or tract of land whereon the said distillery is situated, from the time said spirits are distilled, until the said tax shall be paid: *Provided*, That the tax on all spirits shall be collected at no lower rate than the basis of first-proof, and shall be increased in proportion for any greater strength than the strength of first-proof.]

(Sec. 34. Act of July, 1866.) [*And be it further enacted*, That proof spirit shall be held and taken to be that alcoholic liquor which contains one-half its volume of alcohol of a specific gravity of seven thousand nine hundred and thirty-nine ten thousandths (.7939) at sixty degrees Fahrenheit; and the Secretary of the Treasury is hereby authorized to adopt, procure, and prescribe for use, such hydrometers, weighing and gauging instruments, meters or other means for ascertaining the strength and quantity of spirits subject to tax, and to prescribe such rules and regulations as he may deem necessary to insure a uniform and correct system of inspection, weighing and gauging of spirits subject to tax throughout the United States. And in all sales of spirits hereafter made, where not otherwise especially agreed, a gallon shall be taken to be a gallon of first-proof, according to the foregoing standard set forth and declared for the inspection and gauging of spirits throughout the United States.]

(SEC. 35. Act of July, 1866.) [*And be it further enacted,* That the owner, agent, or superintendent of any distillery established as hereinbefore provided, shall erect, in a room or building to be provided and used for that purpose, and for no other, two or more receiving cisterns, each to be at least of sufficient capacity to hold all the spirits distilled during the day of twenty-four hours, into one of which shall be conveyed each day all the spirits manufactured in said distillery during that day; and such cisterns shall be so constructed as to leave an open space of at least three feet between the tops thereof and the floor or roof above, and of not less than eighteen inches between the bottoms thereof and the floor below, and shall be separated in such a manner as will enable the inspector to pass around the same, and shall be connected with the outlet of the stills, boilers, or other vessels used for distilling, by suitable pipes or other apparatus so constructed as always to be exposed to the view of the inspector; such cisterns and the room in which they are contained shall be in charge of and under the lock and seal of the inspector; and on the third day after the spirits are conveyed into such cisterns the same shall be drawn off into casks or other packages, under the supervision of the inspector, and shall be immediately inspected, gauged, proved, and the casks or packages marked, as herein provided, and be removed directly to the bonded warehouse before mentioned: *Provided,* That the spirits may be drawn off from said cisterns at any time previous to the third day, if so desired by the owner, agent, or superintendent of such distillery; and all locks and seals required by law shall be provided by the Secretary of the Treasury, at the expense of the owner of the distillery, or warehouse, and the keys shall always be in the custody of the inspector or assistant inspector, or the officer having charge of the distillery and warehouse.]

(SEC. 36. Act of July, 1866.) [*And be it further enacted,* That any person who shall knowingly and fraudulently use any false weights or measures in ascertaining, weighing, or measuring the quantities of grain, meal, or vegetable materials, molasses, beer, or other substances to be used for distillation, or who shall fraudulently make false record of the same, or who shall destroy or tamper with any locks or seal which may be placed on any cistern, rooms, or buildings, by the duly authorized officers of the revenue, shall on conviction thereof be imprisoned for the term of two years, and pay a fine not exceeding one thousand dollars, in the discretion of the court; and any person who shall use any molasses, beer, or other substances, whether fermented on the premises or elsewhere, for the purpose of producing spirits, before an account of the same shall have been registered in the proper record book provided for this purpose, shall forfeit and pay the sum of one thousand dollars for each and every offence so committed.]

(SEC. 37. Act of July, 1866.) [*And be it further enacted,* That on all wines, liquors, or compounds known or denominated as wine, made in imitation of sparkling wine or champagne, and put up in bottles in imitation of any imported wine, or with the pretence of being imported wine or wine of foreign growth or manufacture, there shall be levied and paid a tax of six dollars per dozen bottles, each bottle containing more than one pint and not more than one quart, or three dollars per dozen bottles, each bottle containing not more than one pint; said tax to be paid by the manufacturer, owner, or person having possession thereof; and the returns, assessment, collection, and time of collection of the tax on such imitation wines shall be subject to the regulations of the Commissioner of Internal Revenue. And any person who shall willfully and knowingly sell or offer for sale any such wine made after this act takes effect, upon which the tax herein imposed has not been paid, or which has been fraudulently evaded, shall, upon conviction thereof, be subject to a penalty of one thousand dollars, or to imprisonment not exceeding one year, at the discretion of the court.]

(Sec. 38. Act of July, 1866.) [*And be it further enacted*, That every owner, agent, or superintendent of any distillery shall, at all times when required, supply all assistance, lights, ladders, tools, staging, or other things necessary for inspecting the premises, stock, tools, and apparatus, belonging to such person, and shall open all doors, and open for examination all boxes, packages, and all casks, barrels, and other vessels not under the control of the inspector, when required so to do by any duly authorized officer, under a penalty of two hundred dollars for any refusal or neglect so to do.]

(Sec. 39. Act of July, 1866.) [*And be it further enacted*, That all spirits distilled shall, before the same are removed to the bonded warehouse, be inspected, gauged, and proved by the inspector appointed for that purpose, after the same has been drawn into casks or packages, each of not less capacity than twenty gallons, wine measure, and said inspector shall mark, by cutting, branding, or otherwise upon the cask or package containing such spirits, in a manner to be prescribed by the Commissioner of Internal Revenue, the quantity and proof of the contents of such cask or package, with the date of inspection, the collection district, the name of the inspector, and the name of the distiller, and also the number of each cask in progressive order, such progressive number, for every distiller, to begin with number one with the first cask or package inspected after this act takes effect, and subsequently with number one with the first cask inspected on or after the first day of January in each year, and no two or more casks warehoused in the same year by the same distiller shall be marked with the same number, and the officer in charge of the warehouse shall refuse to allow any cask of spirits to be taken out therefrom which has not marked thereon all the several particulars aforesaid, and in the manner required by law. And the inspector or other revenue officer in charge of any distillery shall make a prompt return of all spirits inspected by him in accordance with the provisions of law, and the name of the distiller, to the collector, and a duplicate thereof to the assessor of the district; and any person who shall fraudulently evade or attempt fraudulently to evade the payment of the tax upon any spirits distilled as aforesaid, by changing any marks upon any such cask or package, or in any other manner whatever, or who shall fraudulently put into such cask or package spirits of greater strength than that inspected and certified to by the inspector, shall pay double the amount of tax on each proof gallon of the quantity of such spirits, to be assessed and collected as in case of other taxes, and forfeit and pay as a penalty the additional sum of five hundred dollars for each cask or package so altered or changed, to be recovered as provided by law; and any inspector, assistant inspector, or officer temporarily in charge of any distillery who shall conspire with the proprietor of any distillery or with any other person or persons to defraud the United States of the revenue or tax arising from distilled spirits or any part thereof or who shall, with intent to defraud the United States of such revenue or tax, make any false or fraudulent entry, certificate, or return, or place any false or fraudulent mark upon any cask or package, shall, on conviction thereof, pay a fine of not less than one thousand nor more than five thousand dollars, and be imprisoned for not less than two nor more than five years; and any person who shall fraudulently use any cask or package bearing inspection marks, for the purpose of selling any other spirits than that so inspected, or for selling spirits of a quantity or quality different from that so inspected, shall be imprisoned for a term of six months, or shall pay a fine of one hundred dollars for each cask or package so used, in the discretion of the court; and any person who shall knowingly purchase or sell, with inspection marks thereon, any cask or package, after the same has been used for distilled spirits, or who shall fraudulently omit to erase or obliterate the inspection marks upon any such package or cask at the time of emptying the same, shall forfeit and pay the sum of two hundred dollars for every cask so purchased or used, or on which the marks are not so obliterated. And any person who shall, with fraudulent intent, use any inspector's brands or plates upon any cask or package containing or purporting to contain distilled spirits, or who shall knowingly make or use any counterfeit or spurious brand or plate upon any cask or package of distilled spirits, as aforesaid, shall be deemed guilty of a felony, and, on conviction thereof shall pay a fine of one thousand dollars, and be imprisoned for not less than two nor more than five years, and such cask or package with its contents shall be forfeited to the United States. And any inspector who shall permit any person not employed by him to use any of his brands or plates, or who shall negligently or willfully leave such brands or plates where they can be used by any other person than those who may be in his employ, shall pay a fine not exceeding one thousand dollars in the discretion of the court. And any inspector who shall employ any owner, agent, or superintendent of any distillery or warehouse under his supervision, or who shall employ any person in the service of such owner, agent or superintendent, to use his plates or brands or to discharge any of the duties imposed by law upon such inspector, shall, for each offence so committed, be subject to the fine last mentioned.]

(SEC. 40. Act of July, 1866.) [*And be it further enacted*, That any person or persons who shall add, or cause to be added, any ingredients to any spirits before the tax imposed by law shall have been paid thereon, for the purpose of creating a fictitious proof, shall, upon conviction, be subject to a fine of one thousand dollars for each cask or package so adulterated, and be imprisoned for not less than one nor more than two years, in the discretion of the court, and such cask or package with its contents shall be forfeited to the United States.]

(SEC. 41. Act of July, 1866.) [*And be it further enacted*, That any distilled spirits which have been inspected, gauged, proved, and marked by the inspector, according to the provisions of law, may be removed without the payment of tax from the bonded warehouse owned by the distiller, under such rules and regulations, and upon the execution of such transportation bonds or other security, as the Commissioner of Internal Revenue, subject to the approval of the Secretary of the Treasury may prescribe, and may be transported to any general bonded warehouse used for the storage of distilled spirits, established under the internal revenue laws and regulations, after having been branded as follows: "U. S. bonded warehouse, —— district, ——: for transportation to —— district, ——," (inserting in each case the number of the district and name of the State;) and immediately after the arrival of such distilled spirits at the district of the collector to which it has been transferred, it shall again be inspected and placed in a bonded warehouse; and the tax shall be paid on the difference between the number of proof gallons as stated in the bond given at the place of shipment and the number received at the warehouse, less the allowance for leakage as established by the regulations of the Commissioner of Internal Revenue; and except for actual destruction by unavoidable accident, by the elements, or by the public enemy, no other allowance for loss shall be made; and any distilled spirits entered in a general bonded warehouse shall be subject to such rules and regulations as the Commissioner of Internal Revenue may prescribe, and be chargeable with the same costs and expenses, in all respects, to which imported goods deposited in public store or bonded warehouse may be subject, and shall be in charge of a storekeeper, to be appointed by the Secretary of the Treasury, who, with the owner and proprietor of the warehouse, shall have the joint custody of all the distilled spirits so stored in said warehouse, which shall be at the risk of the owner of the said spirits; and all labor on the same shall be performed by the owner or proprietor of the warehouse, under the supervision of the officer in charge of the same, and at the expense of said owner or proprietor. And the same fees shall be paid for the execution of all papers, instruments, and documents relating to the exportation of any spirits or other merchandise, as are charged to exporters for like services in the custom-house; and all expense and services required in the removal, transfer, and shipment of the same for export shall be paid by the owner thereof: *Provided*, That any distilled spirits may be withdrawn from a bonded warehouse, after having been inspected and gauged by the proper officer, and after the payment to the collector of internal revenue for the district in which the warehouse is situated of the tax imposed by law; and when so delivered, shall be branded "U. S. bonded warehouse, tax paid;" or may be removed from said warehouse without the payment of the tax for the purpose of being exported, or for the purpose of being rectified, or re-distilled, canned, or put into other packages, after the quantity and proof of the spirits to be removed have been ascertained and inspected as required by law, under such rules and regulations and the execution of such bonds or other security as the Commissioner of Internal Revenue, subject to the approval of the Secretary of the Treasury, may prescribe; but such removal of bonded spirits for the purpose of being rectified, re-distilled, or put into other packages, shall be allowed but once on the same spirits; and all spirits so removed for re-distillation, rectification, or change of package, shall be returned to the same warehouse, and shall again be inspected; and the tax shall be paid to the said collector on any deficiency or reduction beyond three per cent. And upon spirits removed under bond for the purpose of being re-distilled or rectified, or change of package as aforesaid, and upon which an allowance shall have been made, as herein provided, the duty upon such allowance shall be paid, together with the duties imposed by law upon such spirits, in case such spirits shall be withdrawn for consumption or sale, or for transportation without being exported. And no drawback shall be allowed on any distilled spirits on which the tax has been paid; but nothing in this section shall be so construed as to prevent the manufacture in bond for exportation, without the payment of taxes, of medicines, preparations, compositions, perfumery, cosmetics, cordials, and other liquors manufactured wholly or in part of domestic spirits, as provided by law.]

(SEC. 42. Act of July, 1866.) [*And be it further enacted*, That any spirits or other merchandise may be removed from bonded warehouse, for the purpose of being exported, upon the order of the superintendent of exports for the port whence the spirits are to be exported; and such order shall state the port to which such spirits are to be shipped, and the name of the vessel, and also the number of proof gallons, and the marks of the packages or casks, and such spirits or other merchandise shall be branded "U. S. bonded warehouse, for export," and shall be put on board of the vessel in or by which they are to be exported, by an officer under direction of the superintendent of exports, and placed under the supervision of an officer of the customs, after a bond with good and sufficient sureties shall have been given in such form and containing such conditions as the Commissioner of Internal Revenue, subject to the approval of the Secretary of the Treasury, may prescribe. And such bond shall be canceled upon the presentation of the proper certificate that said spirits have been landed at the port named in said bond, or at any other port without the jurisdiction of the United States, or upon satisfactory proof that after shipment the spirits have been lost. And at any port where there shall be no superintendent of exports, all the duties and services required of superintendents of exports and drawback shall devolve upon and be performed by the collector of internal revenue designated to have charge of exportations.]

(SEC. 43. Act of July, 1866.) [*And be it further enacted*, That any person or persons who shall execute or sign any false or fraudulent bond, permit, entry, or other document, required by law or regulations; or who shall fraudulently procure the same to be executed; or who shall connive at the execution thereof, by which the payment of any internal revenue tax shall be evaded, or attempted to be evaded, or which shall be executed, or purport to be executed, for the purpose of placing in, or withdrawing from, any bonded warehouse, any spirits or other merchandise for any purpose whatever, or which shall in any way be used or attempted to be used in fraud of the internal revenue laws and regulations, on conviction thereof shall forfeit all property in such spirits or other merchandise to which such instrument relates, or purports to relate; and shall be imprisoned for a term not less than one nor more than five years, at the discretion of the court.]

(SEC. 44. Act of July, 1866.) [*And be it further enacted*, That any person owning any distilled spirits intended for sale, manufactured prior to the time when this act takes effect, exceeding fifty gallons altogether, shall notify in writing the collector of the district wherein such spirits may be stored, held, or owned, within sixty days thereafter, to gauge and prove the same; and upon the receipt of said notice the collector shall cause said spirits to be gauged and proved, and the casks or packages containing the same to be marked by the inspector in the following manner:

Manufactured prior to
————186—.
————Inspector
——District.
Inspected——, 186—.

And no spirits so manufactured, held, or owned, shall be gauged, proved, or marked in any cistern or other stationery vessel, but shall be gauged, proved, and marked only in barrels, casks, or packages in which the same shall have been placed; and the quantity held in leach tubs shall be estimated by the inspector, and, when drawn off into packages, shall be gauged and marked as herein provided. Upon the receipt of the return the collector shall immediately forward to the Commissioner of Internal Revenue a copy thereof; and any person holding or owning such spirits, and refusing or neglecting to notify the collector, as in this section provided, shall forfeit the same and pay the sum of five hundred dollars, to be collected in the manner provided by law for the collection of other penalties. No distilled spirits on which the tax has been paid shall be stored or allowed to remain on any distillery premises under the penalty of a forfeiture of all spirits so found. And all spirits, after being removed from the original package in which they were inspected and gauged into other packages for purposes of rectification, re-distillation, or change of proof, shall again be inspected and gauged and properly branded; and the absence of an inspector's brand shall be taken and held as sufficient cause or evidence upon which any spirits so found may be forfeited. Aud any person who shall change the character of any spirits, either by rectification, mixing, or otherwise, after they have been duly inspected and marked, as hereinbefore provided, and place the same in other packages for consumption or sale without first stamping or branding upon such package, in such manner as the Commissioner of Internal Revenue may prescribe, the word "Rectified," shall forfeit such spirits, and the same may be seized by the collector or deputy collector of the district where such spirits may be found, or by such other collector or deputy collector as may be specially authorized by the Commissioner of Internal Revenue for that purpose. And any person who shall so brand any package containing spirits knowing the taxes thereon have not been paid, shall forfeit such spirits, and shall be deemed guilty of a misdemeanor, and upon conviction, shall be imprisoned for not more than two years, at the discretion of the court.]

(SEC. 45. Act of July, 1866.) [*And be it further enacted*, That all boilers, stills, or other vessels, tools, and implements, used in distilling or rectifying, and forfeited under any of the provisions of this act, and all condemned material, together with any engine, or other machinery connected therewith, and all empty barrels, and all grain or other material suitable for distillation, shall, under the direction of the court in which the forfeiture is recovered, be sold at public auction, and the proceeds thereof, after deducting the expenses of sale, shall be disposed of according to law. And all spirits or spirituous liquors which may be forfeited under the provisions of this act, unless herein otherwise provided, shall be disposed of by the Commissioner of Internal Revenue as the Secretary of the Treasury may direct. And the Commissioner of Internal Revenue is hereby authorized with the approval of the Secretary of the Treasury, to exempt distillers of brandy from apples, peaches, or grapes, exclusively, from such of the provisions of this act, relating to the manufacture of spirits as in his judgment may seem expedient. And any word or words in any and all parts of this act, and of all acts to which this act is additional, indicating or referring to person or persons, shall be taken to include partnerships, firms, associations, bodies corporate or politic, or any other party whatsoever, when not otherwise designated, or manifestly incompatible with the intent thereof.]

(SEC. 46. Act of July, 1866.) [*And be it further enacted*, That any person who shall remove any distilled spirits from the place where the same are distilled, otherwise than into a bonded warehouse as provided by law, shall be liable to a fine of double the amount of the tax imposed thereon, or to imprisonment for not less than three months. All distilled spirits so removed, and all distilled spirits found elsewhere than in a bonded warehouse, not having been removed from such warehouse according to law, and the tax imposed by law on the same not having been paid, shall be forfeited to the United States; or may, immediately upon discovery, be seized, and, after assessment of the tax thereon, may be sold by the collector for the tax and expenses of seizure and sale. And proceedings upon such seizure shall be according to existing provisions of law in relation to distraint, and in conformity with any regulations which shall be made by the Commissioner of Internal Revenue. And the burden of proof shall be upon the claimant of said spirits to show that the requirements of law in regard to the same have been complied with. And any person who shall aid or abet in the removal of distilled spirits from any distillery otherwise than to a bonded warehouse, as provided by law, or shall aid in the concealment of such spirits so removed, shall be liable, on conviction thereof, to a fine of not less than two hundred nor more than one thousand dollars, or to imprisonment for not less than three nor more than twelve months. And any person who shall remove, or shall aid or abet in the removal of any distilled spirits from any bonded warehouse other than is allowed by law, shall be liable to a fine of not more than one thousand dollars, or to imprisonment for not less than three nor more than twelve months.]

(SEC. 47. Act of July, 1866.) [*And be it further enacted*, That every brewer shall, before commencing or continuing business after this act takes effect, file with the assistant assessor of the assessment district in which he shall design to carry on his business a notice, in writing, stating therein the name of the person, company, corporation, or firm, and the names of the members of any such company or firm, together with the place or places of residence of such person or persons, and a description of the premises on which the brewery is situated, and of his or their title thereto, and the name or names of the owner or owners thereof; and also the whole quantity of malt liquors annually made and sold or removed from the brewery for two years next preceding the date of filing such notice.]

(SEC. 48. Act of July, 1866.) [*And be it further enacted*, That every brewer shall execute a bond to the United States, to be approved by the collector of the district, in a sum equal to twice the amount of tax which, in the opinion of the assessor, said brewer will be liable to pay during any one month, which bond shall be renewed on the first day of May in each year, and shall be conditioned that he will pay or cause to be paid, as herein provided, the tax required by law on all beer, lager-beer, ale, porter, and other fermented liquors aforesaid made by him, or for him, before the same is sold or removed for consumption or sale, except as hereinafter provided; and that he will keep, or cause to be kept, a book in the manner and for the purposes hereinafter specified, which shall be opon to inspection by the proper officers as by law required, and that he will in all respects faithfully comply, without fraud or evasion, with all requirements of law relating to the manufacture and sale of any malt liquors before mentioned: *Provided*, That no brewer shall be required to pay a special tax as a wholesale dealer by reason of selling at wholesale, at a place other than his brewery, malt liquors manufactured by him.]

(SEC. 49. Act of July 1866.) [*And be it further enacted*, That there shall be paid on all beer, lager-beer, ale, porter, and other similar fermented liquors, by whatever name such liquors may be called, a tax of one dollar for every barrel containing not more than thirty-one gallons; and at a like rate for any other quantity or for any fractional part of a barrel which shall be brewed or manufactured and sold, or removed for consumption or sale, within the United States; which tax shall be paid by the owner, agent, or superintendent of the brewery or premises in which such fermented liquors shall be made, in the manner and at the time hereinafter specified: *Provided*, That fractional parts of a barrel shall be halves, quarters, sixths and eighths; and any fractional part of a barrel containing less than one-eighth shall be accounted one-eighth; more than one eighth and not more than one-sixth, shall be accounted one-sixth; more than one-sixth and not more than one-quarter, shall be accounted one quarter; more than one-quarter and not more than one-half, shall be accounted one-half; more than one-half and not more than one barrel, shall be accounted one barrel; and more than one barrel and not more than sixty-three gallons, shall be accounted two barrels, or a hogshead.]

(SEC. 50. Act of July, 1866.) [*And be it further enacted*, That every person, owning or occupying any brewery or premises used or intended to be used for the purpose of brewing or making such fermented liquors, or who shall have such premises under his control or superintendence as agent for the owner or occupant, or shall have in his possession or custody any brewing materials, utensils, apparatus, used or intended to be used on said premises in the manufacture of beer, lager-beer, ale, porter, or other similar fermented liquors, either as owner, agent or superintendent, shall, from day to day, enter or cause to be entered, in a book to be kept by him for that purpose, the kind of such fermented liquors, the description of packages, the number of barrels and fractional parts of barrels of fermented liquors made, and also the quantity sold or removed for consumption or sale, and shall also from day to day enter or cause to be entered, in a separate book, to be kept by him for that purpose, an account of all material by him purchased for the purpose of producing such fermented liquors, including grain and malt; and shall render to said assessor or assistant assessor, on or before the tenth day of each month, a true statement in writing, taken from his books, of the whole quantity or number of barrels and fractional parts of barrels of fermented liquors brewed and sold, or removed for consumption or sale, during the preceding month; and shall verify, or cause to be verified, the said statement, and the facts therein set forth, by oath or affirmation, to be taken before the assessor or assistant assessor of the district, according to the form required by law; and shall immediately forward to the collector of the district a duplicate of said statement, duly certified by the assessor or assistant assessor. And said books shall be open at all times for the inspection of any assessor or assistant assessor, collector, deputy collector, inspector, or revenue agent, who may take memorandums and transcripts therefrom.]

(SEC. 51. Act of July, 1866.) [*And be it further enacted*, That the entries made in such books shall, on or before the tenth day of each month, be verified by the oath or affirmation of the person or persons by whom such entries shall have been made, which oath or affirmation shall be written in the book at the end of such entries, and be certified by the officer administering the same, and shall be in form as follows: "I do swear (or affirm) that the foregoing entries were made by me, and that they state truly, according to the best of my knowledge and belief, the whole quantity of fermented liquors brewed, the quantity sold, and the quantity removed from the brewery owned by , in the county of . And further, that I have no knowledge of any matter or thing, required by law to be stated in said entries, which has been omitted therefrom." And the owner, agent, or superintendent aforesaid, shall also, in case the original entries made in his books shall not have been made by himself, subjoin thereto the following oath or affirmation, to be taken in manner as aforesaid: "I do swear (or affirm) that, to the best of my knowledge and belief, the foregoing entries fully set forth all the matters therein required by law, and that the same are just and true, and that I have taken all the means in my power to make them so."]

(SEC. 52. Act of July, 1866.) [*And be it further enacted*, That the owner, agent, or superintendent of any brewery, vessels, or utensils used in making fermented liquors, who shall evade or attempt to evade the payment of the tax thereon, or fraudulently neglect or refuse to make true and exact entry and report of the same in the manner by law required, or to do or cause to be done any of the things by law required to be done by him as aforesaid, or who shall intentionally make false entry in said book or in said statement, or knowingly allow or procure the same to be done, shall forfeit, for every such offence, all the liquors made by him or for him, and all the vessels, utensils, and apparatus used in making the same, and be liable to a penalty of not less than five hundred nor more than one thousand dollars, to be recovered with costs of suit, and shall be deemed guilty of a misdemeanor, and shall be imprisoned for a term not exceeding one year. And any brewer who shall neglect to keep the books, or refuse to furnish the account and duplicate thereof as by law, or who shall refuse to permit the proper officer to examine the books in the manner provided, shall, for every such refusal or neglect, forfeit and pay the sum of three hundred dollars.]

(SEC. 53. Act of July, 1866.) [*And be it further enacted*, That the Commissioner of Internal Revenue shall cause to be prepared, for the payment of the tax aforesaid, suitable stamps denoting the amount of tax required to be paid on the hogshead, barrels, and halves, quarters, sixths, and eighths of a barrel of such fermented liquors, and shall furnish the same to the collectors of internal revenue, who shall each be required to keep on hand, at all times, a supply equal in amount to two months' sales thereof, if there shall be any brewery or brewery warehouse in his district, and the same shall be sold by such collectors only to the brewers of their districts, respectively; and such collectors shall keep an account of the number and values of the stamps sold by them to each of such brewers, respectively: and the Commissioner of Internal Revenue shall allow upon all sales of such stamps to any brewer, and by him used in his business, a deduction of seven and one-half per centum. And the amount paid into the treasury by any collector on account of the sale of such stamps to brewers shall be included in estimating the commissions of such collector and of the assessor of the same district.]

(SEC. 54. Act of July, 1866.) [*And be it further enacted*, That every brewer shall obtain, from the collector of the district in which his brewery or brewery warehouse may be situated, and not otherwise, unless said collector shall fail to furnish the same upon application to him, the proper stamp or stamps; and shall affix upon the spigot-hole or tap (of which there shall be but one) of each and every hogshead, barrel, keg, or other receptacle, in which any fermented liquor shall be contained, when sold or removed from such brewery or warehouse, a stamp denoting the amount of the tax required upon such fermented liquor, in such a way that the said stamp or stamps will be destroyed upon the withdrawal of the liquor from such hogshead, barrel, keg, or other vessel, or upon the introduction of a faucet or other instrument for that purpose; and shall also, at the time of affixing such stamp or stamps as aforesaid, cancel the same by writing or imprinting thereon the name of the person, firm, or corporation by whom such liquor may have been made, or the initial letters thereof, and the date when canceled. Every brewer who shall refuse or neglect to affix and cancel the stamp or stamps required by law in the manner aforesaid, or who shall affix a false or fraudulent stamp thereto, or knowingly permit the same to be done, shall be liable to pay a penalty of one hundred dollars for each barrel or package on which such ommission or fraud occurs, and shall be liable to imprisonment for not more than one year.]

(SEC. 55. Act of July, 1866.) [*And be it further enacted*, That any brewer, carman, agent for transportation, or other person, who shall sell, remove, receive, or purchase, or in any way aid in the sale, removal, receipt, or purchase of any fermented liquor contained in any hogshead, barrel, keg, or other vessel from any brewery, or brewery warehouse, upon which the stamp required by law shall not have been affixed, or on which a false or fraudulent stamp is affixed, with knowledge that it is such, or on which a stamp once canceled is used a second time; and any retail dealer or other person, who shall withdraw or aid in the withdrawal of any fermented liquor from any hogshead, barrel, keg, or other vessel containing the same, without destroying or defacing the stamp affixed upon the same, or shall withdraw or aid in the withdrawal of any fermented liquor from any hogshead, barrel, keg, or other vessel, upon which the proper stamp shall not have been affixed, or on which a false or fraudulent stamp is affixed, shall be liable to a fine of one hundred dollars, and to imprisonment not more than one year. Every person who shall make, sell, or use any false or counterfeit stamp or die for printing or making stamps which shall be in imitation of, or purport to be a lawful stamp or die of, the kind before mentioned, or who shall procure the same to be done, shall be imprisoned not less than one nor more than five years: *Provided*, That every brewer, who sells fermented liquor at retail at the brewery or other place where the same is made, shall affix and cancel the proper stamp or stamps upon the hogsheads, barrels, kegs, or other vessels in which the same is contained, and shall keep an account of the quantity so sold by him, and of the number and size of the hogsheads, barrels, kegs, or other vessels, in which the same may have been contained, and shall make a report thereof, verified by oath, monthly to the assessor, and forward a duplicate of same to the collector of the district: *And provided further*, That brewers may remove malt liquors of their own manufacture from their breweries or other places of manufacture to a warehouse or other place of storage occupied by them within the same district in quantities of not less than six barrels in one vessel without affixing the proper stamp or stamps, but shall affix the same upon such liquor when sold or removed from such warehouse or other place of storage: But when the manufacturer of any ale or porter manufactures the same in one collection district, and owns, occupies, or hires a depot or warehouse for the storage and sale of such ale or porter in another collection district, he may, without affixing the stamps on the casks at the brewery, as herein provided for, remove or transport, or cause to be removed or transported, said ale and porter, in quantities not less than one hundred barrels at a time, under a permit from the collector of the district wherein said ale or porter is manufactured, to said depot or warehouse, but to no other place, under such rules and regulations as the Commissioner of Internal Revenue may prescribe; and thereafter the manufacturer of the ale and porter so removed shall stamp the same when it leaves such depot or warehouse, in the same manner and under the same penalties and liabilities as when stamped at the brewery as herein provided; and the collector of the district in which such depot or warehouse is situated shall furnish the manufacturer with the stamps for stamping the same, as if the said ale and porter had been manufactured in his district: *And provided further*, That where fermented liquor has become sour or damaged, so as to be incapable of use as such, brewers may sell the same for manufacturing purposes, and may remove the same to places where it may be used for such purposes, in casks or other vessels, unlike those ordinarily used for fermented liquors, containing respectively not less than one barrel each, and having the nature of their contents marked upon them, without affixing thereon the stamp or stamps herein required.]

(SEC. 56. Act of July, 1866.) [*And be it further enacted*, That every brewer shall mark, or cause to be marked, in such manner as shall be prescribed by the Commissioner of Internal Revenue, upon every hogshead, barrel, keg, or other vessel, containing the fermented liquor made by him, before it is sold or removed from the brewery, or brewery warehouse, or other place of manufacture, the name of the person, firm, or corporation by whom such liquor was manufactured, and the place where the same shall have been made; and any person, other than the owner thereof, or his agent, who shall intentionally remove or deface such mark therefrom, shall be liable to a penalty of fifty dollars for each cask from which the mark is so removed or defaced.]

(Sec. 57. Act of July, 1866.) [*And be it further enacted,* That every person, other than the purchaser or owner of any fermented liquor, or person acting on his behalf, or as his agent, who shall intentionally remove or deface the stamp affixed, upon the hogshead, barrel, keg, or other vessel, in which the same may be contained, shall be liable to a fine of fifty dollars for each such vessel from which the stamp is so removed or defaced, and to render compensation to such purchaser or owner for all damages sustained by him therefrom.]

(Sec. 58. Act of July, 1866.) [*And be it further enacted,* That the ownership or possession by any person of any fermented liquor after its sale or removal from brewery or warehouse, or other place where it was made, upon which the tax required shall not have been paid, shall render the same liable to seizure wherever found, and to forfeiture; and that the want of the proper stamp or stamps upon any hogshead, barrel, keg, or other vessel in which fermented liquor may be contained after its sale or removal from the brewery where the same was made, or warehouse, as aforesaid, shall be notice to all persons that the tax has not been paid thereon, and shall be prima facie evidence of the non-payment thereof.]

(Sec. 59. Act of July, 1866.) [*And be it further enacted,* That every person who shall withdraw any fermented liquor from any hogshead, barrel, keg, or other vessel upon which the proper stamp or stamps shall not have been affixed, for the purpose of bottling the same, or who shall carry on, or attempt to carry on, the business of bottling fermented liquor in any brewery or other place in which fermented liquor is made, or upon any premises having communication with such brewery or any warehouse, shall be liable to a fine of five hundred dollars, and the property used in such bottling or business shall be liable to forfeiture.]

Penalty Imposed upon Revenue Officers for Becoming Interested in the Manufacture of Tobacco, Cigars, Distilled Spirits, Ale, &c.

(Sec. 60. Act of July, 1866.) [*And be it further enacted,* That any inspector, or revenue agent, who shall hereafter become interested, directly or indirectly, in the manufacture of tobacco, snuff, or cigars, and any assessor, collector inspector, or revenue agent who shall hereafter become interested, directly or indirectly, in the production, by distillation or by other process, of spirits, ale, or beer, or other fermented liquors, shall, on conviction before any court of the United States of competent jurisdiction, pay a penalty not less than five hundred dollars nor more than five thousand dollars, in the discretion of the court. And any such officer interested as aforesaid in any such manufacture at the time this act takes effect, who shall fail to divest himself of such interest within sixty days thereafter, shall be held and declared to have become so interested after this act takes effect.]

Revenue Officers to Render Sworn Returns of Fees, Rewards, &c., received. Penalty for False Statement.

(Sec. 61. Act of July, 1866.) [*And be it further enacted,* That every internal revenue officer whose payment, charges, salary, or compensation shall be composed, either wholly or in part, of fees, commissions, allowances, or rewards, from whatever source derived, shall be required to render to the Commissioner of Internal Revenue, under regulations to be approved by the Secretary of the Treasury, a statement under oath, setting forth the entire amount of such fees, commissions, emoluments, or rewards, of whatever nature or from whatever source received, during the time for which said statement is rendered; and any false statement knowingly and willfully rendered under the requirements of this section, or regulations established in accordance therewith, shall be deemed willful perjury, and punished, on conviction thereof, as provided in section forty-two of the act of June thirty, eighteen hundred and sixty-four, to which this act is an amendment: and any neglect or omission to render such statement when required shall be punished, on conviction therefor, by a fine of not less than two hundred dollars nor more than five hundred dollars, in the discretion of the court.]

(Sec. 62. Act of July, 1866.) [*And be it further enacted,* That so much of this act as changes the existing law relating to distilled spirits and fermented liquors shall take effect from and after the first day of September, eighteen hundred and sixty-six.]

Penalty for Bribery and Attempted Bribery of Revenue Officers.

(Sec. 63. Act of July, 1866.) [*And be it further enacted,* That if any person or persons shall, directly or indirectly, promise, offer, or give, or cause or procure to be promised, offered, or given, any money, goods, right in action, bribe, present or reward, or any promise, contract, undertaking, obligation or security for the payment or delivery of any money, goods, right in action, bribe, present or reward, or any other valuable thing whatever to any officer of the United States, or person holding any place of trust or profit, or discharging any official function under, or in connection with, any department of the government of the United States, after the passage of this act, with intent to influence his decision or action on any question, matter, cause, or thing which may then be pending, or may by law be brought before him in his official capacity, or in his place of trust or profit, or with intent to influence any such officer or person to commit, or aid or abet in committing, any fraud on the revenue of the United States, or to connive at or collude in, or to allow or permit, or make opportunity for, the commission of any such fraud, and shall be thereof convicted, such person or persons so offering, promising or giving, or causing or procuring to be promised, offered or given any such money, goods, right in action, bribe, present or reward, or any promise, contract, undertaking, obligation or security for the payment or delivery of any money, goods, right in action, bribe, present or reward, or other valuable thing whatever; and the officer or person who shall in anywise accept or receive the same, or any part thereof, shall respectively be liable to indictment in any court of the United States having jurisdiction, and shall, upon conviction thereof, be fined not exceeding three times the amount so offered, promised, given, accepted or received, and imprisoned not exceeding three years; and the person convicted of so accepting or receiving the same, or any part thereof, if an officer or person holding any such place of trust or profit, shall forfeit his office or place; and any person so convicted under this section shall forever be disqualified to hold any office of honor, trust or profit under the United States.]

Provisions in relation to Seizure of Goods subject to Forfeiture.

(SEC. 64. Act of July, 1866.) [*And be it further enacted,* That hereafter in all cases of seizure of any goods, wares, or merchandise which shall, in the opinion of the collector or deputy collector, making such seizure, be of the appraised value of three hundred dollars or less, and which shall have been so seized as being subject to forfeiture under any of the provisions of this act, or of any act to which this is an amendment, excepting in cases otherwise provided, the said collector or deputy collector shall proceed as follows, that is to say: He shall cause a list containing a particular description of the goods, wares, or merchandise so seized to be prepared in duplicate, and an appraisement of the same to be made by three sworn appraisers, to be selected by him for said purpose, who shall be respectable and disinterested citizens of the United States, residing within the collection district wherein the seizure was made. The aforesaid list and appraisement shall be properly attested by such collector or deputy collector and the persons making the appraisement, for which service said appraisers shall be allowed the sum of one dollar and fifty cents per day each, to be paid as other necessary charges of collectors according to law. If the said goods shall be found by such appraisers to be of the value of three hundred dollars or less, the said collector or deputy collector shall publish a notice, for the space of three weeks, in some newspaper of the district where the seizure was made, describing the articles, and stating the time, place, and cause of their seizure, and requiring any person or persons claiming them to appear and make such claim within thirty days from the date of the first publication of such notice: *Provided,* That any person or persons claiming the goods, wares, or merchandise, so seized, within the time specified in the notice, may file with such collector or deputy collector a claim, stating his or their interest in the articles seized, and may execute a bond to the United States in the penal sum of two hundred and fifty dollars, with sureties, to be approved by said collector or deputy collector, conditioned that, in case of condemnation of the articles so seized, the obligors will pay all the costs and expenses of the proceedings to obtain such condemnation; and upon the delivery of such bond to the collector or deputy collector, he shall transmit the same, with the duplicate list and description of the goods seized, to the United States district attorney for the district, who shall proceed thereon in the ordinary manner prescribed by law: *And provided, also,* That if there shall be no claim interposed and no bond given within the time above specified, the collector or deputy collector, as the case may be, shall give ten days' notice of the sale of the goods, wares, or merchandise, by publication; and at the time and place specified in said notice, shall sell the article so seized at public auction, and, after deducting the expenses of appraisement and sale, he shall deposit the proceeds to the credit of the Secretary of the Treasury. And within one year after the sale of any goods, wares, or merchandise, as aforesaid, any person or persons claiming to be interested in the goods, wares, or merchandise so sold may apply to the Secretary of the Treasury for a remission of the forfeiture thereof, or any of them, and a restoration of the proceeds of the said sale, which may be granted by the said Secretary upon satisfactory proof, to be furnished in such manner as he shall prescribe: *Provided,* That it shall be satisfactorily shown that the applicant, at the time of the seizure and sale of the goods in question, and during the intervening time, was absent out of the United States, or in such circumstances as prevented him from knowing of such seizure, and that he did not know of the same; and also that the said forfeiture was incurred without willful negligence or any intention of fraud on the part of the owner or owners of such goods. If no application for such restoration be made within one year, as hereinbefore prescribed, then, at the expiration of the said time, the Secretary of the Treasury shall cause the proceeds of the sale of the said goods, wares, or merchandise to be distributed according to law, as in the case of goods, wares, or merchandise condemned and sold pursuant to the decree of a competent court.]

Reorganization of Office of the Commissioner of Internal Revenue.

(Sec. 65. Act of July, 1866.) [*And be it further enacted,* That the office of the Commissioner of Internal Revenue be reorganized so as to include—

One Commissioner of Internal Revenue, with a salary of six thousand dollars, and

One Deputy Commissioner, with a salary of three thousand five hundred dollars; which offices are now already created, and the duties thereof defined by law; and to authorize, under the direction of the Secretary of the Treasury, the employment of the following additional officers and clerks, and with the salaries hereinafter specified, namely:

Two Deputy Commissioners, each with a salary of three thousand dollars.

One Solicitor, with a salary of four thousand dollars.

Seven heads of divisions, each with a salary of two thousand five hundred dollars.

Thirty-four clerks of class four; forty-five clerks of class three; fifty clerks of class two; and thirty-seven clerks of class one.

Fifty-five female clerks.

Five messengers.

Three assistant messengers, and fifteen laborers, and a sum sufficient to pay the additional salaries of officers, clerks, and employes herein authorized is hereby appropriated out of any money in the treasury not otherwise appropriated; and this section shall take effect from and after the thirtieth day of June, eighteen hundred and sixty-six.]

Franking Privilege to certain Internal Revenue Officers.

(SEC. 66. Act of July, 1866.) [*And be it further enacted,* That all official communications made by assessors to collectors, assessors to assessors, or by collectors to collectors, or by collectors to assessors, or by assessors to assistant assessors, or by assistant assessors to assessors, or by collectors to their deputies, or by deputy collectors to collectors, may be officially franked by the writers thereof, and shall, when so franked, be transmitted by mail free of postage.]

Provisions for the Appointment of the "Special Commissioner of the Revenue." His Duties and Salary and Powers.

(SEC. 67. Act of July, 1866.) [*And be it further enacted,* That the Secretary of the Treasury is hereby authorized to appoint an officer in his department who shall be styled "Special Commissioner of the Revenue,"* whose office shall terminate in four years from the 30th day of June, 1866. It shall be the duty of the Special Commissioner of the Revenue to inquire into all the sources of national revenue, and the best methods of collecting the revenue; the relations of foreign trade to domestic industry; the mutual adjustment of the systems of taxation by customs and excise, with the view of insuring the requisite revenue with the least disturbance or inconvenience to the progress of industry and the development of the resources of the country; and to inquire from time to time, under the direction of the Secretary of the Treasury, into the manner in which officers charged with the administration and collection of the revenues perform their duties. And the said Special Commissioner of the Revenue shall from time to time report, through the Secretary of the Treasury, to Congress, either in the form of a bill or otherwise, such modifications of the rates of taxation or of the methods of collecting the revenues, and such other facts pertaining to the trade, industry, commerce, or taxation of the country, as he may find, by actual observation of the operation of the law, to be conducive to the public interest; and, in order to enable the Special Commissioner of the Revenue to properly conduct his investigations, he is hereby empowered to examine the books, papers, and accounts of any officer of

*It is confidently supposed that this important position will be offered to, and accepted by, Hon. David A. Wells, the Chairman of the Commission established by the amendatory act of 1865, who, in his Report submitted through the Secretary of the Treasury to the present Congress, and by his highly useful labors in consultation with the Committee of Ways and Means in the House, and of Finance in the Senate, has given symmetry to the enactments contained in this volume, and added a practical as well as philosophical character and tone to the speculations and discussions of Excise taxation.

the revenue, to administer oaths, examine and summon witnesses, and take testimony; and each and every such person falsely swearing or affirming shall be subject to the penalties and disabilities prescribed by law for the punishment of corrupt and willful perjury; and all officers of the government are hereby required to extend to the said Commissioner all reasonable facilities for the collection of information pertinent to the duties of his office. And the said Special Commissioner shall be paid an annual salary of four thousand dollars, and the traveling expenses necessarily incurred while in the discharge of his duty; and all letters and documents to and from the Special Commissioner relating to the duties and business of his office shall be transmitted by mail free of postage. And section nineteen of an act entitled "An act to amend an act entitled 'An act to provide internal revenue to support the government, to pay interest on the public debt, and for other purposes,' approved June thirtieth, eighteen hundred and sixty-four," approved March third, eighteen hundred and sixty-five, be, and the same is hereby repealed.]

Provisions in relation to Suits against Revenue Officers. Removal of Suits in State Courts to Circuit Courts of the United States, and Proceedings thereupon.

(Sec. 67a. Act of July, 1866.) [*And be it further enacted*, That in any case, civil or criminal, where suit or prosecution shall be commenced in any court of any State against any officer of the United States, appointed under or acting by authority of the act entitled "An act to provide internal revenue to support the government, to pay interest on the public debt, and for other purposes," passed June thirtieth, eighteen hundred and sixty-four, or of any act in addition thereto, or in amendment thereof, or against any person acting under or by authority of any such officer on account of any act done under color of his office, or against any person holding property or estate by title derived from any such officer, concerning such property or estate and affecting the validity of this act, or acts of which it is amendatory, it shall be lawful for the defendant, in such suit or prosecution, at any time before trial, upon a petition to the circuit court of the United States in and for the district in which the defendant shall have been served with process, setting forth the nature of said suit or prosecution, and verifying the said petition by affidavit, together with a certificate, signed by an attorney or counsellor at law of some court of record of the State in which such suit shall have been commenced, or of the United States, setting forth that, as counsel for the petitioner, he has examined the proceedings against him, and carefully inquired into all the matters set forth in the petition, and that he believes the same to be true; which petition, affidavit, and certificate shall be presented to the said circuit court if in session, and if not, to the clerk thereof, at his office, and shall be filed in said office, and the cause shall thereupon be entered on the docket of said court, and shall be thereafter proceeded in as a cause originally commenced in that court; and it shall be the duty of the clerk of said court, if the suit were commenced in the court below by summons, to issue a writ of certiorari to the State court, requiring said court to send to the said circuit court the record and proceedings in said cause; or if it were commenced by capias, he shall issue a writ of habeas corpus cum causa, a duplicate of which said writ shall be delivered to the clerk of the State court, or left at his office, by the marshal of the district; or his deputy, or some person duly authorized thereto; and thereupon it shall be the duty of the said State court to stay all further proceedings in such cause, and the said suit or prosecution, upon delivery of such process, or leaving the same as aforesaid, shall be deemed and taken to be moved to the said circuit court, and any further proceedings, trial, or judgment therein in the State court shall be wholly null and void. And if the defendant in any such suit be in actual custody on mesne process therein, it shall be the duty of the marshal, by virtue of the writ of habeas corpus cum causa, to take the body of the defendant into his custody, to be dealt with in the said cause according to the rules of law and the order of the circuit court, or of any judge thereof in vacation. All attachments made, and all bail and other security given, upon such suit or prosecution shall be and continue in like force and effect as if the same suit or prosecution had proceeded to final judgment and execution in the State court; and if, upon removal of any such suit or prosecution, it shall be made [to] appear to the said circuit court that no copy of the record and proceedings therein in the State court can be obtained, it shall be lawful for said circuit court to allow and require the plaintiff to proceed de novo, and to file a declaration of his cause of action, and the parties may thereupon proceed as in action originally brought in said circuit court; and, on failure of so proceeding, judgment of nolle prosequi may be rendered against the plaintiff, with costs for the defendant: *Provided*, That an act entitled "An act further to provide for the collection of duties on imports," passed March second, eighteen hundred and thirty-three, shall not be so construed as to apply to cases arising under an act entitled "An act to provide internal revenue to support the government, to pay interest on the public debt, and for other purposes," passed June thirtieth, eighteen hundred and sixty-four, or any act in addition thereto or in amendment thereof, nor to any case in which the validity or interpretation of said act or acts shall be in issue: *Provided further*, That if any officer appointed under and by virtue of any act to provide internal revenue, or any person acting under or by authority of any such officer, shall receive any injury to his person or property for or on account of any act by him done under any law of the United States for the collection of taxes, he shall be entitled to maintain suit for damages therefor in the circuit court of the United States, in the district wherein the party doing the injury, may reside or shall be found; and all property taken or detained by any officer or other person under authority of any revenue law of the United States shall be irrepreviable, and shall be deemed to be in the custody of the law, and subject only to the orders and decrees of the courts of the United States having jurisdiction thereof; and if any person shall dispossess or rescue or attempt to dispossess or rescue, any property so taken or detained as aforesaid, or shall aid or assist therein, such person shall be deemed guilty of a misdemeanor, and shall be liable to such punishment as is provided by the twenty-second section of the act for the punishment of certain crimes against the United States, approved the thirtieth of April, Anno Domini seventeen hundred and ninety, for the willful obstruction or resistance of officers in the service of process.]

Repeal of Section 50 *of Act of June* 30, 1864.

(SEC. 68. Act of July, 1866.) [*And be it further enacted*, That the fiftieth section of an act passed June thirtieth, eighteen hundred and sixty-four, entitled, "An act to provide internal revenue to support the government, to pay interest on the public debt, and for other purposes," is hereby repealed: *Provided*, That any case which may have been removed from the courts of any State under said fiftieth section to the courts of the United States shall be remanded to the State court from which it was so removed, with all the records relating to such cases, unless the justice of the circuit court of the United States in which such suit or prosecution is pending shall be of opinion that said case would be removable from the court of the State to the circuit court under and by virtue of the sixty-seventh section of this act. And in all cases which may have been removed from any court of any State under and by virtue of said fiftieth section of said act of June thirtieth, eighteen hundred and sixty-four, all attachments made, and all bail or other security given upon such suit or prosecution, shall be and continue in full force and effect until final judgment and execution, whether such suit shall be prosecuted to final judgment in the circuit court of the Uuited States or remanded to the State court from which it was removed.]

Writs of Error for the Revision of Judgments in State Courts, under Section 25 *of Act of September* 24, 1789.

(SEC. 69. Act of July, 1866.) [*And be it further enacted*, That whenever a writ of error shall be issued for the revision of any judgment or decree in any criminal proceeding where is drawn in question the construction of any statute of the United States, in a court of any State, as is provided in the twenty-fifth section of an act entitled, "An act to establish the judicial courts of the United States," passed September twenty-fourth, seventeen hundred and eighty-nine, the defendant, if charged with an offence bailable by the laws of such State, shall not be released from custody until a final judgment upon such writ, or until a bond, with sufficient sureties, in a reasonable sum, as ordered and approved by the State court, shall be given; and if the offence is not so bailable, until a final judgment upon the writ of error. Writs of error in criminal cases shall have precedence upon the docket of the Supreme Court of all cases to which the government of the United States is not a party, excepting only such cases as the court, at their discretion, may decide to be of public importance.]

This Act of Amendment, &c., to take effect August 1, 1866. *Saving Provisions, &c., for Accrued Taxes and Penalties Incurred, &c.*

(SEC. 70. Act of July, 1866.) [*And be it further enacted,* That this act shall take effect, where not otherwise provided, on the first day of August, eighteen hundred and sixty-six, and all provisions of any former act inconsistent with the provisions of this act are hereby repealed: *Provided, however,* That all the provisions of said acts shall be in force for collecting all taxes, duties and licenses properly assessed or liable to be assessed, or accruing under the provisions of acts, the right to which has already accrued or which may hereafter accrue under said acts, and for maintaining and continuing liens, fines, penalties and forfeitures incurred under and by virtue thereof. And for carrying out and completing all proceedings which have been already commenced, or that may be commenced, to enforce such fines, penalties, and forfeitures, or criminal proceedings under said acts, and for the punishment of crimes of which any party shall be or has been found guilty: *And provided further,* That whenever the duty imposed by any existing law shall cease in consequence of any limitation therein contained before the respective provisions of this act shall take effect, the same duty shall be, and is hereby, continued until such provisions of this act shall take effect; and where any act is hereby repealed, no duty imposed thereby shall be held to cease, in consequence of such repeal, until the respective corresponding provisions of this act shall take effect: *And provided further,* That all manufactures and productions on which a duty was imposed by either of the acts repealed by this act, which shall be in the possession of the manufacturer or producer, or of his agent or agents, on the day when this act takes effect, the duty imposed by any such former act not having been paid, shall be held and deemed to have been manufactured or produced after such date; and whenever by the terms of this act a duty is imposed upon any articles, goods, wares, or merchandise, manufactured or produced, upon which no duty was imposed by either of said former acts, it shall apply to such as were manufactured or produced, and not removed from the place of manufacture or production, on the day when this act takes effect; and the Commissioner of Internal Revenue, under the direction of the Secretary of the treasury, is authorized to make all necessary regulations and prescribe all necessary forms and proceedings for the collection of such taxes and the enforcement of such fines and penalties for the execution of the provisions of this act.]

The Act to be Published in the German Language.

(SEC. 71. Act of July, 1866.) [*And be it further enacted,* That it shall be the duty of the Commissioner of Internal Revenue to have this act, and the acts to which it is amendatory, published in at least one German newspaper in each of the States of the Union where such paper may be published.]

SUPPLEMENT

BEING THE AMENDED

LAW OF 1867.

28

AN ACT

To Amend Existing Laws Relating to Internal Revenue, and for Other Purposes.

Be it enacted by the Senate and House of Representatives of the United States of America, in Congress assembled, That all acts in relation to the assessment, return, collection, and payment of the income tax, special tax, and other annual taxes now by law required to be performed in the month of May, shall hereafter be performed on the corresponding days in the month of March in each year; all acts required to be performed in the month of June, in relation to the collection, return, and payment of said taxes, shall hereafter be performed on the corresponding days of the month of April of each year: *Provided,* That on and after the 1st day of September, 1867, a tax of $2\frac{1}{2}$ cents per pound only shall be levied, collected and paid on any cotton produced within the United States.

SEC. 2. *And be it further enacted,* That apothecaries, butchers, confectioners, and plumbers and gas-fitters, whose annual sales exceed twenty-five thousand dollars, shall pay, in addition to the special tax now required by law, one dollar for every thousand dollars in excess of said twenty-five thousand dollars; and the taxes on such excess shall be assessed and paid in the manner provided in the case of wholesale dealers.

SEC. 3. *And be it further enacted,* That in all suits or proceedings arising under the internal revenue laws, to which the United States is party, and in all suits or proceedings against a collector or other officer of the internal revenue, wherein a district attorney shall appear for the purpose of prosecuting or defending, it shall be the duty of said attorney, instead of reporting to the Solicitor of the Treasury, immediately at the end of every term of the court in which said suit or proceeding is or shall be instituted, to forward to the Commissioner of Internal Revenue a full and particular statement of the condition of all such suits or proceedings appearing upon the docket of said court: *Provided,* That upon the institution of any such suit or proceeding it shall be the duty of said attorney to report to said commissioner the full particulars relating to such suit or proceeding; and it shall be the duty of the Commissioner of Internal Revenue, (with the approval of the Secretary of the Treasury,) to establish such rules and regulations, not inconsistent with law, for the observance of revenue officers, district attorneys and marshals, respecting suits arising under the internal revenue laws, in which the United States is a party, as may be deemed necessary for the just responsibility of those officers and the prompt collection of all revenues, and debts due and accruing to the United States under such laws.

SEC. 4. *And be it further enacted,* That the Commissioner of Internal Revenue, shall have charge of all real estate which has been or shall be assigned, set off, or conveyed, by purchase or otherwise, to the United States, in payment of debts arising under the laws relating to internal revenue, and of all trusts created for the use of the United States, in payment of such debts due them; and, with the approval of the Secretary of the Treasury, may sell and dispose of, at public vendue, upon not less than twenty days' notice, lands assigned or set off to the United States in payment of such debts, or vested in them by mortgage or other security, for the payment of such debts; and in cases where real estate has already become the property of the United States by conveyance or otherwise, in payment of or as security for a debt arising under the laws relating to internal revenue, and such debt shall have been paid, together with the interest thereon, at the rate of one per centum per month, to the United States, within two years from the date of the acquisition of such real estate, it shall be lawful for the Commissioner of Internal Revenue, with the approval of the Secretary of the Treasury, to release by deed, or otherwise convey, such real estate to the debtor from whom it was taken, or to his heirs or other legal representatives.

SEC. 5. *And be it further enacted,* That if the manufacturer of any article upon which a tax is required to be paid by means of a stamp shall have sold or removed for sale any such articles without the use of the proper stamp, in addition to the penalties now imposed by law for such sale or removal, it shall be the duty of the proper assessor or assistant assessor, within a period of not more than two years after such removal or sale, upon such information as he can obtain, to estimate the amount of the tax which has been omitted to be paid, and to make an assessment therefor, and certify the same to the collector; and the subsequent proceedings for collection shall be in all respects like those for the collection of taxes upon manufactures and productions.

SEC. 6. *And be it further enacted,* That it shall be lawful for the Commissioner of Internal Revenue, whenever he shall deem it expedient, to designate one or more of the assistant assessors in any collection district to make assessments in any part of such collection district for all such taxes as may be due upon any specified objects of taxation, and in such case it shall be the duty of the other assistant assessors of such collection district to report to the assistant assessor thus specially designated, all matters which may come to their knowledge relative to any assessments to be made by him. *Provided,* That whenever two or more districts or parts of districts are embraced within one county it may be lawful for such assistant assessor or assessors to make assessment anywhere within such county upon such specified objects of taxation as he may be by said commissioner required: *Provided further*, That such assessment shall be returned to the assessor of the district in which such taxes are payable.

SEC. 7. *And be it further enacted*, That the Commissioner of Internal Revenue, with the approval of the Secretary of the Treasury, is hereby authorized to pay such sums, not exceeding in the aggregate the amount appropriated therefor, as may in his judgment be deemed necessary for detecting and bringing to trial and punishment persons guilty of violating the internal revenue laws, or conniving at the same in cases where such expenses are not otherwise provided for by law. And for this purpose there is hereby appropriated one hundred thousand dollars, or so much thereof as may be necessary, out of any money in the treasury not otherwise appropriated.

SEC. 8. *And be it further enacted*, That hereafter for any failure to pay any internal revenue tax at the time and in the manner required by law, where such failure creates a liability to pay a penalty of ten per centum additional upon the amount of tax so due and unpaid, the person or persons so failing or neglecting to pay said tax, instead of ten per centum as aforesaid, shall pay a penalty of five per centum, together with interest at the rate of one per centum per month upon said tax from the time the same became due, but no interest for any fraction of a month shall be demanded.

SEC. 9. *And be it further enacted*, That the act entitled "An act to provide internal revenue to support the government, to pay interest on the public debt, and for other purposes," approved June thirty, eighteen hundred and sixty-four, as subsequently amended, be, and the same is hereby, amended as follows, viz:

That section twenty-two be amended by striking out, after the words "assistant assessor," and before the word "actually," the words "four dollars for every day," and inserting in lieu thereof the words "five dollars for every day;" and, further, by striking out the following words: "And assistant assessors may be allowed, in the settlement of their accounts, such sum as the Commissioner of Internal Revenue shall approve, not exceeding three hundred dollars per annum, for office rent; but no account for such office rent shall be allowed or paid until it shall have been verified in such manner as the Commissioner of Internal Revenue may require, and shall have been audited and approved by the proper officers of the Treasury Department; and assistant assessors, when employed outside of the town in which they reside, in addition to the compensation which they are now allowed by law, shall, during such time so employed, receive one dollar per day." This amendment shall take effect upon compensation for the month of March, eighteen hundred and sixty-seven, and thereafter.

That section twenty-four be amended by inserting in the proviso to said section, after the word "spirits," wherever it occurs, the words "or other articles."

That section forty be amended by striking out the following words: "That in case a collector shall die, resign, or be removed," and inserting in lieu the following: "That in case of a vacancy occurring in the office of collector by reason of death, or any other cause."

That section seventy-three be amended by striking out all after the enacting clause, and inserting in lieu thereof the following: That any person who shall exercise or carry on any trade, business, or profession, or do any act hereinafter mentioned, for the exercising, carrying on, or doing of which a special tax is imposed by law, without payment thereof, as in that behalf required, shall, for every such offence, besides being liable to the payment of the tax, be subject to a fine or penalty of not less than ten nor more than five hundred dollars. And if such person shall be a manufacturer of tobacco, snuff, or cigars, or a wholesale or retail dealer in liquor, he shall be further liable to imprisonment for a term not less than sixty days and not exceeding two years.

That section seventy-nine be amended as follows: In paragraph four, by striking out the following words: "In quantities of more than three gallons at one and the same time to the same purchaser, or." In paragraph five, by striking out the following words: "In quantities of three gallons or less." In paragraph thirty-one, by adding thereto the following: "*Provided*, That no special tax shall be required of any person for the manufacture of butter or cheese." In paragraph thirty-two, by inserting after the word "garden" and before the word "who," the words "or traveling on foot and peddling fruits, vegetables, pies, cakes, and confectionery."

That section ninety be amended by inserting after the word "cigars," and before the first proviso in said section, the words "and all proceedings relating to forfeiture and sale of distilled spirits shall apply to tobacco, snuff, and cigars."

That section ninety-four be amended as follows:

By striking out in the paragraph relating to gas, the words "and until the thirtieth day of April, 1867."

By striking out the paragraphs relating to "sugar and sugar refiners," and insert in lieu thereof the words:

"On all sugars produced from the sugar cane, and not from sorghum or imphee, other than those produced by the refiner, a tax of one cent per pound.

"On refined sugars, and on the products of sugar refineries not including sirup or molasses, a tax of two per centum ad valorem: *Provided*, That every person shall be regarded as a sugar refiner, and pay the taxes required by law, whose business it is to advance the quality and value of sugar by melting and recrystallization, or by liquoring claying, or other washing process, or by any other chemical or mechanical means, or who shall by boiling or other process extract sugar from or advance the quality or value of molasses, concentrated molasses, or melado;"

Also, in the paragraph relating to wood screws, by striking out the word "ten" and inserting "five;"

Also by striking out the paragraph relating to "gunpowder," and inserting in lieu thereof the following:

"On gunpowder, canister powder, five cents per pound: sporting powder in kegs, one cent per pound; blasting powder, in kegs or casks, one-half cent per pound;"

Also, by striking out all from the words "cigarettes or small cigars," in the first paragraph relating to cigars, down to and including the words "twenty per centum ad valorem on the market value thereof," in the last paragraph relating to cigars, and inserting in lieu thereof the following:

"On cigarettes, cigars, and cheroots of all descriptions, made of tobacco or any substitute therefor, five dollars per thousand."

That section ninety-four be further amended so that in lieu of the taxes now provided by law upon the goods, wares, and merchandise hereinafter mentioned, which shall be produced and sold, or be manufactured or made and sold, or be consumed or used by the manufacturer or producer thereof, or removed for consumption or use, or for delivery to others than agents of the manufacturer or producer within the United States or Territories thereof, there shall be assessed, collected and paid the following taxes, to be paid by the producer or manufacturer thereof, that is to say:

On boots and shoes, made wholly or in part of India-rubber, two per centum ad valorem;

On hats, caps, bonnets, and hoods of all descriptions, two per centum ad valorem;

On hoop-skirts, two per centum ad valorem;

On leather of all descriptions, and goat, deer, calf, kid, sheep, horse, hog and dog skins, tanned or partially tanned, curried, finished or in the rough, two and one-half per centum ad valorem;

On manufactures exclusively of glass, other than window glass, three per centum ad valorem.

On manufactures of wool, or of which wool is the chief component material or the component material of chief value, two and a half per centum ad valorem.

That section ninety-four be amended by adding to the end of said section the following words: "But no tax shall be imposed upon the redyeing or reprinting of cloths or other articles."

That section ninety-six be amended by inserting after the words "and also all goods, wares, and merchandise, and articles," and before the words, "made or manufactured from materials," the words, "not specially named and taxed, and which are."

That section one hundred and three be amended by striking out the word three where it occurs and inserting the words two and a half, and by striking out the words "until the thirtieth day of April, eighteen hundred and sixty-seven."

That schedule B, in relation to stamp duties, named in section one hundred and fifty-one, be amended by striking out of said schedule the words "legal documents," and all thereafter, and inserting in lieu thereof the following: "*Provided*, That the stamp duties imposed by the foregoing schedule (B) on manifests, bills of lading, and passage tickets, shall not apply to steamboats or vessels plying between ports of the United States and ports of British North America. *And provided further*, That all affidavits shall be exempt from stamp duty."

Also by inserting at the end of the last paragraph relating to "probate of will," the following words: "*Provided*, That no stamp either for probate of wills, or letters testamentary, or of administration, or on administrator or guardian bond, shall be required when the value of the estate and effects, real and personal, does not exceed one thousand dollars: *Provided further*, That no stamp tax shall be required upon any papers necessary to be used for the collection from the government of claims by soldiers or their legal representatives of the United States, for pensions, back pay, bounty, or for property lost in the service." The reduction of taxes provided in this section shall take effect on and after March one, eighteen hundred and sixty-seven.

SEC. 10. *And be it further enacted*, That the act amendatory to the act entitled "An act to provide internal revenue to support the government, to pay interest on the public debt, and for other purposes," approved June thirty, eighteen hundred and sixty-four, approved July thirteen, eighteen hundred and sixty-six, be amended as follows, viz:

That section ten (section eleven, page 177 of this work,) be amended by adding after the word "pupils," in the sixth paragraph of said section, the words "but not including distilled spirits, mineral oil, tobacco, snuff, and cigars."

Also, by striking out in the paragraph relating to monuments, after the word "monuments," where it first occurs, the words "of stone."

That section eighteen (section nineteen, page 184 of this work,) be amended by adding thereto the following: "*Provided*, That the exemption herein shall not apply to tobacco, snuff, and cigars manufactured, or spirits distilled, or petroleum refined, either in or for such schools and colleges."

That section nineteen (section twenty, page 184 of this work,) is hereby amended by adding the following thereto: "And no suit for the purpose of restraining the assessment or collection of tax shall be maintained in any court."

That section forty-three (section forty-four, page 197 of this work,) be amended by striking out the last two sentences.

Amend section forty-eight (section forty-nine, page 199 of this work,) of the act relating to internal revenue approved July thirteen, eighteen hundred and sixty-six, so as to insert in the proviso the word "thirds" after word "halves" and before the word "quarters," and also amend it by striking out the words "more than one-quarter and not more than one-half shall be accounted one-half," and insert, "more than one-quarter and not more than one-third shall be accounted one-third and more than one-third and less than one-half shall be accounted one-half:" *Provided*, that fractional parts of barrels containing more than one-quarter and not more than one-half shall be accounted one half and pay tax as such until June 1st, 1867.

SEC. 11. *And be it further enacted*, That on and after March first, eighteen hundred and sixty-seven, in addition to the articles now exempt by law, the articles and products hereinafter enumerated shall be exempt from internal tax, namely:

Alcoholic and ethereal vegetable extracts, when solid and used solely for medicinal purposes;

Bale rope, seines and netting for seines, twine, and lines of all kinds;

Bar, rod, hoop, band, sheet, and plate iron of all descriptions, and iron prepared for the manufacture of steel: *Provided*, That the exemption aforesaid shall be confined exclusively to said articles in the state and condition specified in the foregoing enumeration, and shall not be construed as exempting spikes, nails, or any other manufactures of iron from the taxes now imposed by law;

Brush blocks;

Canned and preserved meats, and shell fish;

Carbolic acid and carbolate of lime, used solely for disinfectants;

Carpet bag and caba frames;

Canned and preserved vegetables and fruits;

Casks, churns, barrels, wooden brushes and broom handles, tanks, and kitts made of wood, including cooperage of all kinds, bungs and plugs, packing boxes, nest boxes, and match boxes, whether made of wood or other materials; wooden hames, plough beams, split-bottom chairs, and turned materials for the same unmanufactured, and saddle-trees made of wood, and match boxes heretofore made. on which a tax has not been paid;

Castings of iron, copper, or brass made for machinery, cars or scales, and castings made to form a part of any article upon which, in a finished state, a tax is assessed and paid;

Cast-iron hollow ware, and cast-iron hollow ware tinned, enameled, japanned, or galvanized;

Clock trimmings, namely: Clock work, clock pillars. sash fastenings for clocks, winding keys, verges and pendulum rods;

Clothing, or articles of dress not specially enumerated, made by sewing, for the wear of men, women, or children, from cloths or fabrics on which a tax or duty has been paid;

Coffee mills, coffee grinders and roasters, and apple-paring machines;

Copper bottoms for articles used for domestic and culinary purposes;

Doors, window sash, blinds, frames, and sills, of whatever material;

Drain, gas, and water-pipe, made of wood or cement;

Frames and handles for saws and buck-saws;

Glue and gelatine, of all descriptions, in the solid state;

Glue and cement, made wholly or in part of glue in the liquid state;

Horse-rakes, horse powers, tedders, hames, scythe snaths, hay forks, hoes, and portable grinding mills;

Horse-blankets, made from cloth, on which a tax or duty has been paid;

Licorice and licorice paste;

Magnesium lamps;

Manufactures of jute;

Molasses, concentrated molasses or melado, sirup of molasses or sugar cane juice, and cistern bottoms;

Oil naphtha, benzine, benzole, or gasoline, marking more than seventy degrees Baume's hydrometer, the product of the distillation, or re-distillation, or refining of crude petroleum, or of crude oil produced by a single distillation of coal, shale, peat, asphaltum, or other bituminous substances;

Palm-leaf and straw, bleached, split, prepared, or advanced by being braided or woven, but not made up into hats, bonnets, or hoods;

Potato hooks, pitchforks, manure and spading forks;

Pottery-ware of all descriptions, including stone, earthen, brown and yellow-earthen, and common or gray-stone ware;

Pumps, garden engines, and hydraulic rams;

Rock and root-diggers, or excavators;

Root-beer, and other small beer;

Salt;

School-room seats and desks, blackboards, and globes of all kinds;

Sleds, wheelbarrows, and hand-carts, and fence made of wood;

Soap, common brown, in bars, sold for less than seven cents per pound;

Saws for cotton gins, when used by the maker in the manufacture of gins;

Soles and heel-taps made of India-rubber, or of India-rubber and other materials;

Shirt fronts or bosoms, wristbands or cuffs for shirts, except those made of paper.

Spiral springs, used in the manufacture of furniture;

Stove polish, or other manufacture exclusively of plumbago, buck saws, stump machines, potato diggers;

Steel of all descriptions, whether made from muck-bar, blooms, slabs, loops, or otherwise;

Scythes;

Straw or binder's board, and binder's cloth, and straw wrapping paper;

Tags for merchandise and direction, of cloth, paper or metal, whether blank or printed; thimble skeins and pipe boxes, made of iron;

Tin ware for domestic and culinary purposes;

Ultramarine blue;

Varnish;

Wagons, carts and drays, made to be used for farming, freighting, or lumber purposes;

Washing, mangling, and clothes-wringing machines, zinc washboards, spinning and flax-wheels, hand-reels, hand-looms, wooden knobs, and beehives;

Provided, That the exemptions aforesaid shall, in all cases, be confined exclusively to said articles in the state and condition specified in the foregoing enumeration, and shall not extend to articles in any other form, nor to manufactures from said articles.

SEC. 12. *And be it further enacted,* That there shall be levied, collected and paid on brandy made from grapes, one dollar per gallon; and if any person shall knowingly manufacture, compound, put up, sell or dispose of, or cause to be manufactured, compounded, put up, sold or disposed of, or aid or assist therein, any fluid as or for, or under, or with the name of brandy made from grapes, which shall not be really such, shall, on conviction thereof, be punished for each offence by a fine not exceeding one thousand dollars, and by imprisonment not exceeding one year, or both said punishments, in the discretion of the court, and any such simulated or compounded fluid as aforesaid, shall be forfeited to the United States.

SEC. 13. *And be it further enacted,* That the act entitled "An act to provide internal revenue to support the government, to pay interest on the public debt, and for other purposes," approved June thirty, eighteen hundred and sixty-four, and as subsequently amended, be further amended as follows, namely:

INCOME.

That section one hundred and sixteen be amended by striking out all after the enacting clause, and inserting, in lieu thereof, as follows: That there shall be levied, collected, and paid annually upon the gains, profits, and income of every person residing in the United States, or of any citizen of the United States residing abroad, whether derived from any kind of property, rents, interest, dividends, or salaries, or from any profession, trade, employment, or vocation, carried on in the United States or elsewhere, or from any other source whatever, a tax of five per centum on the amount so derived over one thousand dollars, and a like tax shall be levied, collected, and paid annually upon the gains, profits, and income of every business, trade, or profession carried on in the United States by persons residing without the United States, and not citizens thereof. And the tax herein provided for shall be assessed, collected, and paid upon the gains, profits, and income for the year ending the thirty-first day of December next preceding the time for levying, collecting, and paying said tax.

That section one hundred and seventeen be amended by striking out all after the enacting clause and inserting, in lieu thereof, the following: That, in estimating the gains, profits, and income of any person, there shall be included all income derived from interest upon notes, bonds, and other securities of the United States; profits realized within the year from sales of real estate purchased within the year or within two years previous to the year for which income is estimated; interest received or accrued upon all notes, bonds, and mortgages, or other forms of indebtedness bearing interest, whether paid or not, if good and collectable, less the interest which has become due from said person during the year; the amount of all premium on gold and coupons; the amount of sales of live stock, sugar, wool, butter, cheese, pork, beef, mutton, or other meats, hay and grain, or other vegetable or other productions, being the growth or produce of the estate of such person, not including any part thereof consumed directly by the family; all other gains, profits, and income derived from any source whatever; except the rental value of any homestead used or occupied by any person or by his family in his own right or in the right of his wife; and the share of any person of the gains and profits of all companies, whether incorporated or partnership, w' o would be entitled to the same, if divided, whether divided or otherwise, except the amount of income received from institutions or corporations whose officers, as required by law, withhold a per centum of the dividends made by such institutions, and pay the same to the officer authorized to receive the same; and except that portion of the salary or pay received for services in the civil, military, naval or other service of the United States, including senators, representatives, and delegates in Congress, from which the tax has been deducted. And in addition to one thousand dollars exempt from income tax, as hereinbefore provided, all national, State, county, and municipal taxes paid within the year shall be deducted from the gains, profits, or income of the person who has actually paid the same, whether such person be owner, tenant, or mortgagor; losses actually sustained during the year arising from fires, shipwreck, or incurred in trade, and debts ascertained to be worthless, but excluding all estimated depreciation of values and losses within the year on sales of real estate purchased two years previous to the year for which income is estimated; the amount actually paid for labor or interest by any person who rents lands or hires labor to cultivate land, or who conducts any other business from which income is actually derived; the amount actually paid by any person for the rent of the house or premises occupied as a residence for himself or his family; the amount paid out for usual or ordinary repairs: *Provided*, That no deduction shall be made for any amount paid out for new buildings, permanent improvements, or betterments, made to increase the value of any property or estate: *And provided, further*, That only one deduction of one thousand dollars shall be made from the aggregate income of all the members of any family, composed of one or both parents and one or more minor children, or husband and wife; that guardians shall be allowed to make such deduction in favor of each and every ward, except that in case where two or more wards are comprised in one family, and have joint property interest, only one deduction shall be made in their favor: *And provided further*, That in cases where the salary or other compensation paid to any person in the employment or service of the United States shall not exceed the rate of one thousand dollars per annum, or shall be by fees, or uncertain or irregular in the amount or in the time during which the same shall have accrued or been earned, such salary or other compensation shall be included in estimating the annual gains, profits, or income of the person to whom the same shall have been paid.

That section one hundred and eighteen be amended by striking out all after the enacting clause and inserting, in lieu thereof, the following: That it shall be the duty of all persons of lawful age to make and render a list or return, on or before the day prescribed by law, in such form and manner as may be prescribed by the Commissioner of Internal Revenue, to the assistant assessor of the district in which they reside, of the amount of their income, gains, and profits, as aforesaid; and all guardians and trustees, executors and administrators, or any person acting in any other fiduciary capacity, shall make and render a list or return, as aforesaid, to the assistant assessor of the district in which such person acting in a fiduciary capacity resides, of the amount of income, gains, and profits of any minor or person for whom they act and the assistant assessor shall require every list or return to be verified by the oath or affirmation of the party rendering it, and may increase the amount of any list or return, if he has reason to believe that the same is understated; and in case any such person, shall neglect or refuse to make and render such list or return, or shall render a false or fraudulent list or return, it shall be the duty of the assessor or the assistant assessor to make such list, according to the best information he can obtain, by the examination of such person, or his books or accounts, or any other evidence, and to add fifty per centum as a penalty to the amount of the tax due on such list in all cases of wilful neglect or refusal to make and render a list or return, and, in all cases of a false or fraudulent list or return having been rendered, to add one hundred per centum, as a penalty, to the amount of tax ascertained to be due, the tax and the additions thereto as a penalty to be assessed and collected in the manner provided for in other cases of wilful neglect or refusal to render a list or return, or of rendering a false and fraudulent return: *Provided,* That any party, in his or her own behalf, or as such fiduciary shall be permitted to declare, under oath or affirmation, the form and manner of which shall be prescribed by the Commissioner of Internal Revenue, that he or she, or his or her ward or beneficiary, was not possessed of an income of one thousand dollars, liable to be assessed according to the provisions of this act; or may declare that he or she has been assessed and paid an income tax elsewhere in the same year, under authority of the United States, upon his or her income, gains, and profits, as prescribed by law; and if the assistant assessor shall be satisfied of the truth of the declaration, shall thereupon be exempt from income tax in the said district; or if the list or return of any party shall have been increased by the assistant assessor, such party may exhibit his books and accounts, and be permitted to prove and declare, under oath or affirmation, the amount of income liable to be assessed; but such oaths and evidence shall not be considered as conclusive of the facts, and no deductions claimed in such cases shall be made or allowed until approved by the assistant assessor. Any person feeling aggrieved by the decision of the assistant assessor in such cases may appeal to the assessor of the district, and his decision thereon, unless reversed by the Commissioner of Internal Revenue, shall be final, and the form, time, and manner of proceedings shall be subject to rules and regulations to be prescribed by the Commissioner of Internal Revenue: *Provided further*, That no penalty shall be assessed upon any person for such neglect or refusal, or for making or rendering a false or fraudulent return, except after reasonable notice of the time and place of hearing, to be regulated by the Commissioner of Internal Revenue, so as to give the person charged an opportunity to be heard.

That section one hundred and nineteen be amended by striking out all after the enacting clause and inserting, in lieu thereof the following: That the taxes on incomes herein imposed shall be levied on the first day of March, and be due and payable on or before the thirtieth day of April, in each year, until and including the year eighteen hundred and seventy, and no longer; and to any sum or sums annually due and unpaid after the thirtieth of April, as aforesaid and for ten days after notice and demand thereof by the collector, there shall be levied in addition thereto the sum of five per centum on the amount of taxes unpaid, and interest at the rate of one per centum per month upon said tax from the time the same became due, as a penalty, except from the estates of deceased insane or insolvent persons: *Provided*, That the tax on incomes for the year eighteen hundred and sixty-six shall be levied on the day this act takes effect.

That section one hundred and twenty-three be amended by striking out all after the enacting clause and inserting, in lieu thereof, the following: That there shall be levied, collected, and paid on all salaries of officers, or payments for services to persons in the civil, military, naval, or other employment or service of the United States, including senators and representatives and delegates in Congress, when exceeding the rate of one thousand dollars per annum, a tax of five per centum on the excess above the said one thousand dollars; and it shall be the duty of all paymasters and all disbursing officers, under the government of the United States, or persons in the employ thereof, when making any payment to any officers or persons as aforesaid, whose compensation is determined by a fixed salary, or upon settling or adjusting the accounts of such officers or persons, to deduct and withhold the aforesaid tax of five per centum; and the pay-roll, receipts, or account of officers or persons paying such tax as aforesaid, shall be made to exhibit the fact of such payment. And it shall be the duty of the accounting officers of the Treasury Department, when auditing the accounts of any paymaster or disbursing officer, or any officer withholding his salary from moneys received by him, or when settling or adjusting the accounts of any such officer, to require evidence that the taxes mentioned in this section have been deducted and paid over to the Treasurer of the United States, or other officer authorized to receive the same: *Provided*, That payments of prize money shall be regarded as income from salaries, and the tax thereon shall be adjusted and collected in like manner: *Provided further*, That this section shall not apply to payments made to mechanics or laborers employed upon public works: And *provided further*, That in case it should become necessary for showing the true receipts of the government under the operations of this section upon the books of the treasury Department, the requisite amount may be carried from unappropriated moneys in the Treasury to the credit of said account; and this section shall take effect upon salary and compensation for the month of March, eighteen hundred and sixty-seven.

SEC. 14. *And be it further enacted*, That there shall be levied, collected, and paid on all distilled spirits, upon which no tax has been paid according to law, a tax of two dollars upon each and every proof gallon, to be paid by the distiller, owner, or any person having possession thereof, and every proprietor and possessor of a still, distillery, or distilling apparatus shall be jointly and severally liable for the taxes imposed by law upon the spirits distilled therein; and the tax shall be a lien upon the spirits distilled, on the distillery used for distilling the same, with the stills, vessels, fixtures, and tools therein, and on the lot or tract of land whereon the said distillery is situated, together with any building thereon, from the time said spirits are distilled until the said tax shall be paid: *Provided*, That the tax upon any spirits distilled and removed from the place where the same were distilled, and not deposited in bonded warehouse as required by law, shall, at any time, upon knowledge of such fact obtained by the assessor or assistant assessor of the district where such spirits were distilled, be assessed by him upon the distiller of the same, and certified or returned to the collector, who shall immediately demand payment of such tax, and upon the neglect or refusal of payment by the distiller, shall proceed to collect the same by distraint. But this provision shall not exclude any other remedy or proceeding provided by law: *Provided further*, That the tax on all spirits shall be collected at no lower rate than the basis of first proof, and shall be increased in proportion for any greater strength than the strength of first proof.

SEC. 15. *And be it further enacted*, That proof spirit shall be held and taken to be that alcoholic liquor which contains one-half its volume of alcohol of a specific gravity of seven thousand nine hundred and thirty-nine (.7939) ten thousandths at sixty degrees Fahrenheit; and the Secretary of the Treasury is hereby authorized to adopt, procure, and prescribe for use such hydrometers, weighing and gauging instruments, meters, or other means for ascertaining the strength and quantity of spirits subject to tax, or for the prevention or detection of frauds by distillers of spirits, and to prescribe such rules and regulations as he may deem necessary to insure a uniform and correct system of inspection, weighing, and gauging of spirits subject to tax throughout the United States. And whenever the Secretary of the Treasury shall adopt and prescribe for use any meter or meters it shall be the duty of every owner, agent, or superintendent of a distillery, to make application to the collector of his district for such meter or meters, to be used in his distillery, and the same shall be furnished and attached to the distillery at the expense of the distiller, whose duty it shall be to furnish all the pipes, materials, labor, and facilities necessary to complete such attachment in accordance with the regulations of the Commissioner of Internal Revenue, who is hereby further authorized to order and require such changes of or additions to distilling apparatus, connecting pipes, pumps or cisterns, or any machinery connected with or used in or on the distillery premises, or may require to be put on any of the stills, tubs, cisterns, pipes, or other vessels such fastenings, locks or seals as he may deem necessary. And in all sales of spirits hereafter made, where not otherwise specially agreed, a gallon shall be taken to be a gallon of first proof, according to the foregoing standard set forth and declared for the inspection and gauging of spirits throughout the United States.

SEC. 16. *And be it further enacted,* That every person, firm, or corporation who distills or manufactures spirits or alcohol, or who brews or makes mash, wort, or wash, for distillation or the production of spirits shall be deemed a distiller. And the making or keeping by any person of grain, mash, wash, wort, or beer, prepared or fit for distillation, together with the possession by such person of a still or other apparatus capable of use for distilling, upon the same premises, shall be deemed and taken as presumptive evidence that such person is a distiller.

SEC. 17. *And be it further enacted,* That hereafter all distilled spirits, before being removed from the distillery, shall be inspected and gauged by a general inspector of spirits, who shall mark the barrels or packages in the manner required by law; and so much of the act approved July thirteen, eighteen hundred and sixty-six, as requires the appointment of an inspector for each distillery established according to law, is hereby repealed: *Provided,* That such other duties as have heretofore been imposed upon inspectors of distilleries, may be performed by such other duly appointed officers as may be designated by the Commissioner of Internal Revenue.

SEC. 18. *And be it further enacted,* That whenever, in the judgment of the collector, there shall be a general bonded warehouse so located as to be conveniently accessible to a distillery, and in the same collection district, the said collector shall direct all spirits which may be stored in the bonded warehouse attached to such distillery to be transferred directly to a general bonded warehouse; and all spirits thereafter produced in such distillery shall be removed to a general bonded warehouse within the time and in the manner heretofore required for removal to the bonded warehouse attached to the distillery.

SEC. 19. *And be it further enacted,* That no spirits shall be removed in any cask or package containing more than ten gallons from any premises or building in which the same may have been distilled, re-distilled, rectified or manufactured, nor from any place of storage, at any other times than after sun-rising and before sun-setting, on pain of forfeiture of such spirits, and every person who shall violate this provision shall be liable to a penalty of one hundred dollars for each cask, barrel or package of spirits removed. Any officer of internal revenue may be specially authorized by the Commissioner of Internal Revenue to seize any property which may by law be subject to seizure, and for that purpose such officer shall have all the power conferred by law upon collectors of internal revenue, and such special authority shall be limited in respect of time, place, and kind or class of property as the said Commissioner may specify.

SEC. 20. *And be it further enacted*, That it shall be lawful for any internal revenue officer to seize and detain any barrels, casks, or packages containing, or supposed to contain, distilled spirits, when such officer has reason to believe the tax imposed by law upon the same has not been paid, or that they are being removed in violation of law, and such packages may be detained by such officer in a safe place until it can be satisfactorily ascertained by the proper officers whether the articles so seized are liable to be proceeded against for violations of the internal revenue laws.

SEC. 21. *And be it further enacted*, That whenever any distilled spirits so found elsewhere than in a bonded warehouse, shall be sold, or offered for sale at a less price than the tax imposed by law thereon, such selling or offering for sale as aforesaid, shall be taken and deemed as prima facie evidence that said spirits have not been removed from a bonded warehouse according to law, and that the tax imposed by law on the same has not been paid, and the same shall, without further evidence, be liable to seizure and forfeiture: *Provided*, That this section shall not apply to spirits sold at public sale by an auctioneer who has paid the special tax as such under such rules and regulations, and upon such public notice as may be prescribed by the Commissioner of Internal Revenue, nor to sales made by judicial or executive officers under the authority or decree of any court.

SEC. 22. *And be it further enacted*, That it shall be the duty of every person who empties or draws off, or causes to be emptied or drawn off, distilled spirits or other article subject by law to tax, from a cask, barrel, or package, bearing any of the marks or brands required by law, or marks intended for or purporting to be, or designed to have the effect of such marks, immediately upon such cask, barrel or package being emptied, to efface and obliterate said marks or brands; and any person who shall violate this provision shall be liable to a penalty of ten dollars for each offence; and any such cask, barrel, or package, from which said marks are not so effaced and obliterated as herein required, shall be liable to forfeiture, and may be seized by any officer of internal revenue wherever found.

SEC. 23 *And be it further enacted*, That in case any bond under which any distilled spirits shall have been withdrawn from a bonded warehouse is forfeited by failure to furnish or produce at the proper time the evidence required by law or regulation that the articles named in the bond were duly received and actually stored in the warehouse or district to which they were shipped, or by other breach of the obligation, the obligors in the bond shall pay the total amount of duties upon the articles removed under the bond, together with fifty per centum upon that amount, and the collector of the district in which such bond is or may be given may forthwith distrain upon any property, real or personal, subject to distraint or seizure, belonging to said obligors; and in case no such property can be found, the collector shall immediately forward the bond to the United States district attorney for the proper district for suit, and notice of the breach of the obligation of any such bond shall be forthwith forwarded by the collector of the district to the Commissioner of Internal Revenue.

SEC. 24. *And be it further enacted*, That the forty-fourth (section 45, page 198 of this work,) section of the act of July thirteen, eighteen hundred and sixty-six, aforesaid, be amended by adding thereto as follows: *Provided*, That when any still used or fit for use in the production of distilled spirits, the same not exceeding one thousand dollars in value, has been or shall be seized for any violation of the laws relating to internal revenue, the same shall not be released by the court to the claimant, or any other intervening party, before judgment; and if declared forfeited, such still shall be so destroyed as to prevent its use for the purpose aforesaid, and the materials thereof shall be sold as other forfeited property. In case of seizure, as above, of a still exceeding in value the sum of one thousand dollars, its release to the claimant or any other intervening party, before judgment, shall be at the discretion of the court.

SEC. 25. *And be it further enacted*, That the owner, agent, or superintendent of any still, boiler, or other vessel used in the distillation of spirits, who shall neglect or refuse to make true and exact entry and report of the same, or to do or cause to be done any of the things by law required to be done concerning distilled spirits, shall in addition to other fines and penalties, now by law provided, forfeit for every such neglect or refusal all the spirits made by or for him, and all the vessels used in making the same, and the stills, boilers, and other vessels used in distillation, and all materials fit for use in distillation found on the premises, together with the sum of five hundred dollars for each offence, to be recovered with costs of suit, and shall be deemed guilty of a misdemeanor, and be subject to imprisonment for a term not exceeding one year; which said spirits, with the vessels containing the same, with all the vessels used in making the same, and all said materials may be seized by the collector and held by him until a decision shall be had thereon according to law: *Provided*, That proceedings to enforce said forfeiture shall be commenced by such collector within twenty days after the seizure thereof. And the proceedings to enforce said forfeiture of said property shall be in the nature of a proceeding *in rem*, in the circuit or district court of the United States for the district where such seizure is made, or in any other court of competent jurisdiction.

SEC. 26. *And be it further enacted*, That if any collector, deputy collector, assessor, assistant assessor, inspector, district attorney, marshal, or other officer, agent, or person charged with the execution or supervision of the execution of any of the provisions of this act, or of the act to which this is amendatory, shall demand, or accept, or attempt to collect, directly or indirectly, as payment or gift or otherwise, any sum of money or other property of value for the compromise, adjustment, or settlement of any charge or complaint for any violation or alleged violation of any of the said provisions, except as expressly authorized by law so to do, he shall be held to be guilty of a misdemeanor, and shall for every such offence be liable to indictment and trial in any court of the United States having competent jurisdiction, and on conviction thereof shall be fined in double the sum or value of the money or property received or demanded, and be imprisoned for a period of not less than one year nor more than ten years.

SEC. 27. *And be it further enacted*, That no distilled spirits which have been forfeited to the government in accordance with law shall be sold for a price less than the amount of the tax required thereon by law at the time of such sale. And if the officer having such spirits in charge shall have been unable, for a period of ninety days, to sell the same for the price equal to the tax, such spirits shall be destroyed, under such rules and regulations as the Commissioner of Internal Revenue may prescribe.

SEC. 28. *And be it further enacted*, That if any person shall falsely represent himself to be a revenue officer of the United States, and shall in such assumed character demand or receive any money or other article of value from any person for any duty or tax due to the United States, or for any violation or pretended violation of any revenue law of the United States, such person shall be deemed guilty of a felony, and on conviction thereof shall be liable to a fine of five hundred dollars, and to imprisonment not less than six months and not exceeding two years, at the discretion of the court.*

SEC. 29. *And be it further enacted*, That no person shall mix for sale naphtha and illuminating oils, or shall knowingly sell or keep for sale or offer for sale such mixture, or shall sell or offer for sale oil made from petroleum for illuminating purposes, inflammable at less temperature or fire test than one hundred and ten degrees Fahrenheit, and any person so doing shall be held to be guilty of a misdemeanor, and on conviction thereof by indictment or presentment in any court of the United States, having competent jurisdiction, shall be punished by a

---

* The reader will not fail to carefully compare the provisions of law from section 22 to section 47 inclusive, of the Act of July 13, 1866, found on page 185 *et seq.* of this work, and the circulars and instructions to inspectors of distilleries, found in the Appendix.

fine of not less than one hundred dollars nor more than five hundred dollars, and by imprisonment for a term of not less than six months nor more than three years.

SEC. 30. *And be it further enacted,* That if two or more persons conspire either to commit any offence against the laws of the United States, or to defraud the United States in any manner whatever, and one or more of said parties to said conspiracy shall do any act to effect the object thereof, the parties to said conspiracy shall be deemed guilty of a misdemeanor, and, on conviction thereof, shall be liable to a penalty of not less than one thousand dollars, and not more than ten thousand dollars, and to imprisonment not exceeding two years. And when any offence shall be begun in one judicial district of the United States and completed in another, every such offence shall be deemed to have been committed in either of the said districts, and may be dealt with, inquired of, tried, determined, and punished in either of the said districts, in the same manner as if it had been actually and wholly committed therein.

SEC. 31. *And be it further enacted,* That all inspectors appointed under the provisions of the act or acts of which this is amendatory, shall be required to give bonds, with security, approved by the Secretary of the Treasury, or assessor of the district, in a sum not less than $5,000, conditioned for the faithful discharge of the duties of such inspectors.

SEC. 32. *And be it further enacted,* That any person who shall sell, give away, or otherwise dispose of any empty cigar box or boxes which have been stamped, without first defacing or destroying such stamp, or shall re-fill any cigar box without first defacing or destroying such stamp, shall, on conviction of either offence, be liable to a penalty of one hundred dollars, or to imprisonment not exceeding sixty days, or both, in the discretion of the court, with the costs of the trial, and it shall be lawful for any cigar inspector or revenue officer to destroy any empty cigar box upon which a cigar stamp shall be found.

SEC. 33. *And be it further enacted,* That the tonnage duty now imposed on all ships, vessels or steamers, engaged in foreign or domestic commerce, shall be levied but once within one year, and when paid by such ship, vessel or steamer, no further tonnage tax shall be collected within one year from the date of such payment.

SEC. 34. *And be it further enacted,* That all acts or parts of acts inconsistent with this act, and all acts and parts of acts imposing any tax upon advertisements, or the gross receipts of toll roads, are hereby repealed: *Provided,* That this act shall not be construed to affect any act done, right accrued, or penalty incurred under former acts, but every such right is hereby saved; and all suits and prosecutions for acts already done in violation of any former act or acts of Congress relating to the subjects embraced in this act, may be commenced or proceeded with in like manner as if this act had not been passed; and all penal clauses and provisions in existing laws, relating to the subjects embraced in this act, shall be deemed applicable thereto.

APPROVED, March 2, 1867.

[Public Resolution No. 8.]

JOINT RESOLUTION

TO AMEND EXISTING LAWS RELATING TO INTERNAL REVENUE.

Be it resolved by the Senate and House of Representatives of the United States of America in Congress assembled, That alcohol made or manufactured of distilled spirits upon which the taxes imposed by law shall have been paid, and burning fluid made or manufactured from alcohol or spirits of turpentine, or camphene upon which the taxes imposed by law shall have been paid, shall be, and hereby are, exempt from tax ; and so much of section ninety-six of the act of June thirtieth, eighteen hundred and sixty-four, as relates to alcohol and burning fluid, is hereby repealed, and all products of distillation, by whatever name known, which contain distilled spirits or alcohol on which the tax imposed by law has not been paid, shall be considered and taxed as distilled spirits.

SEC. 2. *And bè it further resolved,* that paragraph nineteen of section seventy-nine of the act of June thirtieth, eighteen hundred and sixty-four, as amended by the act of July thirteenth, eighteen hundred and sixty-six, entitled "An act to reduce internal taxation, and to amend an act entitled "An act to provide internal revenue to support the Government, to pay the interest on the public debt and for other purposes" approved June thirtieth, eighteen hundred and sixty-four, and acts amendatory thereof, be, and the same is hereby amended by striking out the words "and distillers of burning fluid and camphene."

APPROVED FEBRUARY 5, 1867.

Schedule

OF

MANUFACTURES AND PRODUCTS EXEMPT FROM TAX

Under the Internal Revenue Laws of the United States,

ON AND AFTER MARCH 2D, 1867.

Acids, acetic, boracic, muriatic, nitric, oleic.

Alcohol, made of spirits or materials on which the duty imposed by law has been paid.

Alcoholic and ethereal vegetable extracts, when solid and used solely for medicinal purposes.

Alkaloids, vegetable.

Alum and patent alum.

Alumina, sulphate of.

Aluminous cake.

Aluminum.

Ammoniacal liquor, produced by the manufacture of illuminating gas.

Ammoniacal liquor, products of.

Aniline.

Animal Charco

Anvils.

Articles manufactured in institutions for the blind, deaf, and dumb, and sold to aid in their support, not including distilled spirits, mineral oil, tobacco, snuff and cigars.

Articles manufactured in manual-labor schools, the proceeds being applied exclusively to the support of the institution.

Ashes, pot and pearl.

Awnings, made by sewing, from fabrics or articles upon which a duty or tax has been paid.

Axles made of steel, used exclusively for vehicles, cars, or locomotives.

Bags, paper.

Bags, made by sewing, from fabrics or articles on which a duty or tax has been paid.

Banners, made of bunting of domestic manufacture.

Barrels or casks, other than those used for the reception of fluids.

Barytes, sulphate of.

Baskets, grain or farm, made of splints.

Beds, feather.

Bees-wax, crude or unrefined.

Bleaching powders.

Blocks, vessel.
Blue vitriol.
Boards.
Bolsters.
Bone-dust.
Book-binding.
Books, and all printed matter.
Borax, and boracic acid.
Bows.
Boxes, packing, made of wood.
Boxes, of wood or paper, for friction matches, cigar lights, and wax tapers.
Brass, in ingots, pigs, bars, rods, or sheets.
Bread, and breadstuffs.
Brick, and fire-brick.
Bristles.
Brooms, made from corn, brush, or palmleaf.
Building stone of all kinds, including slate, marble, freestone, and soapstone.
Bullion, prepared for the use of platers and watchmakers.
Bullion, used in the manufacture of wares, watches, and watch cases.
Bunting, and flags of the United States.
Burial cases.
Burning fluid.
Burr stones.
Butter.
Bale rope, seines and netting for seines, twine, and lines of all kinds.
Bar, rod, hoop, band, sheet, and plate iron of all descriptions, and iron prepared for the manufacture of steel: *Provided*, That the exemption aforesaid shall be confined exclusively to said articles in the state and condition specified in the foregoing enumeration, and shall not be construed as exempting spikes, nails, or any other manufactures of iron from the taxes now imposed by law.
Brush blocks.
Candle-wicking.
Car wheels, made of steel.
Castings of all descriptions, made specially for locks, safes, looms, spinning machines, steam engines, hot-air and hot-water furnaces, and sewing machines, not sold or used for any other purpose, and upon which a tax is assessed and paid on the article of which the casting is a part.
Castings, of malleable iron, unfinished.
Cement, Roman and water.
Charcoal, and animal charcoal or carbon.
Cheese.
Chronometers.
Cider.
Circulars.
Clock springs, faces, and hands.
Cloth, redyeing or reprinting of.
Coal, mineral, of all kinds.
Cobalt.
Coffins.
Coke.

Colors, painters' and paper stainers'.

Copper, in ingots, pigs, or bars, rods, or sheets.

Copperas.

Cordage, ropes, and cables, made of vegetable fibre.

Corn-shellers.

Cotton and hay presses.

Cotton-gins.

Crates.

Crucibles, of all kinds.

Crutches.

Cultivators.

Canned and preserved meats, and shell fish.

Carbolic acid and carbolate of lime, used solely for disinfectants.

Carpet bag and cabas frames.

Canned and preserved vegetables and fruits.

Casks, churns, barrels, wooden brushes and broom handles, tanks, and kits made of wood, including cooperage of all kinds, bungs and plugs, packing boxes, nest boxes, and match boxes, whether made of wood or other materials; wooden hames, plough beams, split-bottom chairs, and turned materials for the same unmanufactured, and saddle trees made of wood, and match boxes heretofore made on which a tax has not been paid.

Castings of iron, copper, or brass made for machinery, cars or scales, and castings made to form a part of any article upon which, in a finished state, a tax is assessed and paid.

Cast-iron hollow ware, and cast-iron hollow ware tinned, enamelled, japanned, or galvanized.

Clock trimmings, namely: Clock work, clock pillars, sash fastenings for clocks, winding keys, verges and pendulum rods.

Clothing or articles of dress not specially enumerated, made by sewing, for the wear of men, women, or children from cloths or fabrics on which a tax or duty has been paid.

Coffee mills, coffee grinders and roasters, and apple-paring machines.

Copper bottoms for articles used for domestic and culinary purposes.

Deerskins, smoked, or not oil-dressed.

Drain and sewer pipes, of iron or cement.

Drain tiles.

Doors, window sash, blinds, frames, and sills of whatever material.

Drain, gas, and water-pipe made of wood, or cement.

Earthen and stone water pipes.

Electrotypers, productions of.

Engravers, productions of.

Eyes, artificial.

Fertilizers, of all kinds.

Flasks and patterns used by founders.

Flavoring extracts, solely for cooking purposes.

Flax, and the manufactures thereof.

Flour and meal made from grain.

Frames and handles for saws and buck-saws.

Gas, illuminating, manufactured by educational institutions for their own use exclusively.

German silver, in bars or sheets.

Glue and gelatine, of all descriptions, in the solid state.

Glue and cement made wholly or in part of glue in the liquid state.
Gold-foil and gold-leaf.
Grain cradles.
Grindstones, rough or wrought.
Gypsum, rock and ground.
Hand-rakes.
Hand-saws.
Harrows.
Hay and straw cutters.
Headings.
Hemp or jute, prepared for textile or felting purposes.
Hoops.
Hoop-skirt wire, covered or uncovered.
Hoop skirts, small wares and cut-tape used in the manufacture of.
Horse-rakes.
Horse-rakes, horse powers, tedders, hames, scythe snaths, hay-forks, hoes, and portable grinding mills.
Horse-blankets, made from cloth, on which a tax or duty has been paid.
Hulls of ships and other vessels.
India-rubber springs, made exclusively for railroad cars.
Ink, printers'.
Iron, pig, muck-bar, blooms, slabs, and loops.
Iron bridges, and castings therefor.
Keys, actions, and strings for musical instruments.
*Laths and other lumber.
Lead, in ingots, pigs, or bars.
Lead, nitrate of.
Lead, red and white.
Licorice and licorice paste.
Limbs, artificial.
Lime.
Litharge and orange mineral.
Lithographers, productions of.
Machines driven by horse-power and used exclusively for cutting fire-wood, staves, and shingle-bolts.
Magnesia, calcined, carbonate of magnesia, and magnesium.
Magnesium lamps.
Manufactures of jute.
Molasses, concentrated molasses or melado, syrup of molasses or sugar cane juice, and cistern bottoms.
Malt.
Manganese.
Maps and charts.
Masts, spars, ship and vessel blocks, and tree-nail wedges and deck-plugs.
Match-wood.
Mattresses.
Mead.

---

*While these sheets are passing through the press, we perceive that a bill has been introduced into the House of Representatives, March 20, and passed, to exempt wooden ladders.

Medicinal and mineral waters, of all kinds, sold in bottles or from fountains.

Milk, concentrated.

Mills and machinery for the manufacture of sugar, syrup, and molasses, from sorghum, imphee, beets, and corn.

Millstones.

Molasses, made from beets, corn, sugar-maple, or from sorghum or imphee.

Monuments of stone, of all kinds, not exceeding in value one hundred dollars, and all monuments erected to commemorate the services of Union soldiers, &c.

Morphine.

Mouldings for looking-glasses and picture-frames.

Mounting and machinery of telescopes, for astronomical purposes.

Mowers.

Naphtha, used or consumed for fuel or cleaning on the premises where distilled.

Newspapers.

Nickel.

Oakum.

Oil naphtha, benzine, benzole, or gasoline, marking more than seventy degrees Baume's hydrometer, the product of the distillation, or re-distillation, or refining of crude petroleum, or of crude oil produced by a single distillation of coal, shale, peat, asphaltum, or other bituminous substances.

Oil, paraffine or lubricating, made from crude petroleum, coal, or shale, not exceeding in specific gravity 36 degrees Baume's hydrometer.

Oil, crude, the product of the first and single distillation of coal, shale, asphaltum, peat, or other bituminous substances.

Oil, vegetable, animal, and fish, of all descriptions, not otherwise provided for, including red oil, oleic acid, and admixtures of the same with paraffine oil, not exceeding in specific gravity 36 degrees Baume.

Pail and tub ears and handles.

Paintings, original.

Paints.

Palliasses.

Paper, printing, of all descriptions.

Paper, tarred.

Paraffine.

Palm-leaf and straw, bleached, split, prepared, or advanced by being braided or woven, but not made up into hats, bonnets, or hoods.

Peat.

Petroleum, crude.

Phosphorus.

Photographs, &c., being copies of engravings or works of art, when the same are sold by the producer at wholesale, at a price not exceeding fifteen cents each, or are used for the illustration of books.

Pickles, when sold by the gallon, and not in glass packages.

Pillows.

Pipes, drain and sewer, made of iron or cement.

Pipes, water, made of earthen or stone.

Planters.

Plaster or gypsum.

Ploughs.

Potash, bichromate and prussiate of.

Potato hooks, pitchforks, manure and spading forks.

Pottery-ware of all descriptions, including stone, earthen, brown and yellow earthen, and common or gray-stone ware.

Pumps, garden engines, and hydraulic rams.

Putty.

Quicksilver.

Quinine.

Railroad iron and railroad iron re-rolled.

Railroad chairs and fish plates; railroad, boat, and ship spikes; axe polls; iron axles; shoes for horses, mules, and oxen; rivets, horseshoe nails, nuts, washers, and bolts, vises, iron chains, and anchors, when such articles are made of wrought iron which has previously paid the tax or duty assessed thereon.

Reapers.

Repairs of articles of all kinds.

Residuums drawn from stills after distillation.

Retorts, made of clay.

Rock and root-diggers or excavators.

Root beer and other small beer.

Roofing slates, slabs, and tiles.

Sails, and tents, made by sewing from fabrics or articles on which a tax or duty has been paid.

Saleratus.

Sal soda.

Salt.

Saltpetre.

Salts of tin.

Saws for cotton gins, when used by the maker in the manufacture of gins.

School-room seats and desks, blackboards, and globes of all kinds.

Scythes.

Seed-drills.

Sheathing metal, yellow, in rods or sheets.

Shingles.

Shirt fronts or bosoms, wristbands or cuffs for shirts, except those made of paper.

Shooks.

Silex used in the manufacture of glass.

Slate.

Sleds, wheelbarrows, and hand-carts, and fence made of wood.

Soap valued at not above three cents per pound.

Soap, common brown, in bars, sold for less than seven cents per pound.

Soda, bicarbonate of.

Soda, caustic; crude; aluminate of; silicate of; aluminosilicate of; and sodium.

Soles and heel-taps made of India-rubber or of India-rubber and other materials.

Spelter.

Spindles.

Spiral springs used in the manufacture of furniture.

Spokes, hubs, bows, and felloes; poles, shafts, arms, and wheels not ironed or finished, for carriages or wagons.

Starch.

Statues and groups of statuary, and casts made thereof by the artist from the original designs.

Staves.

Steel of all descriptions, whether made from muck-bar, blooms, slabs, loops, or otherwise.

Steel made from taxed iron, in ingots, bars, rails made and fitted for railroads, sheet, plate, coil or wire.

Steel springs, used exclusively for vehicles, cars, or locomotives.

Stereotypers, productions of.

Stove polish or other manufacture exclusively of plumbago, buck-saws, stump machines, potato diggers.

Stoves composed in part of cast iron, and in part of sheet iron, or of soapstone, fire-bricks, or of freestone, with or without cast iron or sheet iron: *Provided*, That the cast or sheet iron shall have paid the tax or duty previously assessed thereon.

Straw or binder's board and binder's cloth, and straw wrapping paper.

Sugar or syrup made from other articles than the sugar cane.

Sulphur and flowers of sulphur, and sulphur flour.

Tags for merchandise and direction of cloth, paper or metal, whether blank or printed; thimble skeins and pipe boxes, made of iron.

Tar.

Teeth, artificial.

Thimble-skeins and pipe-boxes made of steel.

Threshing machines and separators.

Tiles, made of clay.

Timber, partially wrought and unfinished, for chairs, tubs, pails, and lasts.

Tin cans, used for preserved meats, fish, shell-fish, fruits, vegetables, jams, jellies, paints, oils, and spices.

Tin, in ingots, pigs, or bars.

Tin-ware for domestic and culinary purposes.

Tire, made of steel and used exclusively for vehicles, cars, or locomotives.

Turpentine, crude.

Ultra-marine blue.

Umbrellas and parasols, and sticks, frames, and stretchers for the same.

Varnish.

Verdigris.

Vinegar.

Wagons, carts, and drays made to be used for farming, freighting, or lumber purposes.

Washing, mangling, and clothes-wringing machines, zinc washboards, spinning and flax wheels, hand-reels, hand-looms, wooden knobs and beehives.

Warp, for weaving, braiding, or manufacturing purposes exclusively.

Wheels, not ironed or finished, for carriages.

Whiting and Paris white.

Window-glass, of all kinds.

Wine, made of grapes, currants, or other fruits, or rhubarb.

Winnowing mills.

Wire, made from wire less than No. 20 wire gauge, upon which a tax has been assessed and paid as wire.

Wooden handles, for ploughs, and for other agricultural, household, and mechanical tools and implements.

Wooden tanks and cisterns, for crude mineral oil.

Wooden-ware.

Yarn, for weaving, braiding, or manufacturing purposes exclusively.

Yeast powders and baking powders.

Zinc, in ingots or sheets.

Zinc, oxide of.

MANUFACTURES AND PRODUCTIONS.

The phraseology of official schedules under former Law has been preserved. The reader will in all cases of doubt carefully examine the text of the amended Law of 1867.

Agricultural implements not specially exempted, . .	5 per cent.
Bonnets not made and trimmed by milliners, .	2 per cent.
Boilers, water tanks, and sugar tanks, . . .	5 per cent.
Boots and shoes, made wholly or in part of India rubber, .	2 per cent
Brandy made from grapes, per gallon, . . .	$1 00
Brushes, not specially exempt, ...	5 per cent.
Bullion, gold, in lumps, ingots, or bars, . .	1-2 of 1 per cent.
Bullion, silver, in lumps, ingots, or bars, . .	1-2 of 1 per cent
Candles, ...	5 per cent
Carpetings, not chiefly of wool, ...	5 per cent
Carriages and other vehicles, ...	5 per cent
Cars, railroad, ...	5 per cent
Chemical productions, uncompounded, not otherwise provided for, ...	5 per cent
Chocolate and cocoa, prepared, per pound, . .	1 1-2 per cent
Cigars, cigarettes and cheroots of all descriptions, made of tobacco or any substitute, ...	$5 per M.
Clocks, clock movements and cases, except as specially exempted, ...	5 per cent.
Cloth, and all textile, knitted, or felted fabrics, made of cotton, ...	5 per cent.
Cloth, manufactured of wool, see "wool."	
Cloth, painted, enamelled, shirred, tarred, varnished, or oiled, ...	5 per cent.
Clothing, articles of, made from India rubber or gutta percha, ...	5 per cent.
*Clothing, articles of, made by weaving, knitting, or felting, or from fur or fur skins, ...	5 per cent.
Clothing, articles of, made from fur, valued at $20 or less,	2 per cent.
Clothing, made by sewing, and all other articles of dress not elsewhere enumerated or exempted, . . .	2 per cent.
Coffee, roasted or ground, and all substitutes therefor, per pound, ...	1 cent.

*See Clothing in list of exempt articles.

Article	Rate
Confectionery, valued at 20 cents per pound or less, per pound,	2 cents.
Confectionery, valued at over 20 cents per pound and not over 40 cents, per pound,	4 cents.
Confectionery, valued at over 40 cents per pound, or when sold otherwise than by the pound,	10 per cent.
Copper, zinc, and brass tubes, nails, and rivets,	5 per cent.
Cotton, raw, per pound,	2 1-2 cents.
Cutlery,	5 per cent.
Diamonds, emeralds, precious stones, and imitations thereof, and all other jewelry,	5 per cent.
Fermented liquors, per barrel,	$1 00
Fire-arms,	5 per cent.
Furniture,	5 per cent.
Gas, monthly product not over 200,000 cubic feet, per 1,000 cubic feet,	10 cents.
Gas, monthly product over 200,000 and not over 500,000 cubic feet, per 1,000 cubic feet,	15 cents.
Gas, monthly product over 500,000 and not over 5,000,000 cubic feet, per 1,000 cubic feet,	20 cents.
Gas, monthly product over 5,000,000 cubic feet, per 1,000 cubic feet,	25 cents.
Gas fixtures and chandeliers,	5 per cent.
Glass, manufactures of, exclusively, other than window glass,	3 per cent.
Gunpowder, canister, per pound,	5 cents.
Gunpowder, for sporting, in kegs, per pound,	1 cent.
Gunpowder, blasting, in kegs or casks, per pound,	1-2 cent.
Gun cotton,	5 per cent.
Gutta percha, manufactures of, not elsewhere enumerated,	5 per cent.
Hats, caps, bonnets and hoods of all descriptions,	2 per cent.
Hoop skirts,	2 per cent.
India rubber, manufactures of, not elsewhere enumerated,	5 per cent.
Iron castings not specially exempted, per ton,	$3 00
Iron, cut nails and spikes, not including nails, tacks, brads, or finishing nails, usually sold in papers, per ton,	5 00
Iron, railings, gates, fences, and statuary,	5 per cent.
Iron tubes, wrought, per ton,	5 00
Iron, manufactures of, not specially exempted and not elsewhere enumerated,	5 per cent.
Lamps and lanterns,	5 per cent.
Lead, sheet, lead pipes, and shot,	5 per cent.
Leather, of all descriptions, and goat, deer, calf, kid, sheep, horse, hog, and dog skins, tanned or partially tanned, curried, finished or in the rough,	2 1-2 per cent.
Machinery, including shafting and gearing, and mechanics' tools, not specially exempted,	5 per cent.
Monuments, valued at over $100,	5 per cent.
Oils, essential, of all descriptions,	5 per cent.
Oil, produced from petroleum, marking not less than 36 degrees nor more than 59 degrees Baume, per gallon,	20 cents
Oil, produced from petroleum, marking more than 59 degrees Baume, except naphtha oil, benzine, benzole, or	

gasoline marking more than 70 deg. Baume, per gallon,	10 cents.
Oil, produced from coal, shale, or other bituminous substances, marking not less than 36 degrees Baume, except oil naphtha, &c., as above, per gallon,	10 cents.
Paper, not specially exempted,	3 per cent.
Paper collars, and all articles of dress made of paper,	2 per cent.
Photographs, or other pictures taken by the action of light, not specially exempted,	5 per cent.
Pianos, and other musical instruments,	5 per cent.
Pins,	5 per cent.
Plated and Brittania ware,	5 per cent.
Saddlery, harness, trunks, and valises,	5 per cent.
Safes, fire or burglar-proof,	5 per cent.
Scales,	3 per cent.
Screws, commonly called wood screws,	5 per cent.
Sewing machines,	5 per cent.
Silk, manufactures of,	5 per cent.
Silver-ware,	5 per cent.
Snuff, of all descriptions, per pound,	40 cents.
Soap, valued at over 7 cents per pound, not perfumed; and salt-water soap, made of cocoanut oil, per pound,	1-2 cent.
Soap, perfumed, per pound,	3 cents.
Spices, ground, dry mustard, and all substitutes therefor, per pound,	1 cent.
Spirits, distilled from apples, and peaches, per gallon,	$2 00
Spirits, distilled from other materials, per gallon,	2 00
Steam, locomotive, and marine engines,	5 per cent.
Sugar, on all produced from the sugar cane, and not from sorghum or imphee, other than that produced by the refiner,	1 cent.
Sugar, refined, and in the product of sugar refineries, not including syrup or molasses,	2 per cent.
Thread,	5 per cent.
Tin-ware, except as specially exempted,	5 per cent.
Tobacco, chewing, per pound,	40 cents.
Tobacco, smoking, sweetened, stemmed, or butted, per pound,	40 cents.
Tobacco, smoking, not sweetened, stemmed, or butted, including that made of stems, or in part of stems, per pound,	15 cents.
Tobacco, twisted by hand, and not pressed, sweetened, or otherwise prepared, and fine-cut shorts, per pound,	30 cents.
Turpentine, spirits of, per gallon,	10 cents.
Watches and watch chains,	5 per cent.
Varnish or Japan,	5 per cent.
Wine, produced by being mixed with other spirits, and not otherwise provided for, per gallon,	50 cents.
Wine, made in imitation of imported sparkling wine, when put up in bottles containing not more than one pint, per dozen,	$3 00
Wine, made in imitation of imported sparkling wine, in bottles containing more than one pint, and not more than one quart, per dozen,	6 00

Wool, manufactures of, or of which wool is the chief component material, or component material of chief value, 2 1-2 per cent.
Manufactured articles which are increased in value by being polished, painted, &c., &c., on such increased value, 5 per cent.
Manufactures not elsewhere enumerated nor specially exempted, ... 5 per cent.

GROSS RECEIPTS.

Bridges, ...	2 1-2 per cent.
Canals, ...	2 1-2 per cent.
Express Companies, ...	3 per cent.
Ferries, ...	2 1-2 per cent.
Insurance Companies, ...	1 1-2 per cent.
Lotteries and lottery-ticket dealers, . . .	5 per cent.
Railroads, passengers, and mails, ...	2 1-2 per cent.
Ships, barges, &c., ...	2 1-2 per cent.
Stage coaches, &c., ...	2 1-2 per cent.
Steamboats, ...	2 1-2 per cent.
Telegraph Companies, ...	3 per cent.
Theatres, operas, circuses, and museums, . . .	2 per cent.

SALES.

Apothecaries, butchers, confectioners, plumbers and gas fitters, same as "dealers."

Auction sales, ...	1-10 of 1 per cent.
Brokers, cattle, sales in excess of $10,000, per $1,000, .	$1 00
Brokers, commercial, sales of merchandise,	1-20 of 1 per cent.
Dealers, sales in excess of $50,000, per $1,000, . .	1 00
Dealers in liquor, sales in excess of $50,000, per $1,000, .	1 00

SPECIAL TAXES.

Apothecaries, annual sales not over $25,000, . .	$10 00
Architects and civil engineers, ...	10 00
Assayers, annual assays not over $250,000, in value, . .	100 00
Assayers, annual assays over $250,000 and not over $500,000, .	200 00
Assayers, annual assays over $500,000, ...	500 00
Auctioneers, annual sales not over $10,000, . . .	10 00
Auctioneers, annual sales over $10,000, ...	20 00
Banks and bankers, capital not over $50,000, . . .	100 00
Banks and bankers, capital over $50,000, $2 for eacn additional $1,000, in addition to the $100.	
Billiard rooms, for each table, ...	10 00
Boats, barges, and flats, of capacity exceeding 25 tons and not exceeding 100 tons, ...	5 00
Boats, barges, and flats, of capacity exceeding 100 tons, .	10 00
Bowling alleys, for each alley, ...	10 00
Brewers, annual manufacture less than 500 barrels, . .	50 00
Brewers who manufacture not less than 500 barrels, . .	100 00
Brokers, cattle, annual sales not over $10,000, . . .	10 00

Brokers, commercial,	$20 00
Brokers, custom-house,	10 00
Brokers, land-warrant,	25 00
Brokers, pawn, capital not over $50,000,	50 00
Brokers, pawn, capital over $50,000, $2 for every $1,000 in addition to the $50.	
Brokers, produce,	10 00
Brokers, stock,	50 00
Builders and contractors,	10 00
Butchers, annual sales not over $25,000,	10 00
Butchers, who sell from carts exclusively,	5 00
Circuses,	100 00
Claim agents,	10 00
Confectioners,	10 00
Conveyancers,	10 00
Dealers, retail,	10 00
Dealers, wholesale, annual sales not over $50,000,	50 00
Dealers, retail liquor,	25 00
Dealers, wholesale liquor, annual sales not over $50,000,	100 00
Dentists,	10 00
Distillers of coal oil, burning fluid, and camphene,	50 00
Distillers of spirituous liquor,	100 00
Distillers of apples, grapes, or peaches, distilling 50 barrels, and less than 150 barrels per year,	50 00
Distillers of apples, grapes, or peaches, distilling less than 50 barrels per year,	20 00
Eating-houses,	10 00
Exhibitions, not otherwise provided for,	10 00
Express carriers and agents,	10 00
Gift enterprises,	150 00
Grinders of coffee and spices,	100 00
Horse-dealers,	10 00
Hotels, yearly rental $200 or less,	10 00
Hotels, yearly rental over $200, $5 for every $100, or fractional part thereof, in addition to the $10.	
Hotels, steamers and vessels carrying and boarding passengers,	25 00
Insurance agents, domestic, annual receipts not exceeding $100,	5 00
Insurance agents, domestic, annual receipts exceeding $100,	10 00
Insurance agents, foreign,	50 00
Intelligence office keepers,	10 00
Jugglers,	20 00
Lawyers,	10 00
Livery-stable keepers,	10 00
Lottery-ticket dealers,	100 00
Manufacturers	10 00
Miners,	10 00
Patent agents,	10 00
Patent-right dealers,	10 00
Peddlers, 1st class,	50 00
Peddlers, 2d class,	25 00
Peddlers, 3d class,	15 00
Peddlers, 4th class,	10 00
Peddlers of fish,	5 00
Peddlers of dry goods in original packages, or jewelry,	50 00
Peddlers of distilled spirits, fermented liquors or wines,	50 00
Photographers,	10 00
Plumbers and gas-fitters, annual sales not over $25,000,	10 00
Physicians and surgeons,	10 00
Real estate agents,	10 00

Rectifiers of any quantity not exceeding 500 barrels,	$25 00
Rectifiers of any quantity exceeding 500 barrels, $25 in addition to the $25 for every 500 barrels rectified.	
Stallions and jacks,	10 00
Theatres, museums, and concert halls,	100 00
Tobacconists,	10 00

INCOME.

Income exceeding $1,000,	5 per cent.
Bank dividends, and additions to surplus funds,	5 per cent.
Bank profits, not divided or added to surplus,	5 per cent.
Canal companies, dividends, interest on bonds, and additions to surplus funds,	5 per cent.
Insurance companies, dividends, and additions to surplus funds,	5 per cent.
Railroad companies, dividends, interest on bonds, and additions to surplus funds,	5 per cent.
Salaries of United States officers, exceeding $1,000,	5 per cent.
Turnpike companies, dividends, interest on bonds, and additions to surplus funds,	5 per cent.

LEGACIES AND SUCCESSIONS.

Legacies, lineal issue or ancestor, brother or sister,	1 per cent.
Legacies, descendant of brother or sister,	2 per cent.
Legacies, uncle or aunt, or descendant of same,	4 per cent.
Legacies, great uncle or aunt, or descendants of same,	5 per cent.
Legacies, stranger in blood,	6 per cent.
Successions, lineal issue or ancestor,	1 per cent.
Successions, brother or sister, or descendant of same,	2 per cent.
Successions, uncle or aunt, or descendant of same,	4 per cent.
Successions, great uncle or aunt, or descendant of same,	5 per cent.
Successions, stranger in blood,	6 per cent.

ARTICLES IN SCHEDULE A.

Billiard tables kept for use,	$10 00
Carriages kept for use, for hire, or for passengers, and valued at exceeding $300 and not above $500 each, including harness used therewith,	6 00
Carriages of like description, valued at above $500 each,	10 00
Plate of gold, kept for use, per ounce troy,	50
Plate of silver, kept for use, per ounce troy,	05
Watches, gold, composed wholly or in part of gold or gilt, kept for use, and not over $100 in value,	1 00
Watches, gold, composed wholly or in part of gold or gilt, kept for use, and valued at above $100, each,	2 00

BANK CIRCULATION AND DEPOSITS.

Bank deposits, per month,	1-24 of 1 per cent.
Bank capital, per month,	1-24 of 1 per cent.
Bank circulation, per month,	1-12 of 1 per cent.
Bank circulation, exceeding 90 per cent. of capital, in addition, per month,	1-6 of 1 per cent.
Banks, on amount of notes of any person, State bank, or State banking association, used for circulation, and paid out,	10 per cent.

PASSPORTS.

Passports, each,	$5 00

SCHEDULE OF STAMP DUTIES,

On and after August 1, 1866.

Accidental Injuries to persons, tickets or contracts for insurance against, are exempt from stamp duty.

Affidavits in suits or legal proceedings are exempt from stamp duty.

Agreement or Contract, other than domestic or inland bills of lading. For every sheet or piece of paper upon which either of the same shall be written, ... 5 cts.

If more than one appraisement, agreement or contract shall be written upon one sheet or piece of paper, 5 cents for each and every additional appraisement, agreement or contract.

Agreement, renewal of, same stamp as original instrument.

Appraisement of value or damage, or for any other purpose, for each sheet of paper on which it is written, ... 5 cts.

Assignment of a Lease, same stamp as original, and additional stamp upon the value or consideration of transfer, according to the rates of stamps on Deeds. See "Conveyance."

Assignment of Policy of Insurance, same stamp as original instrument. See "Insurance."

Assignment of mortgage, same stamp as that required upon a mortgage for the amount remaining unpaid. See "Mortgage."

Bank Check, draft, or order for any sum of money drawn upon any bank, banker, or trust company, at sight or on demand, 2 cts.

When drawn upon any other person or persons, companies or corporations, for any sum exceeding $10, at sight or on demand, ... 2 cts.

Bill of Exchange, (Inland), draft, or order for the payment of any sum of money not exceeding $100, otherwise than at sight or on demand, or any promissory note, or any memorandum, check, receipt, or other written or printed evidence of an amount of money to be paid on demand or at a time designated, for a sum not exceeding $100, ... 5 cts.

And for every additional $100, or fractional part thereof in excess of $100, ... 5 cts.

Bill of Exchange, (Foreign,) or letter of credit, drawn in, but payable out of, the United States, if drawn singly, same rates of duty as inland bills of exchange or promissory notes.

If drawn in sets of three or more—for every bill of each set, where the sum made payable shall not exceed $100, or the equivalent thereof, in any foreign currency, ... 2 cts.

And for every additional $100, or fractional part thereof in excess of $100, ... 2 cts.

[The acceptor or acceptors of any Bill of Exchange, or order for the payment of any sum of money drawn, or purporting to be drawn, in any foreign country, but payable in the United States, must, before paying or accepting the same, place thereupon a stamp indicating the duty.]

Bill of Lading or receipt (other than charty party) for any goods, merchandise, or effects to be exported from a port or place in the United States to any foreign port or place, . . . 10 cts.

Bill of Lading to any port in British North America does not require a stamp.

Bill of Lading, domestic or inland, requires no stamp.

Bill of Sale by which any ship or vessel, or any part thereof, shall be conveyed to or vested in any other person or persons, when the consideration shall not exceed $500, . .	50 cts.
Exceeding $500 and not exceeding $1,000, . . .	$1 00
Exceeding $1,000, for every additional amount of $500, or fractional part thereof, ...	50 cts.
Bond for indemnifying any person for payment of any sum of money, when the money ultimately recoverable thereupon, is $1,000 or less, ...	50 cts.
When in excess of $1,000, for each $1,000 or fraction, . .	50 cts.
Bond for due execution or performance of duties of office, .	$1 00
Bond, administrator, or guardian, where value of estate does not exceed $1,000, ...	exempt.
Bond, personal, for securtity for the payment of money. See "Mortgage."	
Bond of any description, other than such as may be required in legal proceedings, or used in connection with mortgage deeds, and not otherwise charged in this Schedule, . .	25 cts.
Bond or Note accompanying a mortgage requires no stamp if the mortgage is stamped. But one stamp is required on those papers, which may be placed on either, and must be the highest rate required upon either.	
Broker's notes. See "Contract."	
Certificates of Measurement or weight of animals, wood, coal, or hay, exempt from stamp duty.	
Certificates of Measurement of other articles, . .	5 cts.
Certificates of Stock in any incorporated company, . .	25 cts.
Certificates of Profits, or any certificate or memorandum showing an interest in the property or accumulations of any incorporated company, if for a sum not less than $10 and not exceeding $50, ...	10 cts.
Exceeding $50 and not exceeding $1,000, . . .	25 cts.
Exceeding $1,000, for every additional $1,000, or fractional part thereof, ...	25 cts.
Certificate. Any certificate of damage or otherwise, and all other certificates or documents issued by any port warden, marine surveyor, or other person acting as such, . .	25 cts.
Certificate of deposit of any sum of money in any bank or trust company, or with any banker or person acting as such:	
If for a sum not exceeding $100, ...	2 cts.
For a sum exceeding $100, ...	5 cts.
Certificate of any other description than those specified, .	5 cts.
Charter, renewal of, same stamp as on original instrument.	
Charter party for the charter of any ship, or vessel, or steamer, or any letter, memorandum, or other writing relating to the charter, or any renewal or transfer thereof, if the registered tonnage of such ship, or vessel, or steamer, does not exceed 150 tons, ...	$1 00
Exceeding 150 tons, and not exceeding 300 tons, . .	$3 00
Exceeding 300 tons, and not exceeding 600 tons, . .	$5 00
Exceeding 600 tons, ...	$10 00
Check. Bank check, ...	2 cts.
Contract. Broker's note or memorandum of sale of any goods or merchandise, exchange, real estate, or property of any kind or description issued by brokers or persons acting as such, for each note or memorandum of sale, . .	10 cts.
Bill or memorandum of the sale or contract for the sale of stocks, bonds, gold or silver, bullion, coin, promissory notes, or other securities made by brokers, banks, or bankers, either	

for the benefit of others or on their own account, for each hundred dollars, or fractional part thereof, of the amount of such sale or contract, ... 1ct.

Bill or memorandum of the sale or contract for the sale of stocks, bonds, gold or siver bullion, coin, promissory notes, or other securities, not his or their own property, made by any person, firm or company not paying a special tax as broker, bank, or banker, for each hundred dollars, or fractional part thereof, of the amount of such sale or contract, . . . 5 cts.

Contract. See "Agreement."

Contract, renewal of, same stamp as original instrument.

Conveyance, deed, instrument, or writing, whereby any lands, tenements, or other realty sold shall be granted, assigned, transferred, or otherwise conveyed to or vested in the purchaser or purchasers, or any other person or persons, by his, her, or their direction, when the consideration or value does not exceed $500, ... 50 cts.

When the consideration exceeds $500, and does not exceed $1,000, ... $1 00

And for every additional $500, or fractional part thereof, in excess of $1,000, ... 50 cts.

Conveyance — the acknowledgment of a deed, or proof by a witness, needs no stamp.

Conveyance—certificate of record of a deed does not require a stamp.

Credit, Letter of. Same as Foreign Bill of Exchange.

Custom-house Entry. See "Entry."

Custom-house Withdrawals. See "Entry."

Deed. See " Conveyance—Trust Deed."

Draft. Same as Inland Bill of Exchange.

Endorsement of any negotiable instrument, ... exempt.

Entry of any goods, wares, or merchandise at any custom-house, either for consumption or ware-housing, not exceeding $100 in value, ... 25 cts.

Exceeding $100, and not exceeding $500 in value, . . 50 cts.

Exceeding $500 in value, ... $1 00

Entry for the withdrawal of any goods or merchandise from bonded warehouse, ... 50 cts.

Gauger's Returns, ... exempt.

Indorsement upon a stamped obligation in acknowledgment of its fulfillment, ... exempt.

Insurance, (Life.) Policy, when the amount insured shall not exceed $1,000, ... 25 cts.

Exceeding $1,000, and not exceeding $5,000, . . . 50 cts.

Exceeding $5,000, ... $1 00

Insurance, (Marine, Inland and Fire.) Policies, or renewals of the same, if the premium does not exceed $10, . . 10 cts.

Exceeding $10, and not exceeding $50, . . . 25 cts.

Exceeding $50, ... 50 cts.

Assignment of policy of insurance, same stamp as original instrument.

Insurance, contracts, or tickets against accidental injuries to persons, do not require stamps.

Lease, agreement, memorandum, or contract for the hire, use, or rent of any land, tenement, or portion thereof, where the rent or rental value is $300 per annum or less, . . **50 cts.**

Where the rent or rental value exceeds the sum of $300 per annum, for each additional $200, or fractional part thereof in excess of $300, ... 50 cts.

Assignment of lease, same stamp as original instrument, and the value or consideration of the transfer at the same rate as a deed. See "Conveyance."

Letters of Administration. See "Probate of Will."

Letter of Credit. Same as Bill of Exchange, "Foreign."

Manifest for custom-house entry or clearance of the cargo of any ship, vessel, or steamer, for a foreign port:

If the registered tonnage of such ship, vessel, or steamer does not exceed 300 tons, ... $1 00

Exceeding 300 tons, and not exceeding 600 tons, . . $3 00

Exceeding 600 tons, ... $5 00

[These provisions do not apply to vessels or steamboats plying between ports of the United States and British North America.]

Measurer's Returns, ... exempt.

Memorandum of Sale, or Broker's Note. See "Contract."

Mortgage of Lands, estate, or property, real or personal, heritable, or movable whatsoever, a trust deed in the nature of a mortgage, or any personal bond given as security for the payment of any definite or certain sum of money exceeding $100, and not exceeding $500, ... 50 cts.

Exceeding $500, and not exceeding $1,000, ... $1 00

And for every additional $500, or fractional part thereof in excess of $1,000, ... 50 cts.

Upon each assignment or transfer of a mortgage, a stamp duty equal to that upon a mortgage for the amount remaining unpaid.

Order for payment of money, if the amount is $10 or over 2 cts.

Passage Ticket on any vessel from a port in the United States to a foreign port, not exceeding $35, . . . 50 cts.

Exceeding $35, and not exceeding $50, ... $1 00

And for every additional $50, or fractional part thereof in excess of $50, ... $1 00

[Passage tickets to ports in British North America do not require stamps.]

Pawner's Checks, ... 5 cts.

Power of Attorney, for the sale or transfer of any stock, bonds, or scrip, or for the collection of any dividends or interest thereon, ... 25 cts.

Power of Attorney or proxy for voting at any election for officers of any incorporated company or society, except religious, charitable, or literary societies, or public cemeteries, 10 cts.

Power of Attorney to receive or collect rent, ... 25 cts.

Power of Attorney to sell and convey real estate, or to rent or lease the same, ... $1 00

Power of Attorney for any other purpose, ... 50 cts.

[Power of Attorney or other papers relating to applications for bounties, arrearages of pay, or pensions, or receipts therefor, require no stamp. See, also, Warrant of Attorney.]

Probate of Will, or letters of Administration, where the estate and effects for or in respect of which such probate or letters of administration applied for shall be sworn or declared not to exceed the value of $1,000, ... exempt.

Exceeding $1,000, and not exceeding $2,000, ... $1 00

Exceeding $2,000, for every additional $1,000, or fractional part thereof, ... 50 cts.

"*Provided*, That no stamp tax shall be required upon any papers necessary to be used for the collection from the Government of claims by soldiers or their legal representatives of the United States, for pensions, back pay, bounty, or for property lost in the service." The reduction of taxes provided in this section shall take effect on and after March 1, 1867, ... 50 cts.

Promissory Note. See "Bill of Exchange," Inland.

Deposit note to mutual insurance companies, when policy is subject to duty, ... exempt

Renewal of a note subject to same duty as an original note.

Protest of note, bill of exchange, acceptance, check, or draft, or any marine protest, ... 25 cts

Quit Claim Deed to be stamped as a conveyance, except when given as a release of a mortgage by the mortgagee to the mortgagor, in which case it is exempt; but if it contains covenants *may* be subject as an agreement or contract.

Receipt for satisfaction of any mortgage or judgment or decree of any court, ... exempt

Receipts for the payment of any sum of money or debt due, or for a draft or other instrument given for the payment of money, exceeding $20, not being for satisfaction of any mortgage or judgment or decree of court. See "Indorsement." . . . . 2 cts

Receipts for the delivery of property. . . . . . exempt

Renewal of Agreement, contract, or charter, by letter or otherwise, same stamp as original instrument.

Sheriff's Return on writ, or other process, ... exempt

Trust Deed, made to secure a debt, to be stamped as a mortgage.

Warehouse Receipts, ... exempt

Warrant of Attorney accompanying a bond or note requires no stamp if the bond or note is stamped.

Weigher's Returns, ... exempt.

Writs and other process in any criminal or other suits commenced by the United States or any State, ... exempt.

*Official documents, instruments, and papers issued by officers of the United States Government, ... exempt.

*Official instruments, documents, and papers issued by the officers of any State, county, town, or other municipal corporation, in the exercise of functions strictly belonging to them in their ordinary governmental or municipal capacity, exempt.

GENERAL REMARKS.

Revenue stamps may be used indiscriminately upon any of the matters or things enumerated in Schedule B, except proprietary and playing card stamps, for which a special use has been provided.

Postage stamps cannot be used in payment of the duty chargeable on instruments.

It is the duty of the maker of an instrument to affix the stamp thereto and to cancel the same in the manner required by law. Proper cancellation is essential.

Under the provisions of section 158, an instrument subject to stamp duty, but issued without a stamp or with an insufficient one, may be so stamped by the Collector as to be as valid to all intents and purposes (*except as against rights acquired in good faith before such stamping and the recording of the instrument, if a record be required*) as if properly stamped when made or issued. Such an instrument issued at a time when and in a place where no collection district was established may be stamped by the party who issued it or by any party having an interest therein at any time prior to January 1, 1867, and the legal effect of the stamp thus affixed will be the same as though affixed by the Collector. When orignals are lost the necessary stamps may be affixed to copies.

Certificates of Loan, in which there shall appear any written or printed evidence of an amount of money to be paid on demand, or at a time designated, are subject to stamp duty as "Promissory Notes."

When two or more persons join in the execution of an instrument, the stamp to which the instrument is liable under the law may be affixed and cancelled by either of them; and "when more than one signature is affixed to the same paper, one or more stamps may be affixed thereto representing the whole amount of the stamp required for such signatures."

No stamp is required on any warrant of attorney accompanying a bond or note when such bond or note has affixed thereto the stamp or stamps denoting the duty required; and whenever any bond or note is secured by mortgage, but one stamp duty is required on such papers, such stamp duty being the highest rate required for such instruments, or either of them. In such case a note or memorandum of the value or denomination of stamp affixed should be made upon the margin or in the acknowledgment of the instrument which is not stamped.

Particular attention is called to the change in section 154, by striking out the words "or used;" the exemption thereunder is thus restricted to documents, &c., *issued* by the officers therein named. Also to the changes in sections 152 and 158, by inserting the words "and cancelled in the manner required by law."

Attention is also called to the amendments of March 2, 1867, in text. The Schedule has been made to conform as nearly as possible to the changes in the Law, both in phraseology, rate and otherwise.

The Income Tax for 1867.

THERE is no part of the official duty of an assessor and his assistants of greater importance than the assessment of the tax on annual incomes. The officer meets with many obstacles in the performance of his work, and there are inherent difficulties in the matter, both in ascertaining the true income of the tax-payer, and establishing the proper basis of assessment: not to speak of the strong temptation to, and the frequent instances of concealment, fraud and downright perjury. The editor proposes to submit a succinct analysis of the provisions of law, which have just been enacted (March, 1867,) and append some of the rules and instructions, heretofore established by the department, and a few suggestions drawn from his own experience in administering the system. Immediate instructions are to be expected also from the Commissioner of Internal Revenue. (Vide letter of Commissioner, of March 6, 1867, appended.)

LAW OF MARCH 4, 1867.

1. The tax is levied upon the gains, profit and income from January 1, 1866, to December 31, 1866, of every resident of the United States, or citizen residing abroad.

2. All gains are included, whether derived from rents, interest, dividends, salaries, professions, trade, employment, vocation (wherever carried on) or from any source, or from any kind of property.

3. The tax is 5 per cent. in all such gains, &c., over $1,000, and is assessed as of March 1st, 1867, and payable on or before April 30, 1867.

4. In the estimate shall be included :

(a) Interest upon notes, bonds, or other U. S. securities.

(b) Profits realized from sales of real estate within the year, or within two years previous to the year 1866.

(c) Interest received or accrued on all notes, bonds, or mortgages, or other interest bearing form of indebtedness whether paid or not, if collectable, less interest due from the tax-payer.

(d) All premiums on gold and coupons.

(e) Amount of sales of live stock, sugar, wool, butter, cheese, pork, beef, mutton, or other meats, hay and grain, or other farm products, not including what is used in the family.

(f) All other profit or income from other sources.

5. The tax-payer may *deduct*, (or there is exempt)

(a) The rental value of a homestead used and occupied by himself, in his own right, or in the right of his wife.

(b) The income received from institutions or corporations who have withheld and paid over the tax upon dividends.

(c) That portion of the salary or pay for services in the military, naval, or other service of the United States, from which tax has been already deducted.

(d) All national, municipal, state and county taxes, paid within the year by the person liable, whether owner of premises, &c., tenant, or mortgagor.

(e) Losses from fire, shipwreck, or incurred in trade and worthless debts, excluding all estimated depreciation of values and losses within the year on sales of real estate purchased two years previous.

(f) Amount paid for labor or interest by tenant of lands, or who hires labor to cultivate land, or who conducts other business from which income is derived.

(g) Amount paid for rent of house or premises occupied as a residence for self or family.

(h) Amount paid for usual or ordinary repairs, not including amount paid for new buildings, permanent improvements, or betterments.

6. But the deduction shall be made of $1,000 from aggregate incomes of all the members of any family, composed of one or both parents, and one or more minor children or husband and wife.

7. Guardians may make such deductions in favor of each and every ward, except when two or more wards are in one family, and have joint property interest, but one deduction shall be made on their account.

8. When salary in United States service shall not exceed the rate of $1000 per annum, or shall be by uncertain or irregular fees, such salary shall be included in the estimate of income.

9. The income return must be made by all persons of lawful age, on or before the prescribed time, and in the prescribed form, and in the district of residence.

10. Guardians, trustees, executors and administrators must return the income of those they represent, in the residence of the fiduciary.

11. The list or return must be sworn to.

12. The assessor may increase a return which he has reason to believe understated.

13. In case of refusal or neglect to make return or in case of false or fraudulent return, the assessor or assistant may estimate it by examination of books or papers, &c., and add 50 per cent. in case of neglect or refusal; and in case of false or fraudulent return he may add 100 per cent. as penalty.

14. The tax with penalty so added is assessed and collected as in other cases of false or fraudulent returns.

15. A party may declare under oath or affirmation that he is not possessed of an income of $1000 liable to be assessed, or that he has paid his income tax elsewhere.

16. If the list has been increased by the assistant assessor, the party may exhibit his books and accounts, and prove the amount of income to which he is liable, such oaths not being conclusive.

17. A person aggrieved by the action of an assistant assessor may have his appeal to the assessor, whose decision shall be final till reversed by the Commissioner of Internal Revenue.

18 No penalty shall be assessed for refusal or neglect to make the income return till reasonable notice of time and place of hearing, regulated by the Commissioner of Internal Revenue.

19. The income tax shall be assessed on March 1, and be due and payable April 30, in each year, till 1870; and for neglect to pay after April 1, an additional sum of 5 per cent. on the unpaid tax with interest at one per cent. per month.

20. Upon the salaries of officers in the civil, military, naval or other service of the United States, including members of Congress, there shall be levied a tax of 5 per cent. on the excess of $1000, and paymasters of United States, in making their payments, shall deduct this 5 per cent., and the auditing officers of the Treasury, in settling the accounts of paymasters, shall require evidence that these taxes have been deducted and paid over.

21. Prize money shall be deemed income from salaries.

22. The tax on salaries shall not apply to mechanics or laborers on public works.

Acting upon these plain provisions of law in relation to this subject, assistant assessors will, on the 1st of March in each year, canvass their several divisions, and with the necessary assistance provided for by the Department, see to it, that every person, guardian, &c., who, from the best information the officers can obtain, is probably liable to some income tax, makes his proper returns; and the greatest diligence and faithfulness will be required of him in this behalf. He will be furnished with the proper blanks, in adequate terms, but he can do much in furthering his labors, even before blanks are received, by making a list of all the persons in his division, who are probably liable, and giving them notice to be prepared to fill up the formal returns. The directions for assessing the income tax of 1865, are here applied. Most of them are pertinent and applicable. Profits from sales of mining claims are held to be *incomes.* (Letter of Commissioner, Aug. 9, 1866.)

If an assistant assessor paid out of his income any sums for printing or traveling expenses, necessarily incurred in the prosecution of his official business, he may deduct the amount so paid from his taxable income, provided the same was not refunded to him. This, however, would not include expenses for food and lodging. (Letter of Commissioner, June 13, 1866.)

The recipient of a pension should return the entire amount of the same as income for the year when received. (Letter of Commissioner, Aug. 6, 1866.)

The reader will compare the notes on p. p. 127–132, inclusive, upon the subject of the income tax.

If a manufacturer, merchant, &c., has invariably estimated his stock on hand, as a mode of ascertaining the gains or profits of the year for which income is to be calculated, he should continue to do so.

If there is reason to believe that the tax-payer has made a fraudulent return of his income, his books and accounts should be thoroughly inspected, and if an attempt or intent to defraud appears, the assistant assessor or assessor should make the assessment, with 100 per cent. penalty, and report the case at once to the collector for prosecution. If, however, no evidence of attempted fraud appears, but merely ignorance, or innocent even, the party should be allowed to amend his return, and no penalties should be imposed. (Int. Rev. Rec., Vol. III., p. 109.)

Important Circular from Commissioner Rollins.

TREASURY DEPARTMENT, Office of Internal Revenue,
Washington, March 6, 1867.

The following has just been issued from the office of internal revenue:

The act approved March 2, 1867, amending existing laws relating to internal revenue, requires the assessment of annual taxes heretofore made in the month of May, to be made on the corresponding days in the month of March. The principal changes in the law respecting the income tax are those increasing the exemption from $600 to $1,000, and the repeal of the tax of 10 per cent. on sums above $5,000, so that the law now imposes a uniform tax of 5 per cent. on incomes in excess of $1,000. Profits on sales of real estate purchased since December 31, 1863, are made taxable as income. Attention is also called to that portion of the act of July 13, 1866, which repealed the tax on musical instruments, yachts, and certain carriages heretofore taxed in schedule A. Instructions and rulings concerning the assessment of the annual taxes will be issued in a few days. When the present number of assistant assessors is insufficient for the proper assessment of the annual taxes, an additional number will be appointed upon the request of the assessors. Care should be taken to specify the division for which they are needed. It will be some days before a supply of income blanks can be printed, and in the meantime, assessors who have any of the forms No. 24, prepared for use last year, can adopt them for the present service. Form 24½ can be used with the alteration of dates only. A limited number of last year's blanks can be furnished from this office to those assessors who desire to use them while waiting for the preparation of the new blanks.

E. A. ROLLINS, *Commissioner.*

The Internal Revenue Department, with great promptness, has already commenced dispatching to agents and other officers, pamphlet editions of the amendatory internal revenue act, which was not signed by the President until noon of the 4th instant. Blanks for the return of incomes, under the new law, have been prepared, and are now in press.

Instructions for Assessment of 1866. *Income.*

1. Farmers will not be required to make return of produce consumed in their own immediate families.

2. The farmer's profits from sales of live stock are to be found by deducting from the gross receipts for animals sold, the purchase-money paid for the same. If animals have been lost during the year by death or robbery, the purchase-money paid for such animals may be deducted from the gross income of the farm.

3. No deduction can be made by the farmer for the value of services rendered by his minor children, whether he actually pays for such services or not. If his adult children work for him and receive compensation for their labor, they are to be regarded as other hired laborers in determining his income.

4. Money paid for labor, except such as is issued or employed in domestic service, or in the production of articles consumed in the family of the producer, may be deducted.

5. No deduction can be allowed in any case for the cost of unproductive labor. If house servants are employed a portion of the time in productive labor, such as the making of butter and cheese for sale, a proportionate amount of the wages paid them may be deducted.

6. Expenses for ditching and clearing new land are plainly expenses for permanent improvements, and not deductible.

7. The whole amount expended for fertilizers applied during the year to the farmer's lands may be deducted, but no deduction is allowed for fertilizers produced on the farm. The cost of seed purchased for sowing or planting may be deducted.

8. If a person sells timber standing, the profits are to be ascertained by estimating the value of the land after the removal of the timber, and adding thereto the amount received for the timber, and from the sum thus obtained deducting the estimated value of the land on the first day of January, 1862, or on the day of purchase, if purchased since that date.

9. Where no repairs have been made by the tax-payer upon any building owned by him during the preceding five years, nothing can be deducted for repairs made during the year for which income is estimated.

10. A farmer should make return of all his produce sold within the year, but a mere executory contract for a sale is not a sale; delivery, either actual or constructive, is essential. The criterion by which to judge whether a sale is complete or not is to determine whether the vendor still retains in that character a right over the property; if the

property were lost or destroyed, upon which of the parties, in the absence of any other relation between them than that of vendor and vendee, would the loss fall.

11. Tax-payers frequently claim deductions for losses from depreciation in the value of stocks or other property of a like nature. No deduction can in any case be allowed for depreciation of value of such property until it is actually disposed of and a loss realized.

12. Costs of suits and other legal proceedings arising from ordinary business are to be treated as other expenses of such business, and may be deducted from the gross profits thereof.

13. Money paid for a substitute in the army or navy cannot be deducted from income. Money received by a substitute for acting as such must be returned by him as income.

14. Where physicians are obliged to keep a horse for the transaction of business, they may deduct so much of the expense so incurred as is fairly referable to the business done.

15. Expenses for medical attendance, store bills, &c., are not proper subjects for deduction. Expenses of repairs of implements, tools, &c., used in business, may be deducted.

16. Only one deduction of $600 [$1,000] is allowed from the aggregate incomes of all the members of any family composed of parents and minor children, even though one parent only may be living. It is not essential that the children live with the parents. Husband and wife are regarded as members of the same family, though living separately, unless separated by divorce, or other operation of law, such as to break up the family relations.

17. If the members of a family have separate incomes, the returns may be made separately by the proper parties, and a ratable proportion of the $600 [$1,000] deducted from the income of each. The parent, as the natural guardian of the minor child, is required to make return for him. But where any other guardian or trustee has been appointed, the return should be made by the latter. If the minor has no guardian or trustee, he should make return himself. If he refuse or neglect, an independent assessment must be made as in other cases, omitting penalty.

18. If a tax-payer has a minor child in the civil service of the government, receiving a salary, such parent should include in his income return so much of the salary of his child as is not subject to salary tax.

19. Voluntary contributions to bounty funds are not considered as taxes, and cannot be deducted.

20. Rent of a homestead actually paid may be deducted, but the rental value of property owned by the tax-payer is not a subject of deduction. Any person claiming a deduction on account of expense for room rent must satisfy the assessor that the room or rooms occupied by him constitute his home, and that he has no residence elsewhere, and this being shown, he may be allowed to deduct what he actually pays for rent of such rooms. When rent is included and deducted as an expense of business, it must not be again deducted as rent, nor should a

person hiring a house and sub-letting a portion of it be allowed to deduct more than the excess of his payments over his receipts.

21. Among the national, State, county, and municipal taxes deductible from income are comprised such internal revenue taxes as have not been included in expenses of business, and such municipal taxes as are assessed ratably upon all the persons liable to such assessment. But assessments made by municipal authorities upon the inhabitants of a particular locality of a town or city on account of special improvements in or upon the streets adjoining the premises of such inhabitants, the same not being assessed ratably, are not considered as taxes deductible from income.

22. Marriage fees, gifts from members of a congregation to their pastor, &c., are taxable as income when the gifts or donations are in the nature of compensation for services rendered, whether in accordance with an understanding to that effect at the time of settlement, or with an annual custom.

23. Gifts of money, when clearly not in the nature of payment for services rendered, or other valuable consideration, are not liable to taxation as income. Amounts received on life insurance policies, and damages recovered in actions of tort, are exempt from income tax.

24. Lawyers and physicians may return either the actual fees received during the year, without regard to the time when they accrued, or the amounts due to the business of the year. But when the tax-payer has heretofore adopted one method, he cannot now be allowed to make use of the other.

25. If the manufacturer or dealer has been in the practice of estimating his annual profits by taking inventories of stock, he should take the *cost* value of such stock, unless he has taken the market value in making previous returns. Whichever method has been adopted by the tax-payer should be adhered to uniformly.

26. If interest accrued during the year on notes, bonds, &c., is good and collectible at the end of the year, it should be returned as income whether actually collected or not.

27. The fact that income is devoted to the payment of debts does not release the same from liability to income tax.

28. If an inventor sell his invention at once for a gross sum, he should return as income the whole amount, less the expenses actually incurred in perfecting the invention, or in procuring a patent right. But no allowance can be made for the labor or personal expenses of the inventor. If he sell only a portion of his right during the year, he may deduct a proportionate amount of such expense.

29. Wherever the salary or pay received by any person in government employ does not exceed $600 [$1,000] per annum, or is made up of fees, or is uncertain or irregular in the amount or time, and has not therefore been subjected to salary tax, it should be returned as income.

30. Incomes of persons who died after December 31 are taxable,

and should be returned by executors or administrators, and also all income which accrued in 1865 to persons who died within that year. Income which accrued from the estates of such persons in 1865 after the date of decease should be returned by the heirs or other persons who received the benefit of the same.

31. Residents should make return in the district where they reside at the time of making return. The residence required under section 116 for the purpose of taxing income is held to be a residence during the year for which income is "derived." If any person subject to income tax resides abroad, his return should be made in the district where he last resided.

A guardian residing abroad should return the income of his ward in the district where the ward resides.

32. Citizens of the United States residing abroad are subject to tax upon their entire incomes from all sources whatever; and the same is true of foreigners residing in this country.

33. The term "real estate" includes all lands, tenements, and hereditaments, corporeal and incorporeal. Profits on sales of real estate purchased in a previous year need not be returned as income, nor can losses on such sales be deducted therefrom.

34. A lease for years or for life is personal estate, and any profits on the sale of such lease are taxable as income for the year of sale.

35. Where any portion of a legacy has been transferred by the executor to the legatee, so that the executor in his capacity of guardian or trustee has no longer any control of the profits arising from such legacy, the return of such profits as income must be required of the legatee.

36. The payment of legacy or succession tax on the bequest of an annuity does not relieve the annuitant from liability to income tax on his annuity.

37. Where an income exceeds $5,000, $600 will be exempt, $4,400 subject to tax at five per cent., and the remainder at ten per cent.*

38. All expenses for insurance upon property and all actual losses in business may be deducted from the gross income of the business of the year. But losses sustained after December 31, 1865, cannot reduce the income for the year. Losses incurred in the prosecution of one kind of business may be deducted from gains in another, but not from those portions of income derived from fixed investments, such as bonds, mortgages, rents, and the like. Assessors should also be careful not to allow the deduction of amounts claimed to have been lost in business, when in reality they should be regarded as investments or expenditures, as when merchants expend money in farming or gardening for recreation or adornment rather than pecuniary profit.

39. Dividends from which the tax of five per cent. has been withheld should be returned as income, inclusive of the tax withheld, and

* Repealed Stat., 1867.

after the total tax has been assessed, the amount of tax withheld may be deducted therefrom.

40. Coupons on railroad bonds should be returned as income for the year in which they mature, if they are good and collectible.

41. Scrip dividends of companies named in sections 120 and 122 are taxable as income at their nominal value; scrip dividends of other companies should be returned at their market value at the time when received.

Appendix.

DECISIONS, RULINGS, Etc.,

MADE BY

COMMISSIONER AND SECRETARY OF TREASURY,

Under the Amendments of July 13, 1866.

SPECIAL TAXES.

1.

Special Tax on Agents of Foreign Insurance Companies in the United States.

The Liverpool and London and Globe Insurance Company is a foreign company, and its agents in this country are liable to a special tax of fifty dollars.

2.

Public Agents for Dispensing Liquors under Maine Liquor Law, Exempt from Special Tax under certain conditions.

No special tax as liquor dealers is required of a county, city, or town agent, appointed under what is popularly known as the "Maine Liquor Law," for sales made in strict accordance with the provisions of said law.

3.

Drawing and Preparation of Papers to be used in Government Claims, Subjects Parties to Special Tax as Conveyancers.

A person who makes it his business or any part of his business to prepare papers to be used by another in the prosecution of claims before any of the executive departments of the federal government, is liable as a conveyancer, unless he have paid a special (formerly license) tax as a lawyer or as a claim agent.

4.

Special Tax on Hotels. How to Estimate Rental Value.

The special tax of a hotel keeper is based upon the annual rent or rental value of that portion of the premises which is actually used for hotel purposes. Barber's saloons, billiard rooms, and liquor, cigar, and newspaper stands are the usual concomitants of a hotel, and in assessing the special tax of a hotel keeper, no deduction should be made from the rent or rental value of the entire premises on account of any portion of the said premises being occupied for such purposes.

5.

Special Tax on Boats, Barges, or Flats.

By the last proviso to section 103 of the act in force, (section 74 of the Department Compilation), an annual special tax, in lieu of enrollment fees or tonnage tax, is imposed upon all boats, barges and flats, of a capacity exceeding twenty-five tons, not used for carrying passengers, nor propelled by steam or sails, and which are floated, or towed by tug boats, or horses, and used exclusively for carrying coal, oil, minerals, or agricultural products to market.

The term *used exclusively for carrying coal, &c., to market*, is understood to apply to those boats employed exclusively in transporting such merchandise from the place of original deposit, or production, to the first place of consignment or sale, as well as from one market to another.

Boats, barges, and flats used exclusively in transporting the articles named between the shore and a vessel, or from one vessel to another, are liable to a special tax under said proviso. This tax, however, is *in lieu* of enrollment fees or tonnage tax, and should not be assessed upon boats which have already paid taxes under the customs laws.

6.

Manufacturers Selling at Places other than their Factories.

By section 74, of the Act of June 30, 1864, as amended, it is provided that no special tax shall be required for the sale, by manufacturers or producers, of their own goods, wares, and merchandise, at the place of production or manufacture, or at their principal office or place of business, *provided* no goods, wares, or merchandise, except as samples, are kept at such office, or place of business. This is understood to authorize a manufacturer or producer to sell goods, wares, and merchandise of his own manufacture or production *at any time* at the places and in the manner above mentioned without paying a special tax as dealer, even though he has discontinued the manufacture or production, and the time covered by his license as a manufacturer has expired.

7.

Special Tax Receipts not Transferable.

Special tax receipts cannot be transferred from one party to another as licenses were. It is only in case of death that the receipt is transferable, and then only to legal representatives. (Letter of Commissioner, Oct. 30, 1866.)

8.

Surplus Earnings not basis of Special Tax on Banks.

The surplus earnings of an incorporated bank is no part of its capital, under the provisions in relation to special taxes; and any excess paid on that basis is remitted on application to the Department. (Letter of Commissioner, Nov. 12, 1866.)

9.

Transfer of Licenses.

Licenses granted prior to act of July 13, 1866, may be transferred and assigned. It is otherwise under that act providing for special tax receipts. (Letter of Commissioner, Nov. 12, 1866.)

10.

Reassessment of Licenses based on Amount of Sales.

In case the rate of tax is increased by the act of July 13, 1866, upon wholesale liquor dealers, (*i. e.* from $50 to $100) reassessments should be made only in cases where the former license tax already paid is less than $100. Any amounts due within the year beyond that sum is assessed monthly. When the sales exceed $50,000 the total amount of tax for the year should never be more than $50 in excess of one-tenth per cent. of the sales. (Letter of Commissioner, Sept. 13, 1866.)

11.

Commercial Brokers' Special Tax.

The agent of a single manufacturer or dealer is exempt from tax as a "commercial broker," in respect of soliciting orders for such manufacturer or dealer. The agent is also exempt from broker's tax on sales. But the amount of the orders filled by the dealer, through the agent, should be included in the dealer's basis of special tax. (Letter of Commissioner, Jan. 9, 1867.)

12.

Distillation of Spirits from Sour Wine.

The distillation of spirits from sour wine, imported, on which the import duty has been paid, subjects the party to all the requirements of a distiller as to special tax or otherwise. If he "treats" such spirits, selling the article as Cognac brandy, he is also a rectifier, and such rectifying cannot be carried on in the same premises as the distillation. (Letter of Commissioner, Sept. 29, 1866.)

13.

Distillers of Cider, Peach, and Grape Brandy.

Distillers of brandy from apples, peaches, or grapes, exclusively, are not required to comply with the conditions imposed upon other distillers.

But the tax of $2 per gallon, must be paid on all brandy distilled from lees and inferior wine remaining after the manufacture of inferior wine. (Letter of Commissioner, Sept. 27, 1866.) (See section 12, law of 1867.)

14.

When Brewers should pay Tax as Liquor Dealers.

The *special tax* required of *liquor dealers*, is not imposed upon brewers, selling their own products at other places than the brewery; but any amount due as license, must be paid. (Letter of Commissioner, Dec. 1, 1866.)

15.

Construction of Terms "Annual Receipts of Insurance Agents."

The terms "annual receipts of any person (as insurance agent) shall not exceed $100," refer to the individual receipts of such agent as distinct from the receipts for the company for which he acts; [compensation and not premiums, &c.] (Letter of Commissioner, Nov. 5, 1866.)

16.

Special Tax of Manufacturers and Dealers.

A manufacturer can sell his own products at the place of manufacture, in the manner of a dealer; but nowhere else as a dealer without additional tax; and the sale of any of his products at the principal office in the manner of a dealer takes away his privilege of selling said products, even by samples, at said office, without additional tax. It follows that if he sell his own products at his principal office (not the place of manufacture) as a dealer,—all such sales must be included with his sales as a dealer of other merchandise at said office. (Letter of Commissioner, Oct. 26, 1866.)

17.

When Owners of "Water" and other Mills are liable to Special Tax.

The owners of water, steam, grain, and saw-mills are liable to special tax as manufacturers, if their manufactures exceed $1,000 annually. (Letter of Commissioner, Dec. 18, 1866.)

18.

Special Tax of Butchers and Dealers in Shell Fish.

The law imposes a special tax of $5 upon persons who sell shell or other fish, &c., &c., and there is no provision enabling butchers, whatever amount of special tax they pay as such, to sell fish, by reason of paying said special tax.

The butcher who pays a special tax of but $5 is as much a butcher within the meaning of section 65 as the butcher who pays $10, and is entitled to same immunities of that section. (Letter of Commissioner, Sept. 20, 1866.)

19.

Special Tax of Exhibitors, &c.

The proviso to paragraph 38, section 79, indicates liability on the part of the manager of the company (exhibiting, &c.,) rather than on the part of the owner of the building, under paragraph 37 of that section. (Letter of Commissioner, Nov. 15. 1866.)

20.

Grinders of Coffee, Spices, &c.

The retailers of coffee, spices, or mustard, may after the sale is effected *grind* the same in small quantities without charge or receiving pay for so doing and incur no liability to the special tax imposed upon the "grinders of coffee and spices." A tax of one cent per pound is imposed upon the roasting of coffee, &c.; and a similar tax upon the same when *ground* by the manufacturer or dealer. The tax upon coffee, &c., when both roasted and ground is therefore two cents per pound. Any hardship in this is matter, rather for the legislature. (Letter of Commissioner, Nov. 2, 1866.)

21.

Concerning Special Taxes under Act of July 13, 1866.

TREASURY DEPARTMENT, Office of Internal Revenue,
Washington, July 31, 1866.

Attention is hereby called to the changes made in the internal revenue laws relating to licenses, by the act of July 13, 1866, which act goes into effect, so far as special taxes provided for in said act are concerned, on the 1st of August, 1866.

Licenses are abolished, and a "special tax" is substituted therefor.

By the provisions of section eighty, it becomes the duty of assessors to re-assess any person, firm, or company, holding license, for any excess of the special tax substituted therefor over the license tax which has been paid, from the 1st day of August, 1866, ratably, up to the 1st day of May, 1867.

Under these provisions, persons having a license as wholesale dealers in liquor, brewers, distillers, and proprietors of gift enterprises, will be liable to re-assessment from the 1st day of August, 1866. Every wholesale dealer in liquors, for instance, who has paid but $50 for his license, will be immediately liable to re-assessment for the nine months ending May 1, 1867, the amount of re-assessment being $37.50.

A special tax is to be assessed from the same date against distillers of burning fluid and camphene, grinders of coffee and spices, and peddlers of liquors. Peddlers traveling by public conveyances are classed as peddlers of the fourth class Persons whose business it is to manufacture cigars, snuff, or tobacco in any form, should be immediately assessed a special tax as tobacconists, without reference to the amount of their products; but where such persons now hold license as manufacturers, they will not be subject to the special tax until the expiration of their present licenses as manufacturers, unless they are engaged at the same time in the manufacture of other articles, in such manner as to be liable to special tax both as manufacturers and as tobacconists. But no special tax is imposed upon journeymen employed in a cigar manufactory.

Persons now licensed as tobacconists should be assessed a special tax as wholesale dealers when their sales exceed twenty-five thousand dollars.

Any person who is engaged in the manufacture or preparation for sale of any articles or compounds, or who puts up for sale in packages, with his name or trade-mark thereon, any articles or compounds, is liable, under the new law, to special tax as a manufacturer.

Producers of ornamental and fruit trees, and charcoal, selling the same at wholesale, by themselves or authorized agents, at places other than the place of production, are exempt from special tax in respect thereof.

All boats, barges, and flats, not used for carrying passengers, nor propelled by steam or sails, which are floated or towed by tug-boats or horses, and used exclusively for carrying coal, oil, minerals, or agricultural products to market, will be assessable under the new law with an annual special tax, from and after the expiration of the time covered by their present enrollment fees and tonnage duties, in lieu of such fees and duties. Such boats, of a capacity exceeding twenty-five tons, and not exceeding one hundred tons, will be subject to a special tax of five dollars, and when exceeding one hundred tons, to a special tax of ten dollars, said tax to be assessed and collected as other special taxes provided for in the act. The above special tax on boats, barges, and flats, does not, however, affect the liability of the proprietors to special tax as express carriers or agents, when doing business as described in paragraph fifty of section seventy-nine of the act of June 30, 1864, as amended by the act of July 13, 1866.

Wholesale dealers are required, as soon as the amount of their sales within the year exceeds fifty thousand dollars, to make monthly return of sales to the assistant assessor, and pay the tax on sales monthly, as other monthly taxes are paid; and in estimating the amount of sales, any sales made by or through another wholesale dealer, need not again be estimated and included as sold by the party for whom the sale was made. Wholesale dealers now holding license based on a certain amount of sales, will be liable to make monthly returns of sales as soon as their sales exceed the amount named in the license; wholesale dealers in liquors, as soon as their sales shall reach an amount which is less than the basis of their license by the sum of thirty-seven thousand and five hundred, dollars.

The bond required of lottery dealers is further conditioned, by the new law, that the dealer will pay the tax imposed by law on the gross receipts of his sales, and the managers of *any* lottery, now or hereafter existing, can give the bond required.

Cattle brokers should be assessed on the excess of sales over ten thousand dollars, in the same manner as of wholesale dealers.

Under the new law, "every person (other than one having paid the special tax as a commercial broker, or cattle broker, or wholesale dealer, or retail dealer, or peddler,) whose occupation it is to buy or sell agricultural or farm products, and whose annual sales do not exceed ten thousand dollars, is to be regarded a produce broker."

The payment of the special tax of a hotel-keeper permits the person so keeping a hotel, &c., to furnish the necessary food for the animals of travelers or sojourners, without the payment of an additional special tax as a livery-stable keeper.

Lawyers, who have paid a special tax as such, are exempted under paragraph twenty-five from paying the special tax as real-estate agents.

If the annual receipts of an insurance agent shall not exceed $100, a special tax of $5 only, is imposed under the new law; and the paragraph relative to *insurance brokers* is omitted. No special tax is imposed by the new law for selling tickets or contracts of insurance against injury to persons while traveling.

Apothecaries, who have paid the special tax as such, are not required by the new law to pay the tax as retail dealers in liquor, in consequence of selling or of dispensing upon physicians' prescriptions the wines and spirits officinal in the United States or other national pharmacopœias, in quantities not exceeding half a pint of either at one time, nor exceeding, in aggregate cost value, the sum of three hundred dollars per annum.

No special tax is required of a common carrier, by the new law, where the gross receipts do not exceed the sum of one thousand dollars per annum. Draymen and teamsters, owning only one dray or team, will not be liable to this tax.

By proviso to section forty-seven of the act of July 13, 1866, brewers are exempted from special tax as wholesale dealers, when selling at wholesale, even at a place other than their breweries, malt liquors manufactured by them.

Manual-labor schools and colleges are exempt from special tax, as manufacturers, where the proceeds of the labor of such institutions are applied exclusively to the support and maintenance of such institutions. (Section eighteen.)

There is no provision in the new law for refunding license taxes where they exceed the special taxes provided by said law in respect to the same business.

No person doing a business requiring payment of special tax under the new law should be assessed therefor if he now holds a license covering a business of the same nature, unless the special tax provided for exceeds the license tax, in which case the difference of tax should be assessed immediately.

Receipts for special taxes will be furnished from this office. No more licenses will be furnished. With slight alteration, receipts for special taxes may be used as receipts for license taxes assessed under former laws. E. A. Rollins, *Commissioner.*

MANUFACTURES Etc.

22.

Floating Houses not liable to anufacturers Tax.

Floating houses, or square boxes, caulked and made water tight, so as to float, with building erected on it for oyster stand, are not liable to 5 per cent. tax as a manufacture. (Letter of Commissioner, Oct. 26, 1866.)

23.

Construction of Section 94 *in relation to Clothing, &c., as Articles of Dress.*

By section ninety-four of the act of June 20, 1864, as amended by the act of July 13, 1866, there is imposed on clothing, gloves, mittens, moccasins, caps, felt hats, and other articles of dress for the wear of men, women and children, not otherwise assessed and taxed, a tax of two per cent ad valorem, to be paid by every person making, manufacturing or producing for sale clothing, gloves, mittens, moccasins, caps, felt hats, and other articles of dress, or furnishing the materials, or any part thereof, and employing others to make, manufacture or produce them.

Under this provision, it is held that any person, firm, company, or corporation, owning or hiring a factory, workshop or other place of production, and managing or controlling the business, either by personal oversight or by an agent, overseer, or foreman, and making for sale any of the before mentioned articles, is the manufacturer and liable to make returns of the goods manufactured and sold or used, &c., and pay taxes thereon in the district where the factory, workshop, or place of manufacture or production is located.

But where such person, firm, &c., do not manufacture the above enumerated articles for sale, but for other parties who furnish the material in whole or in part, and to whom the articles or goods are returned when so made or finished, upon the payment of a stipulated price for manufacturing, making, or furnishing, he or they are not held liable for the payment of the tax on such articles or goods.

Parties receiving materials to be manufactured for others will make returns to the assessors of their several districts, of the kind and quality of goods made by them, and the names and places of business or residence of the parties furnishing the materials. The assessor receiving these returns will transmit copies of the same to the assessors of the districts where the owners of the goods or parties furnishing the materials reside or have their place of business. (Letter of Commissioner, Nov. 13, 1866.)

24.

What Saws were Exempt under Act of 1866.

The exemption of "hand saws," applies only to the common small saws ordinarily used by joiners and carpenters, and not to pit saws, cross-cut saws, and wood saws with frames, which are subject to the general provisions of the ninety-sixth section of the law. (Letter of Commissioner, Dec. 15, 1866.)

25.

Tin Roofing Not Liable.

The covering of the roofs of buildings with tin is not liable to any tax. (Letter of Commissioner, Dec. 8, 1866.)

26.

Deductions under Section 86.

Under section 86 of the act of 1864, manufacturers were allowed to deduct from their gross sales of products, "the freight, commission, and other expenses of sale, *bona fide* paid;" but under the law of July 13, 1866, no deductions are allowed. A manufacturer, however, who sells his goods on time without interest, may be allowed to reduce such sales to cash value at the time the sales are made. (Letter of Commissioner, Oct. 2, 1866.)

27.

Exemption of Yarn and Warp for Weaving.

Yarn and warp for weaving, &c., on which the tax did not accrue, prior to July 13, 1866, are exempt from tax: cloth, therefore, manufactured since that date, is liable to tax on its entire value, unless evidence satisfactory to the assessor is produced, showing that a tax or duty had actually been paid on the yarn or warp used in its manufacture; in which case the value of the yarn or warp so used may be deducted. (Letter of Commissioner, Oct. 2, 1866.)

28.

What Boxes, Bottles, Cans, &c., can be Deducted under Section 86 as Amended.

Boxes, bottles, cans, spools, &c., used in putting up goods for sale, cannot be deducted from sale value; that part of section 86 under which these deductions were formerly allowed, having been repealed by the act of July 13, 1866. (Letter of Commissioner, Oct. 10, 1866.)

29.

No Tax on the Bleaching of Fabrics as Independent Process of Manufacture.

A tax does not accrue on the bleaching of fabrics, when the same have not previously paid tax. The tax accrues on the full value of the bleached fabrics, when sold. (Letter of Commissioner, Oct. 10, 1866.)

30.

Exemption of Manufacturers under Section 93.

A manufacturer who personally engages in his business is not debarred from the exemptions of section 93, from the fact that he employs apprentices or journeymen to assist him. (Letter of Commissioner, Sept. 10, 1866, and Sept. 21, 1866.)

31.

What Deductions shall be made Monthly on Manufactures of Less than $3,000.

The deduction of $83⅓ monthly, may be made when it is not certain that the annual product will not exceed $3,000, otherwise the entire amount should be taxed. (Letter of Commissioner, Nov. 16, 1866.)

32.

Tax upon India Rubber Boots and Shoes.

India rubber boots and shoes under the law of July, 1866, were liable at the rate of five per cent. ad valorem, on "articles of wearing apparel manufactured from India rubber." (Letter of Commissioner, Oct. 10, 1866.)

NOTE.—They were exempted by amendatory Act of 1867. q. v.

33.

How Cologne Water is to be Taxed.

Under the law of 1866, cologne water was regarded as perfumery, and when put up into bottles, &c., it should be stamped as provided in schedule "C." When put up and sold by the gallon, &c., it pays five per cent. ad valorem, under section 94.

34.

What the term "Wooden Ware" includes.

Under amendment of July, 1866, the exemption of "wooden ware," did not include zinc or metallic washboards, mop-handles with iron or metallic heads, wooden faucets, or well and chain buckets. (Letter of Commissioner, Oct. 16, 1866.) (Compare new law of 1867.)

35.

Mode of Taxing Articles of Clothing, Knit or Woven.

No change was made under the law of 1866 in the mode of taxing articles of clothing, manufactured or produced directly by weaving or knitting, except in the rate of tax. (Letter of Commissioner, Oct. 27, 1866.)

36.

Exemption of Melodeon Actions, &c., &c.

Melodeon actions, organ boards, reeds, &c., fitted to be enclosed in the boards, &c., made and sold to melodeon and organ manufacturers exclusively for that purpose, who pay the tax on the finished instrument, are exempt from tax, under the amendment of 1866. (Letter of Commissioner, Sept. 8, 1866.)

37.

What is Included in the Term Flax, and the Manufactures thereof.

Under the exemption of "Flax, and the manufactures thereof," is not included crash, diaper, sheetings, &c., the warps of which are cotton, or other materials, and the filling flax yarn. So with the articles for the wear of men, women and children. They are not manufactures of flax entirely, and exemptions are to be construed strictly. (Letter of Commissioner, Sept. 11, 1866.)

38.

Ibidem.

The same ruling is made in case of cord or cordage, made from flax thread or yarn. The thread is exempt, but not the secondary manufacture. (Letter of Commissioner, Sept. 22, 1866.)

39.

Repacking and Reinspection of Cigars.

When satisfactory evidence that cigars have been properly inspected, is presented, and have paid the tax imposed upon them, they may be repacked, reinspected, and restamped. (Letter of Commissioner, Oct. 10, 1866)

40.

No Constructive Bonded Warehouses for Cigars.

No constructive bonding of cigars is allowable. When the tax does not accrue on cigars until after a sale has been effected, the actual price received must be returned for taxation. (Letter of Commissioner, Nov. 5, 1866.)

41.

What Deductions may be made from the Finished Locomotive.

Under the amendment of 1866, the builder of a finished locomotive, may deduct, the taxes previously paid on the boiler tubes, wheels, tire, axles, bell shafts, cranks, wrists, or head lights, that is to say, the taxes paid on these articles as separate and distinct manufactures in themselves, but not on the materials out of which they are constructed; but not on any casting used in the construction of a boiler engine, locomotive or cars: nor upon any wheels, springs, tire or axles, made of steel. (Letter of Commissioner, Sept. 19, 1866.)

42.

Tax on Iron, Brass, Steel and Copper Wire and Castings—Deductions for Freight and Commission.

OFFICE OF INTERNAL REVENUE,
Washington, Aug. 27, 1866.

SIR:—In answer to your letter of the 23d inst., I have to say that the tax on wire, whether made of iron, steel, brass or copper, is 5 per cent ad valorem as a manufacture not otherwise provided for. There is, however, in the 10th section of the new law, a provision exempting wire made from wire less than No. 20 wire gauge, upon which a tax has been assessed and paid as wire, and also a proviso that no manufactured wire shall pay a greater tax than that imposed on No. 20 wire gauge.

When wire less than No. 20 on which a tax of five per cent ad valorem has been paid, is afterwards drawn to a greater degree of fineness, no additional tax is to be assessed thereon. Wire, however, on which no tax has been previously paid as wire, is liable to a tax of five per cent upon the price at which it is sold, whether that price is sixty cents, one dollar or two dollars per pound. The law imposes a tax of five per cent ad valorem. The assessment of the tax must be at that rate. The amount of tax depends upon the value of the wire. This is a variable quantity, subject to the fluctuations of the market, supply and demand. The rate is fixed, being imposed by the law, at 5 per cent ad valorem—it cannot be changed except by a change of the law. You are not to assess the same amount only of tax on wire sold at one dollar per pound as on wire sold at sixty cents per pound.

The tax on the former is 5 cents and on the latter 3 cents, unless in the one case the wire has been re-drawn from wire less than No. 20 wire gauge on which a tax has been previously paid as wire.

Castings of iron of all descriptions not otherwise provided for, are subject to a tax of $3 per ton under the new law.

The castings otherwise provided for are (1) malleable iron castings, unfinished, and (2) castings made specially for locks, safes, looms, spinning machines, steam engines, hot air and hot water furnaces, and sewing machines.

These castings when not sold or used for any other purpose, and when a tax is assessed and paid on the article of which the casting is a part, are exempt from taxation.

Castings of all descriptions made for articles, machines or instruments, other than those specially enumerated are liable to tax.

The words "castings of all descriptions" includes castings of brass and other metals or combinations of metals, as well as castings of iron.

No deductions for freight, commissions, or other expenses of sale are allowed under the act of July 13th, 1866.

Yours respectfully,

THOMAS HARLAND,
Dep. Commissioner.

43.

Additional Tax upon Clothing from Taxed Cloth made from Yarn and Warps.

When a party manufactures cloth from yarn and warps, and makes such cloth into garments he is liable to tax; first on the cloth manufacture and then upon the garments made from it.

The same principle applies to wire cloth and articles manufactured from it. (Letter of Commissioner, Sept. 28, 1866.)

44.

Tax upon Sprays, Branches, and Wreaths.

Sprays, branches or wreaths made from buds and flowers, on which no tax or duty has been paid, are taxable at the rate of five per cent on their full value when sold or used, otherwise when the tax has been previously paid.

The proviso of section 94 as amended by act of July, 1866, is not applicable to sprays of artificial flowers. (Letter of Commissioner, Sept. 27, 1866.)

45.

Value of Spools are Liable to Tax upon Spooled Thread.

The value of spools on which tax has been paid, cannot be deducted from sales of thread on spools. (Letter of Commissioner, Oct. 6, 1866.)

46.

Increased Value on Dyed Yarns and Warps.

Yarn or warp exempted from tax by law are not liable to any tax, when dyed or colored. But yarn and warp, and thread, and twine, on which a tax or duty has been previously paid are taxable on increased value when dyed or otherwise more completely finished or fitted for use or sale. (Letter of Commissioner, Nov. 21, 1866.)

47.

What is Regarded as Taxable Building Stone.

By the act of July 13, 1866, building stone of all kinds is exempted from tax: but doors and window-caps and sills are regarded as manufactures of stone, liable to tax when sold or used: but caps and bases for pillars and cornice (though ornamental) are regarded as building stones and exempt from tax. (Letter of Commissioner, Oct. 25, 1866.)

48.

Payment of Tax by Parties who furnish Materials.

Under the provisions of act of July 13, 1866, relative to the payment of the tax by the parties who furnish the material in the manufacture of clothing or other articles of dress which are taxable at the rate of 2 per cent., it is held not applicable to cases, when materials are furnished for the manufacture of constituent parts of clothing: but the manufacturer is held liable to the tax, and not the parties who furnished the materials. (Letter of Commissioner, Jan. 4, 1867.)

49.

Mattresses and Palliasses Exempt.

All mattresses and palliasses, whether made with spiral springs or otherwise, are, under the amendment of 1866, exempt from tax. (Letter of Commissioner, Dec. 14, 1866.)

50.

Curtains Not Taxable on Increased Value on Account of Addition of Tax Paid Tassels.

Tassels on which the tax has been paid, and which are not made part of the curtain, need not be returned for taxation as part of such curtain. (Letter of Commissioner, Nov. 17, 1866.

51.

Exemption of Articles of Dress, &c.

All articles of dress for the wear of women and children, made or trimmed by dressmakers or milliners, are exempt from the two per cent. tax, though the products of such dressmakers or milliners may exceed $1000 per year. (Letter of Commissioner, Oct. 17, 1867.)

52.

Provisions in Relation to Tax on Photographs.

Under amendment of July, 1866, photographs or other sun pictures, not specially exempted, are subject to ad valorem tax of 5 per cent.

And sun pictures on which the tax has been paid, when more completely finished, by painting, &c., are liable to a tax of 5 per cent. on their increased value. When an artist takes a photograph, as the outline of the picture he designs to paint, subsequently destroying such photograph, he substantially produces a "work of art," and is not liable to any tax. (Letter of Commissioner, Oct., 1866.)

53.

Cheese Boxes under the Act of 1866 *are not "Packing Boxes."*

Cheese boxes necessary to put the cheese into market cannot be regarded as "packing boxes," and are not exempt. (Letter of Commissioner, Oct. 12, 1866.)

54.

Photograph Albums are not "Books."

Photograph albums cannot be regarded as "Books," and are therefore not exempt as such. (Letter of Commissioner, Aug. 18, 1866.)

55.

Tax on Printed Envelopes.

Printed envelopes are not exempt as "printed matter," but are liable to tax on entire value. If printed after made and sold, they are liable to additional tax on increased value. (Letter of Commissioner, Sept. 27, 1866.)

56.

What is included under term "Packing Boxes."

Under the term "packing boxes," exempt from tax, may be included all that class of boxes in which goods, before or after sale, are commonly transported or shipped, and which are not for transportation enclosed in other packages. (Letter of Commissioner. Nov. 1, 1866.)

57.

Tax on Brass and Composition Castings.

Brass and composition castings, not specially exempted, are liable to an ad valorem tax of 5 per cent. under section 94 of amended law of 1866. (Letter of Commissioner, Oct. 31, 1866.)

58.

Liability to Tax of Cloths Dyed and Printed—Increase value under Sec. 94—Repairs.

Office of Internal Revenue,
Washington, January 15, 1867.

Sir:—Your letter of the 11th inst., calling my attention to a communication of yours under date of October 29th, on the subject of cloths dyed and printed, and asking for a decision as to their liability to tax, has been received.

Samples of different kinds of cloths accompanied your letter, grouped under four different heads, with descriptions of each; but there seems to be but one question raised, viz: whether the dyeing or printing of cloths which have become unsaleable on account of changes in style or fashion, or which have depreciated in value from the length of time they have been on hand, renders such cloths liable to taxation either under Sec. 94 or Sec. 95 (act of June 20, 1864, as amended).

In answer to the question thus raised I have to say, that the taxing of increased value under Sec. 95, is limited to articles, &c., which are not specially provided for. Cloths made or manufactured, and cloths dyed, printed, or bleached, are specially provided for in Sec. 94; therefore, whatever liability there may be in the case is to be found in Sec. 94.

Originally Sec. 94 provided for taxing repairs, as well as for taxing manufacturing. Dyeing, printing and bleaching may be either, according to the article to which the process is applied and the end to be secured. The coloring or bleaching of dresses, shawls, bonnets and other articles of clothing or dress which have become impaired by use, accident or decay, is clearly a repair, and therefore exempt from taxation under the amendatory act of July 13th, 1866, which exempts repairs of articles of all kinds.

The dyeing, printing, or bleaching of cloths or articles which have never been used, nor suffered decay, waste, injury, or partial destruction thereby, is a process of manufacturing, and taxable by express provision, on the increased value added by the process provided a tax or duty shall have been paid on the cloths or articles before the same were re-dyed, printed or bleached.

The cloths, &c., may be domestic fabrics or foreign manufactures; and the tax previously paid may have been upon cloths merchantable, but which have not been subjected to the final or finishing process of dyeing, printing, &c., or they may already have been once dyed, printed or bleached. The liability is the same in either case; and the increased value, whether it is more or less, is taxable.

That there is some increased value, I presume no one would seriously pretend to deny. It is contrary to reason and experience for persons to incur the expense of dyeing, printing, bleaching, &c, unless, there was a probability, amounting nearly to a certainty, that the owners would realize more for the goods after they were colored and printed, than they would otherwise receive.

The question is not whether they may realize the original value of the goods, or whether their sale involves to the owners profits or losses. The law taxes the manufacturer or producer on his goods, wares and articles upon their value, or increased value, whether he makes or loses money.

The increased value given to cloths, &c , by dyeing, printing or bleaching, is not to be determined in such cases by comparing their value when dyed, &c., with their original cost. The values immediately before and after dyeing, &c., are the bases of comparison. This value will, at least, equal the cost of dyeing, printing or bleaching, and may be more.

The rule of this office is to tax the dyer, printer or bleacher when he purchases goods, and dyes, prints, or bleaches them, or receives from manufacturers or dealers new goods on which a tax or duty has been paid to be dyed, printed or bleached, or cloths which have become unsaleable, not from use, accident or decay, but from change of style, color, print or fashion, to be re-dyed, printed, or bleached, five per cent. on increased value. But the re-dyeing of dresses, shawls and other articles of clothing which have become impaired by use, accident or decay, is regarded as repairs, and therefore exempt from taxation.

Yours respectfully,

THOMAS HARLAND, *Dept. Commissioner.*

S. LASAR, Esq.

59.

Construction of term "Barrels, &c., for reception of Fluids."

By the excise act of July 13, 1866, "barrels and casks other than those used for the reception of fluids," are exempt from tax. Under this provision, barrels and casks not capable of holding fluids, and which are used for packing flour, lime, nails, dry paints, &c., are exempt from tax. But kegs in which white lead, ground in oil, is packed, are generally substantial articles, made water tight, and which are not entitled to exemption. (Letter of Commissioner, Oct. 18, 1866.)

60.

Small Oil Cans for Oiling Machinery not Exempt.

By the act of July 13, 1866, tin cans used for oil are exempt from tax. Under this designation are not included the small vessels commonly used for applying oil to machinery, &c. (Letter of Commissioner, Dec. 27, 1866.)

61.

What Yarn is Taxable.

Under the terms "yarn for weaving, braiding, and manufacturing purposes exclusively" includes *all* yarns for whatever purpose the same may be used. (Letter of Commissioner, Dec. 31, 1866.)

62.

Tax on "Holland Shades."

"Holland shades" not being specially provided for in the law of 1866, are taxable at the rate of 5 per cent. on their full value, unless they are sold at a price not exceeding five per cent. above the cost of materials used in their manufacture; in which case they are exempt. (Letter of Commissioner, Sept. 20, 1866.)

63.

Tax on Chairs, Chair-stuff, Legs of Pianos, &c.

Chairs manufactured from taxed chair-stuff, are taxable on the increased value only. It should be borne in mind, however, that chair-stuff is not taxable unless finished, and bored, or mortised, ready to put together. The cost of taxed legs and cases of pianos, may be deducted from the value of pianos of which they form a part; but no deduction has been allowed for the cost of taxed lyres. Cords, tassels, and fringes, made wholly of taxed thread, yarn, or warp, are taxable on increased value only, but if they are made in part of article other than thread, yarn, or warp, they are taxable on entire value when sold or used. (Letter of Commissioner, Oct. 16, 1866.)

64.

Tax on Charcoal and Foundry Facings.

Under the present excise law charcoal and mineral coal are exempt from tax; but foundry facings are regarded as a manufacture from charcoal, and taxable at the rate of five per cent. ad valorem, under the general provision of section 94. (Letter of Commissioner, Dec. 3, 1866.)

65.

Illuminating, Lubricating and other Mineral Oils.

Illuminating, lubricating, and other mineral oils, marking between thirty-six degrees and fifty-nine degrees, inclusive, Baume's hydrometer, the product of the distillation, re-distillation, or refining of crude petroleum, are taxable at the rate of twenty cents per gallon, without regard to the specific gravity of the petroleum from which they are produced. (Letter of Commissioner, Feb. 1867.)

Cotton Motes.

The article known as cotton motes is subject to a tax of three cents per pound. (Letter of Commissioner, Feb. 1867.)

66.

Kaolin and China Clay Exempt.

Kaolin or china clay being a preparation of clay by washing the crude material and freeing it from extraneous matter, and impurities is not a manufacture taxable. (Letter of Commissioner, Jan. 1867.)

STAMP DUTIES.

67.

Stamp Duty on Leases, or Contracts for Rent or use of Real Estate based on Annual value.

The stamp duty upon a lease, agreement, memorandum or contract for the hire, use, or rent of any land, tenement or portion thereof, is based upon the annual rent or retail value of the property leased, and the duty is the same whether the lease be for one year, for a term of years, or for the fractional part of a year only.

68.

Stamp Duty on Bills, Single or Obligatory.

A bill single or a bill obligatory, *i. e.*, an instrument in the form of a promissory note, under seal, is subject to stamp duty as written or printed evidence of amount of money to be paid on demand or at a time designated, at the rate of five cents for each one hundred dollars or fractional part thereof.

69.

Stamp Duty on Writ or other Process on Appeal to Court of Record.

A fifty cent stamp is required upon a writ or other process on appeal from a Justice's court or other court of inferior jurisdiction to a court of record ; and this stamp covers all the papers necessary to the taking of the appeal and to the entry of the action in the court of appellate jurisdiction.

70.

Conveyance from Municipal Corporations, &c., of Lands sold for Taxes exempt from Stamp Duty.

A conveyance of lands sold for unpaid taxes issued since August 1st, 1866, by the officers of any county, town, or other municipal corporation in the discharge of their strictly official duties, is exempt from stamp tax.

71.

Assignment or Transfer of Mortgage or Insurance Policy, liable to Stamp Duty.

The assignment or transfer of a mortgage or of a policy of insurance is subject to stamp tax, whether there be a sale or not ; such for instance as a transfer from the legal owner to the equitable one

72.

Jurat to an Affidavit exempt from Stamp Duty in certain cases.

The jurat to an affidavit of the correctness of a return of property for taxation when made before an assessor of State, County, Town, or other municipal taxes, is exempt from tax duty if the administration of the oath is part of the Assessor's official duties.

73.

Registry of a Judgment exempt from Stamp Duty.

No stamp is necessary upon the registry of a judgment, even though the registry is such in its legal effect as to create a lien which operates as a mortgage upon the property of the judgment debtor.

74.

Assignments for benefit of Creditors liable to Stamp Duty.

An assignment of real or personal property or of both for the benefit of creditors, should be stamped as an argument or contract.

75.

Stamp Duties on Protests accrues for each and every Note, Bills of Exchange, Drafts, &c.

A stamp duty of twenty-five cents is imposed upon the "protest of every note, bill of exchange, check or draft," and upon every marine protest. If several notes, bills of exchange, drafts, &c., are protested at the same time and all attached to one and the same certificate, stamps should be affixed to the amount of twenty-five cents for each note, bill, draft, &c., thus protested.

76.

Duplicate &c., Leases all require Stamps.

When leases are executed in duplicate, triplicate, &c., all require stamps as original, but mere copies are exempt. If notes are given for the consideration of a lease, they must be stamped as well as the lease. (Letter of Commissioner, Sept. 11, 1866.)

77.

Stamp Tax on Note Endorsements, &c.

The endorsement of a partial payment on the back of a note is regarded as a new memorandum, not subject to stamp duty.

The agreement to waive protest and notice of protest signed by the party making it is subject to stamp duty as a contract or agreement. (Letter of Commissioner, July 6, 1866.)

78.

Stamp Tax on Substituted Notes.

New promissory notes substituted for others that had been destroyed after having been properly stamped, and not renewals of notes payable at different dates, do not require to be stamped. It would be otherwise if *new notes*, of different dates or otherwise changed, were given. (Letter of Commissioner, Nov. 28, 1866.)

79.

Stamp Tax on Special Powers, &c., in Deeds.

Extraordinary powers, special covenants, &c., sometimes inserted in deeds, and not contained in common forms, are liable to same stamp as if issued separately. (Letter of Commissioner, Nov. 15, 1866.)

80.

Relative to the Taxes upon Canned Meats, Vegetables, &c.

By the amendatory act of July 13, 1866, a stamp duty is imposed upon "every can, bottle, or other single package containing meats, fish, shell-fish, fruits, vegetables, sauces, sirups, prepared mustard, jams, or jellies contained therein, and packed or sealed, made, prepared, and sold, or offered for sale, or removed for consumption, in the United States, on or after the first day of October, eighteen hundred and sixty-six."

While it is believed that it was the purpose and intent of Congress to impose a stamp tax upon the above-named articles, if sold or offered for sale or removed for consumption in the United States, on or after October 1, 1866, regardless of the time of their manufacture or production, that intent is so imperfectly expressed as to render it doubtful whether, under a proper construction of the language of the statute, such a tax can be collected.

Internal Revenue officers are therefore instructed not to interfere with the possession or sale of such articles, of domestic manufacture or production, when satisfactory evidence is furnished that they were prepared and passed out of the possession of the producer prior to the first day of October.

Oysters and other shell-fish are often removed from the shell, and, without undergoing any process for their preservation, are placed, in a raw state, in tin or other vessels, for the sole purpose of transportation in ice. When put up in this manner, and for this purpose only, they are not regarded as *canned* within the meaning and intent of the law, and no stamps will be required upon them.

Articles named in schedule C, when imported, or of foreign manufacture, are liable to the stamp tax *in addition* to the import duties thereon. When, however, such imported articles, except playing cards, lucifer or friction matches, cigar lights, and wax tapers, are sold in the original and unbroken packages in which the bottles or other enclosures were packed by the manufacturer, the person so selling them is not subject to any penalty on account of the want of a proper stamp; but when such packages are opened, the articles should not, under any circumstances, be offered or exposed for sale until they have been appropriately stamped. E. A. ROLLINS, *Commissioner.*

81.

Assignment of Lease—Assignment of Rents, &c.

An assignment of a lease within the meaning and intent of Schedule B, is an assignment of the leasehold or of some portion thereof by the lessee, or by some person claiming by, from, or under him, such an assignment as subrogates the assignee to the rights, or some portion of the rights, of the lessee, or of the person standing in his place. A transfer by the lessor of his part of a lease, neither giving nor purporting to give a claim to the leasehold, or to any part thereof, but simply a right to the rents, &c., is subject to stamp tax as a contract or agreement only.

82.

Jurats Administered by Revenue Officers.

The words "or used" were stricken out of section 154, by the act of July 13th, 1866. When a Notary Public or Justice of the Peace administers the oath to an assistant assessor, upon his monthly account for services, a five cent stamp should be affixed to the jurat. No stamp will be required when the oath is administered, and the jurat issued by an assessor, assistant assessor, collector, deputy collector, revenue agent, or inspector.

83.

Subscription Lists, Contracts, Promissory Notes.

When a subscription is for a purpose in which there is a community of interest among the subscribers, the list should be stamped as a contract, or agreement, at the rate of five cents for each sheet or piece of paper upon which it is written.

When there is no community of interest, and the subscription is conditional, each signer executes a separate contract, requiring its appropriate amount of stamps; this amount depends upon the number of sheets or pieces of paper upon which the contract is written.

When each of the subscribers contracts to pay a certain and definite sum of money on demand, or at a time designated, the separate contract of each should be stamped at the same rate as a promissory note.

84.

Payment for and affixing of Stamps—Penalties.

The law does not designate which of the parties to an instrument shall furnish the necessary stamp, nor does the Commissioner of Internal Revenue assume to determine that it shall be supplied by one party rather than by another; but if an instrument subject to stamp duty is issued without having the necessary stamps affixed thereto, it cannot be recorded, or admitted, or used as evidence, in any court, until a legal stamp or stamps, denoting the amount of tax shall have been affixed as prescribed by law, and the person who thus issues it is liable to a penalty, if he omits the stamps with an intent to evade the provisions of the internal revenue act.

85.

Bills of Sale of Vessels—Contract for Transfer of Property.

The stamp tax upon a bill of sale, by which any ship or vessel, or any part thereof, is conveyed to, or vested in, any other person or persons, is at the same rate as that imposed upon conveyances of realty sold; a bill of sale of any other personal property should be stamped as a contract or agreement.

86.

Stamp Tax on Canned Goods, &c.

All canned goods sold or offered for sale after October 1, 1866, were required to be stamped as specified in Schedule "C," of act of July 13, 1866. When they have been packed in cases, and it would be difficult to unpack them, the law will be substantially complied with, by enclosing to the purchaser a sufficient number of cancelled stamps. (Letter of Commissioner, Oct. 3, 1866.)

87.

Stamp Tax on Syrup in Cans.

Syrups when put up in cans, bottles, &c., are liable to a stamp tax of one cent, when the packages with their contents do not exceed two pounds in weight respectively. When exceeding two pounds in weight, one cent for every additional pound or fractional part thereof. When not put up in cans, bottles, &c., they are liable to an *ad valorem* tax of 5 per cent. (Letter of Commissioner, Oct. 11, 1866.)

88.

Stamp Tax in the late Insurrectionary States in force from October 1, 1862.

The first act imposing a stamp tax upon certain specified instruments, took effect, so far as said tax is concerned, October 1st, 1862. The impression which seems to prevail to some extent, that no stamps are required upon any instruments issued in the States lately in insurrection, prior to the surrender, or prior to the establishment of collection districts there, is erroneous.

Instruments issued in those States since October 1st, 1862, are subject to the same taxes as similar ones issued at the same time in the other States.

89.

Administrators, Executors, and Guardians' Bonds.

The official bonds of administrators, executors, and guardians, are subject to a stamp tax of one dollar each, as bonds for the due execution, or performance of the duties of an office.

90.

Instruments to which the U. S. is a party.

No stamp is required upon an instrument to which the United States is a party, if it is signed and executed by a person representing the Government; if not signed by such a person stamps should be affixed.

91.

Receipt of Attorney for Note or Claim for Collection.

No stamp is required upon the receipt of an attorney for a note or other claim left with him for collection.

92.

Cancellation of Stamps.

Each stamp when used should be separately cancelled.

93.

Basis of Stamp Duty on Conveyance of Realty—Actual Consideration or Value.

The *actual* "consideration or value," and not the mere nominal consideration, determines the amount of stamp tax upon a conveyance of realty sold.

94.

Marriage Certificates, when, and when not, Liable.

A marriage certificate issued by the officiating clergyman or magistrate, to be returned to any officer of a state, county, city, town, or other municipal corporation to constitute part of a public record, requires no stamp; but if it is to be retained by the parties, a five cent stamp should be affixed.

95.

Landlord Notice to Tenant to Quit.

A notice from landlord to tenant to quit possession of premises, requires no stamp.

96.

Bond to Convey Real Estate.

A bond to convey real estate, requires stamps to the amount of twenty-five cents.

97.

Receipts taken by Administrators, Executors, and Guardians.

Receipts taken by administrators, executors, guardians, trustees, &c., to be used as vouchers upon the settlement of their accounts, are subject to the same stamp taxes as other receipts.

98.

Transfer of Mortgages--Endorsements on Negotiable Instruments.

Upon every assignment or transfer of a mortgage, a stamp tax is required equal to that imposed upon a mortgage for the amount remaining unpaid; this tax is required upon every such transfer in writing, whether there is a *sale* of the mortgage or not; but no stamp is necessary upon the endorsement of a negotiable instrument, even though the legal effect of such endorsement is to transfer a mortgage by which the instrument is secured.

99.

When Partition Deeds may become Taxable.

Partition deeds between tenants in common need not be stamped as conveyances, inasmuch as there is no sale of realty, but merely a marking out, or a defining of the boundaries of the part belonging to each; but where money or other valuable consideration is paid by one co-tenant to another for equality of partition, there is a sale to the extent of such consideration, and the conveyance by the party receiving it, should be stamped accordingly.

100.

Renewal of Insurance Policies—Definition.

An instrument which operates as the renewal of a policy of insurance, is subject to the same stamp tax as the policy itself; but such a receipt as is usually given for the payment of the monthly, quarterly, or annual premium, is not a renewal within the meaning of the statute. The payment simply prevents the policy from expiring, by reason of non-performance of its conditions: a receipt given for such a payment requires a two cent stamp, if the amount received exceeds twenty dollars, and a two cent stamp only.

But when the time of payment has passed, and a tender of the premium is not sufficient to bind the Company, but a new policy or a new contract in some form, with the mutuality essential to every contract, becomes necessary between the insurer and the insured, the same amount of stamps should be used as that required upon the original policy.

101.

Insurance Permits changing terms of Policies.

A permit issued by a life insurance company changing the terms of a policy as to travel, residence, occupation, &c., should be stamped as a contract or agreement.

102.

Mortgage, when Taxable as Contract.

A mortgage given to secure a surety from loss, or given for any purpose whatever, other than as security for the payment of a definite and certain sum of money, is taxable only as an agreement or contract.

SAVINGS INSTITUTIONS.

(Circular No. 53.)

103.

Treasury Department, Office of Internal Revenue, }
Washington, Sept. 17, 1866. }

As the amendatory act of July 13, 1866, takes effect on the first day of August, 1866, all Savings Banks will be required to make the return of tax on their deposits for the month of July, 1866, in manner and form as heretofore. The return for said month should be made to the proper assistant assessor, and the tax paid to the collector in accordance with Circular No. 48, July 20, 1866.

The returns of the above-named institutions, from the first day of August, 1866, will be made on the first day of January, 1867, and semi-annually thereafter, in the manner set forth in form No. 106.

The benefit of the exemptions in the proviso to section 110, act of June 30, 1864, as amended July 13, 1866, is confined to Provident Institutions, Savings Banks, Savings Funds, or Savings Institutions having no capital stock, and doing no other business than receiving deposits to be loaned or invested for the sole benefit of the parties making such deposits without profit or compensation to the company.

In ascertaining the taxable amount of deposits, all sums of five hundred ($500) dollars and upward, in the name of any one person, are to be included.

In determining the "average amount of deposits" subject to taxation for the period covered by the return, these institutions will be allowed, in order to facilitate the making of such return, to take the amount on deposit on the first days of January and July of each year, prior to the time of making their returns, as the correct average deposit, or to take such period between those dates as may be satisfactory to the Assessor of the district where such institution is located. The total amount of deposits at the date fixed upon should always be stated in the return.

The term "United States' Securities" includes all interest-bearing obligations of the United States, owned and held by the bank as an investment.

The proviso to section 120, act of June 30, 1864, as amended July 13, 1866, so far as it relates to the interest paid to depositors in Savings Banks or Savings Institutions, is construed to apply only to such savings Institutions as are described in the proviso to section 116, act of June 30, 1864 as amended July 13, 1866. All others are liable to the five per cent. tax imposed by section 120 aforesaid, on the dividends or interest declared or paid by them to depositors and stockholders.

E. A. ROLLINS, *Commissioner.*

104.

Liabilities of Savings Institutions—Tax on the Average of Deposits over $500—Surplus and Reserved Earnings.

ASSESSOR'S OFFICE, 3d District of Massachusetts,
Boston Dec. 6, 1866.

SIR: A wide difference of opinion prevails among the managers of Savings Banks in regard to the exact requirements of the present law in the matter of tax. It is contended that the law requiring returns to be made on the first Monday of January and July in each year, subjects such institutions to a tax of one-twenty-fourth of one per cent. semi-annually, on the amount of deposits of $500 and upwards existing on said first Mondays of January and July, respectively; and that they are liable to no further or greater tax.

Par 71 per 40 of the present law provides that "there shall be levied collected, and paid, a tax of one-twenty-fourth of one per cent. each month, &c.," and at the close of par. 162 p. 92, it is provided that the "annual or semi-annual interest allowed or paid to depositors in Savings Banks or Savings Institutions shall not be considered a dividend."

In regard to the first point I claim the intent of the law to be that such institutions shall on the first Monday of January or July in each year, return the aggregate amount of their monthly deposits of $500, and over, as they existed on the last day of each month preceding, and pay the tax thereon at the rate of one-twenty-fourth of one per centum; or return the average amount of the six months preceding and pay a tax thereon of ¼ of 1 per cent.

In regard to the second case, I suppose no tax is chargeable upon dividends, as such—as the principal part of such dividends are either paid directly, or credited in account, to depositors.

There is generally a large surplus of gain, on savings of the preceding six months in excess of the dividend, which is credited to no individual account, but carried to account of reserved profits, and may not be divided for many years.

"The Provident Institution for Savings" in Boston, at the July dividend in 1866, credited "Profit and Loss" with more than $110,000 reserved profits.

Are gains in this form by such institutions taxable? and if so, at what rate? Very respectfully,

WM. S. KING, *Assessor.*

Hon. E. A. ROLLINS,
Commissioner of Internal Revenue.

OFFICE OF INTERNAL REVENUE,
WASHINGTON, Dec. 13, 1866.

SIR:—Your letter of 6th inst., relative to Savings Banks, is received.

As regards the manner of making returns of tax on the deposits of such Institutions as are enumerated in the proviso to section 110, act

June 30, 1864, amended July 13, 1866, I refer you to Circular No. 53 of this office, issued Sept. 17, 1866. (Record Vol. IV., p. 102.)

You will see from this that the Institution is allowed to take the amount of deposits on the first days of January and July of each year, as the correct average for the six months preceding—but in case this time is not satisfactory to the Assessor, he can fix some other period between the first days of January and July, as giving an amount which can be taken as the correct average for the six months. This management was made at the solicitation of the New York Savings Banks, to facilitate making the returns, and as it gives the Assessor discretionary power to determine what day the deposits shall be taken as a fair average for the six months, it cannot give the Banks any undue advantage.

Replying to your second question I have to say, that, under the proviso to section 120, act of June 30, 1864, as amended July 13, 1866, the amount of "annual or semi-annual interest allowed, or paid to the depositors in Savings Banks, or Savings Institutions" is not considered a dividend, and is, therefore exempt from the tax of five per cent. imposed by said section.

The proviso last aforesaid is construed to apply only to such Savings Institutions as are described in the proviso to section 110, act June 30, 1866, as amended, &c., viz:—"Provident Institutions, Savings Banks, Savings Funds, or Savings Institutions, having no capital stock, and doing no other business than receiving deposits to be loaned or invested for the sole benefit of the parties making such deposits without profit or compensation to the Association or Company: All others are liable to the dividend tax of five per cent.

Where this class of Savings Institutions makes an addition to its surplus fund of earnings in excess of the amount of interest paid, or allowed, to depositors, as in the case you mention, such profits are clearly subject to the tax under section 120 aforesaid.

In order to be exempt from tax the interest or earnings must be either paid to the depositors or credited to their individual account.

Very respectfully,

THOS. HARLAND, *Deputy Commissioner.*

WM. S. KING, Esq., *Assessor, 3d Dist., Boston, Mass.*

105.

Savings Banks and Provident Institutions—Dividend Tax.

The undistributed earnings of Provident Institutions, Savings Banks, Savings Funds, and Savings Institutions, having no capital stock, and doing no other business than receiving deposits to be loaned, or invested for the sole benefit of the parties making such deposits, without profit or compensation to the association or company, fall within the proviso to section 120, of the act in force, (162 of Compilation) and are exempt from dividend tax. Although the entire amount of annual or semi-annual interest, may not be paid to the depositors or credited upon their several accounts at the time the dividend is declared, it will eventually be disposed of in this manner, and the depositors alone will receive the benefit of the business. (Letter of Commissioner, Jan. 7, 1867.)

DISTILLED SPIRITS.

106.

Provision of Section 68, *Act* 1864, *amended by Act* 1865, *limiting time for commencing proceedings for Forfeiture of Spirits—Repealed by Act of July*, 1866.

Section 68, of the act of June 30th, 1864, as amended by the act of March 3d, 1865, limiting the time for commencing proceedings to enforce a forfeiture of liquors, the vessels containing it, and the vessels used in making it to thirty days, was repealed by section 9 of the act of July 13, 1866.

107.

Spirits may remain an unlimited time in Bond, but Tax must be paid unless removed according to law.

The time during which spirits may remain in bond without payment of tax is not limited, but the tax must be paid before they are removed from the warehouse, unless removed in pursuance of law.

108.

Manufacture of Saleratus on Distillery premises.

No other article except saleratus can be manufactured upon the premises where spirits are distilled.

109.

An Assessor has no authority to remove an Inspector of Distilleries, but must report to Commissioner.

An assessor has no authority to remove an inspector and appoint another person temporarily in his place. Where an inspector is derelict in his duty, or is interested in a distillery, the case should immediately be reported to the Commissioner of Internal Revenue.

110.

Sale of Brewers' Stamps by Collectors.

Collectors are not authorized to sell stamps denoting the amount of tax upon fermented liquors to any one outside their respective districts, nor to any one within their districts except brewers.

111.

Inspection by General Inspector of Spirits withdrawn from Bonded Warehouse.

All spirits withdrawn from a bonded warehouse should be inspected by a general inspector.

112.

Countersinking and affixing of Beer Stamps.

The purpose of countersinking for beer stamps is to protect the brewer by preventing the stamp from becoming detached. If brewers prefer to affix their stamp without countersinking, there is no legal objection to the practice.

113.

Liabilities of Distillers of Spirits from Fruits, such as Cherries, Blackberries, &c.

The distillers of other fruits, such as cherries, blackberries, &c., are not entitled under the law to the benefit of the low rates of special tax imposed upon distillers of apples, peaches and grapes, nor has the Commissioner of Internal Revenue any discretionary power to exempt the distillers of such other fruits, from any of the provisions of the law relating to the manufacture of spirits.

114.

Wine and Spirits produced from Rhubarb.

Wine produced from rhubarb by fermentation is exempt from tax, but spirits produced from rhubarb by distillation are subject to a tax of two dollars per gallon. The exemption of "wine made of grapes, currants, or other fruits and rhubarb," applies to fermented liquors only.

115.

Special 48 *applies to Spirits, and not Coal Oil.*

The provisions of special 48, from the Internal Revenue office, are applicable to transactions in spirits only, and not to coal oil removed in bond. (Record, Vol. V., p. 20.)

116.

Destruction of Bonded Merchandise and Cancellation of Bond.

Where merchandise shipped in bond is clearly proved to have been destroyed by fire or other unavoidable accident, the tax will be remitted and the bond cancelled.

117.

Per diem Compensation of Inspectors of Distilleries when under seizure or not running.

So long as an inspector has charge of spirits in a bonded warehouse, he is entitled to his regular per diem compensation, although the distillery itself may not be in operation, but when the warehouse or the distiller's spirits therein are under seizure, they are not in the custody of the inspector, and he has no claim for a per diem compensation.

118.

Inspector of Spirits can act only in his own District and must act in person.

An inspector can lawfully act as such only within his own district; he cannot deputize another person to use his stencils.

119.

Tax-paid Spirits cannot remain in Bonded Warehouse.

Spirits upon which the tax has been paid should not be allowed to remain in a bonded warehouse, but should be removed at once upon payment of the tax.

120.

Brandy distilled from Imported Wines liable to Full Tax.

Brandy produced by distilling imported wines, is subject to a tax of two dollars per gallon without any deduction of the import duties upon the wines.

121.

Wines put up as American Wines, exempt—Wines put up on pretence of being Foreign Wines, liable.

Wines put up as American wines, with no pretence whatever that they are imported wines or wines of foreign growth or manufacture, are not subject to tax under section 36 of the act of July 13, 1866; but if there be any such pretence, they are liable under said section, even though the bottle bear the name of a firm in the United States.

122.

Returns and Payment of Tax on Spirits.

That part of the act of June 30, 1864, which allowed distillers who distill or manufacture less than one hundred and fifty barrels per year, to make returns and pay taxes on the first day of each and every month, instead of the first, eleventh and twenty-first, was repealed by the act of July 13, 1866. By the last named act all distillers, except distillers of apples, peaches, and grapes, are required to make tri-monthly returns

123.

Party Improving Whiskey by Passing it through Still, Liable as a Rectifier.

A person becomes liable, not as a distiller, but as a rectifier, by reason of passing whiskey, upon which the tax has been paid, through the copper still, for the sole purpose of improving it.

124.

Two Inspectors Required by a Distillery that runs constantly.

Assistant Inspectors must be employed at each distillery which runs so constantly that one Inspector cannot be present all the time it is running.

125.

Distillers' Warehouses—Assistant Inspectors.

A distiller can establish as many warehouses, class A, for the storage of his products as he may elect ; but if the number is so great as to withdraw the attention of the Inspector from a strict supervision of the distillery, one or more assistants should be appointed, as provided in section 29 of the act of July 13, 1866, (129 of Compilation.)

126.

Rectifiers not liable to tax on their Productions.

Rectifiers are not required to pay a five per cent. ad valorem tax upon compound or imitation liquors manufactured by them for sale.

127.

Wines and Imitation Wines.

A tax of fifty cents per gallon is imposed upon all liquors known or denominated as wine, not made from grapes, currants, rhubarb, or berries, produced by rectification, or mixed with other spirits, or into which any matter whatever may be infused, to be sold as wine or by any other name, and not otherwise provided for in the Internal Revenue Laws. Such spirits need not be inspected and gauged by an inspector, but all persons engaged in the manufacture of them should make their returns and pay their taxes at the same time, and in the same manner as the manufacturers of other articles.

128.

Cider, Ale, Beer, and Wine, exempt from the Tax on Distilled Spirits.

Cider, ale, beer, and wine contain alcohol, but they are produced by fermentation ; and inasmuch as they are not produced by distillation, they are not subject to the tax upon distilled spirits.

129.

Spirits cannot be Refined in Bonded Warehouses of Distillers.

Spirits may be refined upon removal in bond, but cannot be refined in the distiller's bonded warehouse.

130.

Apple Distillers may distill Brandy from pure Apple Cider.

Brandy distilled from pure apple cider is included in the exemption made in reference to "distillers of brandy from apples, peaches, or grapes exclusively."

131.

Definition of Capacity of a Still under Section 24, Act July 13, 1866.

The capacity of a still, as the term is used in section 24, of the act of July 13, 1866, (section 122 of Compilation) is not the quantity which the distiller may seem practicable to operate on his still or boiler, but is the full measurement of the vessel.

132.

Bonded Spirits removed from Warehouses for Re-distillation, Rectification, &c., must in all cases whatever be returned to the same Warehouse.

Bonded spirits removed for re-distillation, rectification, or change of package, under the provisions of section 40, of the act of July 13, 1866, must be returned to the same warehouse, and a change in the ownership does not remove the necessity of such return.

133.

The General Inspector must inspect all Spirits produced by Apple Distillers, and re-inspect Bonded Spirits Rectified or Re-distilled.

The duty of inspecting bonded spirits which have been removed for the purpose of being rectified, re-distilled, canned or put into other packages and then returned, and of inspecting spirits manufactured from apples, peaches, or grapes belong to the general inspector.

134.

Apple and Peach Distillers must give Bond.

Distillers of brandy and other spirits from apples, peaches or grapes, are not exempted from the provisions of section 24, of the act of July 13, 1866, (section 122 of Compilation) requiring distillers to give bonds.

135.

Tax on Fresh Beer produced by creating a new fermentation of Flat Ale.

If a brewer purchase his products from another brewer before it has fermented, and mixes it with flat beer for the purpose of creating a new fermentation, the purchaser who thus manufactures a saleable article of beer must pay a tax on the full amount sold by him, or removed for consumption or sale; but such product sold before fermentation need not be included in the monthly account of beer, &c., sold by the person who sells it.

136.

Power of Commissioner in authorizing Collectors or Deputies to make Special Seizures.

Section 48, of the act of June 30, 1864, as amended by the act of July 13, 1866, provides that goods, wares, merchandise, &c., may, under certain circumstances, be seized by the collector or deputy collector of the proper district, or by such other collector or deputy collector as may be specially authorized by the Commissioner of Internal Revenue. This does not make it the duty of the Commissioner to designate any one collector to make general seizures, but confers upon him special authority to designate any collector or deputy collector not "of the proper district," whenever in his opinion the exercise of such authority becomes necessary or expedient.

137.

Re-inspection of Spirits and Liquors—Absence of Inspection Marks on Packages of Spirits, presumptive of Nonpayment of Tax or Fraud.

It is only when spirits are removed from an inspected package for the purpose of rectification, re-distillation or change of proof, that a re-inspection is necessary. When removed for other purposes, as when a dealer puts them up in other packages for sale, a second inspection is unnecessary ; but if such packages bear no inspection marks or brands, it will be presumed that no tax has been paid upon the spirits therein contained, and the person in whose possession they are found, should be prepared to rebut the presumption.

138.

Liabilities of Druggists or Chemists in Distilling, Recovering or Producing Alcohol—Special Tax.

No special tax is imposed for any still, stills, or other apparatus used by druggists or chemists for the recovery for phamaceutical and chemical or scientific purposes, of alcohol, which has been used in those processes, but if used for its production, the usual taxes should be assessed and collected.

139.

Marking of Spirits in Bond prior to September 1st, 1866.

Spirits manufactured prior to September 1st, 1866, and which are in bonded warehouses, need not be proved, gauged and branded. Provision is made in the law and in the regulations for marking such liquors when withdrawn from the warehouses, and those marks are sufficient.

140.

Inspection of Alcohol made from Tax-paid Whiskey.

When whiskey is removed from an inspected package and made into alcohol, it should be again inspected after its character has thus been changed, and the packages containing it should be properly branded.

141.

Distillery Inspectors must engage in no other Business.

A stiller or beer runner cannot at the same time act as inspector of a distillery. An inspector can engage in no other business while employed as inspector, either for the distiller or for any other party.

142.

Medicated Spirits produced by distillery Drugs, Roots, &c., Liable to Tax of $2 per Gallon.

The product of stills though medicated by distilling drugs, roots, &c., is nevertheless liable to a tax of two dollars per gallon.

143.

Distillers of Spirits from Apples, Grapes, and Peaches exclusively, not required to pay per diem Compensation of Inspectors.

Persons employed in the distillation of spirits from apples, grapes, and peaches exclusively, are not required to pay per diem compensation to inspectors.

144.

Regulations for Distillers and Refiners of Coal or Mineral Oils.

(Circular No. 53.)

Office of Internal Revenue,
Washington, October 17, 1866.

By the act of June 30, 1864, as amended by the act of July 13, 1866, a tax is imposed upon illuminating, lubricating, or other mineral oils; and it is further provided "that distillers of illuminating, lubricating, or other mineral oils, naphtha, benzine, benzole, or gasoline, shall be subject to all the provisions of law applicable to distillers of spirits, with regard to special taxes, bonds, returns, assessments, removing to and withdrawing from warehouses, liens, penalties, forfeitures, drawbacks, and all other provisions designed for the purpose of ascertaining the quantity distilled and securing the payment of taxes, so far as the same may, in the judgment of the Commissioner of Internal Revenue, and under regulations prescribed by him, be deemed necessary for that purpose."

Under this authority, the Commissioner of Internal Revenue hereby prescribes that every person who refines, distills, or re-distills petroleum or other bituminous substances, or refines crude oil, produced by a single distillation of coal, shale, asphaltum, peat, or other bituminous substances, shall give a bond. (Form 28.) This bond must be taken by the collector, who will bear in mind that bonds already given under the provisions of former laws will not suffice.

Each distiller or refiner must keep a book, in form and manner set forth in Form 25, which form is hereby prescribed, showing the quantity and description of the oil produced, the quantity placed in bond, and the quantity not placed in bond, and consequently subject to tax, and the quantity and description of oil sold by him, with the name and place of business or residence of the person to whom sold. If desired by the distiller, the account of sales may be kept in a separate book.

A return will be made on Form 26, on or before the tenth day of each month, instead of tri-monthly as heretofore, showing the product of the preceding month, the quantity bonded, and the quantity subject to tax; and the tax is to be paid, like other monthly taxes, on or before the last day of the month in which the return is made.

By the act of July 13, 1866, section 10, paraffine oil, and lubricating oil made from petroleum, coal, or shale, not exceeding in specific gravity 36 deg., is exempt from tax, but such oil is made subject to the same inspections as illuminating oil: it therefore, follows that the entire product of the distillery or refinery must be inspected and gauged by an inspector appointed under the provision of section 58, act of June 30, 1864.

The establishment of bonded warehouses, for the storage of mineral oil, and the withdrawal of the same therefrom, will be governed by the regulations of March 1, 1865, issued by the Secretary of the Treasury, until otherwise directed.

Distillers and refiners of mineral oil are, by these regulations, released from the restrictions placed upon distillers of spirits by the present law, so far as relates to establishing bonded warehouses for the storage of their products, employing inspectors for each distillery at a per diem compensation, providing receiving cisterns, &c. They can also remove the oil produced by them directly from the distillery or refinery to a general bonded warehouse, Class A, as in the case of removal of distilled spirits. E. A. ROLLINS, *Commissioner*.

MISCELLANEOUS.

145.

No Deduction for Salary Tax on Compensation of Inspectors of Distilleries.

No tax on salary is to be withheld from the compensation of inspectors of distilleries, and assessments on the distillers for their services, are to be entered upon the monthly lists (Letter of Commissioner, Oct 18, 1866.)

146.

Power of Revenue Inspectors.

A revenue inspector cannot make seizures or act in the capacity of deputy collector. (Letter of Commissioner, Nov. 26, 1866.)

147.

No Office Furniture allowed to Assessors, &c.

No payment is made to assessors or their assistants, for office furniture, rent of the same, nor for fuel and lights. (Letter of Commissioner, Dec. 11, 1866.)

148.

Hours of Service need not now be stated in Assistant Assessors' Bills.

Assistant assessors are not required to specify in their bills the hours employed as under former law. (Letter of Commissioner, Nov. 15, 1856.)

149.

Liabilities of Auctioneers for Sales, &c.

Under the amendments of July, 1866, sales of Auctioneers made for or on account of judicial officers and executors and administrators are not liable to tax. (Letter of Commissioner, Aug. 9, 1866.)

150.

Mode of Determining Special Tax on Boats, &c.

In assessing the special tax upon boats, barges and flats under the last proviso to section 103, (section 74 of Compilation) the capacity is to be determined by the customs admeasurement.

151.

No Tax on Receipts for Transporting Property.

The tax of two and one-half per cent imposed by section 103, upon gross receipts for transportation of passengers, freight, &c., is no longer assessed upon receipts for transporting *property* by amendment of July 13, 1866. (Letter of Commissioner, Sept. 20, 1866.)

152.

Farmers Exempt as Peddlers.

Under the present rules of the office, a person conveying slaughtered calves and sheep to market in wagons, to sell by the carcass or quarter, to butchers keeping a stall or stand, would be liable as a peddler, unless he were a farmer, selling meat from animals raised upon his farm, in which case he would be exempt. (Letter of Commissioner, Dec., 1866.)

153.

Duties of Deputy Collectors in the Payment of Money.

Deputy collectors are bound by law to pay over daily all monies received by them, and they cannot lawfully deposit them in any bank. He is considered an "officer" or "agent" of the treasury, under internal revenue law, section 12, and act of June 14, 1866, section 3. (Solicitor of Secretary of Treasury, Aug. 25, 1866.)

154.

Regulations of United States as to Inspection of Liquors do not Relieve from State Laws.

United States laws and regulations concerning the inspection and gauging distilled spirits do not relieve liquor dealers from the obligations of State laws. (Letter of Commissioner, Oct. 5, 1866.)

155.

Spirits Under Proof.

Distilled spirits under "proof," are liable to full tax. (Letter of Commissioner, Dec. 1866.)

156.

Re-inspection of Spirits.

All spirits or liquors removed from the original package must be re-inspected and marked. So with all spirits changed by rectification or mixing. (Letter of Commissioner, Nov. 20, 1866.)

157.

Shares of Informers in Revenue Frauds.

The schedule of informers' shares prescribed in treasury circular of August 14, 1866, is applied to proceeds resulting from forfeitures as well as penalties, fines and proceeds of forfeitures.

(Circular Instructions.)

TREASURY DEPARTMENT, August 14, 1866.

The act amendatory of the Internal Revenue Law, which went into effect on August 1, contains the following provisions:

"And where not otherwise provided for, such share as the Secretary of the Treasury shall, by general regulations, provide, not exceeding one moiety nor more than five thousand dollars in any one case, shall be to the use of the person, to be ascertained by the Court which shall have imposed or decreed any such fine, penalty or forfeiture, who shall first inform of the cause, matter, or thing whereby such fine, penalty, or forfeiture shall have been incurred: and when any sum is paid without suit, or before judgment, in lieu of fine, penalty, or forfeiture, and a share of the same is claimed by any person as informer, the Secretary of the Treasury, under general regulations to be by him prescribed, shall determine whether any claimant is entitled to such share as above limited, and to whom the same shall be paid, and shall make payment accordingly. It is hereby declared to be the true intent and meaning of the present and all previous provisions of internal revenue acts granting shares to informers that no right accrues to or is vested in any informer in any case until the fine, penalty, or forfeiture in such case is fixed by judgment or compromise, and the amount of proceeds shall have been paid, when the informer shall become entitled to his legal share of the sum adjudged or agreed upon and receive, *Provided* That nothing herein contained shall be construed to limit or effect the power of remitting the whole or any portion of a fine, penalty, or forfeiture conferred on the Secretary of the Treasury by existing laws."

Under the authority here conferred, the following schedule of informer's shares is hereby prescribed:

Of the first five hundred dollars of any penalty the informer shall receive	50 per cent.
Of the next fifteen hundred dollars	40 per cent.
Of the next two thousand dollars	30 per cent.
Of the next two thousand dollars	25 per cent.
Of the next two thousand dollars	20 per cent.
Of the next two thousand dollars	15 per cent.
Of the next two thousand dollars	10 per cent.
Of all above twelve thousand dollars, and not exceeding fifty-five thousand dollars	5 per cent.
THUS: If the penalty is five hundred dollars, the informer will receive	$250 00
If one thousand dollars	450 00
If two thousand dollars	850 00
If three thousand dollars	1,150 00
If four thousand dollars	1,450 00
If five thousand dollars	1,700 00
If six thousand dollars	1,950 00
If seven thousand dollars	2,150 00
If eight thousand dollars	2,350 00
If nine thousand dollars	2,500 00
If ten thousand dollars	2,650 00
If eleven thousand dollars	2,750 00
If twelve thousand dollars	2,850 00
Of every additional one thousand dollars up to fifty-five thousand dollars	50 00

H. McCULLOCH, *Secretary of the Treasury.*

158.

Circular relative to Informers' shares under the Internal Revenue Law.

TREASURY DEPARTMENT,
Washington, Sept. 26, 1866.

Doubts having been expressed as to whether the Schedule of Informers' Shares, prescribed in the Circular Instructions issued by this Department on August 14, 1866, (IV. RECORD. p. 2), is to be applied to proceeds resulting from forfeitures, as well as to penalties, said Schedule is hereby declared to be, and to have been from its issue, applicable to all informers' shares or fines, penalties, forfeitures, and proceeds of forfeitures, accruing under the provision of Internal Revenue Law cited in the above-mentioned Circular.

H. McCulloch, *Secretary of the Treasury.*

159.

Brokers' Sales—Sales through another Broker.

The last proviso to section 99 (70 of the Compilation) is "That in estimating sales of goods, wares, and merchandise, for the purposes of this section, any sales made through another broker upon which a tax has been paid, shall not be estimated and included as sold by the broker for whom the sale was made.

Broker to Return Entire Amount of Sales.

Every broker should be required to state in his returns the entire amounts of all his sales, *including those made through other brokers;* from that amount he may deduct the amount of sales made by him through other brokers, and upon which a tax has been paid, and should himself pay a tax upon the remainder. He should be required to state in his return when, where, and by whom, the sales deducted by him were made; and the assistant assessor should ascertain, by correspondence or otherwise, whether his representations are correct.

160.

Assistant Assessors and Elective Officers.

Office of Internal Revenue,
Washington, Aug. 20, 1866.

It has been represented to this office that in some instances assistant assessors have used their official positions to secure their nomination to the local office, and it is urged that their relation to the tax-payer is such that they may use it to their personal advantage in this respect if so disposed; it is also believed that the position of a candidate for office before the people is unfavorable to that strict impartiality which is so essential to the proper discharge of the duties of an assistant assessor. The Secretary of the Treasury has, therefore, directed that notice be issued that the acceptance of a nomination to an elective office by any assistant assessor will be taken as evidence that he no longer wishes to retain his position. Assessors are instructed to promptly report the name of any assistant who may accept, or who is known to be seeking any nomination for such office, in order that a successor may be forthwith appointed.

Thomas Harland, *Acting Commissioner.*

161.

Tax on Advertisements.

When railroad tickets, envelopes, signs or placards, are made the medium of public advertisements for which the publisher receives pay, such advertisements are liable to a tax of three per cent. on the gross receipts. (Letter of Commissioner, Dec. 17, 1866.) (See new provisions of 1867.)

162.

Tobacco, Re-manufacture of.

Broken plug tobacco on which tax has been paid, cannot be re-manufactured into smoking tobacco, without the payment of the proper tax upon the latter, being a manufacturer of an article of different grade and tax. (Letter of Commissioner, Dec. 19, 1866.)

163.

Successions. No Tax on when Estate passed before Enactment of Law.

There is no successive tax on the proceeds of realty passing to children under will of the father upon the decease of the mother, in 1855. The real estate was converted into personalty before taxes accrued. (Letter of Commissioner, July 30, 1866.)

164.

Ibidem. How Assessed, and on what Value.

A succession tax is assessable on clear value of the estate when it comes into the possession of the successor.

165.

Limitation of Re-assessments.

Treasury Department, Office of Internal Revenue,
Washington, February 27, 1867.

Sir:—In reply to your letter of the 22d instant, calling for the views of this office as to the effect of the concluding portion of paragraph 38 of the amended revenue laws, in reference to re-assessments, I have to say, that such re-assessments may be made for fifteen months after the passage of the act of July 13, 1866, for any of the causes indicated in said paragraph, occurring during any period anterior to the passage of said act; and for like causes occurring since July 13, 1866, such re-assessment may be made at any time within fifteen months from the passage of the act, or from the delivery of the list to the collector by the assessor for collection. Very respectfully,

E. A. Rollins, *Commissioner.*

C. N. Emerson, Esq., *Assessor, 10th Dist., Pittsfield, Mass.*

166.

Tax on Bank Dividends.

Treasury Department, Office of Internal Revenue,
Washington, February 26, 1867.

Sir—It has come to the knowledge of this office that many of the National Banks pay the local taxes (State and Municipal) assessed upon their shares, deducting the amount so paid from their earnings, thus reducing the amount subject to the tax of five per cent., under sections 120 and 121 of the Internal Revenue Act of June 30, amended July 13, 1866.

The decision of the Supreme Court is to the effect that said taxes may be imposed upon the *shares* of National Banks, as being the personal property of the *shareholders*, and they cannot, therefore, be deducted by the Bank as an *expense* of the Bank, as if the taxes were assessed upon the Corporation.

Assessors will instruct the banks that taxes paid for the shareholders, cannot be deducted in ascertaining the amount of net gains.

It also appears that some National Banks withhold from their returns of *dividends and surplus profits*, the amounts carried to surplus fund, as required by the National Currency Act. This is erroneous, as the law requires the tax to be paid upon the *entire* net earnings, including amounts paid stockholders, and "all undistributed sums, or sums made or added during the year, to their surplus or contingent fund." (See sections 120 and 121 aforesaid.)

This tax upon the additions to the surplus, should not be confounded with that once required to be paid upon surplus as a part of the Banks capital, it being a tax upon the profits of the business, without regard to the disposition made of the same. Very respectfully,

E. A. ROLLINS, *Commissioner.*

C. N. EMERSON, ESQ , *U. S. Assessor* 10*th Dist.*, *Pittsfield, Mass.*

167.

Concerning Seizures of Property in the Custody of Transportation Companies.

TREASURY DEPARTMENT, Office of Internal Revenue,
Washington, Feb. 5, 1867.

In order to avoid giving cause of complaint to transportation companies, collectors and deputy collectors are instructed, when they seize property in the custody of an agent of any transportation company, to address and deliver to such agent a written statement, giving, for the purpose of fully identifying the property seized, an inventory of the different articles, mentioning the brands, numbers, and marks thereon, including, when it is known, the name and residence of the ostensible owners.

They should also, in the same statement, specify in general terms that the property is seized for violation of the internal revenue laws.

If the property is removed from the custody of the company, that fact should be stated in the paper, that the company may be able to show that the property has properly passed from their possession.

This statement should be signed by the seizing officer as collector or deputy collector, giving his full address. Where it is required, the seizing officer should show that he is an officer authorized by law to make seizures.

When the property is forfeited, the collector should inform the company. If, however, it is released upon compromise or otherwise, it should be returned to the company, unless the company consent that it be given up directly to the claimant.

E. A. ROLLINS, *Commissioner.*

Miscellaneous Rulings, Decisions and Correspondence upon Manufactures.

Assessors and others desirous of obtaining a thorough and intelligent knowledge of the various decisions under former laws, many of which are fully applicable to the present act, will not fail to consult the following numbered decisions of the Internal Revenue Department to be found collected in Boutwell's Manual, Ed. 1863, viz. :

No. 2. Tanning of leather.
No. 3. Tanning leather and making of shoes.
No. 7. Manufactures of clothing.
No. 22. Ship and boat building.
No. 25. Newspapers, circulation, &c.
No. 36. Manufacture of clothing, (referred to in the note on the subject of increased values.)
No. 40. Agents of manufacturers.
No. 41. Publishers of printed books.
No. 42. Job printers, lithographers and engravers.
No. 46. Manufacturers and employes.
No. 49. Place of manufacture.
No. 55. Manufacturers of cabinet ware and furniture.
No. 56. Manufacturers of stone, marble and slate.
No. 69. Taxable value of articles sold at places other than the place of manufacture.
No. 71. Definition of manufactures, "commercial value."
No. 77. "Manufacture of patented articles." (This decision has been essentially modified.)
No. 81. Tanned leather when curried or finished.
No. 83. Custom made clothing.
No. 85. Mode of ascertaining "increased values." Also No. 164, Nov. 9, 1865, same subject.
No. 118. Manufactures of stone, marble and slate.
No. 119. Manufactures made under contract prior to July 1, 1862 Also series 1, No. 5, Boutwell 177, "Manufacturers' returns."
No. 132. July 9, 1864: Liability of manufacturers to license and to pay excise duties.
No. 133. July 9, 1864: Articles taxable under act of June 30, 1864.

No. 142. Manufactures and place of manufacture. (Oct. 18, 1864.)

No. 143. Sept. 6, 1864: Manufacture of printed books.

No. 144. Sept. 21, 1864: "Deductions" under section 86, law of 1864.

No. 147. Oct. 20, 1864: "Thread, yarn and warps," and fabrics made therefrom.

Circular No. 24. Oct. 26, 1864: "Goods made for the United States from materials furnished by Government."

Circular 25. Day on which manufacturers' duties shall be payable. (December 1, 1864.)

No. 154. May 9, 1865: Manufactured soda water sold from fountains.

No. 157. July 26, 1865: Photographs and sun pictures.

No. 162. Oct. 31, 1865: Marble and building stone.

No. 163. Nov. 6, 1865: Liability of manufacturer and producer of exempt articles from duty under section 96. (This is an important decision and in view of the largely increased list of the exempt articles, it is printed in full, *infra.*)

"Special" No. 31, February 3, 1866. "Taxation ot articles manufactured in the States lately in insurrection, remaining in the possession of the manufacturers or producers," and Decision No. 168, of February 26, explaining Special No. 31. Also special No. 16, of June 23, 1865, and Regulations of Treasury of June 27, 1865, *in Appendix.* The above decisions, &c., made since the early part of the year 1864, (and not contained in Mr. Boutwell's Manual of 1863,) should be on the files of every officer of the law, to be studied carefully in connection with the present act. The assessor especially should be intimately familiar with them, that he may intelligently perform his important duties, and save the Department from continual annoyance, and himself from the just reproach of incompetency and ignorance.

We also append the following rulings, instructions, and correspondence, drawn from various sources, and well worthy of the attentive examination of all officers of the internal revenue law, and persons liable to duty. Many of them are of course, now inapplicable, but all are important as part of the history of the revenue law.

The soldering together of tin plate for roofing is not held to be a manufacture. (Boutwell, No. 118.)

Sheet iron stoves are a manufacture, and subject to duty, on entire value when complete, of six per cent. ad valorem. (*Ibidem*, No. 120.)

A manufacturer must make his returns to the assessor of the district where his place of manufacture is *located*, though he may reside and make his sales in another district. When the manufacturer effects his own sales by himself or his authorized agent the tax does not accrue on removal from the place of manufacture to the place of sale, but only when sales of the goods are actually made. (*Ibidem*, No. 121.)

The manufacturer of *farina* is subject to a duty of six per cent. ad valorem. (*Ibidem*, No. 122.)

Cotton lines or ropes, made from taxed yarn are only liable to tax on their increased value. (*Ibidem*, No. 147.)

Every distinct shop used by a railroad company for making or repairing of machinery or apparatus for its own use is regarded as a manufactory. (*Ibidem*, No. 148.)

Hides prepared by tanners for saddle-tree covers are held to be a manufacture and subject to duties. (*Ibidem*, No. 151.)

Cordage is a manufacture, and subject to an ad valorem duty of six per cent. (*Ibidem*, No. 154.)

Balusters are taxable as a distinct manufacture. (*Ibidem*, No. 156.)

The grinding of dye woods is not considered a manufacture. (*Ibidem*, No. 161.)

Boot tops and uppers of shoes, manufactured as such, (independent of the finished boot or shoe,) are held subject to duty. (*Ibidem*, No. 163, also 169.)

Watch cases are taxable on their full value as a manufacture when made or sold as a separate part of the business of making watches. (*Ibidem*, No. 164.)

Stereotype plates are held to be manufactures, and the duties must be collected in the district where manufactured. (*Ibidem*, No. 165.)

Grinding and preparing salt for table use is taxable on increased value. (*Ibidem*, No. 166.)

Ribbons made for general use are regarded as fabrics of the nature of cloth, and when a tax has been paid on the thread or yarn or warp, the ribbons are to be assessed only on the increased value. (*Ibidem*, No. 175.)

The owners and cutters of clothing, shirts and shirt-fronts are to be regarded as the manufacturers, and not the mere operatives who make them up and return them. (I. Int. Rev. Rec., 67.—II. *Ibidem*, 186.—Letter of Commissioner, Nov. 28, 1865.)

A change in the character of a manufacture may change its liability to duty, as a change from soured wine, &c., to vinegar. (I. Int. Rev. Rec., 100.)

A builder's or contractor's license covers his business if he makes no articles subject to duty as manufactures; but if he makes such articles to an amount exceeding $1,000 annually, he must also have license as a manufacturer; in such case the amount of business covered by the manufacturer's license may be deducted from the amount of his contracts. (I. Int. Rev. Rec. 45.)

As to the mode of returning manufactures and products, consult particularly Decision No. 144 and Circular No. 44.

As to who are liable to pay the tax on manufactures and deductions, see the United States vs. Stevens, and *als*. (II. Int. Rev. Rec., 54.

Letter of Commissioner to Smith & Wesson. Assessor's Circular, cited II. Int. Rev. Rec., 130. Letter of Commissioner, Oct. 23, 1865, cited II. Int. Rev. Rec., 156.)

The producers of articles exempt from tax, are to be licensed as manufacturers and not as dealers. (Decision No. 163.)

The following rulings and decisions in Vol. III. of Int. Rev. Rec. in relation to specific matters, may be consulted: stoves, 3; cheese, 3, 12, 140; harness, 3; artificial eyes, 12; shoddy, 13, 124; flasks, 13, 117; shooks, 13; tax paid materials, 14, 94, 140; wheels, &c., 14, 94; horse blankets, 14, 124; white lead, 36; hoop skirt wire, 36, 53; increased values, 38, 94, 100, 102, 117; horse shoes, 44; carriages, 45; belts and buckles, 52; tape, 53; matches, 60; work on ships, 70, 100; wood mouldings, 93; flax and thread, 94; fire arms, 94; (matter of parts of pistols) modified, 145; piano actions, 94.

"In answer to your letter of the 28th ult., asking for a ruling from this office in relation to shirts woven in a continuous web, and then cut into suitable lengths and finished; also in relation to balmoral skirts woven in a similar manner with appropriate stripes at proper intervals; and shawls and blankets woven in the same manner, I have to say that the proper mode of taxing in all these cases will be to assess a tax on the thread or yarn, whether sold for such purposes or used by the manufacturer who spins it and afterwards consumes or uses it in weaving shirt, balmoral skirt, shawl or blanket webs.

"The webs or rather the shirts, skirts, shawls and blankets, are then to be taxed on their entire value, according to the 7th paragraph of Decision No. 147. If such webs are sold before the shirts, skirts, shawls, and blankets are cut and bound or otherwise finished more completely, and fitted for use, the additional tax for such finishing, &c., should be only on their increased value.

"This ruling is on the supposition that these webs are not mere fabrics, but are woven expressly for these articles, and are mainly, if not entirely, unfitted for any other use." (Letter of Commissioner, December 3, 1864.)

"From this examination I am satisfied that, when Piano Cases and other parts of the Piano have been assessed, and a duty paid thereon, the finished articles into which such previously taxed parts enter are correctly assessed on their increased value, under the proviso relative to furniture previously taxed in the rough or unfinished state, section 94.

"Whenever, therefore, the assessor or assistant assessor of the district, where such parts were increased in value by being more completely finished, or fitted for use or for sale, is satisfied that the same have been returned for a revenue tax, you will assess such Pianos a duty of five per centum, ad valorem, upon the increased value only. That value can be ascertained by deducting from the value of the finished Pianos, when sold or removed for sale, &c., the cost prior to the last manufacture of the part or parts so previously returned.

"When piano cases, or other parts of pianos are made in your dis trict, and sold or removed for sale, &c., you should assess them for a tax. By so doing, uniformity and equality will be secured, and I believe this mode of assessment is clearly authorized by the terms of law." (Letter of Commissioner, Oct. 22, 1864.)

"The painting of window sashes is taxable as increased value. Otherwise with the setting in of glass." (Letter of Commissioner, Dec. 22, 1864.)

"Shoddy, yarn, and blankets are separate and distinct manufactures, and each is taxable at the rate of five per cent., ad valorem.

"If a person is engaged in the manufacture of shoddy, and converts the same into yarn, which he finally weaves into blankets, he is liable under the law to pay a tax on each manufacture." (Letter of Commissioner, Jan. 3, 1865.)

"Paper bags are subject to a duty of five per cent., ad valorem, if their value exceeds by five per cent. the value of the paper from which they are made, notwithstanding such paper has been previously taxed." (Letter of Commissioner, Jan. 5, 1865.)

"In the case of a marine engine, the assessment is to be made on the engine and boiler separately, the former at the rate of three, and the latter at the rate of five per cent., ad valorem.

"But I know of no provision of the law, by which either could be taxed on increased value, because a tax had been previously paid on material, or parts, which are in themselves considered and taxed as manufactures. The locomotive is taxed on its full value notwithstanding the wheels, the axles, the tires, springs, castings, &c., have all been previously taxed. The carriage maker pays in like manner an ad valorem tax on the sale price of his product, though every article used in its structure (and they are numerous) has paid one or two previous taxes. So of various and almost every other complex machine or instrument.— Why should a steam engine form an exception to the rule? I know of no reason or law for it, and therefore hold that the tax must be assessed on the full value." (Letter of Commissioner, Jan. 28, 1865.)

"If the company purchase machine made horse shoes on which a tax of five per cent. has been paid, and toe and cork them, they are liable to the five per cent. additional tax on the increased value by toeing and corking. But the expense of fitting and setting the shoe should not be included in estimating the increased value." (Letter of Commissioner, Sept. 16, 1864.)

"Taxable articles made to order, or for sale are to be assessed without regard to the use to which they may be applied. New wheels, put into an old locomotive are therefore taxable." (Letter of Commissioner, Sept. 28, 1864.)

"Patented articles, which are made by manufacturing companies for their own use, with the consent of the patentee, are not exempt from taxation on the ground that he invented the article and procured the patent while in the employ and at the expense of the company. If the inventor is not exempt for the product of his brain, they cannot be for the product of their cash." (Letter of Commissioner, Jan. 3, 1865.)

"When a person or firm engaged in manufacturing any goods, wares, merchandise or articles, are personally and constantly engaged in the manual labor, or the oversight of the machinery brought into operation for the production of such goods, &c., they are entitled to the exemption named in the conditions of section 93, though apprentices or journeymen may be employed in the process of production." (Letter of Commissioner, Oct. 10, 1864.)

"Chair manufacturers cannot deduct from the value of the chairs the cost of split cane used by them on which an excise duty has been paid." (Letter of Commissioner, March 7, 1865.)

"Wall paper is a manufacture more completely finished or fitted for use, and is therefore liable to the duty upon the increased value, under section 95." (Letter of Commissioner, March 20, 1865.)

"If a man makes a thousand or ten thousand spindles, each equally fitted for any one of the like number of cotton machines, part of which he uses himself in the construction of said machines, part of which he sells, he is liable to tax on all, according to the principles laid down in Special No. 9, and according to the proviso of the 93d section of the act of June 30, 1864, and the first clause of the 94th section of same act." (Letter of Commissioner, November 26, 1864.)

"The increase of one-fifth, or twenty per cent. of the rates of duty authorized by the 5th section of the act of March 3, 1865, amendatory of the act of June 30, 1864, applies *only* to duties imposed in the 94th section of the last named act, and does not apply to duties imposed by the provisions of the 95th section of the said act." (Letter of Commissioner, May 22, 1865.)

"Whenever it is impracticable to obtain from patentees the returns of articles manufactured for them by other parties, or when they neglect or refuse to make such return, the manufacturers themselves may be assessed for such articles, the value to be determined by actual sales and by the contract price for manufacture. Decision No. 77 is modified by this ruling. The government cannot be deprived of its lien." (Letter of Commissioner, April 25, 1865.)

"Your letter of June 24, in relation to the duty upon hoop skirts, has been received. In answer I have to say, that when the wire is made by one party, covered by another, and the skirts manufactured by a third party, the first is liable to a duty on the wire, the second is liable to a duty on the increased value of it when covered, and a third is liable to a duty upon the entire value of the skirts when finished or sold, or removed for sale.

"But when the whole process is performed by the same manufacturer, he is liable to a duty upon the value of the covered wire, and then upon the entire value of the skirts when finished; and when one party makes the wire and pays the duty on it, and a second party covers it and manufactures the skirts, said second party is liable to a duty first upon increased value of the wire given by covering, and then upon the entire value of manufactured skirts." (Letter of Commissioner, July 12, 1865.)

"Heels, which are made as stated in your letter, are a taxable manufacture and liable under the general provision of section 94, of the act of June 30, 1864, as amended March 3, 1865, to a duty of six per cent., ad valorem; but a boot or shoe-maker, who makes the heels which he consumes in the manufacture of boots and shoes, is not liable to duty on such heels." (Letter of Commissioner, August 10, 1865.)

"Hats made from material purchased six months ago may not be worth more than the cost of the material. This fact, however, would not exempt them from duty under the provision of the 96th section, before alluded to." (Letter of Commissioner, August 28, 1864.)

"Thread or yarn which is spun and used by the same manufacturer in making tapes, which are used only in the manufacture of hoop skirts, is exempt from duty." (Letter of Commissioner, Sept. 1, 1864.)

"Prior to June 30, 1864, box shooks were considered liable to an excise tax, but as the internal revenue act of that date exempts shooks from duty in an unqualified manner, this office in its rulings has thought proper to exempt alike all shooks, whether cask or box, and to hold the party making or finishing the boxes liable for the duty upon the entire value of the finished article." (Letter of Commissioner, July 26, 1864.)

"Your letter of the 18th inst., with the accompanying paper, has been received, describing two different modes by which shoe binding is made, and wishing to be informed how these different kinds of binding are to be taxed. In answer, I have to say, that a tanned skin finished up by being striped with blacking, thereby forming alternate stripes of white and black of suitable width for shoe binding, is not a new manufacture, and is not subject to any tax other than that which the law imposes upon finished sheep skins. But when a tanned skin is cut into strips of the width desired for bindings, and the strips are afterwards passed through a machine by which they are shaved down to an even thickness and are then pasted or glued together, so as to make a continuous belt, and are wound into rolls of a given number of yards, and in this form sold as shoe bindings, and so known in the market, they can no longer be regarded as skins; nor can this binding properly be taxed as tanned sheep skins, or taxed on the increased value. Such shoe binding must be regarded and taxed as a new and distinct manufacture, on the full value, six per cent." (Letter of Commissioner, Oct. 24, 1864.)

"By special provision of the 94th section, 'all furniture or other articles *made of wood*, previously assessed and a duty paid thereon, shall be assessed a duty of five per cent., ad valorem, upon the increased value only thereof when sold in a finished condition.' By another provision of the same section, *iron* furniture, statuary, &c., is subject to a duty of six per cent. ad valorem. Neither of these provisions applies to the case under consideration. It becomes necessary therefore, to tax this furniture, made partly of wood and partly of castings, in the same manner as other machines, instruments or articles are taxed into whose structure iron castings largely enter as material or component parts. See the late Commissioner's opinion in the case of Osborne and *al.* vs. Collector Halsey." (Letter of Commissioner, Dec. 4, 1864.)

"Carriages, &c., are liable to duty on their entire value, though the wheels, axles, springs, &c., used in their production, have previously paid tax." (Int. Rev. Rec., Feb. 10, 1865.)

"In answer I have to say that timber partially wrought and unfinished (sawed or blocked out,) for hubs, spokes and felloes, is exempt from duty under section 96. But when hubs and spokes are turned or shaved, and felloes planed and bent, and thus substantially finished, though the hubs and felloes may not be bored or mortised, or the tenons cut upon the spokes, they are liable to a duty of 6 per cent. on their value when sold or removed for sale.

"A party who makes wheels from hubs, spokes and felloes of his own manufacture, is required to pay duty on the wheels only when sold or removed for sale or use. It is not proposed to tax the hubs, spokes and felloes, then again the wheels, and again the finished carriage, when a manufacturer makes the entire wood-work of a carriage or wagon." (Letter of Commissioner, Jan. 27, 1865.)

"Your letter of Jan. 13, in relation to deduction on increased value, has been received. In a letter from this office to Assessor Ritchie of Boston, Mass., dated Dec. 21, 1865, it was decided that the commission of 3 per cent. may be deducted when the goods are sold by the manufacturer or producer. The person who increases the value of an article can be regarded as the *manufacturer or producer* of that article only so far as he has increased its value, and he is therefore entitled to the above commission on that amount only.

"You wish to know whether this decision applies to articles taxed under section 94, or only to those taxed under section 95.

"A party who buys cotton warps on which the duty has been paid, and consumes them in manufacture of satinet, for example, is required to pay tax on the value of the satinet above the cost of the warps used in its production; and when he sells such satinets at a place other than the place of manufacture, he may be allowed to deduct a commission of three per cent. from the gross sales, less the cost of the warps and other deductions allowed by law and the rulings of this office." (Letter of Commissioner, Jan. 25, 1865.)

"Your letter of Dec. 19, in relation to harness, bedsteads, and monuments, has been received. You wish to know whether a harness-maker in making his monthly return may be allowed to deduct the cost of harness saddles and collars, on which a duty has been paid, from the amount of his sales, and whether a cabinet-maker may deduct from his sales the cost of castors and articles of iron used in the manufacture of bedsteads, and also whether a manufacturer of grave stones and monuments may deduct from the value of a monument the freight on it from the place of manufacture to the place of delivery, and also the cost of setting it up. In answer I have to say that the making of harness collars being generally considered as a distinct manufacture, a harness-maker who buys collars, on which the duty has been paid, and sells them with harnesses of his own manufacture, may deduct from the amount of his sales the cost of such collars, but the saddle becoming a fixed part of the harness its cost cannot be so deducted, though a duty may have been paid on it. A cabinet-maker cannot be allowed to deduct from his sales the cost of castors and articles of iron used in the manufacture of bedsteads. A party who manufactures a monument may be allowed to deduct from its value, freight from the place of manufacture to the place of delivery, and also the cost of setting it up, if such cost is included in the price received for the monument." (Letter of Commissioner, December 23, 1864.)

"Belting is liable to tax on full value." (Int. Rev. Rec. April 21, 1866.)

"Wood mouldings used for finish upon the eaves of buildings, whether made for general sale or to order, are liable to a duty of six per cent. on their value when sold." (Letter of Commissioner, May 22, 1866.)

"Wood mouldings are liable to duty as manufactures. When more completely finished by gilding or enameling they are subject to a duty of six per cent. on increased value under section 94 as 'articles made of wood.'" (Int. Rev. Rec. March 24, 1866.)

"Boards simply planed, grooved and beveled, do not lose their distinctive name as lumber and are not taxable." (Letter of Commissioner, March 12, 1866.)

"Your letter of April 19, in relation to pews, pulpits, doors, &c., has been received. You wish to know whether contractors, who furnish, or furnish and set up, general inside finish for public and private buildings, such as pews, sheathing, doors, pulpits, door-casings, &c., should be required to pay duty on them as manufacturers. In answer I have to say, that contractors who make and sell, or manufacture and use in the construction of buildings, doors, sash and blinds, are subject to the same liabilities as other manufacturers of those articles, but this office has not held that sheathing, pews, pulpits, doors, casings, &c., were liable to duty when made and used by contractors in the construction of buildings. Pulpits, however, manufactured and kept on hand for sale are liable to duty when sold or removed for sale." (Letter of Commissioner, April 23, 1866.)

"Slate in the block, rough and unwrought, is exempt from duty, but slate for building purposes, when dressed, hewn, or finished, is liable to duty. But this office is of opinion that slate sawed out and partially wrought for mantels and other articles, should not be taxed until finished for the purpose for which it is intended." (Letter of Commissioner, Feb. 16, 1866.)

"Iron stoops are 'structures,' and not liable to duty. But the railings, steps, or other castings used therein are liable." (Int. Rev, Rec., April 7, 1866.)

"Flasks and patterns of the character described in the second paragraph of printed Decision, No. 169, whether m by foundrymen or others for their own use, or to order for others, are manufactures." (Letter of Commissioner, April 25, 1866.)

"Articles manufactured in one district and removed to another, to be set up, are to be taxed where manufactured." (Int. Rev. Rec,, April 21, 1866.)

As to tax on artificial flowers, &c., see Int. Rev. Rec., May 19, 1866.

Miscellaneous Rulings and Decisions as to Stamps.

"Under the law the stamp duty on probate of will and letters of administration, must correspond to the estate for, or in respect of which such probate or letters are applied for. When the will devises the real estate to the executors in trust for specific purposes, or directs its sale, or subjects it to the payment of the debts, the value of that estate must be included as a basis for the estimate of stamp duty.

"When under the laws of the State, the administrator taking letters, has an office or duty to perform in respect to the real estate, the same rule obtains. It is otherwise when the personal estate only does, or can come under the authority or cognizance of the administrator of such." (Letter of Commissioner, December 29, 1864.)

"State and city securities are exempt from stamp duty." (Letter of Commissioner, December, 29, 1864.)

"Stereoscopic views taken as original pictures of mountain scenery, buildings, &c., must be stamped under Schedule 'C' of the law." (Letter of Commissioner, June 30, 1865.)

"The bond given by a guardian of minor heirs of a deceased soldier in order to obtain the pension, &c., is subject to stamp duty of $1.00." (Vol. I. Int. Rev. Rec., September 9, 1864.)

"Your letter of the 3d instant, in relation to the stamp duty upon a subscription list for a map of the State of Massachusetts, has been received. In reply I have to say that such subscription list as the one enclosed by you is liable to stamp duty as an agreement or contract, and each person signing the same is liable to the duty and should affix and cancel a five cent stamp." (Letter of Commissioner, June 6, 1865.)

"When a merchant ships goods and takes a receipt therefor and obtains upon the receipt three bills of lading, the receipt and each bill of lading require stamps." (Vol. II. Int. Rev. Rec., Oct. 28, 1864.)

"Yours of the 21st, containing inquiries as to the cancellation of stamped paper, is received. All stamped paper is cancelled whenever used, and the use of the paper by filling the blanks or attaching a signature, is equivalent to the ordinary form of cancelling an adhesive stamp by writing initials and date upon it. The entire paper is regarded as the stamp, and of course no part of it can be "cut out" or separated from the remainder, and retain any value as a stamp. Any portion cut and attached to another paper is worthless, and such use of it is *prima facie* fraudulent." (Rulings of the Department, June 23, 1865.)

"Where a bond is secured by two mortgages, the stamp duty required to validate all the instruments will be double, (if governed by the mortgages,) what it would have been in the case of one mortgage. If, however, the stamp appropriate to a bond be affixed to the same, then the bond will be valid, though the mortgages might not be." (Vol. 1., Int. Rev. Rec. July 15, 1865.)

"In the case of a subscription list where the heading involves a promise to pay the sums annexed, the party signing is liable to the stamp duty required on promissory notes, *unless* he pay the amount annexed his name at the time of signature; in which case the signing of his name should be regarded as a mere part of a memorandum. When the heading of the list involves a condition on which the subscribers will pay the sums annexed their names, then each signature is held to create an agreement, subject to a duty of five cents." (Vol. II., Int. Rev. Rec., July 22, 1865.)

"Your letter of the 8th inst., inquiring whether it is necessary for shippers of goods to foreign and domestic ports to place stamps upon the dray receipts, in addition to the one placed upon the original bills of lading, is received. I reply, that stamps should be affixed to such receipts by *some person*, and that the person who signs and issues an *unstamped* receipt of that character thereby makes himself liable to a penalty. This Bureau does not undertake to decide who shall pay for a stamp annexed to a receipt in any particular case. That question may be decided by some local law or private contract. The dray receipts mentioned by you are not covered by the stamps affixed to the bills of lading but should themselves be stamped like any other receipt for goods delivered." (Rulings of the Department, July 14, 1865.)

"If a mortgage executed years ago is assigned at the present time, the assignment must be governed by the law now in force. If the mortgage has been reduced by payments, the amount of stamps to be affixed to the assignment depends upon the amount actually due on the mortgage when the assignment is made, not on the sum secured by the mortgager, without regard to deductions made by subsequent payments." (Vol. II. Int. Rev. July 29, 1865.)

"Domestic bills of lading are considered as receipts for the delivery of property, and should be stamped as such." (Int. Rev. Rec. Vol. II., Aug. 26, 1865.)

"Complaints having been made in some instances that there were deficiencies in packages of Internal Revenue stamps forwarded by direction of this office, notice is *hereby given* that, in order to secure consideration of such claims, persons receiving stamps will hereafter be required to *open the packages when received in the presence of two witnesses;* and should a deficiency exist, duplicate *affidavits* of the facts in the case must be forwarded to this office *without delay.*" (Rulings of Dept., Sept 9, 1865.)

"In reply to the questions submitted in your letter of September 30, I answer as follows:

1. It is not proper for inspectors of tobacco, snuff and cigars, to put their names on cigar stamps with a stencil or other stamp, but they *must write* their names.

2 It is the duty of such inspector to mark the weight on each package marked and inspected by them, date of inspection, State and district.

3. Said inspectors may employ deputies or assistants to do the work of weighing packages, affixing stamps, &c., provided the work is done in the presence and under the immediate supervision of the inspectors.

4 I consider it a part of your duty as revenue inspector, to examine the manner in which inspectors of tobacco, snuff, and cigars do their work, and to report at this office any irregularities which the inspectors refuse or neglect to correct upon your advice." (Rulings of the Department, Oct. 5, 1865.)

"Your letter of the 14th inst., has been received. You state the following case: A merchant ships a load of goods and takes a receipt for the same properly stamped. Upon this receipt he obtains three bills of lading, two of which the shipper takes, and one the ship owner retains with the receipt. You inquire how many, if any, of these bills of lading should be stamped. I reply that a domestic bill of lading is subject to the same stamp duty as a receipt. If it is issued in triplicate the duplicate and the triplicate should each be stamped the same as the original. The fact that a stamp is affixed to the shipping receipt in no way changes the liability of the bills of lading." (Rulings of the Department, Oct. 15, 1865.)

"I reply to your letter of the 5th inst., that it was formerly held by this office that the receipt given for a stamped check was exempt from stamp duty. It is now held, however, that the receipts for a check, note, draft, or order, when received as the *payment* of a sum of money, or of a debt due exceeding twenty dollars, is subject to a stamp duty, the same as a receipt for money paid." (Rulings of the Department, Dec. 8, 1865.)

Stamp Duty on Bonds.

OFFICE OF INTERNAL REVENUE, Washington.

"I reply that the law requiring stamps upon conveyances, bonds, notes, etc., took effect Oct. 1, 1862, and that no stamps are necessary upon instruments issued prior to that date.

"A bond for the *payment* of money is subject to stamp duty at the rate of five cents for each one hundred dollars, or each fractional part thereof, as 'written or printed evidence of an amount of money to be paid on demand or at a time designated;' a personal bond, given *as security* for the payment of any definite or certain sum of money exceeding one hundred dollars, and not exceeding five hundred dollars, is subject to a stamp duty of fifty cents, and to fifty cents additional for each additional five hundred dollars or fractional part thereof.

"An instrument subject to stamp duty, but issued and used unstamped prior to August 1st, 1864, may be made valid by stamping it as required by section 163 of the act of June 30, 1864; if issued since that date, the case falls under section 158 of said act as amended by the act of March 3, 1865." (Ruling of Commissioner, Jan. 30, 1866.)

Stamping of Deeds.

OFFICE OF INTERNAL REVENUE, Washington.

"Your letter of the 31st ult., enclosing one from Messrs. Rutledge & Young, has been received. They write that during the existence of slavery manumission was impossible, and gifts to slaves were impossible. At the same time there were a large number of slaves held in nominal servitude only, who were allowed to enjoy their own earnings, and because they could not hold their property in their own names, they were accustomed to select some white persons in whom they reposed confidence, and such persons took the title absolutely in their own names, without any declaration of trust. Now that slavery has ceased to exist, and the freedmen have become capable of taking, holding and granting title to lands, they propose to have their property conveyed and confirmed to them by deed. No consideration passes, and a nominal one only is expressed in the deeds. You inquire if such conveyances are subject to stamp duty.

"In reply I have to say that a stamp duty is imposed only upon conveyances of *realty sold.* In the case stated there is no *sale;* the purpose and effect of such deeds is merely to place the *legal* title where the *equitable* one is. No stamp, therefore, is necessary, unless the deed contain covenants, in which case it should be stamped as any agreement. Neither in such cases is there any succession tax. The grantee acquires no additional property by such a transfer; the deed simply confirms the pre-existing equitable title." (Ruling of Commissioner, Feb. 10, 1866.)

Regulations for Completing the Collection of Taxes Returned to Collectors, for Rendering Final Accounts of the Same as Provided in Section 33 of the Act of June 30, 1864, and for the Abatement of Erroneous and Uncollectible Taxes.

TREASURY DEPARTMENT, Office of Internal Revenue,
WASHINGTON, February 26, 1866.

The act of July 1, 1862, provided that each collector should complete the collection of all sums assigned to him for that purpose, pay over the same into the Treasury, and render his final account as often as he may be required, and within six months from and after the day when he should have received the collection lists.

The act of June 30, 1864, as amended by the act of March 3, 1865, does not re-enact the limitation of six months but leaves the time to the discretion of this department.

In view of the difficulties and delays incident to the organization of the internal revenue system, this particular requirement of the law has not been heretofore vigorously enforced; but the interests of the Government now demand its strict enforcement.

It is, therefore, hereby prescribed that at the close of each quarter, collectors must render their final accounts for all lists which they may have held for six months or more. From and after April 1, 1866, no credit will be allowed for lists which have been held for six months or longer, and at the close of each quarter thereafter collectors will deposit the money for all amounts remaining uncollected on such lists, for which no claims have been presented to the Commissioner.

In the adjustment of their accounts, collectors will be credited with all taxes uncollectible on account of their being erroneous, or being due from insolvent or absconding persons, upon presenting satisfactory proof in each case.

Abatement for Error in Assessment.

Claims for credit on account of error must be made out in Form 47, and sustained by the affidavits of persons cognizant of the facts, or of the parties against whom the taxes have been reported, and by the certificates of the assistant assessors. The affidavits must contain full and explicit statements of all the material facts and circumstances relating to the claims in support of which they are offered. It should be stated whether the error originated with the tax payer, or with an officer of internal revenue, whether the tax was excessive in amount, while correct in kind, or wrong both in amount and kind, or in kind only, or whether a tax had been reported for collection when none was due.

One affidavit, certified to by the assistant assessor, may in many cases be sufficient to verify several claims. For example, all the duplicate assessments upon the same liability, clerical mistakes, and other errors, the proof of which is entirely documentary and patent, and obvious to any person who may examine the lists, may be scheduled on a sheet of the size of blank 47, and be attached to it, so that a single affidavit of a clerk or other person cognizant of the facts may verify the whole.

Abatement for Inability to Collect.

Claims on account of the insolvency or absconding of the parties taxed must be made on Form 53, and sustained by the affidavits of the deputy collector, and the certificates of collector and assessor. A collector making his own collections in any division will use Form 53, making his affidavit thereon, and treating the schedule in all respects as if made by a deputy.

Collectors or deputy collectors using Form 53 will state, in a concise but clear manner, the reason for non-collection under the head of "Cause of inability to collect." For example, "Insolvent before demand could be legally made." "Died before receipt of list, and estate insolvent." "Left for parts unknown before the tax could be collected." "No property liable to seizure under the law." "Property would not pay expense of distraint."

Claims to be Scheduled on Form 48.

At intervals of not less than one month, all taxes claimed to be uncollectible, either from error or insolvency, will be put into a single schedule on new Form 48, grouped under captions designating the lists to which they belong, whether annual or monthly, or on Form 58 or 60. The natural order of the months should be strictly observed. The captions should be written in red ink across the center of the schedule.—The amount claimed should be placed only in the column headed "Amount claimed." The other two columns, ruled for dollars and cents, must be left blank. Each schedule must be verified by the certificate of the assessor and collector, and accompanied, in all cases, by affidavits on Form 47 or 53.

Affidavits should be numbered by collectors to correspond to the claims in the schedule supported by them. Those covering several claims should be marked on their backs with the number of those claims.

Duplicates should be kept by collectors, without fail, of all schedules transmitted to this office. These in connection with proper check marks placed upon the lists, will prevent duplicate applications for the abatement of the same tax. Before transmitting any schedule the collector should compare it with his lists, and check on the lists each claim contained in the schedule, with intelligible abbreviations, showing the date of the application, and its nature, whether for insolvency or for error, and when notice of action is received, checks should be applied to the lists, showing the nature and date of such action in each case. In designating page and line, the collector and the assessor will each have reference to the pages and lines of the lists as found in his own office.

Numbering the schedules and the claims contained in them should be carefully attended to for convenience of reference The schedules presented under these regulations will be numbered in continuation of those presented under Circular 21 ; and all claims presented to the office at one time should be numbered as on one schedule, and the claims in each will be numbered from one to the last in that schedule

Refunding of Taxes Improperly Collected.

Claims for refunding must be made on blank Form 46, verified by affidavits and certificates of the assistant assessor, assessor and collector.

The collector must certify to the date of payment of the amount claimed. Claims for refunding should not be entered in schedules, and may be presented as often as desired; but unless they are presented to the proper revenue officers within six months from the date of the payment of the tax, the Commissioner will not be bound to investigate them, and may refer the claimants to their remedy at law.

The post office address of parties making claims for refunding must be given; otherwise, the claims cannot be paid if allowed.

Whenever any person who has taken out a license presents a claim for the refunding of the amount during the period for which the license was issued, the collector, before signing his certificate to the claim, will require the claimant to deposit the license with him, or to furnish proof that it has been destroyed. If it should be decided that the tax cannot be refunded, the license will be returned.

General Remarks.

If any claim on Form 46 or 47 is presented without the certificate of the assistant assessor, the reason for the omission must be given.

If in any case, after a full investigation, the assessor and collector, either or both, cannot certify to the facts set forth in the affidavits, they should state the reason for their dissent, and allow the party to corroborate his statements by such other proof as he may be able to furnish.

Members of firms making affidavits must swear, each for himself, to the fact set forth, including that of membership, and subscribe his own name and not that of the firm.

Affidavits may be made before any internal revenue officer, or before the chief clerk of an assessor, without fee or stamp; but when made before the chief clerk it must be accompanied by the assessor's or collector's certificate, verifying the chief clerkship, and the absence of the assessor at the time. Any other person administering an oath or affirmation must show, by seal or certificate from the proper authority, that he is qualified to do so, and the affidavit and certificate must each be stamped.

Credits should not be taken by collectors for taxes supposed to be uncollectible until notice of abatement is received from the Commissioner. When taxes are abated the amounts are at once credited to collectors upon the books of this office, and schedules of the same are sent to them, with authority to take credit for the sums abated in their next quarterly accounts.

When credit is given on account of insolvent or absconding persons, although the collector is thereby released from the obligation created by receipting for the amount credited, the obligation to pay still remains upon the assessed parties. Collectors should bear this fact in mind, and not consider themselves as released from obligation to collect in such cases whenever it shall be in their power. If, pending action for abatement of an erroneous assessment, the tax should be collected, the collector, upon receiving an order abating the same, will return the amount to the assessor on Form 58, and will make an affidavit on Form 46, giving the date of payment, and naming the assessment list, upon which it is returned a second time, and have it properly certified to by the assessor and assistant assessor, when a draft for the amount will be drawn in favor of the party. If a claim for an uncollectible tax should be paid pending action, or after it has been abated, it should be returned as above on Form 58.

Schedules of all taxes abated, refunded, or allowed as uncollectible, will be sent to assessors to be kept on file for public inspection.

Regulations concerning the Disposition of Moneys paid to Collectors after Judgment, and on Compromises.

TREASURY DEPARTMENT, Office of Internal Revenue,
Washington, January 20, 1866.

The following Regulations are issued as supplementary to those of the Secretary of the Treasury of June 20 and June 27, 1865, "for the guidance of collectors under the provisions of the 19th, 44th, and 179th sections of the act of June 30, 1864," in order to correct some practical errors of account in the disposition of moneys paid to collectors after judgment recovered in court, or upon compromises.

It is believed that all cases of the kind alluded to are embraced in one or the other of the three classes described below, and collectors are instructed to dispose of the moneys in each of the cases named as hereinafter directed, viz:

1st. When proceedings are instituted for forfeiture or for the recovery of penalties, and the case is prosecuted to final judgment in court.

The law requires the portions of all fines, penalties, and forfeitures belonging to the Government to be paid to the collector, and when any such payment is made to him by order of court, he will deposit the amount immediately to the credit of the Treasurer of the United States, with his other collections, enter it upon his abstract of collections for the current month, (against No. 288,) and return it to the assessor on Form 58, that it may be included in the monthly list.

2d. When a delinquent tax-payer proposes, after an investigation of his business by a revenue officer, to pay the tax found due, with the assessed penalty and a certain sum in lieu of penalties and forfeitures.

In cases of this kind, the assessor should determine the amount of the tax and the assessed penalty, and return the same to the collector on a special or monthly list, as in the case of other assessments. When these amounts are paid to the collector he will enter them upon his cash book, and also upon his abstract, like other collections.

The amount of the tax and assessed penalty will not be deposited to the credit of the Secretary of the Treasury, but the amount paid in lieu of fines, penalties, and forfeitures should be so deposited, to await his final award and distribution. When the award is made, the Secretary will issue a draft in favor of the informer, if any, for his moiety, and another draft in favor of the collector for the moiety belonging to the Government. The collector will deposit this draft to the credit of the Treasurer of the United States, with his other collections, and enter the amount in his cash book, in his abstract, (against No. 289,) and on Form 58, as directed in the case of moneys paid to him by order of court.

3d. When a delinquent tax-payer, liable to prosecution for fines, penalties, and forfeitures, deposits with the collector a gross sum, either prior to or pending an investigation, in order to avoid seizure, or to release his property from seizure.

There may be occasionally a case in which the circumstances will appear to justify a proceeding of this sort, though obviously such cases will and should be rare. When, however, the circumstances are such as seemingly to justify the collector in accepting a gross sum for taxes and penalties as a condition of refraining from or releasing a seizure, so that the business of the delinquent may go on, he will deposit the entire amount received to the credit of the Secretary of the Treasury.

The case will be investigated by the assessor of the district, who will determine the amount of tax due, and the assessed penalty, if any. He will transmit the assessment to the collector on a special or monthly list, as in the case of other assessments. On the receipt of such list the collector will report the amount of the assessment to the Commissioner, to whom the several proceedings in the case should be promptly reported from time to time, as they are taken.

When the case is finally determined by the Secretary of the Treasury he will distribute the deposit as follows:

One draft in favor of the collector for the tax and assessed penalties. This will be applied to the payment of the assessement, and the proper entries made in the cash book and abstract.

One draft in favor of the collector for the moiety of the penalty belonging to the Government. The amount of this draft will be entered in the cash book, abstract, (against No. 289,) and on Form 58, as directed in the case of moneys deposited by order of court.

One draft in favor of the informer, if any, for his moiety of the penalty, accepted in lieu of fines, penalties, and forfeitures.

If the amount deposited should be in excess of all the taxes and penalties accepted, the excess will be refunded to the delinquent by draft from the Secretary.

It will be obvious to collectors, from the foregoing regulations, that while moneys paid in the 2d and 3d cases remain on deposit to the credit of the Secretary of the Treasury, they should not be reported in Form 22, nor should they be included in receipts on form 23½.

In transmitting to the Secretary the original certificate of deposit to the credit of the Secretary of the Treasury on account of fines, penalties, or forfeitures, collectors will be careful to distinguish both on the face of the certificate of deposit and on form 43, accompanying it, the name of each offender, and the particular amount of fine, penalty, or forfeiture received from him.

E. A. Rollins, *Commissioner.*

Decision Relative to the Mode of Determining "Increased Values" under Sections 94 and 95, and the Persons Liable for the Tax to be Assessed thereon.

Treasury Department, Office of Internal Revenue,
Washington, November 9, 1865.

The 95th section of the act of June 30, 1864, provides: That whenever a manufactured article on which an excise or impost duty has been paid is increased in value, or more completely fitted for use or sale by being polished, painted, varnished, waxed, oiled, gilded, electrotyped, galvanized, plated, &c., &c., the tax is to be levied, collected, and paid upon the amount of such increased value.

The conditions stated in the section authorizing this mode of assessing the tax are: 1. The article must be a manufactured article; 2. An impost or excise duty must have been previously paid thereon; 3. The article must be one not specially provided for under any other section of the law; and, 4. The original character or purpose for which the article was intended to be used must not be changed. When all of these conditions concur, the tax is properly assessed on the increased value. If one or more of these conditions are wanting, if the article is not a manufactured article, or if no tax has been paid upon it, or if it is specially provided for otherwise, or if the original character or purpose for which it was intended to be used is changed, it cannot properly be taxed under section 95 on increased value.

The law itself points out the mode of ascertaining the increased value for all purposes of this section. It declares that the amount of such increased value is to be ascertained by deducting from the value of the finished article when sold, or removed for sale, delivery, or consumption, the cost or value of the original article to the person, firm or company liable to the duty imposed upon the increased value thereof.

Take an example: A. buys an unfinished article for which he pays $3; more completely finishes and fits it for use or sale, by any of the processes enumerated in section 95, at a cost of $2.50; adds a profit of twenty-five per cent., ($1.38,) and sells the article for $6.88.

Now, with the rule given above, this problem is one of very easy solution. Deducting from the price of the finished article when sold ($6.88,) the cost of the original article, ($3,) we have $3.88, the "increased value," on which a tax of 5 per cent. is to be assessed and paid.

But suppose a like article is sent by some dealer or other person to B. to be finished, &c., and returned, and B. receives $2.50 for the material and labor he expends upon the article in finishing it, &c., but does not know the cost of the original article or the price for which the finished article is to be sold, no sale as yet having been made; what is the increased value in this case? How is it to be determined, and who is liable for the tax?

I am aware that it is strongly contended that the increased value in this case is merely the $2.50 which B, receives for finishing, &c.; that this sum B. should return and pay the tax thereon of 12½ cents. Not so. It does not satisfy the requirements of the law. It taxes A. on $1.88 more than his neighbor with whom he comes in competition pays upon; and it is, by the same amount,a short return to the Government. The law makes provision for such cases as this. It regards the finisher, &c., as the employe furnished with materials, or part thereof, paid for manufacturing, making, or finishing the goods, and returning them when so made or finished to the owner. In such cases the law regards the owner as the manufacturer or producer—the party liable for the tax on the finished article when sold, or removed for sale, delivery or consumption. His *sales* constitute the basis for the assessments—the value from which the *cost* of the original article is to be deducted to ascertain the increased value.

The finisher, &c., has only to return the amount of his work for each month, and name in his returns the party or parties for whom the labor or finishing is performed. These returns are to be sent to the assessor of the district within which the parties reside or have their place of business for whom the finishing, &c., is performed, that he may forthwith proceed to ascertain the amount of increased value according to one of the modes I have pointed out, that the tax due thereon may be paid by the party or parties liable for the tax. Sections 83 and 93 clearly authorize this mode of assessment and provide for such cases.

If, however, it is more convenient for the parties interested that the tax shall be assessed upon and paid by the finisher, to be collected afterwards by him of the owner, as authorized by the 83d section, then the increased value may be determined by deducting from the *fair market value* of the finished article the market value of the original article. These values, I presume, can at all times be ascertained with sufficient accuracy to satisfy the Government, and will do no injustice to the taxpayer, who is disposed to accept the easiest mode of ascertaining his liabilities, and is ready to remove rather than multiply obstacles in the way of assessing the Government tax.

Repairs of engines, cars, carriages, or other articles liable to tax on "increased value" under section 94, are to be assessed on the *cost* of such repairs. There being no sale of the articles in such cases, the cost of repairing is the only practical measure of increased value.

The *mode of ascertaining* the increased value and assessing the tax on articles taxed on increased value under section 94, is the same as that under section 95, but the rate of tax is six per cent. instead of five per cent. E. A. Rollins, *Commissioner.*

Regulations concerning the Tax on Tobacco, Snuff, and Cigars, &c.

Treasury Department, Office of Internal Revenue,
Washington, July 30, 1866.

1. By the act of July 13, 1866, the following rates of tax were imposed on manufactured tobacco, cigars, cigarettes, cheroots, and snuff, to wit:

On cavendish, plug, twist, fine-cut chewing tobacco, and all other kinds of manufactured tobacco, not elsewhere enumerated, per pound, ...	40 cents.
On fine cut shorts, per pound, ...	30 cents.
On tobacco twisted by hand, or reduced from leaf into a condition to be consumed, without the use of any machine or instrument, and without being pressed, sweetened, or otherwise prepared, per pound, ...	30 cents.
On smoking tobacco, sweetened, stemmed, or butted, per pound,	40 cents.
On all other kinds of smoking tobacco, and imitations, including that made of stems, per pound, ...	15 cents.
On snuff of all descriptions, manufactured of tobacco, or any substitute for tobacco, when prepared for use, per pound,	40 cents.
On cigars, cigarettes and cheroots of all descriptions, per thousand, ...	$5 00.

2. Smoking tobacco, if manufactured or cut in such a manner as to include the entire stem, and without being sweetened, is liable only to a tax of fifteen cents per pound. If any portion of the leaf is removed, whether it be from the top by cutting across the stem, or from the side or sides by cutting in the direction of the stem, and such portion so removed is manufactured, either with or without sweetening, such tobacco is liable to the duty of forty cents per pound.

4. The tax on tobacco, snuff, and cigars, accrues upon the sale or removal from the place of manufacture, unless removed to a bonded warehouse; and a return of all tobacco, snuff, and cigars which have been manufactured, as well as of that upon which the tax has accrued, must be made on or before the tenth day of each month.

All manufactured tobacco, snuff, and cigars, before being used or removed for consumption, must be inspected and marked or stamped; and all cigars must be packed in boxes or paper packages, except where the maker of cigars is authorized to sell in bulk, or unpacked, after the same have been counted by an assistant assessor or an inspector, and a certificate has been received therefor. In this case the purchaser is required to pack the same in boxes or packages, make return of them, and, unless removed to a bonded warehouse, pay the tax thereon within fifteen days.

5. The 87th section of the act of June 30, 1864, as amended by the act of July 13, 1866, requires every person, firm, company, or corporation, before commencing, or if already commenced, before continuing the manufacture of tobacco, snuff, or cigars, to make to the assessor or assistant assessor a statement, (Form No. 36,) subscribed under oath or affirmation, of the number of machines, &c., used, and the number of persons employed, &c., and also to give bond (Form No. 40,) to the collector of the district, with approved sureties, for the faithful performance of all the requirements of the law. The collector will give to the manufacturer of tobacco or cigars, on receiving his bond, a certificate (Form 41,) showing the number of different machines used by him, and the number of men employed in making cigars, on which the amount of said bond has been determined. Blank forms for such statement, bond, and certificate, will be furnished from this office, and assessors and collectors are particularly charged with the execution of these provisions of the law.

6. The assistant assessor of each division is required to record in a book, to be kept for that purpose, the name of every person, firm, company, or corporation engaged in the manufacture of tobacco, snuff, or cigars in his division, with the place where the manufacture is carried on, and the place of residence of the person or persons engaged therein; and under the name of each manufacturer he will enter also an abstract of his monthly returns. A similar record for the entire collection district is required to be kept by each assessor.

7. The manufacturer's statement or inventory required to be made on the first day of January of each year, or at the time of commencing business, and the account of all his purchases and sales kept in book form, are to be made under the new law substantially as required heretofore. An additional and important item, however, is to be entered in his book each month viz: the total amount of goods manufactured, as well as goods sold and removed.

An abstract of all purchases, sales, and removals must be furnished to the assistant assessor on Form No. 62, on or before the tenth day of each month.

8. Section 90 of the act of June 20, 1864, as amended by the act of July 13, 1866, provides that manufactured tobacco, snuff, or cigars, may be transferred without payment of the tax to a bonded warehouse, established in conformity with law and Treasury regulations, under such rules and regulations and upon the execution of such transportation bonds or other security as may be prescribed by the Commissioner of Internal Revenue, subject to the approval of the Secretary of the

Treasury; said bond or other security to be taken by the collector of the district from which such removal is made.

9. Section 92 of the act of June 30, 1864, as amended by the act of July 13, 1866, requires that every cigar-maker shall procure from the assistant assessor of the divison in which he resides, a permit [Form 71] authorizing him to carry on the business of cigar-making; and if he makes cigars in any other division than the one in which he resides, he must procure the endorsement of the assistant assessor of such other division to be made upon his permit. This section also requires every person making cigars under such permit to keep an accurate account in a book of all cigars made by him, for whom made, and their kind or quality, and on the first Monday of every month to deliver to the assistant assessor of the division a copy of such account, verified by oath or affirmation.

Assistant assessors are particularly charged to see that these provisions of law are complied with; that every cigar-maker in his division has a permit—keeps account of the number, kind, and quality of cigars made by him, and, if made for any other person, the name of the person for whom the same are made, and his place of business—and that on the first Monday of each month he delivers a copy to him of such record.

The assistant assessor is also particularly charged to see that every manufacturer of tobacco, snuff, or cigars furnishes the sworn statement as required by section 87, and makes his inventory and keeps an accurate account, in book form, of his purchases, manufactures, sales, removals, &c., as required by section 90; and any neglect on the part of assistant assessors in these particulars, or of inspectors, personally to perform the duties assigned to them, will be deemed just cause for removal from office.

10. Before cigars, cigarettes, or cheroots are removed for sale or consumption, they must be inspected and have a stamp affixed to the box or package in which they are contained.

On the first Monday of each month, or oftener if required by the assessor, the inspector must return to the assessor of his district a separate and distinct account of the weight and kind of tobacco or snuff inspected by him, the number of cigars, cigarettes, and cheroots inspected and stamped, and their appraised value. He is required also to give in his return the names of the persons, firms, companies, and corporations for whom he has inspected any tobacco, snuff, or cigars, and keep an accurate account of all stamps used or placed on boxes or packages containing cigars.

11. It will be the duty of every officer through whose hands cigars, may pass while in bond, to see if the number and apparent value of the same correspond with the number and value contained in the bond and stated in the permit given by the collector.

All cigars, on being withdrawn from bond for consumption, must be inspected and stamped by the inspector of the district in which the bonded warehouse is situated. This will be necessary in all cases, in order to protect the cigars from liability to seizure and forfeiture

Cigars, cigarettes, and cheroots which shall be in bonded warehouses on the first day of August, 1866, will be subject to the tax of ten dollars per thousand.

12. By the recent Tariff act, it is made the duty of officers of the customs to inspect and stamp all imported cigars before they are withdrawn for consumption. But under the ninety-first section of the act of June 30, 1864, as amended by the act of July 13, 1866, all imported cigars which are sold or pass out of the hands of the importer without the inspection marks or stamps affixed, are liable to seizure and forfeiture, and it will be the duty of internal revenue officers to take notice of any infringement of the law in this respect, in regard to imported cigars equally as in the case of cigars of domestic manufacture.

13. By the eighty-ninth section it is provided, that in all cases where tobacco, snuff, or cigars are manufactured on commission or shares, or where the materials are furnished by one party and manufactured by another, or where the manufactured articles are received in payment for material furnished, the assessor may assess the taxes on articles so made upon the party for whom they are made, or to whom they are delivered, or upon the person or party making the same, as the assessor shall deem best for the collection of the revenue.

This section gives discretionary power to the assessor, which he is expected to use. In all cases where the person making cigars is a recognized manufacturer, having given bond for the performance of all the requirements of the law, the tax on all articles made for him should be assessed upon him. But where they are made for parties who are not known as manufacturers and have not given bond, the tax should, if possible, be collected from the maker of the articles.

In every case where an assessor receives a return sent to him from the assessor of another district, he should acknowledge the receipt of such return and immediately proceed to assess the tax on the same, as though the cigars had been manufactured in his district. If the person or party for whom the articles were manufactured is not found in his district, he will immediately notify the assessor from whom he has received the return, of such fact, that the taxes may be collected of the maker of the same.

E. A. Rollins, *Commissioner.*

Sale of Cigars in Bulk, Packing, Inspection, and Stamping of same.

Office of Internal Revenue,
Washington, Dec. 29, 1866.

Sir: Your letter of the 24th inst. is received, in which you inqure substantially whether a manufacturer of cigars can put them up loose in cases containing 20,000 more or less, have them inspected and stamped in that condition, and pay the tax upon the price which he receives, the purchaser being allowed afterwards to have them repacked in small boxes and re-stamped without incurring any liability.

To this inquiry I have to state that by the act of June 30, 1864, as amended by subsequent acts, all cigars are required to be packed in boxes or paper packages, before used or removed for consumption, inspected and stamped in a manner to denote the kind, quantity, or number contained in each package, with date of inspection, and the name of the inspector, and the collection district where the same were manufactured.

Any manufacturer of cigars who shall allow his cigars to pass out of his hands, except into a bonded warehouse, without the inspection marks or stamps affixed, is liable to have them seized, ferfeited and sold for the benefit of the United States. To this requirement of law there is a single exception.

A manufacturer of cigars may apply to the assistant assessor or inspector of the district to have his cigars counted, and on receiving a certificate of the number, he may sell and deliver such cigars to any purchaser in the presence of said assistant assessor or inspector, in bulk, or unpacked without payment of the tax. In this case the purchaser is required to pack the cigars in boxes or packages, have them inspected and marked or stamped, make a return of them to the assessor, and pay the tax on them to the collector of the district where they were manufactured.

The mode of packing preparatory to inspection, if not clearly defined, is sufficiently indicated by the language of the law. They cannot be packed or sold in bulk, except as above indicated.

They must be packed in boxes or paper packages. These boxes, or packages, must be such as are ordinarily used, and put up in the manner or style generally adopted for placing them upon the market. Ordinarily cigars are put in packages or boxes of 25, 50 or 100, sometimes 250 or 500, seldom more than 1,000, unless they are intended to be repacked.

The tax upon cigars is so much per thousand, and if the manufacturer packs more than 1,000 in a box, they must be regarded as cigars in *bulk*. And even that number, or half of that number, if thrown together loosely, or not packed with that care ordinarily employed for putting cigars in a saleable condition, they are to be regarded as being in bulk, and not packed as the law requires, and therefore not in a condition to be inspected or branded.

Very Respectfully,
THOMAS HARLAND.

Duties of Assistant Assessors in Charge of Distilleries.

TREASURY DEPARTMENT, Office of Internal Revenue,
Washington, January 1, 1866.

The following rules are prescribed for the guidance of officers supervising distilleries:

Inventories of Distillable Material, Barrels, and Distilled Spirits on hand

1. The assistant assessor, on commencing his duties, should take an inventory of the kind and quantity of grain, or other distillable material, on the premises of the distiller for purposes of distillation.

He should also take an inventory of the number of new and old barrels on the premises, giving the number of each kind.

He should also take an inventory of the distilled spirits on the premises, whether in barrels or in cisterns, giving the number of inspected and uninspected barrels of spirits, and the inspection marks on each inspected barrel, viz: the name of the inspector, the date of inspection, the proof and the number of gallons of spirits it contains. He should ascertain personally, or through the inspector, the proof and number of gallons of spirits in each cistern, and include them in his inventory. He should also ascertain from the proprietors of the distillery the quantity of spirits in bond or in store belonging to them, together with the number of barrels in each lot, and the inspection marks on each barrel; and he should include this information in the inventory.

He should also take an inventory of the number or kind of stock (as swine or neat cattle) on the premises, stating whether they are owned by the distiller, or brought there to be fed.

He should submit the inventories, when completed, to the agent, owner, or superintendent, of the distillery for certificates of their correctness. If the certificates are refused, he should note the fact upon the inventories, which, without delay, he should copy in his diary and send to the assessor of the district, who should file them as records of his office.

Diary.

2. He should make the records hereinafter prescribed in his diary, each day, never amending it by erasure or interlineation, but, if he has any correction to make, stating it in a foot note, letting his original entry stand untouched. On retiring from office, he should turn his diary over to the assessor of the district.

Record of Distillable Material brought on the Premises.

3. He should know, and record each day in his diary, in tabular form, the quantity and kind of grain, mill-feed, molasses, or other substances, brought into the distillery upon that day for distillation.

Record of Barrels brought on the Premises.

4. He should know and record the number of new and old barrels brought on to the premises daily, and he should state, after personal examination, that there is no inspector's mark remaining on any old barrel.

Record of Contents of Mash Tubs.

5. He should record the quantity and kind of grain ground each day, and, separately, the quantity put into the mash tub; and, where

there is more than one mash tub, he should designate them by numbers (as tub No. 4;) he should have this information of his own knowledge, where possible; otherwise, from the masher or miller; but he should never take it from the owner, agent, or superintendent. He should enter in his record the capacity of each mash tub, and he should make a new record when a change is made in the capacity of the tubs.

Record of Miller and Masher.

6. He should record each day the names of the miller and the masher on that day.

Record of Fermenting Tubs.

7. He should number each fermenting tub, (as No. 2 or No. 5,) and should record the capacity of each, and the number of each tub into which the mash is run, and the hour (as 9.30 a. m.) when the mash is run off.

He should record how many fermenting tubs are full each night, specifying them by their numbers, as No. 1, No. 2, &c.

He should record the number of each fermenting tub as its contents are run into the receiving cistern, the time when this is done, and the name of the man then in charge of the still; and he should give the number of hours in which the stills run every twenty-four hours, and should specify, as near as may be, the quantity and proof of the spirits produced during that time, taking his data, when possible, from personal inspection.

Record of Barrels Filled.

8. He should record the number of barrels filled from each day's distillation, stating whether the barrels were old or new, and how many of each were filled.

What constitutes a Day.

9. He should regard the day as consisting of twenty-four hours, and as commencing at midnight.

Record of Inspections.

10. He should record the day on which the barrels so filled are inspected, giving the name of the inspector, and stating that he saw the barrels properly marked by him with such marks as are required in section 59 of the internal revenue law and the regulations of the Commissioner of Internal Revenue.

He should record, not in his diary, but in a book to be kept for that purpose, the inspection marks put on each package inspected in the distillery each day by the inspector, and should preserve the book for reference, turning it over to the assessor on retiring from office.

Record of Spirits Removed

11. He should record the number of barrels of spirits removed from the premises each day, stating whether by railroad, canal, river, &c.,

stating whether for sale, storage, or bonding; if for sale, stating to whom consigned or sold; if tax-paid and stored, stating where stored; if for bonding, stating in what bonded warehouse, and in all cases recording the quantity and proof of each barrel, with date of inspection and name of inspector, to be taken from the barrels themselves.

Numbering Barrels of Spirits.

12. He should number each barrel removed with stencil plate and paint, or brush and paint, marking the first barrel removed after his entry upon his duties in that distillery as No. 1, and continuing the numbering consecutively until the first of the next January, when he will again commence with No. 1, thus making a new series of numbers for each calendar year.

Stock Record.

13. He should record each day the number and kind of animals (as swine or neat cattle) brought on to the premises on that day, stating whether purchased or brought there to be fed, also the number sent away, and whether slaughtered, sold, or returned to the owner.

Record of Slop Sold.

14. He should record each day the number of barrels of slop sold on that day, if any.

Record of Grain Sold or Feed Cut, &c.

15. He should record the kind and quantity of grain fed out to cattle, the kind and quantity sold, and, where a grist mill is connected with the still, and they use the same grain for both still and mill, the quantity of flour, meal, shipstuffs, middlings, &c., sold, or removed for sale each day.

Record of Accidents.

16. He should record the fact if a mash is spoiled, or partially spoiled, and state what is done with it; if it is run he should give separately the quantity and quality of its product as above.

He should record any unusual proceeding or accident which may increase or decrease the product of the still.

Distillers' Bonds.

17. He should at the time of entering upon his duties at the distillery, ascertain, and record in his diary the amount of the distiller's bond, the names of the sureties, their residences, and the amount for which each security justified, where they have been put under oath. And he should, on ascertaining the amount of the penal sum named in the bond, compare it with the amount of the monthly tax, and if it be not double that amount, should, at once, in writing, call the attention of the collector of the district to that fact.

Tri-Monthly Report.

18. He should submit his report on Form 50 to the owner, agent,

or superintendent of the distillery, and ask a certificate of its correctness. If it is refused, he should note the fact by inserting the words "declined to sign," in the blank left in Form 50 for this signature.

Trial Balance of Spirits Made and Removed.

19. He should enter upon a page in his inspection book, in parallel columns, the footings of each of those columns of his returns on Form 50 which show the number of gallons of spirits made, and the quantity removed during the ten days for which report is made.

On Entries in the Distiller's Book.

20. He should see that the entries in the distiller's book are made on each day that the distillery is in operation; that they are correct on all points; that they conform literally to what is required in section 57 of the internal revenue act now in force; and that the quantities of all kinds mentioned in the entries have been ascertained by actual weighing or measurement. He should, at the end of each ten days, compare these entries with those made by himself in his diary; and should, if any error exists, require that it be corrected by new entry, or by a foot note—but he should not permit any erasure when entries are once made. He should, also, in administering the oath to the agent, owner, or superintendent of the distillery, or the book-keeper, as to the truth of these entries, use the forms prescribed in sections 62 and 63, and in all points exact a full and literal compliance with their provisions. He should also be sure that the person proposing to sign as agent, owner, superintendent, or book-keeper, is properly and legally entitled to sign as such, before administering the oath.

Distillers' Tri-Monthly Accounts.

21. When the tri-monthly accounts of the distillery are rendered to him, he should see that they are made out in all points in the form and manner specified in section 57, and Form 14; also, by personal inspection that they are a correct transcript of the entries in the distiller's book.

If the accounts are found correct in all points, he should administer the oath in the form and manner provided by law.

No person, except the agent, owner, superintendent, or book-keeper, should be allowed to verify the tri-monthly account, under any circumstances. The assistant should also see that a duplicate of the tri-monthly account is forwarded to the collector immediately after it is verified.

Concerning the Transportation of Spirits in Bond.

TREASURY DEPARTMENT, Office of Internal Revenue,
Washington, January 16, 1867.

Under former statutes and regulations, if a person who had executed a bond for the transportation of distilled spirits to a bonded warehouse, paid the amount of tax due upon such spirits to the collector holding the bond, such payment was accepted as sufficient to warrant the cancellation of the bond.

It is, however, so clearly the intention of the act of July last that all spirits removed under transportation bond shall be deposited in bonded warehouse; and the statute so explicitly declares the forfeiture of all spirits, which shall be found elsewhere than in bonded warehouse, not having been removed therefrom in pursuance of law, that it is believed to be no longer necessary to tolerate this practice. At the same time, it would be regarded as oppressive, if seizure should be made of spirits which were placed in the market without going into warehouse where the shipper had been in the habit of making this disposition of spirits, and of canceling his bond by the payment of the tax.

Collectors will, therefore, notify all persons who may hereafter execute bonds for transportation of spirits to bonded warehouse, that such spirits will be seized if found elsewhere than in transit to the warehouse for which a permit is issued, and collectors will seize all spirits which may be found in their respective districts branded for transportation, and which are evidently not in regular course of transit to the proper warehouse, unless it shall appear to their satisfaction that the transportation of such spirits was commenced prior to the 20th instant.

The sooner all distillers, and persons engaged in the purchase and sale of distilled spirits, are made aware that only those spirits which have been regularly withdrawn from warehouse upon payment of the tax can be regarded as legitimate objects of traffic, the better will it be for the interests of the Government and of all honest distillers. Collectors will also notify all persons who may hereafter execute transportation bonds that in no event will the bonds be canceled except upon proof of the receipt of the spirits into the proper warehouse, or proof of some special circumstances which have rendered a literal compliance with the condition of the bond impossible.

E. A. ROLLINS, *Commissioner.*

Regulations for Distillers and Refiners of Coal or Mineral Oils.

TREASURY DEPARTMENT, Office of Internal Revenue,
Washington, October 17, 1866.

By the act of June 30, 1864, as amended by the act of July 13, 1866, a tax is imposed upon illuminating, lubricating, or other mineral oils; and it is further provided "that distillers of illuminating, lubricating, or other mineral oils, naphtha, benzine, benzole, or gasoline, shall be subject to all the provisions of law applicable to distillers of spirits, with regard to special taxes, bonds, returns, assessments, removing to and withdrawing from warehouses, liens, penalties, forfeitures, drawbacks, and all other provisions designed for the purpose of ascertaining the quantity distilled and securing the payment of taxes, so far as the same may, in the judgment of the Commissioner of Internal Revenue, and under regulations prescribed by him, be deemed necessary for that purpose."

Under this authority, the Commissioner of Internal Revenue hereby prescribes, that every person who refines, distills, or re-distills petroleum or other bituminous substances, or refines crude oil, produced by a single distillation of coal, shale, asphaltum, peat, or other bituminous substances, shall give a bond. (Form 28.) This bond must be taken by the collector, who will bear in mind that bonds already given under the provisions of former laws will not suffice.

Each distiller or refiner must keep a book, in form and manner set forth in Form 25, which form is hereby prescribed, showing the quantity and description of the oil produced, the quantity placed in bond, and the quantity not placed in bond, and, consequently subject to tax, and the quantity and description of oil sold by him, with the name and place of business or residence of the person to whom sold. If desired by the distiller, the account of sales may be kept in a separate book.

A return will be made on Form 26, on or before the tenth day of each month, instead of tri-monthly as heretofore, showing the product of the preceding month, the quantity bonded, and the quantity subject to tax; and the tax is to be paid, like other monthly taxes, on or before the last day of the month in which the return is made.

By the act of July 13, 1866, section 10, paraffine oil, and lubricating oil made from petroleum, coal, or shale, not exceeding in specific gravity 36 degrees, is exempt from tax, but such oil is made subject to the same inspection as illuminating oil; it therefore follows, that the entire product of the distillery or refinery must be inspected and gauged by an inspector, appointed under the provisions of section 58, act June 30, 1864.

The establishment of bonded warehouses, for the storage of mineral oil, and the withdrawal of the same therefrom, will be governed by the regulations of May 1, 1865, issued by the Secretary of the Treasury, until otherwise directed.

Distillers and refiners of mineral oil are, by these regulations, released from the restrictions placed upon distillers of spirits by the present law, so far as relates to establishing bonded warehouses for the storage of their products, employing inspectors for each distillery at a per diem compensation, providing receiving cisterns, &c. They can also remove the oil produced by them directly from the distillery or refinery to a general bonded warehouse, Class B, without first placing it in a bonded warehouse, Class A, as in the case of removal of distilled spirits.

E. A. Rollins, *Commissioner.*

DISTILLERIES.

WASHINGTON, March 5.

The following circular, addressed to assessors and collectors, concerning distilleries has just been issued:

TREASURY DEPARTMENT, Office of Internal Revenue,
Washington, March 4, 1867.

Section 17 of the Act of Congress approved March 2, 1867, provides that "hereafter all distilled spirits, before being removed from the distillery, shall be inspected and gauged by a general inspector of Spirits; who shall mark the barrels or packages in the manner required by law. And so much of the act approved July 13, 1866, as requires the appointment of an inspector for each distillery established according to law, is hereby repealed: *Provided,* That such other duties as have heretofore been imposed upon inspectors of distilleries may be performed by such other duly apointed officers as may be designated by the Commissioner of Internal Revenue. Section 18 of the same act provides that whenever in the judgment of the collector there shall be a general bonded warehouse so located as to be conveniently accessible to a distillery, and in the same collection district, the said collector shall direct all spirits which may be stored in the bonded warehouse attached to such distillery to be transferred directly to general bonded warehouse, and all spirits thereafter produced in such distillery shall be removed to a general bonded warehouse within the time and in the manner before required for removal to the bonded warehouse attached to the distillery."

Under these provisions, collectors will forthwith require the distillery inspectors to deliver up their "inspector's records" brands, and the keys of the cistern-rooms and distillery bonded warehouses. Wherever a general bonded warehouse may be conveniently accessible to a distillery, the collector will at once direct the transfer of all spirits stored in the distillery bonded warehouse under the supervision of an officer to be detailed by him. Transportation bonds will not be required in such cases, but the usual warehouse entries must be made. In this case, the keys of the cistern-room will be delivered to an assistant assessor, to be designated by the assessor of the district where a general bonded warehouse is not conveniently accessible. The use of distilleries as bonded warehouses will be continued, and the collector will at once appoint a proper person as a storekeeper to have charge of the same, who will keep the keys of the cistern, as well as of the warehouse. The duties and compensation of storekeepers are prescribed in series 2 to 9. As the law now requires all spirits before being removed from the distillery to the bonded warehouse to be inspected and marked by a general inspector, collectors must immediately take measures, when necessary, to have general inspectors appointed within convenient distances to the distilleries. Assessors will immediately designate a sufficient number of assistant assessors for the efficient supervision of all the distilleries in their respective districts. And it shall be the duty of such assistant assessors to visit the distilleries assigned to them daily, if possible, and especially to ascertain the capacity of each distillery, and take such measures as will enable them to determine the daily production of each. Whatever officer has charge of the keys of the cistern room must be present whenever spirits are drawn off from the cistern; and after being inspected by the General Inspector, must superintend their removal to the bonded warehouse. The general inspector must make a return of the spirits so inspected both to the collector and assessor on the day of inspection.

E. A. Rollins, *Commissioner*.

Brewers and their Returns.

For full statement of the requirements and returns of brewers, their notices of intention to carry on business, bonds, books of record, affixing and cancellation of stamps, how fermented liquor may be removed without stamps, the bottling of the same, marking of the casks, penalties, and the stamp account of the collector, &c., see Department series 2, No. 6.

Cotton.

For regulations concerning the weighing and marking of cotton, the assessment and collection of the tax thereon, and the removal of cotton under bond, see series 2, No. 5, and "Additional Regulations" of Sept. 25, 1866.

INSTRUCTIONS TO ASSESSORS AND COLLECTORS.*

Concerning Proceedings for Assessment. The Annual List.

The annual list will include the annual taxes upon income, articles in Schedule A, and licenses dating from May 1. These items, and no others, will be entered on the annual list.

---

* It will not be forgotten that these instructions, &c., were of course issued from the Department under former laws, and before the late amendments. The greater portion of them are fully applicable to the new law, and *all* will be of great importance for reference, comparison, &c., to revenue officers, who will make the required modifications in the light of such new instructions as may be hereafter issued by the Commissioner. The same remark applies to the rulings, decisions, and correspondence, contained herein.—Ed. (See Preface.)

Each assistant assessor will complete his annual list and forward it to the assessor on or before the thirtieth day of May; and the complete list should be delivered by the assessor to the collector on or before the thirtieth day of June in each year.

In preparing the list the assessor must observe the requirements of sections 18 and 19. The notice for receiving and determining appeals must be advertised or posted in each county as directed in section 19. But if the assessor is unable, from any cause, to attend the appeals at the time named in the notices, one of the assistant assessors or a clerk of the assessor should attend, and if any appeals are filed he may adjourn the hearing to a subsequent day.

Monthly List.

The monthly list should be completed by the assistant assessor and forwarded to the assessor on or before the fifteenth day of each month; and the assessor should deliver the same to the collector on or before the twentieth day of each month. In making up this list, assessors will pay particular attention to those taxes which have already been sent forward on special lists, as all such taxes must be included in the collector's receipt for the monthly list.

Assessors should, every month, post into a blank book the returns of manufacturers, distillers, brewers, tobacconists, &c., so as to show the business of each for a series of months, and to enable a comparison to be readily made of the amounts *produced*, with the amounts *sold*. It is of great importance that this account be kept accurately, and the comparison made frequently, so as to keep a proper check on those making retu

Special Lists.

Special lists will be made up, from time to time, by the assistant assessor and transmitted to the assessor, as the occasion may arise; but in all such cases the items will be included and receipted for in the monthly list next completed. Annual taxes, the returns for which are not received in time for the annual list, and monthly or quarterly taxes, the returns for which are not received in time to be entered in the current monthly list, will be forwarded to the assessor, and by him to the collector, on a special list, in order that there may be no delay in the collection. Receipts for transmission to the Commissioner will not be taken for special lists, but the rule which governs receipts on Form 11½ may be adopted. Assessors will retain copies of all special lists transmitted, and will exercise the utmost care that all assessments on such lists shall be entered on the proper monthly list.

Whenever a change of collectors occurs, the assessor should take receipts on Form 23½ from the outgoing collector for all special lists and duplicate returns transmitted to him, and for unassessed penalties collected by him, since his last receipt. Such assessments should not be included in the monthly list presented to the new collector.

Duplicate Returns.

In all cases where, under the provisions of the law, return is made by the tax-payer in duplicate, the assistant assessor will make the proper entry in his assessment book, so that the tax will be included in his next monthly list, and will immediately transmit the duplicate return to the collector.

Unassessed Penalties.

On or before the fifteenth day of each month the collector will make out and furnish to the assessor a detailed statement, on Form 58, of all unassessed penalties, including moieties of penalties belonging to the Government which are paid to collectors by order of court, and duties on passports, collected by him during the calendar month next preceding, and he will also report at the same time all taxes which may have been allowed to him during the month as uncollectible after the same have been collected, and all taxes which may have been collected after the same have been allowed as uncollectible.

These detailed reports will be kept on file in the assessor's office, and the amount will be entered at the foot of the next monthly list and included in the aggregate thereof, for which the collector will receipt on Form 23½.

Concerning Proceedings for Collection.

Within twenty days after receiving the annual list from the assessor, the collector must advertise in one newspaper in each county in his district, and by notices to be posted in at least four public places in each county, stating the time and place within said county at which he or his deputy will attend to receive the duties, which time must not be less than ten days after the publication of said notice.

At the expiration of ten days from the advertised time, it is the duty of the collector to serve demands upon all persons who have neglected to make payment. Form 9 has been prepared for this purpose, and for the issuing and service thereof the collector is entitled to a fee of twenty cents, and to four cents for each mile actually and necessarily traveled in serving the same. No travel fee can be charged when the notice is sent by mail, and none for the distance traveled in returning when personal service is made.

If payment is not made within ten days after the service of demand, the collector will proceed to collect the duties, with the penalty of ten per centum and the proper costs and expenses, by distraint.

Railroads, Theaters, Brokers, &c.

The duties upon the gross receipts of railroads, theaters, &c., as enumerated in section 109, are payable as soon as the amount is ascertained, and the penalty attaches upon a failure to pay within ten days, and section 99 applies the same rule to the tax upon brokers' sales. In all cases where returns for taxes of this description are made to the assessor in time to be first returned to the collector on the monthly list, a notice may be issued to the tax-payer in the manner above directed for the tax on manufactures and products. (Form 17.) When the duplicate return is received by the collector on a later day than that on which the monthly list is received, he will immediately issue a demand, (Form 21,) and if the amount of the duty is not paid within ten days he will distrain for the tax and the penalty of ten per centum.

Lotteries.

By the terms of section 111 the proprietors, managers, or agents of lotteries are required to pay the taxes on their gross receipts on or before the twentieth day of each month; but in case of default it is further provided that collection shall be made in the manner prescribed in relation to manufactures. Collectors are therefore advised to proceed for the collection of this tax in the mode pointed out under the head of manufactures and products.

Auctioneers.

Auctioneers are required to return the amount of their sales to the assessor within ten days after the end of each month, and the tax is payable at the same time. In default of payment collection is to be made in the manner prescribed in the general provisions of the act.

Legacies.

It is provided in section 125, that a list shall be rendered to the assessor by the executor, administrator, or trustee, before paying any legacy or distributive share, and that the tax thereon shall be immediately paid to the collector. In case of any default, the tax is to be assessed as in other cases, and the collector may proceed by suit against the person who has the actual or constructive possession of the property in respect of which the tax is assessed. Inasmuch as the tax is only required to be paid before payment or distribution, and not at any stated time, in ordinary cases this suit would be brought against the legatee or distributee.

Instead of this proceeding by suit, the collector may proceed against the executor or administrator by distraint, in the manner pointed out in section 28, as amended by the act of March 3, 1865, whenever, in his judgment, this course may be the best for the interests of the Government. For this purpose, demand may be made at any time after the list containing the assessment is received; and the penalty of ten per centum will attach if the tax is not paid within ten days.

Successions.

The 150th section of the act of June 30, 1864, requires that the duty upon successions shall be collected by the same officers, in the same manner, and by the same processes as are prescribed by law for the collection of direct taxes assessed upon lands; but the act of March 3, 1865, (amendment to section 28,) substantially repeals this provision by enacting that if any person liable to pay any duty shall neglect or refuse to pay the same after demand, the collector may levy upon all property belonging to such person for the payment of the sum due, with interest and penalty for non-payment. In this case, if payment is not made within ten days after demand the penalty of ten per centum must be added.

Whenever separate assessments are made against separate tracts of land, in accordance with section 146, and it becomes necessary to pursue the land into the possession of a *bona fide* purchaser, the respective tracts will be held chargeable only with the amount of duty separately assessed in respect thereof.

Annual Taxes on Monthly or Special Lists.

Annual taxes which have been omitted from the list, and which are subsequently returned on a monthly or special list, may be demanded immediately after the receipt of the list in which they are assessed, and the penalty of ten per centum must be added if the amount is not paid within ten days.

Forms and Accounts for Collectors acting as Disbursing Agents. Estimates on Form 42, (formerly Form A.)

These are to be made out monthly, and transmitted to the Secretary of the Treasury on or before the 5th day of each month for the expenses of the current month; that is, the estimate to be sent on or before the 5th of January (which will be called the January estimate) will be for the amounts required to pay salaries of collectors and assessors, and pay of assistant assessors and assessors' clerks, for January, commissions of collectors for December, and such bills for expenses and other items as may have been approved and ordered paid by the Treasury Department. Assessors will return to the collectors before the *first* of the month a statement showing the amount needed for the month to pay assistant assessors and clerk hire.

The salaries of assessor and collector will be entered on the estimate from the last column of the table of salaries in this circular.

Under the head of assistant assessors the net amount will be entered; that is, the gross amount due, less the tax, which is to be deducted as directed in the paragraph on salary tax in this circular.

Under the head of assessors' clerk hire the gross amount will be entered as directed in the paragraph on salary tax in these regulations.

The collectors acting as disbursing agents will enter as nearly as possible the exact amount under each head. In entering the amounts to be allowed in this office the cents will not be carried out, so that the sums allowed will often be a fraction of a dollar in excess of the exact amount to be paid.

If, after making all proper payments, there remains a balance on hand, that amount should be deducted from the *footing* of the next estimate.

In filling out the estimate on Form 42, the last column should in all cases be left blank by the collector, in order that it may be filled by the Commissioner.

Commissions.

The amount on which commissions are to be estimated by the collectors for any month will be the amount actually deposited during that month. When the estimates are passed upon by the Commissioner, the commissions will be calculated on the amount for which certificates of deposit are received here during the month. These two amounts will often differ, but as the commissions are to be readjusted at the close of the year, collectors will receive the full amount due them when the final adjustment for the year is made. The amounts allowed from month to month are regarded simply as an advance on account.

Commissions on collections in the month of December should be included in the January estimate, and so on—the estimate for each month including commissions on the collections made in the previous month.

In estimating collectors' commissions, the following rule will be observed: For one month the limit will be three per cent. on the first $8,333⅓, one per cent. on the next $25,000, one-half of one per cent. on the next $50,000, and one-eighth of one per cent. on all over $83,333⅓. From the amount thus calculated ten per cent. will be withheld, to enable the accounting officers to comply with section 26.

If the collector remains in office till the close of the year, the amount so retained will be paid to him with the balance of commissions due him. If he goes out of office before the close of the year, the commissions will be divided between him and his successor, according to the amounts collected by each.

Monthly account current.

Collectors, as disbursing agents, will send a monthly account current on Form 44, (formerly Form D.)

This should be made out for the month for which the estimate was made, and not the month in which the disbursements were made. The account current for each month is intended to show what disposition has been made of the draft sent to pay the expenses of that month. For example, the account current for January should be made out as follows:

The United States should be charged with—

1. Salaries paid assessor and collector for January.
2. Amount paid assistant assessors for services rendered in January.
3. Amount paid assessor for clerk hire for January.
4. Collector's commissions on collections deposited in December.
5. Any bills for stationery, postage, &c., approved by the proper officers of the Treasury Department, or any orders of the same which may have been paid since the rendering of the last account current.

These are the regular charges against the Government to be entered on the January account current.

If by any delay or neglect it should happen that bills for services performed prior to January should not be paid until after the account current for December has been made up and sent on, such bills should be entered on the January account. But no effort should be spared to have *all* bills of assistant assessors, of assessors for salary and clerk hire, and of collectors for salary and commissions, paid within fifteen days after the close of each month, so that they can be entered on the account current in which they belong.

The United States should be credited on the January account current with—

1. The balance from last month.
2. The draft sent for the amount allowed on the January estimate.

This account current, thus made out, accompanied with the prescribed vouchers and abstracts, should be sent to this office on or before the 15th day of February, and so on. The account current for each month should be sent on or before the 15th of the month following.

It is intended that the draft for each month's expenses shall reach the collector by the first of the month following. That is, the January draft should be received by the first of February.

Assessors will see that their assistant's bills are rendered promptly and sent to the collectors for payment immediately after the close of the month. If it is necessary to secure the prompt rendering of these bills, the charges for persons assessed may be deferred for one month; that is, the charges for January may be put in the February bill.

Salaries of Collector and Assessor.

According to the law, the salaries of collectors and assessors are due quarterly.

The amount due each quarter is $375. The amount due each month will bear the same proportion to $375 that the number of days in the month bears to the number of days in the quarter.

The following table, compiled by the disbursing clerk of the Treasury Department, will guide collectors acting as disbursing agents in making payments for these salaries:

Salary each Month, at $1,500 a Year.

Months.	Gross.	Taxable.	Tax, five per cent.	Balance.
July,	$126.36	$75.81	$3.79	$122.57
August,	126.36	75.81	3.79	122.57
September,	122.28	73.38	3.67	118.61
October,	126.36	75.81	3.79	122.57
November,	122.28	73.38	3.67	118.61
December,	126.36	75.81	3.79	122.57
January,	129.16	77.50	3.87	125.29
February,	116.68	70.00	3.51	113.17
March,	129.16	77.50	3.87	125.29
April,	123.63	74.18	3.71	119.92
May,	127.74	76.64	3.83	123.91
June,	123.63	74.18	3.71	119.92

This account will be supported by vouchers as follows:

Payments to Assessors.

Collectors acting as disbursing agents will pay the assessors only their salary proper, and clerk hire. The vouchers for clerk hire will be made out on Form 54, with all the blanks properly filled. These must be entered on Form 92, together with the salary of the assessor. The assessor will fill out the oath and receipt on Form 92 for the whole amount. Both the schedule and the separate vouchers will be taken by the collector. There will be allowed for assessor's clerk hire, each month, a sum not exceeding one-twelfth of the annual allowance, and no more of this must be paid than is actually expended. If less than the monthly allowance is paid for any month, the deficiency may be paid for any subsequent month during the year. (See paragraph on clerk hire in section 3 of these regulations.)

Payments to Collectors.

The proper vouchers for a collector's salary and commissions are his receipts, which should be given by him as collector to himself as disbursing agent.

Collectors acting as disbursing agents will make no payments to their predecessors, unless specially directed so to do.

Revenue Agents and Inspectors.

Revenue agents and inspectors will send their accounts monthly to the Commissioner of Internal Revenue to be audited and paid, unless they receive special directions to the contrary.

Quarterly Account of Collectors.

This will be rendered on Form 79, immediately after the close of each quarter. In this account collectors will credit the United States with—

1. The balance due the United States on the last account

2. The annual and monthly lists which have been receipted for by the collector during the quarter.

According to instructions contained in Series 2, No. 1, dated January 1, 1866, the annual and monthly lists will contain all the taxes for which the collector will receipt.

They will charge the United States with—

1. All moneys deposited to the credit of the Treasurer of the United States within the quarter.

2. All orders for abatement of taxes on account of error or insolvency issued by the Commissioner of Internal Revenue, and dated within the quarter.

3. Certificates of release under section 97. It is not probable that any more claims under this head will be presented.

Under the head of cash deposited, no amount must be included, unless the certificate of deposit for the same is dated within the quarter covered by the account. If a certificate is omitted in making up the amount to be entered on any account, it may be entered on a subsequent account as an item under "Errors in former account."

A schedule of the certificates of deposit for the quarter should be forwarded with each quarterly account showing the date, number, and amount of each certificate, the place of deposit, and the sum of the whole.

This account, with the vouchers, should be forwarded to the Commissioner of Internal Revenue within twenty days after the close of each quarter.

Quarterly Account of Expenses.

This will be rendered on Form 91 within fifteen days after the close of each quarter. In this account collectors will charge the United States with—

1. Their quarterly salary, in gross.
2. Commissions for the quarter.

These will be calculated on the sum total deposited to the credit of the Treasurer of the United States during the quarter. The limit will be, for each quarter, three per cent. on the first $25,000, one per cent. on the next $75,000, one-half of one per cent. on the next $150,000, and one-eighth of one per cent. on all over $250,000.

3. Expenses for stationery and blank books for the quarter.
4. Expenses for postage for the quarter.
5. Expenses for express and of depositing money for the quarter.
6. Expenses for advertising for the quarter.

They will credit the United States with—

1. The amount received from the collector acting as disbursing agent on account of salary for the quarter.
2. The amount received from the same on account of commissions for the quarter.
3. Such other moneys as may have been received by him on this account.
4. The tax on salary and commissions.

Vouchers for Stationery, Blank Books, Postage, Express, Depositing Money, and Advertising.

Vouchers for these items will be entered on Form 85, and the oath on the form must be filled. The bills must in all cases be made out in detail, showing the date, price, quantity, and character of each article purchased or expense incurred.

All bills must be receipted by the parties giving them. The receipt of a clerk will not be accepted. Bills given by a firm must be receipted by a member of the firm, or a duly authorized agent of the firm. Express bills may be receipted by a regular agent of the company.

The proper vouchers for postage are the receipted bills of the postmaster. These should be furnished in all cases in which it is possible to obtain them. Where these cannot be obtained, the certificate of the collector, showing the amount of postage used in the discharge of his official business should be sent. The receipt of a deputy for postage will not be accepted, unless accompanied by a receipted bill of a postmaster.

Bills for depositing money should show the amount deposited, the rate per thousand, and the points between which it was transported. Bills for sending money from deputies to the collector will not ordinarily be allowed, as they are part of the expense of collecting, which must be paid out of the commissions.

Collectors will send their money to the depository in the cheapest manner consistent with safety.

The size of envelopes purchased should be given, or a specimen sent. Bills for printing and advertising should be accompanied by a specimen of the printing and a copy of the advertisements. Handbills and posters will be treated as advertisements.

Collectors will have no blanks printed at the expense of the Government, without first obtaining authority from the Commissioner of Internal Revenue.

Charges for furniture, gold pens, penknives, and for expenses of fitting up offices, will not be allowed to collectors or assessors.

Collectors will, as far as possible, supply their deputies with stationery and postage. When deputies are compelled to purchase for immediate use, they should obtain receipted bills made out in detail, the same as is required of the collector. These should be given to the collector. Collectors in purchasing stationery and blank books for Government uses, are expected to exercise the same economy as if purchasing for their private business. A statement must be made, at the close of each fiscal year, and at such other times as may be required.

Collector's Inventory on going out of Office.

A collector on going out of office will turn over to his successor all blank books, stationery, postage stamps, post office envelopes, and all other property in his possession belonging to the Government; and will file, with his final quarterly account of expenses on Form 91, an inventory thereof, with the receipt of his successor for the same attached.

Duplicates, Etc.

Collectors will retain in their office duplicates of all accounts, schedules, abstracts, and vouchers which they send to this office.

All accounts transmitted by the collector should be dated and receipted by the collector who sends them. All schedules or abstracts should show the number of the district and the name of the collector.

Assessor's Salary and Clerk Hire.

The assessor's salary proper and his clerk hire are to be paid monthly by the collector acting as disbursing agent, as directed in part I. of these regulations. See also paragraph on clerk hire in part III.

Assessors will, at the bottom of their accounts, credit "The United States" with the sums received of the collectors as disbursing agents and the tax on salary.

Accounts and Vouchers.

The several charges must in all cases (except salary and clerk hire) be accompanied by proper vouchers, which must be regularly filed, numbered, and endorsed to correspond with the numbers and names in the account. These vouchers must be made out against the assessors in their official capacity, and not against the "United States," as has been the practice in many cases. Assessors' accounts should be made against the "United States."

In cases where there is not sufficient room on Form 82 to enter each voucher separately, including his assistants' accounts on Form 84, the assessor will make a schedule or list of the bills of his assistants, and enter the same in one item. The schedule must give the name of the assistant, number of his division, the time embraced in the account and the amount.

The assessor's account and vouchers must be transmitted to the Commissioner of Internal Revenue by mail within fifteen days after the close of each quarter.

Any accounts and vouchers which are not plainly and correctly stated and properly receipted, will be returned for correction or suspended; and corrected vouchers must be furnished with the next quarterly account.

Duplicates.

Duplicate accounts and vouchers are not required to be sent to this office, but they should be retained by the assessor and filed in his office.

Commissions.

The law requires the commissions of assessors to be computed for the fiscal year ending June 30.

For the year ending June 30, 1865, and for any subsequent year, commissions will be allowed on the excess over $100,000 received on the assessments for each fiscal year.

The adjustment of commissions is to be made by the Fifth Auditor of the Treasury, based upon the amount of internal revenue received on the assessments or lists of the assessor for the fiscal year, or part of the year.

In order to allow commissions to assessors, the Auditor requires the certificate of the Commissioner, showing the amount of revenue collected on the assessments for the period of time for which commissions are claimed. The amount so collected is ascertained from the collectors' reports on Forms 50 and 51, or on Forms 86 and 87. When these reports are not promptly and correctly made, the adjustment of assessor's commissions must necessarily be delayed, except in those districts where the receipts are known to be $1,200,000 or upwards per annum; in which cases the assessor will be allowed his commissions up to the maximum, or at the rate of $2,500 per annum.

Each assessor will keep an accurate account of all miscellaneous expenses, postage, express charges, advertising, hand-bills and posters, clerk hire, stationery and blank books, and stationery and postage for assistants

Assessor's Inventory on Going Out of Office.

An assessor going out of office must render, with his final account, an inventory in detail of all stationery, blank books, postage stamps, or post office envelopes, and all other property in his possession belonging to the Government, together with the receipt therefor of his successor.

Assessors' Certificates.

Assessors must certify to the correctness of their accounts under oath.

General Remarks.

The estimates and accounts must be properly completed and transmitted as directed within the prescribed time.

An early payment of moneys due to the collectors, assessors, and assistant assessors will depend upon the promptness and accuracy with which their accounts are rendered, and upon the sufficiency of the vouchers furnished.

Collectors and assessors desiring any information concerning their allowances, or any matters pertaining to their accounts, will address the Commissioner of Internal Revenue.

Collectors and assessors, upon receiving notice that any items have been suspended in the adjustment of their accounts for the want of proper vouchers or schedules, should send the required vouchers or schedules to the Commissioner of Internal Revenue with their next account, accompanied by a statement that they have been so suspended.

All letters received by collectors or assessors from any office of the Treasury Department, should be answered to the office from which they are received. This suggestion is rendered necessary by the practice of some officers, who have written to the Commissioner of Internal Revenue in answer to letters received from the fifth auditor.

Instructions concerning the Assessments of Tax on Legacies Distributive Shares, and Successions.

TREASURY DEPARTMENT, Office of Internal Revenue,
Washington, February 15, 1866.

Inasmuch as, through the failure of assessors and assistant assessors to exercise due vigilance in the assessment of legacy and succession duties, much revenue is lost to the Government which is justly due, the following instructions are issued:

Assistant assessors should make it a practice to call at stated periods upon clerks, registers, and other officers having the custody of probate records, and upon officers having charge of the registers of deaths within their respective divisions, and examine such records to ascertain the liability to taxation of legatees, distributees, and successors interested in the estates of persons deceased. They should also examine records of deeds, in order to learn if any real estate has been conveyed without valuable and adequate consideration. (Sec. 132.)

A form of notice for legacy and succession taxes has been issued, (Form 96,) which assessors and assistant assessors can send to persons whose duty it is or may be to make returns, and which may be deposited in probate and other public offices frequented by persons interested in these taxes.

Legacies and Distributive Shares.

1. Where the whole amount of the personal property of an estate, payable to legatees or distributees, exceeds the sum of one thousand dollars in actual value, the same is subject to duty or tax without regard to the amount or value of each legacy or share. But when the whole amount does not exceed one thousand dollars, no tax is chargeable.

2. Shares in personal estate are to be returned by the executor or administrator where the decedent had his legal residence at the time of his death.

3. Where legacies are given or granted by will or deed to the husband or wife of the person who died possessed, for the use of such husband or wife during life, and after his or her death to other persons, the value of the beneficial interest at the time when any distribution or payment is first to be made by virtue of said will or deed is to be estimated, and the tax or duty will be assessed as of that value.

4. Expectancies in personal property are taxable on their present worth; but no distributive shares of *personal* property are taxable unless they come from the estate of a person who has died since July 1, 1862. If the person from whose estate they are derived died prior to June 30, 1864, (and since July 1, 1862,) you will of course tax the legacies according to the rates prescribed in section 111 of the act of July 1, 1862; and those shares which arise from the estates of persons who have died since June 30, 1864, tax by the rates prescribed in section 124 of the act of June 30, 1864.

5. Where legacies are made payable at the expiration of a life or lives in being, the value of the legacy will be estimated by the Carlisle tables of life annuities, which are appended to these instructions.

6. Where a legacy is made payable on a future contingency, the value of the legacy is to be estimated by a consideration of the time, certain or ascertainable by the annuity tables, when the legacy will become vested.

7. Where money is directed to remain in the hands of executors, trustees, or grantees, the interest thereof to be paid annually during a life or lives in being to another person than to the husband or wife of the decedent, and after the termination of such life or lives, the principal to be paid to other person or persons, it will be proper to calculate by approved tables the present value of the annual payments, and to assess the tax or duty on that value, according to the relationship, at the rate prescribed in the 124th section of the excise law. From the whole sum directed to remain in the hands of the said executor, trustee, or grantee, yielding interest, deduct the value of the annual payments ascertained as aforesaid, and assess a tax or duty on the remainder at the prescribed rate.

8. Where the time at which a legacy or a sum of money payable by deed after the death of the testator or grantor is remote and certain, the present worth of the beneficial interest can be estimated in a similar manner.

9. Where a legacy or sum of money given or granted as aforesaid is payable at a remote period, with interest in the meantime, to the legatee, it is to be considered as payable presently for all the purposes of tax or duty.

10. Where a legacy or sum of money given or granted as aforesaid is payable without interest at a future and uncertain period, as at marriage, or at the discretion of the executor or trustee, or when the habits of the beneficiary shall have become reformed, the earliest period at which the legatee may become entitled to the legacy or sum of money ought to be assumed as the day at which it is payable, and its value estimated and tax or duty assessed accordingly.

11. If between the death of the decedent and the time of making the return, a life interest in personal property is terminated by the death of the person having the life interest, you will, nevertheless, estimate the value of his life interest without regard to his death.

12. Where the legacy or gift by deed, taking effect after the death of the testator or donor, is of a specific article of personal property subject to tax or duty, the tax or duty will be assessed on the value of such article, and must be paid by the executor or trustee, or person having the same in charge, before the delivery thereof to the legatee or donee.

Successions to Real Estate.

1. Sections 127 and 132 impose a tax on all successions of real estate by deed, will, or laws of descent, whether arising from the acts of persons who died before or since the 30th of June, 1864. But by section 137 it would seem that succession cannot be taxed if any person possesses any intervening interests which prevent the legal possession or immediate right to possession. But a mere right to possess, which cannot without a suit at law debar the party from the present possession, is not, by reason of provisions in section 131 to be regarded as an in-

cumbrance or estate intervening between inheritance or devise and possession.

2. The executor or administrator does not return for taxation *real estate*, but return thereof is to be made by the devisee or heirs-at-law, except in cases arising under sections 138 and 139, where the duty is payable by the person having control of the funds. If the estate is to be held in trust for life or a term of years, the trustee returns the interest which is intrusted to him; and when that trust expires, the person who legally takes possession is to return what is *now* a remainder or reversion in expectancy.

3. In cases where real estate is devised to one person for life with remainder to another, the life tenant should be required to pay the tax upon the value of his life estate immediately upon his entering into possession; and the remainder man will be taxed upon the full value of the real estate at the termination of the life estate.

4. The same rule applies to property which was incumbered by a life estate at the passage of the act of June 30, 1864. In this case, as in all others, the devisor should be named in the return as the "*predecessor.*"

5. The value of a life interest is to be computed according to the age of beneficiary at the time when the testator died. No regard is to be paid to the state of health of a life tenant in estimating probabilities of life.

6. Succession returns should always contain a sufficiently distinct description of the several parcels of estate, to enable the assessor properly to estimate the value thereof, and also to enable any person who may examine the records in the assessor's office to determine whether the tax has been assessed upon any particular parcel.

7. Each and every described parcel must be separately valued, according to the market value, at the time the successor becomes entitled in possession.

8. All succession taxes must be assessed and paid in the collection districts in which the real estate lies. *Returns* may, however, be made in the district in which the successor lives; and when any real estate returned lies in another district, the assessor will transmit the return to the assessor of such other district.

9. The valuation of successions must always be in accordance with the judgment of the assistant assessor of the division where the estate lies, subject of course to that of the assessor.

10. In cases where several heirs succeed to an estate which for any cause remains undivided, a single return, if this course be preferred, may be made therefor by any successor in behalf of himself and the other heirs, provided that the fact be made known to and approved by the assessor.

11. Succession duties and returns are in all cases due immediately after the successor becomes entitled in possession, or to the receipt of the income of the estate. E. A. Rollins, *Commissioner.*

Example.

John Brown died in 1860, leaving Whiteacre to his widow during her life, remainder to his brother William for life, remainder to his son George, in fee. The widow died in July, 1864, and William took possession of Whiteacre, being 60 years old. William died in May, 1865, and George immediately took Whiteacre in fee. The rental value of Whiteacre is estimated at $1,000 at the time William took his succession. His probability of life at that time was 14.34 years, and if his return had been made promptly, he would have been taxed on the then present worth of an annuity of $1,000 for that term, which by the tables (3d column) is 9.4368+1,000=9436.80, and his neglect in not making a return ought not to benefit his estate. He should be taxed forthwith on a valuation of 9436.80, and the assessment should be dated as of the day when John Brown's widow died. George has a perpetuity, and the actual value of Whiteacre should be estimated, and he be taxed thereon as of the day when William died.

CARLISLE TABLES.

AGE.	Expectancy of life in years and hundredths.	Present value of annuity of $1.00 for the number of years and hundredths of years found in second column at 6 per cent.	Present value of $1.00 to be received at the end of the number of years and hundredths of years, as found in second column, interest at 6 per cent.	AGE.	Expectancy of life in years and hundredths.	Present value of annuity of $1.00 for the number of years and hundredths of years found in second column at 6 per cent.	Present value of $1.00 to be received at the end of the number of years and hundredths of years, as found in second column, interest at 6 per cent.
0	38.72	14.9202	.104788	51	20.39	11.5846	.304922
1	44.68	15.4325	.074045	52	19.68	11.3701	.317792
2	47.55	15.6225	.062645	53	18.97	11.1482	.331108
3	49.82	15.7521	.054874	54	18.28	10.9201	.344791
4	50.76	15.8008	.051953	55	17.58	10.6805	.359172
5	51.25	15.8252	.050490	56	16.89	10.4364	.373815
6	51.17	15.8213	.050722	57	16.21	10.1839	.388967
7	50.80	15.8029	.051830	58	15.55	9.9287	.404275
8	50.24	15.7742	.053551	59	14.92	9.6788	.419268
9	49.57	15.7385	.055689	60	14.34	9.4368	.433789
10	48.82	15.6972	.058168	61	13.82	9.2154	.447078
11	48.04	15.6523	.060860	62	13.31	8.9900	.460612
12	47.27	15.6055	.063670	63	12.81	8.7636	.474184
13	46.51	15.5573	.066559	64	12.30	8.5245	.488530
14	45.75	15.5072	.069566	65	11.79	8.2793	.503231
15	45.00	15.4558	.072650	66	11.27	8.0211	.518737
16	44.27	15.4028	.075832	67	10.75	7.7552	.534690
17	43.57	15.3501	.078996	68	10.23	7.4813	.551125
18	42.87	15.2956	.082267	69	9.70	7.1926	.568446
19	42.17	15.2384	.085695	70	9.18	6.9022	.585867
20	41.46	15.1778	.089331	71	8.65	6.5945	.604328
21	40.75	15.1151	.093095	72	8.16	6.3045	.621730
22	40.04	15.0500	.097002	73	7.72	6.0341	.637953
23	39.31	14.1972	.101248	74	7.33	5.7894	.652634
24	38.59	14.9068	.105592	75	7.01	5.5887	.664681
25	37.86	14.8307	.110157	76	6.69	5.3762	.677427
26	37.14	14.7521	.114876	77	6.40	5.1833	.688999
27	36.41	14.6685	.119892	78	6.12	4.9971	.700173
28	35.69	14.5829	.125024	79	5.80	4.7763	.713420
29	35.00	14.4982	.130105	80	5.51	4.5719	.725687
30	34.34	14.4123	.135258	81	5.21	4.3604	.738376
31	33.68	14.3240	.140560	82	4.93	4.1601	.750394
32	33.03	14.2343	.145938	83	4.65	3.9508	.762940
33	32.36	14.1366	.151789	84	4.39	3.7565	.774590
34	31.68	14.0344	.157932	85	4.12	3.5548	.786687
35	31.00	13.9291	.164255	86	3.90	3.3859	.796820
36	30.32	13.8174	.170957	87	3.71	3.2354	.805855
37	29.64	13.7021	.180796	88	3.59	3.1403	.811562
38	28.96	13.5833	.185000	89	3.47	3.0453	.817268
39	28.28	13.4579	.192530	90	3.28	2.8948	.826304
40	27.61	13.3289	.200208	91	3.26	2.8789	.827255
41	26.97	13.2043	.207741	92	3.37	2.9661	.822024
42	26.34	13.0737	.215580	93	3.48	3.0532	.816793
43	25.71	12.9395	.223635	94	3.53	3.0928	.814415
44	25.09	12.8032	.231812	95	3.53	3.0928	.814415
45	24.46	12.6576	.240548	96	3.46	3.0374	.817744
46	23.82	12.5059	.249646	97	3.28	2.8948	.826304
47	23.17	12.3454	.259278	98	3.07	2.7284	.836290
48	22.51	12.1751	.269494	99	2.77	2.4799	.851206
49	21.81	11.9889	.280669	100	2.28	2.0685	.875891
50	21.11	11.7946	.292324				

Instructions Concerning the Exemption of Articles and Products from Taxation under the 10th Section of Act of July 13, 1866.

TREASURY DEPARTMENT, Office of Internal Revenue,
Washington, September 8, 1866.

The following constructions having been adopted by this office with regard to the exemptions authorized by section eleven are printed as a guide to officers of internal revenue to aid them in determining questions which may arise in the application of the law to the various manufactures involved therein.

E. A. ROLLINS, *Commissioner.*

Barrels and Casks other than those used for the Reception of Fluids.

Under this head all dry barrels are exempt from taxation, such as flour barrels, and barrels and casks for packing lime, plaster, cement, nails, dry paints, rice, tobacco, sugar, &c.

But all barrels and casks made water-tight, and used for packing beef, pork, lard, pickled fish, wet paints, &c., are taxable, though not used for or intended to hold fluids alone.

Packing Boxes made of Wood.

The term "packing boxes" is to be understood and taken in its technical and mercantile signification.

That signification implies boxes used by the manufacturer, merchant, or jobber, to enclose goods after they have been sold in order to secure safe and easy transportation. Boxes used for putting up goods before sale, and without which the goods could not be offered for sale, and which are sold as part and parcel of the goods, are not technically known as packing boxes. Thus, boxes for putting up cigars, spices, starch, salt, shoes, &c., are not packing boxes.

Packing boxes made of paper or other material than wood, except those made for friction matches, cigar lights, and wax tapers, are taxable.

Building Stone.

This exemption applies only to the ordinary stone, and not to articles manufactured from stone, marble, or slate. It does not exempt fire-places, mantle-pieces, window caps, window sills, or other manufactures which are recognized as articles of traffic and manufactured for sale or upon special order as circumstances may require.

All manufactures of stone, marble, or slate not especially exempt, are liable to an ad valorem tax of five per cent.

Flax and the Manufactures Thereof.

By the 96th section of the act of June 30, 1864, flax prepared for textile or felting purposes, until actually woven, is exempt from tax. And by the 10th section of the act of July 13, 1866, flax, and the manufactures thereof, are exempt from tax.

This exemption of flax and the manufactures thereof includes and covers all the exemptions of flax prepared for textile or felting purposes, &c. The question has been raised whether articles or fabrics made in part of flax and in part of other materials are exempt from taxation, and how far the words "manufactures thereof" extend. The primary manufacture of flax consists in separating the fine fibres or skins of the plant by hackling and combing. The article thus obtained is the flax of commerce, and this the law exempts The manufactures from flax are thread, and cloth or fabrics, and these also are exempt.

If a manufacturer takes the raw material flax, and by a continuous process, or by a succession of processes, weaves, knits, or felts a cloth, a fabric, or an article, his product is exempt from tax; it is a manufacture of flax.

But a manufacturer who makes articles of dress for the wear of men, women, or children, from cloth or fabrics purchased in the market, or purchased from the manufacturer thereof, is not entitled to exemption from tax.

He does not manufacture from flax, but his products are all the result of a secondary manufacture, and are all made from materials which render them liable to taxation under other express provisions of law.

Again, a manufacturer who makes cloths, fabrics, or articles partly of flax and partly of other materials, is not to be regarded as a manuacturer of flax, nor are such mixed products exempt from taxation.

Exemptions are to be construed literally; such is declared to be the intent of the law, as appears from the proviso at the end of the 10th section, in these words: "*Provided*, That the exemptions aforesaid shall, in all cases, be confined exclusively to said articles in the state and condition specified in the foregoing enumeration, and shall not extend to articles in any other form, nor to manufactures from said articles." This proviso is restrictive, and confines the exemptions to the precise articles named, and the articles must be in the state and condition specified.

In the case under consideration, the exempted articles are (1) flax, and (2) the manufactures of flax, or the articles made of flax, and not any subsequent manufactures from said articles.

Crash, diapers, sheetings, &c., the warps of which are cotton or other material, and the filling flax yarn, are liable to a tax of 5 per cent. ad valorem.

Cloths or fabrics made as above, when dyed, colored, printed, or bleached, if previously assessed and the tax paid thereon, are liable to a tax of 5 per cent. on the increased value only. In no case is a proportionate part of the increased value to be assessed. If liable at all, the entire amount of increased value is taxable.

Hulls of Ships and other Vessels.

The act of June 30, 1864, imposed a tax of 2 per cent. on the hulls of all ships, barks, brigs, schooners, sloops, sailboats, steamboats, canal boats, and all other vessels or water craft.

The exemption in the new law specifies only the hulls of ships and other vessels. Boats propelled by oars cannot be regarded as vessels. They are not therefore exempted from tax under this provision, but are liable to a tax of 5 per cent. under the general provision of the 94th section as manufactures not otherwise provided for.

Medicinal and Mineral Waters.

This provision will exempt soda water however sold, but does not exempt sarsaparilla, pop, root, and like beer.

These are taxable under the general provision of the 94th section at the rate of 5 per cent. ad valorem.

Cordage, Ropes, and Cables, made of Vegetable Fibre.

The terms "cordage" and "cables" exempt from taxation all ropes and lines made and used for the rigging and tackle of vessels or water craft.

Rope differs from twine or line mainly in size. It is difficult to define the precise distinction and show where the line or twine becomes a rope.

The law expressly provides for taxing thread and twine, and cords and lines are regarded as taxable when not used as a part of the rigging or tackle of vessels.

Common usage, and the language employed ordinarily to characterize the article, must be the assessor's guide in settling the question of liability in each case where exemption is claimed under the language of the statute.

Printing Paper of all Descriptions, and Tarred Paper for Roofing and other Purposes.

The exemptions under this head are to be confined strictly to the descriptions of paper named.

Paper technically known as printing paper is exempt. All other kinds, whether writing paper, wrapping paper, drawing paper, blotting paper, filtering paper, paper hangings, and the like, are taxable. And paper made for tarring, if sold dry, is liable to a tax.

Photographs and other Sun Pictures.

Copies of engravings or works of art, when the same are sold by the producer at wholesale at a price not exceeding fifteen cents each, or are used for the illustration of books, are exempt. All other photographs and sun pictures are subject to an ad valorem tax of 5 per cent. upon the price at which the photographer sells his pictures. The law recognizes no other basis of taxation where the tax does not accrue till after a sale.

A photographer who colors a picture or otherwise ornaments it, thereby increasing its value or increasing the price received for it, will not satisfy the law by returning the price which he would have received for the picture without such coloring or ornamentation. Nothing short of the actual price received by the photographer or artist satisfies the requirements of the law.

Repairs of Articles of all Kinds.

This exemption does not extend to the materials used in making repairs when such materials are, in themselves, taxable manufactures. Neither does it exempt constituent parts of machines or instruments when such parts are, in themselves, separate and distinct manufactures, and are made to supply the place of some corresponding part which has been broken or worn out. Castings of iron or other metals, unless specially exempt, are equally liable to tax when used for repairs as when used in a new article or machine.

Residuums.

Under this head, resin drawn from the still after distillation of crude turpentine is exempt from duty. But pitch, a compound of resin and tar, is taxable.

Umbrellas and Parasols, and Sticks and Frames for the same.

By the act of June 30, 1864, section 96, umbrella stretchers were exempt from duty. The other parts of an umbrella or parasol, such as the frame, the handle, the stock, or the stick, were taxable when made as separate and distinct manufactures, and sold in the market as commercial articles.

The new law exempts the finished umbrella and parasol, and also the sticks and frames made for the same, and the question is raised whether the handle, which is a part of the stick, and which is generally manufactured as a separate and distinct article, is also exempt from taxation under the new law.

To this inquiry it may be said that, while the law enumerates sticks, frames, and stretchers as part of the umbrella or parasol, the most important part, and the one on which the greatest amount of skill and labor is expended is left out, and it must be presumed intentionally so by Congress, viz: the handle; and that no door might be left open for exempting any article by construction, the proviso before quoted was placed at the end of the section. It follows, therefore, that umbrella and parasol handles not being found in the list of exempted articles, and being in themselves a well known article of manufacture and traffic, they are taxable, whether made and sold, *or used* by the manufacturer in the production of sticks, umbrellas, or parasols.

Bullion.

Under section 10 of the act of July 13, 1866, the "value of bullion used in the manufacture of wares, watches, and watch-cases, and bullion prepared for the use of platers and watchmakers," is exempt from internal tax.

All bullion which is used by manufacturers is not therefore exempt from tax, but only such as is used and prepared under the provisions of the above-named section.

Bullion used in the manufacture of jewelry is not exempt. Gold and silver rings, bracelets, pins, chains, &c., are regarded as jewelry; but gold pens, thimbles, spectacle frames, &c., are regarded as wares.

Wooden Ware.

The question has been raised with regard to the term "wooden ware," as used in the act of July 13, 1866, and the extent to which articles made wholly or in part of wood, are exempt from taxation under this provision.

The use of the singular number "ware," instead of wares, shows an intention to limit the term to articles of a particular kind or class, and to such as are technically known as "wooden ware," and not to include all articles of wood, however different in kind. There are various other provisions of the same law which go to show that the term "wooden ware" is to be limited strictly to its technical signification, and cannot be applied to manufactures of wood in general.

Section 94 provides for taxing furniture and other articles made of wood, not otherwise provided for, 5 per cent. ad valorem.

Section 10 exempts barrels and casks when not used for fluids; packing boxes made of wood; baskets made of splints; crutches and artificial limbs; various agricultural implements made of wood; constituent parts of wheels and carriages or wagons made of wood; wooden handles for agricultural, household, and mechanical tools and implements; pail and tub ears and handles; and wooden tanks and cisterns for crude mineral oil. These articles were not thought to be covered by the term wooden ware, otherwise there would have been no necessity to have enumerated them and to have declared them specifically exempt.

The conclusion is therefore inevitable that wooden ware, as used in the section of the new law referred to, can only be construed to exempt such articles or implements of kitchen or household use as are made exclusively of wood, and technically known as wooden ware, to wit: tubs, pails, chopping boards and trays, wooden plates, bowls, dishes, spoons, knives, ladles, rollers, pins, moulds, prints, pats, mortars, pestles, dippers, ironing boards, pastry and meat boards, wash boards, clothes sticks, clothes horses, &c., &c.

Other articles made of wood, such as churns, boxes, kegs, firkins, fish-kits, measures, saw frames, ladders, pumps, &c., &c., are liable to an ad valorem tax of 5 per cent.

NOTE.—The reader will remark that by the late amendments of March 2, 1867, (q. v.,) a large number of additional articles are made exempt from taxation, and the foregoing circular will be read in view of these changes.

Regulations for the establishment of Bonded Warehouses under the Internal Revenue Acts, for the Entry, Withdrawal, Transportation, and Exportation of the Merchandise deposited therein, and for the keeping of proper Accounts thereof by Assessors, under Law of July 13, 1866.

TREASURY DEPARTMENT, Office of Internal Revenue,
Washington, Oct. 20, 1866.

Warehouses, in which merchandise may be stored in bond under the internal revenue laws, will be known and designated as bonded warehouses Class A, and bonded warehouses Class B.

A warehouse, Class A, may be a storeroom or building, approved by the Secretary of the Treasury, in the possession of any distiller of spirits, or mineral oil, or any manufacturer of tobacco, snuff, cigars, or friction matches, in which he may store merchandise of his own manufacture. No merchandise will be stored in bonded warehouse, Class A, except such as is manufactured or produced by the owner or occupant of the warehouse.

A warehouse, Class B, may be any storeroom or building, approved by the Secretary of the Treasury, in the possession of any person who may desire to engage in the business of storing spirits, mineral oil, tobacco, snuff, cigars, or friction matches. Owners or occupants of bonded warehouses of this class will receive on storage any merchandise that is allowed to be stored in bonded warehouse by internal revenue laws, provided they shall not be allowed to receive friction matches on storage with spirits or oil, and shall also receive any goods which may be seized or distrained by any collector of internal revenue, subject to the limitation hereinafter stated.

Goods seized or distrained shall be received in warehouses of this class on the order of the collector, if of the same character as goods otherwise deposited in such warehouse, and the proprietor or owner of such warehouse shall be liable for the safe-keeping of such merchandise as for other goods; and no charges for labor, storage, or other expenses shall exceed in any case the regular rates for such objects at the place in question.

Mode of Establishing Bonded Warehouses.

Bonded warehouses of either of the above classes will be established as follows: The owner or occupant will make application to the Collector of Internal Revenue for the district, describing the premises, the location, and capacity of the same, and setting forth the purpose for which the warehouse is proposed to be used; whether for storing his own merchandise, or for general storage of merchandise in bond. The application will also state the class of articles for the storage of which the warehouse is to be used. This application should be accompanied by a sketch or diagram showing the relative position of the warehouse to the distillery, refinery, or factory, and other surrounding buildings. In case the warehouse is intended for the storage of petroleum, the collector must be particular to certify as to whether the location is such as to endanger life or property in the immediate vicinity, in case of fire, as required by regulations of the Secretary of the Treasury. The application, to entitle it to consideration, must be accompanied by a certificate, properly stamped, signed by the officers of two or more insurance companies, that the premises offered are suitable, and may be insured at a moderate rate.

The collector shall thereupon examine and inspect the premises and report in writing the particulars in relation to location, construction, and dimensions, the means provided for securing custody of the merchandise which may be deposited in the same, and all other facts having a bearing on the subject, together with a statement of his own views and opinions, which, together with the application and the insurance certificates, he will transmit to the Commissioner of Internal Revenue. If the report be satisfactory, the application will be granted, and the owner or applicant will be required to give bond. If a bonded warehouse, Class A, the form will be that known as Form A.

The penal sum in the bond should always be sufficient to cover the tax on the amount of merchandise that will be stored therein at any one time, and the security should always be increased whenever the tax on the quantity stored exceeds the penal sum named in the bond. If a bonded warehouse, Class B, the form will be that known as Form B.

General Regulations in regard to Warehouses of both the foregoing classes.

The building, or portion of a building, used as a bonded warehouse, must be under the lock of the officer of internal revenue, in addition to the lock of the owner, which locks must be of different character. All the means of ingress to or egress from the building must be under the control of the Government officer.

Where only a portion of a building is to be used as a bonded warehouse, care is to be taken that the portion so used shall have no communication with or inlet from the remainder of the building.

All labor on the goods deposited in these stores must be performed by the owner or occupant of the warehouse, and the warehouse will be subject to such further rules as the Department may deem necessary, from time to time, for the safe keeping of the goods and protection of the revenue, and may be discontinued as a bonded warehouse by the Commissioner of Internal Revenue, subject to the approval of the Secretary of the Treasury, when, in his opinion, the public interests may require. All arrangements in regard to the rates of storage and the price of labor on goods deposited in warehouses, Class B, must be made between the depositor and the owner or occupant of the store, and all amounts due for storage and labor must be collected by the latter; the collector of internal revenue looking only to the custody of the merchandise for the security of the revenue.

Warehouses, Class A, established by distillers of spirits, for the storage of their products, will be in charge of the inspector, appointed by the Secretary of the Treasury, in accordance with the provisions of section 27 of the act of July 13, 1866.

Warehouses, Class A, established by refiners or distillers of mineral oil, or manufacturers of tobacco, snuff, cigars, cigar lights, tapers, or lucifer or friction matches; and all warehouses, Class B, will be placed in charge of an officer appointed by the collector of internal revenue, for the district in which the warehouse is situated, and who will receive a compensation, to be fixed by said collector, and approved by the Commissioner of Internal Revenue, to be paid monthly, by the owner or occupant of the warehouse, and will be designated as a storekeeper.

Should the amount of business at any one warehouse require, in the judgment of the collector, the services of more than one officer, the owner or occupant will be required to pay monthly such additional sum as will be equivalent to the salary of such officer or officers. One officer may, however, have charge of as many warehouses, not including distillers' warehouses, class A, as, in the judgment of the collector, he can superintend efficiently.

Where a single officer has charge of more than one warehouse, the proportion of his compensation to be paid by each proprietor or occupant will be determined by the collector.

The compensation of a storekeeper will, in no case, exceed four dollars per day, unless by special permission of the Commissioner of Internal Revenue, upon application of the collector of the district.

Great care will, in all cases, be taken by collectors and other officers in inquiring into the safety and suitable character of buildings or premises offered as bonded warehouses, with special reference to the class of goods intended to be deposited therein, and into all other facts material to the subject.

The owner or occupant of a bonded warehouse will in no case have access to it, except in presence of the officer in charge.

After stores or premises have been approved and placed under internal revenue locks, the collector will retain the right of ordering additional fastenings, to be provided by and at the expense of the owners or occupants having charge of the premises.

Should the owner or occupant of any building, room, or premises designated as a bonded warehouse, neglect or refuse to pay to the collector the sum required by these instructions for the salary of an officer or officers, as the case may be, or fail or refuse to comply with any law regulating the storage of merchandise, or any rules or regulations issued by this Department, or by the collecter, for the safety of the goods stored, the collector will refuse permission to deposit goods in such store, and report the facts at once to the Commissioner of Internal Revenue for his action

The proprietors or occupants of warehouses, on ten days' notice from the collector, may be required to renew their bonds; and, if they fail so to do, no more goods will be sent to such warehouses, and those within the same will be withdrawn at their expense.

The owner or occupant of any warehouse will have the right to relinquish the business at any time, with the approval of the collector of the district, and on notice to the owners of the merchandise deposited therein, and paying the expense of its removal to other warehouses, when his bond will be cancelled.

Collectors will report the date and reasons for the discontinuance of a bonded warehouse of either class, to the Commissioner of Internal Revenue, as soon as such discontinuance takes place and the bonds are cancelled.

Mode of Depositing Goods in a Bonded Warehouse, Class A.

An entry for the warehousing of merchandise in any warehouse, Class A, established in the foregoing manner, will be in the form known as Form "C."

The entry must be made in duplicate. The merchandise described therein, having been inspected according to law, the storekeeper will superintend the reception and storing of the same in the warehouse, retaining one entry and transmitting the other, together with his certificate that the goods have been received by him in warehouse, and a certificate of inspection, (Form H, hereinafter provided,) to his collector.

No transportation or other bond is required in this case.

Mode of transporting goods from a refinery, or manufactory, to a bonded warehouse, Class B, or from one bonded warehouse to another.

Mineral oil, tobacco, snuff, cigars, cigar lights, wax tapers, or friction matches, and brandy distilled from apples, peaches, or grapes exclusively, may be transported, under the regulations hereinafter provided, from the distillery, refinery, or manufactory, to any general bonded warehouse, Class B, or from the bonded warehouse in which they are first deposited, to any other bonded warehouse, Class B, established in conformity with these regulations.

Distilled spirits, except those above named, can, in no case, be allowed to be removed from the distillery in bond without first having been placed in the warehouse, Class A, required to be established by all distillers of spirits in accordance with the terms of section 27 of the act of July 13, 1866.

Cotton removed under bond cannot be placed in bonded warehouse upon its arrival at the point of delivery, but must be delivered to the collector of internal revenue, for the district where received, by whom it will be held in custody, at the expense of the owner, until the tax and all charges incurred for storage have been paid.

Whenever it is desired to transport goods, receivable in bonded warehouses under these regulations, from a distillery, refinery, or manufactory, to a bonded warehouse in another district, or from one bonded warehouse to another, as above provided, application must be made to the collector of internal revenue for the district in which the goods are situated for a permit so to do, the merchandise having been first duly inspected, in cases where such inspection is required by law.

The application will be in the form known as Form "D."

Upon the receipt of this application, the collector will exact from the applicant a transportation bond, with good and sufficient sureties in at least double the amount of duties upon said merchandise, in the form known as Form "E."

Upon this bond being duly executed, the collector will grant a permit in the Form "F."

This permit will be executed in duplicate, one of which the collector will give to the applicant, and the other he will forward by mail to the collector of internal revenue for the district to which the goods are designed to be transported, unless the transportation shall be from one portion of a collection district to another portion of the same district, in which case one of the permits shall be sent to the storekeeper in charge of the warehouse for which the goods are destined.

Goods removed under this bond and permit must be deposited in the bonded warehouse to which they were permitted to be removed.

It will be the duty of the owner or consignee, on the arrival of the merchandise, or any part thereof, at the place where the warehouse for which it is destined is situated, immediately to notify the internal revenue collector in charge of said warehouse of its arrival, and to deliver the merchandise to him, and make entry thereof in Form "G."

This entry must be made in duplicate, and forwarded to the storekeeper in charge of the warehouse. The merchandise described therein having been duly inspected, the storekeeper will see the goods stored in the warehouse, retaining one entry and transmitting the other, together with his certificate that the goods have been received by him in warehouse, and a certificate by the inspector of his inspection of the same, to his collector.

The certificate of the inspector will be in the Form "H."

On the receipt of the entry, and of the certificates of the storekeeper and inspector, the collector will take from the owner or consignee of the merchandise a warehouse bond (Form J) for the same; and thereupon will make out duplicate certificates of the merchandise received, and that the same has been inspected, gauged, weighed, or gauged and proved, as the case may be, and stating the quantity thereof; and that a proper warehousing bond has been taken for the same; which certificate will be in the Form "I."

This certificate, in duplicate, will be delivered to the owner or consignee of the merchandise, who will procure it to be countersigned by the assessor of the district in which the warehouse is situated.

If the quantity received should be deficient, that is, less than the quantity described in the permit given for transportation, and the parties allege that the deficiency arose from leakage, they will execute an affidavit to that effect before the collector in charge of the warehouse. This affidavit, with the certificates showing that the goods have been deposited in warehouse, will be forwarded to the collector of the district from which the goods were removed.

Upon the delivery to the collector of internal revenue who received the transportation bond, of the said affidavit, and the certificate issued to the owner of the merchandise, or his consignee, he will cancel said bond, provided the said affidavit and certificate show to the satisfaction of the collector that the whole quantity of goods bonded, after making the allowance for leakage permitted by law and regulation, has been placed in bonded warehouse. If there be any deficiency, the amount of duties thereon must be collected.

Upon a deposit of any goods in a bonded warehouse, Class B, the owner or consignee will be required to execute a bond conditioned to pay the duties on the merchandise so deposited, or to withdraw the same in the manner prescribed by law and regulations. This bond may be executed for one lot of merchandise, or may be continuing for a period not exceeding six months, if executed in an amount sufficient to secure the duties on all the merchandise which may be stored in the warehouse under it; *provided*, that such continuing bond shall in any case be made to cover but one class of merchandise. The said bond will be in Form "J."

The collector will keep an accurate account of the merchandise warehoused under every such bond, and in no case allow the aggregate amount of duties on goods stored to exceed at any time half the amount stated in the bond. If the bond is given to secure but one lot of merchandise, the blank in the bond will be filled by a description of that lot. If it be a continuing bond, the period for which it is to continue will be stated.

Mode of Withdrawing Goods from a Bonded Warehouse.

Goods deposited in a bonded warehouse may be withdrawn therefrom—

1. On payment of the duties.
2. For redistillation, rectification, canning, or change of package.
3. For exportation.
4. For removal to another bonded warehouse.

1. *On Payment of the Duties.*

When goods are to be withdrawn from a bonded warehouse for consumption, the parties will make an entry for withdrawal similar to the entry for withdrawal for exportation, except that the fact of the withdrawal being for consumption instead of exportation will be set forth. The collector having charge of the warehouse will collect the amount of duties due on said merchandise, and will deposit the amount so collected with his general collections, and enter the amount on his monthly abstract; or, if the goods are subject to a stamp duty, he will see that the proper stamps are affixed.

The duties having been fully paid, the collector will issue a permit for their delivery, which must be presented to the assessor or an assistant assessor of the district for his certificate that the same has been presented, and that the duties paid thereon have been entered in the bonded account of the district, and no storekeeper will deliver any merchandise from the bonded warehouse wherein it is stored except upon presentation of a permit on Form "K."

The duties having been fully paid, the collector will cause the barrels, or other packages, to be marked with the words "U. S. bonded warehouse, tax paid;" and if desired, he will issue a certificate, under his seal of office, describing the several packages by their marks or brands, and showing that the duties thereon have been fully paid.

2. *Removal for Redistillation, Rectification, or Change of Package.*

Distilled spirits and mineral oil may, after proper inspection, be removed from a warehouse for the purpose of being redistilled, rectified, or put into other packages; and must, in such cases, be returned to the warehouse and be again inspected; and the duty must be paid to the collector on any deficiency or reduction, beyond three per cent. in the case of distilled spirits, and five per cent. in the case of mineral oil, in the number of proof gallons received at the warehouse, as aforesaid. Collectors will observe that the same lot of spirits or oil can be withdrawn but once for either of the purposes named above, and that the tax upon the allowance made, together with the tax upon the quantity withdrawn, must be paid in case of its withdrawal, after return to the warehouse, for consumption, or for transportation without being exported.

Spirits or oil withdrawn from warehouse for the purpose of being placed in cans or other packages must in all cases be reinspected after the process is completed; and if placed in cans or packages intended to be hermetically sealed, the sealing of such packages must always take place in the presence of an inspector.

Spirits withdrawn for the purpose of being rectified, redistilled, or otherwise changed in proof, can be returned to warehouse below first proof if desired, and be withdrawn therefrom for consumption without rendering the owner liable to payment of tax on the wine gallons withdrawn.

In case spirits at less than first proof are placed in bonded warehouse, and are afterward withdrawn for redistillation, rectification, or change of packages, the bond given at the time of withdrawal should be for the same number of proof gallons as the wine gallons withdrawn; and the parties should be required to account for any discrepancy on their return to warehouse, beyond the loss to which they are legally entitled in cases of exportation.

The entry in these cases will be under Form "K."

On receipt of this entry, the collector will permit the withdrawal of the merchandise, after proper inspection, exacting a bond, in a penalty of at least twice the amount of the tax, with two good and sufficient sureties as by Form "L."

The owner of distilled spirits or mineral oil, who desires to remove for redistillation, rectification, or change of package, during a given period, may give a bond to cover all such removals during that period.

The storekeeper will keep an accurate account of the number of gallons, as certified by the inspector, removed from and returned to the warehouse under each bond, and promptly certify each removal and return to his collector. When all removed is accounted for, after making the allowance for loss, as established by law, or by the Commissioner of Internal Revenue, the bond will be cancelled.

3. *Removal for Exportation.*

Distilled spirits, mineral oil, tobacco, snuff and cigars, and friction matches, may be removed from a bonded warehouse of either class, for the purpose of immediate exportation, in the following manner:

Any person having merchandise stored in a bonded warehouse, situated at a port of entry, and desiring to withdraw the same for exportation, will notify the collector of customs, by making the proper entry given in Form "N."

When merchandise is withdrawn for exportation, the owner or his authorized agent, other than a custom-house broker, transacting his business and cognizant of the facts, must take oath or affirmation before the collector of customs as by Form "O."

The export entry must be made in the name of the real owner or party in interest.

The entry having been duly made and the oath taken, the owner or exporter must enter into a bond, with two sufficient sureties, in a penal sum equal to double the amount of the estimated duties, to produce the required proof of the exportation of the goods, known as Form "P."

The time mentioned in the bond must be *six months* if the exportation is to Canada; if to any other place not beyond the Cape of Good Hope, *one year;* and if beyond the Cape of Good Hope, *two years.*

Upon the execution of this bond, the collector of customs will deliver to the parties a permit known as Form "Q."

If the goods thus to be removed are in a bonded warehouse, the collector of internal revenue will cancel the warehouse bond upon the production of a certificate of shipment and clearance of the merchandise from the collector of customs, known as Form "R."

Upon the receipt of this order, the storekeeper will deliver the goods to the proper officer of the customs, and they will be dealt with thereafter in all respects as are imported goods withdrawn from bonded warehouse for exportation.

If the goods thus to be removed are in a bonded warehouse at a place other than the port from which they are to be exported, a duly authorized application must be made to the collector of internal revenue, for the district in which the goods are situated, for a permit so to do, the merchandise having been first duly inspected in cases where such inspection is required by law. The application will be made on Form known as Form "S."

Upon the receipt of the application, the collector will exact from the applicant a transportation bond for export, for the purpose of exportation with good and sufficient sureties in at least double the amount of duties upon said merchandise, on Form known as Form "T." Upon this bond being duly executed, the collector will grant a permit known as Form "U."

This permit must be executed in duplicate, one given to the applicant, and the other must be sent by mail to the collector of internal revenue having charge of exportations at the port from which the goods are designed to be exported.

Immediately on the arrival of the merchandise at the port, the owner or consignee must give notice thereof to the collector of internal revenue having charge of exportation, who will take charge of said merchandise and deliver the same to the proper officer of the customs.

The exporter must make an entry for exportation at the custom-house, whereupon the collector of customs will direct the proper officer to receive the merchandise; and the same will be dealt with thereafter in all respects as are imported goods withdrawn from bonded warehouse for exportation. In case such merchandise cannot be immediately exported, the collector of internal revenue will direct the same to be placed in a bonded warehouse, and the same may be withdrawn therefrom in the same manner as other merchandise for exportation. The merchandise will be removed from the conveyance by which it arrives to the warehouse under the supervision of an officer detailed by the collector of internal revenue. All expenses and fees consequent upon such removal and storage must be paid by the owner. The order for such removal will be on Form "V."

On the receipt of the merchandise the store-keeper will enter a description of the same, the name of the owner, and place whence transported, in a book to be kept by him for that purpose.

The export entry having been made, and the usual bond not to reland the merchandise within the United States, having been executed, the collector of customs will issue a certificate of clearance.

This certificate, in duplicate, shall be delivered to the owner or consignee of the merchandise.

If the quantity exported should be deficient—that is, less than the quantity described in the permit given for transportation—and the parties allege that the deficiency arose from leakage, they will execute an affidavit to that effect before the collector of customs. This affidavit, with the certificates showing that the goods have been exported, will be forwarded to the collector of the district from which the goods were removed.

Upon the delivery to the collector of internal revenue who received the transportation bond of the said affidavit and the certificates issued to the owner of the merchandise, or his consignee, he will cancel said bond, provided the said oath and certificates show to his satisfaction that the whole quantity of goods bonded, after making the allowance for leakage permitted by law and regulation, has been exported. If there be any deficiency, the amount of duties thereon must be collected.

4. *Removal from one Bonded Warehouse to another.*

Goods may be withdrawn from one bonded warehouse for removal to another bonded warehouse, or to a bonded warehouse, Class 2, established under section 168 of the act of June 30, 1864; or for removal from warehouse, Class 2, situated in the Atlantic States, to the Pacific coast, for export only, in the manner and under the transportation bonds hereinbefore required.

Inspection.

The law requires that all distilled spirits and mineral oil shall be inspected, gauged, proved, and marked before removal from the distillery to a warehouse, and that all such merchandise shall be again inspected, &c., after its arrival at another bonded warehouse, and leakage shall be allowed in accordance with the regulations prescribed by the Commissioner of Internal Revenue. In like manner, all manufactured tobacco, cigars, and snuff must be inspected and marked before removal from the manufactory to a bonded warehouse, and must be again inspected after arrival at another warehouse. The collector of internal revenue for the district will be held responsible for the discharge of these duties by the proper officer.

Return of Bonded Goods by Assessors and Collectors.

In order to insure uniformity of returns from collectors and assessors of districts where goods are produced and placed in bond, or received in bond from other districts, the following regulations will be observed.

The returns on Forms 60 and 61 are restricted to merchandise *placed in bond;* and if, for any month, the collector has nothing to report on Form 61, he will, nevertheless, transmit it in blank to the assessor. The previous instructions upon this subject having been misunderstood in some instances, collectors are again reminded that they should report on Forms 60 and 61, only those articles which are *produced* in their respective districts, and that bonded goods received from other districts should not be returned on those forms.

Assessor's Account of Bonded Goods.

Each assessor in whose district goods are placed in bond, whether produced in the district or received in bond from other districts, will keep an account of such goods with the collector. This account will be kept so as to show the duties to which the merchandise described in the various entries is liable.

The assessor will charge the collector with the duties on all goods received from other districts, and with the duties on all goods produced in the district and placed in bond. To insure accuracy in this account, the collector should notify the assessor when goods produced in his district are placed in bond; and the assessor will compare the amount so reported with the returns of the manufacturers and producers made to him. In case of any discrepancy the assessor will make such investigation as may be necessary to ascertain the facts, but the bonded account will be made up to correspond with the notification received from the collector.

Whenever a collector cancels a bond, he will deliver to the assessor of his district all the evidence upon which such cancellation took place. Such evidence will consist of certificates of other collectors, (*Form I*,) certificates and affidavits of leakage, or certificates of clearance received from collectors of customs, or orders from superintendents of exports for the delivery of goods for exportation.

The assessor will credit the collector in his bonded account with the several amounts to which the evidence submitted shows him to be entitled. No credits will be given except on presentation of the evidence required in proper form. He will also credit him in the bonded account with the duties received on all goods when withdrawn from bond by payment of tax, which must be reported monthly, on Form 93, as follows, to wit:

On or before the 10th day of each month, the collector will transmit to the assessor of his district a monthly statement on Form 93, showing the amount of duties collected by him on account of bonded goods during the preceding month, giving in detail the number of gallons or pounds, and the rate and amount of tax for each case in which collections were made.

Upon the receipt of this statement, the amount will be included in the aggregate of the monthly list for the month in which such collections were made. If from any cause said statement is not received until such list has been delivered to and receipted for by the collector, the aforesaid aggregate amount of collections will be entered on the next succeeding monthly list, and be receipted for on Form 23½.

The bonded account will be balanced monthly by being credited with the duties on the goods reported by the collector monthly as remaining in bonded warehouse, and under bond for transportation, exportation, redistillation, or change of package and unaccounted for at the end of the month; and the amount so credited will be carried forward and placed to the debit of the account for the month next succeeding.

From the bonded account kept by the assessor he will prepare and transmit to the Commissioner, before the 15th day of each month, an aggregate statement, on Form 94, of the bonded account for the preceding month.

This statement is in the form of an account current, and will show—

1. The amount of merchandise in warehouse, brought forward from the preceding monthly statement, and entered therein under No. 10.

2. The amount of merchandise that has been removed in bond and

is yet unaccounted for, brought forward from the preceding statement, being entered there under No. 9.

3. Amount reported on Form 61, accompanied by that Form.

4. Amount received from other districts, with a statement in detail, showing the date and amount of each receipt, and the district whence it came.

5. Amount received by other collectors. This entry must be accompanied by the receipts of said collectors, properly scheduled and numbered.

6. Amount exported. This entry should be accompanied by the orders of superintendents of exports, and certificates of collectors of customs, properly scheduled and numbered.

7. Amount allowed for leakage or loss by redistillation. To be accompanied by the certificates of inspectors, and affidavits of owners or consignees, properly scheduled and numbered.

8. Amount withdrawn from bond on payment of duties, accompanied by the collector's statement on Form 93.

9. Amount removed on transportation bonds and not accounted for at the end of the month. To be accompanied by the collector's inventory in detail.

10. Amount remaining in warehouse at the end of the month, with the collector's inventory in detail.

Allowance for Leakage.

The amount allowed for actual leakage on distilled spirits transported in bond will not exceed one per centum for any distance not exceeding one hundred miles; one and one-half per centum for any distance exceeding one hundred and not exceeding two hundred miles; two per centum for any distance exceeding two hundred and not exceeding three hundred miles; two and one-half per centum for any distance exceeding three hundred and not exceeding four hundred miles; three per centum for any distance exceeding four hundred and not exceeding five hundred miles; and three and one-half per centum for any distance exceeding five hundred miles; and the amount allowed for leakage will in no case exceed three and one-half per centum; except when spirits are transported to California, via Cape Horn, in which case proven leakage, to the extent of seven per centum on spirits, and ten per centum on alcohol, eighty per centum over proof, will be allowed but in no case will leakage be allowed, except upon spirits actually bonded for warehousing or transportation.

Leakage will be allowed on mineral oil, transported in bond, according to the following schedule:

When transported one hundred and not exceeding two hundred miles, one per centum; over two hundred and not exceeding three hundred miles, two per centum; over three hundred and not exceeding four hundred miles, three per centum; over four hundred and not exceeding five hundred miles, four per centum; over five hundred miles, five per centum; but no more than five per centum will be allowed in any case, whatever may be the distance transported, except when oil is transported to California via Cape Horn, when proven leakage to the extent of ten per centum will be allowed.

Actual loss, not to exceed three per centum on spirits, and five per centum on mineral oil, will be allowed on withdrawals for redistillation, rectification, or change of packages. This loss must be proved by the certificates of inspectors, who inspect or gauge the articles, before they are removed from the warehouse, as well as after their return thereto; and also by the affidavit of the owner that the loss occurred by redistillation or change of packages, and not otherwise; and that no part of the deficiency was taken, withdrawn, or withheld illegally.

When spirits or other merchandise, except cotton, are removed in bond, to districts where no bonded warehouse has been established, the collector of such district should not receive payment of the tax on such merchandise, or issue his certificate of receipt of such goods, or recognize, in any manner, their receipt in his district. In such cases, transportation bonds, securing the tax upon merchandise removed, can be cancelled only by payment of the tax on the full quantity removed, to the collector holding the bond; no allowance for loss by leakage being made, unless the goods are deposited in the warehouse, in accordance with the conditions of the bond.

Section 24 of the act of June 30, 1864, as amended by section 9 of the act of July 13, 1866, (Par. 18 of the compilation,) provides that when taxes are collected on cotton and distilled spirits, which have been removed in bond, commissions upon one-half the amount collected shall be allowed to the officers of the district where collected, and upon one-half to the officers of that whence removed.

As it would be exceedingly difficult, and frequently impracticable, to trace distilled spirits to the time of collections being made thereon, in calculating commissions under this provision the amount collected in any district upon spirits withdrawn from warehouses, Class B, will be apportioned among the several districts, from which spirits have been received, in proportion to the number of gallons received from such districts, respectively, and the amount thus assigned to a particular district will be assumed to be the amount collected upon spirits received from that district. Thus, if 10,000 gallons produced in the receiving district, and 5,000 gallons each received in bond from each of two other districts, are placed in warehouses, Class B, and the quarterly collections show that the tax has been paid on 10,000 gallons, amounting to $20,000, the officers of the receiving district will be entitled to the full commissions upon one-half of this sum, and one-half of the commissions upon the other half of this amount, while the officers of the shipping districts will be entitled to commissions upon one-half of the amount of $5,000 each.

These commissions will be adjusted quarterly, from the collectors' monthly reports, on Form 93, and the assessors' monthly statements, on Form 94.

In the case of cotton, as the tax is supposed, in all cases, to be paid in the district to which it is removed, the officers of each district will be allowed commissions on one-half the tax on the quantity for which cancelled bonds for the removal of this article are transmitted to this office.

Collectors will be careful to observe that goods withdrawn from bonded warehouse for transportation, exportation, or consumption, must be branded "U. S. bonded warehouse, for transportation to ——— district," for "export," or "tax paid," as provided by law, and in accordance with the facts in each case.

All actual loss of spirits or coal oil from leakage or evaporation while in bonded warehouse will be allowed upon the proper certificate of the inspector. Loss from destruction by fire, or other unavoidable accident, while in warehouse or in transit, will be allowed only upon presentation of satisfactory proof of such loss to the Commissioner; and no credit for such loss should be taken on the bonded account until the collector is notified of the allowance by the Commissioner.

All claims for loss by leakage must be accompanied by the certificate of the inspector, stating the difference between the amount delivered and the amount bonded; and also by the affidavit of the owner or consignee, showing the distance the goods have been transported, and that no part of the same has been taken, withdrawn, or withheld illegally, and that the discrepancy is caused solely by leakage while in transit; and no claim for loss by leakage will be considered or allowed by collectors in cancelling bonds unless supported by the evidence herein required.

No loss will be allowed for shrinkage in weight of tobacco during transit, or while stored in bond; but where packages are delivered to the storekeeper in good condition, corresponding in numbers, marks, and marked weights with the permit, showing no signs of having been opened or tampered with, the collector will issue his certificate of receipt, and take the warehousing bond for the full number of pounds named in the permit; and when these conditions are complied with, no further inspection at the time of receipt will be required.

In case the tobacco so received is afterwards exported in the original packages, they will be assumed to contain the quantity named in the permit. If withdrawn for consumption, the tax must be paid on the quantity as originally bonded.

As collectors have, in many instances, held bonds uncancelled long after maturity, they are reminded that such a practice is at variance with the rules of this office, and that in future they are expected to require parties to comply with the conditions of the bond, and produce the evidence for its cancellation within the time allowed, and that no extension of time can be granted except upon the approval of the Commissioner.

These regulations will take effect and be in force on and after the 1st day of December, 1866. E. A. ROLLINS, *Commissioner.*

Approved: H. McCULLOCH, *Secretary of the Treasury.*

REGULATIONS AS TO STAMPS.

* *Cancellation.*

In all cases where an *adhesive* stamp is used for denoting the stamp duty upon an instrument, the person using or affixing the same must write or imprint thereupon *in ink* the initials of his name, and the date on which the same is attached or used. When stamps are printed upon checks, &c., so that in filling up the instrument, the face of the stamp is and must necessarily be written across, no other cancellation will be required.

All cancellation must be distinct and legible, and except in the case of proprietary stamps from private dies, no method of cancellation which differs from that above described will be recognized by this office as legal and sufficient.

Stamping of Instruments by collectors prior to the issuing of the same, and by collectors and parties interested after they have been issued.

Any person having an instrument about to be issued, may present it to the collector, who, under the authority conferred upon him by section 162, will so stamp it as to place the sufficiency of that particular instrument beyond all question so far as stamp duties are concerned. The provisions of the section can in no case be applied to an instrument *after* it has been issued or used. The collector should decline to stamp or impress an instrument, under this section, until the stamp duty with which *he* thinks it chargeable has been paid. In cases of reasonable doubt he is recommended to obtain the opinion of this office before affixing his stamp, unless immediate action is essential to the interests of the parties concerned.

Any person who has made, signed, or issued an instrument subject to stamp duty unstamped or insufficiently stamped, or any person having an interest therein, may present it to the collector of the revenue of the proper district, who, upon payment of the price of the proper stamp required by law, a penalty of fifty dollars, and, where the whole amount of the tax denoted by the stamp required exceeds fifty dollars, on payment also of interest at the rate of six per centum from the day on which such stamp ought to have been affixed, is required by law to affix the stamp and to note upon the margin of the instrument the date of his so doing, and the fact that such penalty has been paid. This duty is obligatory upon the collector and he has no legal right to refuse to perform it.

---

*See Schedules at beginning of this work.

When there is a difference of opinion respecting the stamp proper to be affixed, the collector should affix such a one as the applicant prefers: the applicant takes the risk of the validity of his instrument. In such cases, however, it is advisable to refer the question to this office.

When an instrument is presented to a collector to be stamped, under the provisions of section 158, he is authorized to remit the penalty if it shall be proven to his satisfaction that such instrument was issued without the necessary stamp by reason of accident, mistake, inadvertence, or urgent necessity, and without any willful design to defraud the United States of the duty, or to evade or delay the payment thereof; *provided* such instrument is presented to him for that purpose, and the stamp tax chargeable thereon is paid, within twelve calendar months after the first day of August, 1866, or within twelve calendar months after the making or issuing thereof.

An instrument stamped by the collector in conformity with the foregoing instructions is as valid to all intents and purposes (except as against rights acquired in good faith before such stamping and the recording of the instrument, if a record be required) as if properly stamped when made and issued.

An instrument issued unstamped at a time when, and in a place where, no collection district was established, may be stamped by the party who issued it, or by any party having an interest therein, at any time *prior to January 1st*, 1867, and the legal effect of the stamp thus affixed will be the same as though affixed by the collector.

When the originals are lost, the necessary stamps may be affixed to copies in all cases which fall under section 158 or 162.

Each collector will keep a record of all instruments stamped or impressed by him under the provisions of sections 158 and 162, in which must be given the names of the parties to each instrument, the date of its execution, and a sufficient description of its nature to show the reasons for impressing or affixing the particular stamp. A certified copy of this record will be transmitted to this office at the close of each month during which any entry is made. If however, during any month the only instruments stamped or impressed have first been submitted to this office for instructions, the transmission of such copy may be deferred until a subsequent month.

The following is a suitable form for such record, and for the sake of uniformity should be adopted by all collectors:

No.	Names of Parties.	Date of Instrument.	Description of Instrument.	When stamped.	How stamped.	Penalty remitted or amount collected.

The whole amount of penalties paid to collectors for validating unstamped instruments should be returned on Form 58, with other unassessed penalties, and the money should be deposited to the credit of the Treasury of the United States with other collections.

That part of the act of July 1, 1862, which relates to stamp duties upon certain instruments therein specified, took effect October 1, 1862. The stamp laws have been amended and changed from time to time since that date, viz: by the amendatory act of March 3, 1863, which took effect upon its passage; by the act of June 30, 1864, which, so far as pertains to stamp duties upon instruments, took effect October 1, 1864; by the amendatory act of March 3, 1865, which took effect upon its passage, and by the amendatory act of July 13, 1866, which, so far as regards such duties, took effect August 1, 1866. Instruments should be stamped according to requirements of the law in force at the time they were made, signed, or issued, and collectors and others, when affixing stamps to instruments which were issued unstamped, should bear this fact strictly in mind.

A person who holds an unstamped conveyance founded upon a "confederate currency" consideration, will be allowed to affix such stamps thereto as he may think sufficient, and no prosecution will be instituted by the direction of this office for the recovery of a penalty for failure to stamp it according to the nominal *amount* of such consideration. If the parties interested elect to stamp it according to the actual *value* of the consideration in United States currency at the date of its delivery, they will be allowed to do so, *taking their own risk of the sufficiency of the stamp.*

The validity of a deed is a question for the courts. It is one of importance to the parties, but not to this office, any farther than the insufficiency of the stamp may affect the revenue.

The foregoing is applicable to other instruments as well as to deeds.

Penalties.

A penalty of fifty dollars is imposed upon every person who makes, signs, or issues, or who causes to be made, signed, or issued, any paper of any kind or description whatever, or who accepts, negotiates, or pays, or causes to be accepted, negotiated, or paid, any bill of exchange, draft, or order, or promissory note, for the payment of money, without the same being duly stamped, or having thereupon an adhesive stamp for denoting the tax chargeable thereon, canceled in the manner required by law, with intent to evade the provisions of the revenue act.

A penalty of two hundred dollars is imposed upon every person who pays, negotiates, or offers in payment, or receives or takes in payment, any bill of exchange or order for the payment of any sum of money, drawn or purporting to be drawn in a foreign country, but payable in the United States, until the proper stamp has been affixed thereto.

A penalty of fifty dollars is imposed upon every person who fraudulently makes use of an adhesive stamp to denote the duty required by the revenue act, without effectually canceling and obliterating the same in the manner required by law.

It is not lawful to record any instrument, document, or paper required by law to be stamped, or any copy thereof, unless a stamp or stamps of the proper amount have been affixed and canceled in the manner required by law; and such instrument or copy and the record thereof are utterly null and void, and cannot be used or admitted as evidence in any court until the defect has been cured as provided in section 158.

All willful violations of the law should be reported to the United States district attorney within and for the district where they are committed.

General Remarks.

Revenue stamps may be used indiscriminately upon any of the matters or things enumerated in schedule B, except proprietary and playing card stamps, for which a special use has been provided.

Postage stamps cannot be used in payment of the duty chargeable on instruments.

It is the duty of the maker of an instrument to affix the stamp thereto, and to cancel the same in the manner required by law. Proper cancellation is essential.

Suits are commenced in many States by other process than writ, viz: summons, warrant, publication, petition, &c., in which cases these, as the original processes, severally require stamps.

The jurat of an affidavit, taken before a justice of the peace, notary public, or other officer duly authorized to take affidavits, is held to be a certificate, and subject to a stamp duty of five cents, except when taken in suits or legal proceedings.

Certificates of Loan in which there shall appear any written or printed evidence of an amount of money to be paid on demand, or at a time designated, are subject to stamp duty as "Promissory Notes."

When two or more persons join in the execution of an instrument, stamp to which the instrument is liable under the law may be affixed and canceled by either of them; and "when more than one signature is affixed to the same paper, one or more stamps may be affixed thereto, representing the whole amount of the stamp required for such signatures."

No stamp is required on any warrant of attorney accompanying a bond or note, when such bond or note has affixed thereto the stamp or stamps denoting the duty required; and, whenever any bond or note is secured by mortgage, but one stamp duty is required on such papers—such stamp duty being the highest rate required for such instruments, or either of them. In such case a note or memorandum of the value or denomination of the stamp affixed should be made upon the margin or in the acknowledgment of the instrument which is not stamped.

Particular attention is called to the change in section 154, by striking out the words "or used;" the exemption thereunder is thus restricted to documents, &c., *issued* by the officers therein named. Also to the changes in sections 152 and 158, by inserting the words "and cancelled in the manner required by law."

The acceptor or acceptors of any bill of exchange, or order for the payment of any sum of money drawn or purporting to be drawn in any foreign country but payable in the United States, must, before paying or accepting the same, place thereupon a stamp indicating the duty.

It is only upon conveyances of realty *sold* that conveyance stamps are necessary. A deed of real estate made without valuable consideration need not be stamped as a conveyance, but if it contains covenants, such, for instance, as a covenant to warrant and defend the title, it should be stamped as an agreement or contract.

When a deed purporting to be a conveyance of realty sold, and stamped accordingly, is inoperative, a deed of confirmation, made simply to cure the defect, requires no stamp. In such case, the second deed should contain a recital of the facts, and should show the reasons for its execution.

A conveyance of realty sold subject to a mortgage should be stamped according to the consideration, or the value of the property *unencumbered*. The consideration in such case is to be found by adding the amount paid for the equity of redemption to the mortgage debt. The fact that one part of the consideration is paid to the mortgagor and the other part to the mortgagee does not change the liability of the conveyance.

A receipt for a sum of money exceeding twenty dollars and not being for satisfaction of any mortgage, or judgment or decree of court, is subject to a stamp duty of two cents; but no stamp is necessary upon a receipt for a *package* of money as distinguished from a receipt for a specified sum. If, however, the amount contained in the package is named in the receipt and exceeds the sum of twenty dollars, a stamp should be used.

A mere *copy* of an instrument is not subject to stamp duty unless it is a certified one, in which case a five-cent stamp should be affixed to the certificate of the person attesting it; but when an instrument is executed and issued in duplicate, triplicate, &c., as in the case of a lease of two or more parts, each part has the same legal effect as the other, and each should be stamped as an original.

Written or printed assignments of agreements, bonds, notes not negotiable, and of all other instruments the assignments of which are not particularly specified in the foregoing schedule, should be stamped as agreements.

When, as is generally the case, the caption to a deposition contains other certificates in addition to the jurat to the affidavit of the deponent, such as a certificate that the parties were or were not notified, that they did or did not appear, that they did or did not object, &c., it is subject to a stamp duty of five cents.

When an attested copy of a writ or other process is used by a sheriff or other person in making personal service, or in attaching property, a five-cent stamp should be affixed to the certificate of attestation.

The stamp duty upon the probate of a will, or upon letters of administration, is based upon the sworn or declared value of all the estate and effects, real, personal, and mixed, undiminished by the debts of the estate for or in respect of which such probate or letters are applied for.

When the property belonging to the estate of a person deceased lies under different jurisdictions and it becomes necessary to take out letters in two or more places, the letters should be stamped according to the value of all the property, real, personal, and mixed, for or in respect of which the particular letters in each case are issued.

Cigar lights and playing cards in the hands of manufacturers and dealers should be stamped according to the rates fixed by the law now in force. The fact that they were manufactured prior to August 1, 1866, and are stamped in accordance with the law in force at the time of manufacture, does not relieve them from payment of the increased rates by affixing additional stamps.

No stamp tax is imposed upon any uncompounded medicinal drug or chemical, nor upon any medicine compounded according to the United States or other national pharmacopœia, or of which the full and proper formula is published in any of the dispensatories now or hitherto in common use among physicians or apothecaries, or in any pharmaceutical journal now issued by any incorporated college of pharmacy, *unless* sold or offered for sale or advertised under some other name, form, or guise than that under which they are severally denominated and laid down in such pharmacopœias, dispensatories, or journals.

No stamp tax is imposed upon medicines sold to or for the use of any person, which may be mixed and compounded for said person according to the written recipe or prescription of a physician or surgeon. But all medicinal articles whether simple or compounded by any rule, authority, or formula, published or unpublished, which are put up in a style or manner similar to that of patent or proprietary medicines in general, or advertised in newspapers or by public handbills, for popular sale and use, as having any special proprietary claim to merit, or to any peculiar advantage in mode of preparation, quality, use, or effect, whether such claim be real or pretended, are liable to the tax.

Stamps appropriated to denote the duty charged upon articles named in Schedule C, and in the amendments thereto, cannot be used for any other purpose; nor can stamps appropriated to denote the duty upon instruments be used in payment of the duties upon articles enumerated in this Schedule.

When proprietary stamps from a private die are used, if they are so affixed to the boxes, bottles, or packages, that, in opening the same, or in using the contents thereof, they shall and must be unavoidably and effectually destroyed, no cancellation is necessary; but if they cannot be so affixed, they should be cancelled in the ordinary manner by writing or imprinting thereon the initials and date. When general proprietary stamps are used, they must be cancelled by writing or imprinting thereon the date and the initials of the party using or affixing them.

When proprietary medicines and preparations, perfumery, and cosmetics are stamped according to their retail price or value in the immediate vicinity of the place of manufacture, no additional stamps are necessary upon them, whatever may be the price at which they are offered.

Any person who offers or exposes for sale any of the articles named in Schedule C, or in any of the amendments thereto, whether they are imported or of foreign or domestic manufacture, is to be deemed the manufacturer thereof, and subject to all the duties, liabilities, and penalties imposed by law in regard to the sale of domestic articles without the use of the proper stamp or stamps for denoting the tax paid thereon. The stamp tax upon such articles imported or of foreign manufacture is in addition to the import duties, but when such imported articles, except playing cards, lucifer or friction matches, cigar lights, and wax tapers, are sold in the original or unbroken packages in which the bottles or enclosures were packed by the manufacturer, no penalty is incurred for want of the proper stamp. When the packages are opened stamps should be affixed.

Regulations for the purchase of Stamps.

Revenue stamps may be ordered from this office in amounts of not less than fifty dollars. Purchasers desiring smaller amounts should make application to a collector of internal revenue, or deputy collector, assessor, assistant treasurer of the United States, postmaster, or other dealer in stamps. Payments to this office should be made in the form of a *duplicate* certificate of a United States assistant treasurer or designated depositary of a deposit made on account of stamps. Revenue stamps may likewise be obtained of any national bank which is a designated depositary at the rates of commission at which they are furnished from this office. They will also be deposited with the assistant treasurers and designated depositaries other than national banks

General Stamps.

The following commission, *payable in stamps*, will be allowed in purchases of general stamps, Schedule B:

On	purchases of	$50	or more,	2	per centum.
"	"	$100	"	3	"
"	"	$500	"	4	"
"	"	$1,000	"	5	"

By the 153d section of the excise law, all stamps denoting duties under Schedule B, may be used indiscriminately.

If any revenue stamps for which the owner may have no use are returned to this office in good order and free of expense, others will be given in exchange, at a discount of one per cent. Stamps that have been improperly or unnecessarily used and cancelled, when returned to

49

this office for exchange, must be attached to the instruments on which they were used, and accompanied by an affidavit setting forth the facts, when other stamps will be given for them, at a discount of one per cent. The papers to which the stamps are affixed will be retained by the office. Stamps spoiled in transportation, or rendered useless by any modification of the law, will be exchanged free of charge. When the affidavit is made before a person who has no official seal, his authority to administer oaths generally should be certified to by the clerk of a court of record under the seal of the court.

Where the facilities for procuring and distributing stamps are deemed insufficient in the southern States, the Commissioner of Internal Revenue will, on application, furnish to a collector or assessor, assistant treasurer, designated depositary, or postmaster of the United States, a suitable quantity for the supply of the proper district, and will allow the highest rate of commissions allowed by law to any purchaser of common stamps for cash. Such stamps will be furnished under section 170 of the excise law; and the officer applying to be furnished with such stamps will give bond with three sufficient sureties, conditioned for the faithful return, whenever so required, of all quantities or amounts undisposed of, and for the payment, monthly or otherwise, according to instructions, for all quantities and amounts sold or not reported as remaining on hand. No bond will be accepted for a less sum than five hundred dollars ; and no more agencies will be established in the northern States.

Persons to whom stamps shall be furnished under this section will be expected to conform to the following rules :

Agents for the sale of stamps will make return under oath to this office on Form 55, on the first day of each month, of the amount of stamps sold during the preceding month, and of the amount actually on hand and unsold.

Each collector shall supply his deputies with adhesive stamps, and sell them to other parties within his district who may make application therefor, allowing the same commission as specified above. The collector may require such security from his deputies as he sees fit for the stamps placed in their hands, as he alone is responsible, and is to make returns and payment for them to this office.

Orders may be made from time to time for such stamps as are desired, in no case to exceed three-fourths of the penal sum designated in the bond.

Every agent will be charged upon the books of this office with the stamps furnished him, and credited with the amount of each remittance for the sale of stamps, and five per cent. commission on the same.

Stamped Paper.

An arrangement has been made with the American Phototype Company, of New York, to print Internal Revenue stamps upon bank checks and other instruments which may be furnished them by various parties for that purpose. Persons ordering will send to this office, as heretofore, the duplicate certificate of deposit in some designated depository, stating what kind of stamps they desire; an order then will be sent to the phototype company for the amount, adding the same commission as upon general stamps. The price which the company shall charge to the public for printing such stamps is to be such as may be agreed upon between themselves and the parties ordering the same; but is not to exceed one cent for each impression containing not more than six stamps, excepting clearing-house receipts and other documents which ordinarily contain more than six stamps.

A contract has also been made with Messrs. Butler & Carpenter, of Philadelphia, to furnish similar stamps, to be printed on bank checks and other instruments, from steel plates. The extra expense in the latter case is to be arranged between Butler & Carpenter and the purchasers, subject to the decision of the Commissioner of Internal Revenue in case of dissatisfaction with the rates charged. The documents to be stamped should be furnished in *sheets*, as the stamps could not be conveniently printed in a bound book.

All stamps will hereafter be forwarded by express, unless ordered by mail, at the expense of the person ordering the same, under a contract with the Adams Express Company, at the following rates, viz: Between any two points in the territory of the Adams Express Company, and reached by it, twenty-five (25) cents per one thousand dollars; between any two points in the territory of the Southern Express Company, except to points within the States of Arkansas and Texas accessible as aforesaid, thirty-five (35) cents per one thousand dollars, (it being understood that the territory of the Southern Express Company includes the states of North and South Carolina, Georgia, Alabama, Mississippi, Louisana, Texas, Arkansas, Tennessee, and that part of the State of Virginia lying south of Richmond and west of Lynchburg;) between any two points in the State of Texas or in the State of Arkansas, or between any two points severally in those two States respectively, reached by the lines of the Southern Express Company in manner aforesaid, fifty (50) cents per one thousand dollars; between any two points in the territory of another express company than the Adams and the Southern Express Companies, reached as aforesaid, thirty-five (35) cents per one thousand dollars; between any two points, one of which is in the territory of one express company and the other within the territory of another express company, reached as aforesaid, excluding herefrom the States of Texas and Arkansas, sixty (60) cents per one thousand dollars; between any two points, one of which is in the State of Texas or Arkansas, and the other in any of the other States, eighty-five (85) cents per one thousand dollars. The above amounts in all cases to be computed on the *face value* of the stamps; and any fractional part of one thousand dollars shall be paid for as one thousand dollars.

Proprietary Stamps—Schedule C.

Any proprietor of an article named in Schedule C may furnish a design for a stamp, which, if approved, will be engraved by the Government engravers at the cost of the proprietor.

In such case, the proprietor will be entitled to the commission specified in the 161st section of the excise law, viz: On amounts purchased at one time of not less than fifty nor more than five hundred dollars, five per centum; on amounts over five hundred dollars, ten per centum.

If the designs do not exceed in superficial area $\frac{13}{16}$ of an inch for the denomination of one and two-cent stamps, or $\frac{63}{64}$ of an inch for the denomination of three and four-cent stamps, these being the sizes established by the office for the above specified denominations, there will be no additional charge to purchasers. If, however, proprietors desire to increase the size of the stamps for the denominations above mentioned, then an additional charge will be made for the additional cost of paper and printing. This additional charge will be ten cents per thousand for stamps of $3\frac{1}{8}$ inches superficial area, and in the same proportion for other sizes.

All dies and plates will be retained by, and be under the exclusive control of, the Government.

The general stamp must be canceled by writing, stamping, or printing thereon the initials of the proprietor of the stamped article, and the date of canceling; while the private stamp must be so affixed on the package that in opening the same the stamp shall be effectually destroyed.

Where printing in more than one color is desired, the additional expense must be borne by the proprietor

Each stamp must bear the words, or a proper abbreviation of them, "United States Internal Revenue;" also, in words and figures, the denomination of the stamp.

Manufacturers of friction or other matches, cigar lights, or wax tapers, who desire to avail themselves of the provisions of the 161st section of the law, and receive stamps on a credit of not exceeding sixty days, will be furnished, on application to this office, with a blank bond in proper form, to be filled up and executed by them.

The manufacturers of proprietary articles will be required to use the general proprietary stamps until stamps are furnished from their own designs. The same commission will be allowed on the general proprietary stamps as on stamps under Schedule B.

All stamps denoting duties under Schedule C, excepting those from private designs, may be used indiscriminately.

Every correspondent is requested to give the State, as well as Town and County, of his residence. E. A. Rollins, *Commissioner.*

TABLE

Showing the Amounts to be Charged for Licenses now a Special Tax for Fractional Parts of a Year.

FOR THE USE OF ASSISTANT ASSESSORS AND OTHERS.

12 MONTHS.	11 MONTHS.	10 MONTHS.	9 MONTHS.	8 MONTHS.	7 MONTHS.	6 MONTHS.	5 MONTHS.	4 MONTHS.	3 MONTHS.	2 MONTHS.	1 MONTH.
5 00	4 58	4 17	3 75	3 33	2 92	2 50	2 08	1 67	1 25	83	42
10 00	9 17	8 33	7 50	6 67	5 83	5 00	4 17	3 33	2 50	1 67	83
12 50	11 46	10 42	9 38	8 33	7 29	6 25	5 21	4 17	3 13	2 08	1 04
15 00	13 75	12 50	11 25	10 00	8 75	7 50	6 25	5 00	3 75	2 50	1 25
20 00	18 33	16 67	15 00	13 33	11 67	10 00	8 33	6 67	5 00	3 33	1 67
25 00	22 92	20 83	18 75	16 67	14 58	12 50	10 42	8 33	6 25	4 17	2 08
50 00	45 83	41 67	37 50	33 33	29 17	25 00	20 83	16 67	12 50	8 33	4 17
75 00	68 75	62 50	56 25	50 00	43 75	37 50	31 25	25 00	18 75	12 50	6 25
100 00	91 67	83 33	75 00	66 67	58 33	50 00	41 67	33 33	25 00	16 67	8 33
200 00	183 33	166 67	150 00	133 33	116 67	100 00	83 33	66 67	50 00	33 33	16 67
300 00	275 00	250 00	225 00	200 00	175 00	150 00	125 00	100 00	75 00	50 00	25 00
500 00	458 33	416 67	375 00	333 33	291 67	250 00	208 33	166 67	125 00	83 33	41 67
1,000 00	916 67	833 33	750 00	666 67	583 33	500 00	416 67	333 33	250 00	166 67	83 33

Index to Law of 1864,

AS AMENDED JULY 13, 1866.*

A

* This Index gives a succinct view of the Law as it was before the late amendments of 1867. The reader will for himself carefully compare the provisions of the amendments of 1867, and note the changes and additional exemptions therein made. Where the Schedules are referred to, those of Law of 1867 as amended will be examined

B

Index to Law of 1867.

Contents of Appendix.

www.ingramcontent.com/pod-product-compliance
Lightning Source LLC
LaVergne TN
LVHW020104110826
845151LV00001B/53

* 9 7 8 1 4 2 5 5 4 4 0 7 2 *